T0387675

Forgotten Minorities in Organizations

A Volume in Research in Human Resource Management

Series Editors

Dianna L. Stone
Universities of New Mexico, Albany, and Virginia Tech
James H. Dulebohn
Michigan State University

Research in Human Resource Management

Dianna L. Stone and James H. Dulebohn, Editors

Forgotten Minorities in Organizations (2023)
edited by Dianna L. Stone, Brian Murray,
Kimberly M. Lukaszewski, and James H. Dulebohn

Leadership: Leaders, Followers, and Context (2022)
edited by James H. Dulebohn, Brian Murray, and Dianna L. Stone

*Research Methods in Human Resource Management:
Toward Valid Research-Based Inferences* (2020)
edited by Eugene F. Stone-Romero and Patrick J. Rosopa

Diversity and Inclusion in Organizations (2020)
edited by Dianna L. Stone,
James H. Dulebohn, and Kimberly M. Lukaszewski

The Only Constant in HRM Today is Change (2019)
edited by Dianna L. Stone and James H. Dulebohn

The Brave New World of eHRM 2.0 (2019)
edited by James H. Dulebohn and Dianna L. Stone

*Human Resource Management Theory and
Research on New Employment Relationships* (2016)
edited by Dianna L. Stone and James H. Dulebohn

Human Resource Strategies for the High Growth Entrepreneurial Firm (2016)
edited by Robert L. Heneman and Judith Tansky

IT Workers Human Capital Issues in a Knowledge Based Environment (2006)
edited by Tom Ferratt and Fred Niederman

Human Resource Management in Virtual Organizations (2002)
edited by Robert L. Heneman and David B. Greenberger

Innovative Theory and Empirical Research on Employee Turnover (2002)
edited by Rodger Griffeth and Peter Hom

Forgotten Minorities in Organizations

Editors

Dianna L. Stone
*Universities of New Mexico, Albany,
and Virginia Tech*

Brian Murray
University of Dallas

Kimberly M. Lukaszewski
Wright State University

James H. Dulebohn
Michigan State University

INFORMATION AGE PUBLISHING, INC.
Charlotte, NC • www.infoagepub.com

Library of Congress Cataloging-in-Publication Data

CIP record for this book is available from the Library of Congress
http://www.loc.gov

ISBNs: 979-8-88730-184-6 (Paperback)

979-8-88730-185-3 (Hardcover)

979-8-88730-186-0 (ebook)

Copyright © 2023 Information Age Publishing Inc.

All rights reserved. No part of this publication may be reproduced, stored
in a retrieval system, or transmitted, in any form or by any means, electronic,
mechanical, photocopying, microfilming, recording or otherwise, without written
permission from the publisher.

Printed in the United States of America

CONTENTS

CHAPTER 1

MOTIVES FOR DOMINATING AND EXCLUDING FORGOTTEN MINORITIES IN ORGANIZATIONS

Dianna L. Stone
Universities of New Mexico, Albany, and Virginia Tech

Kimberly M. Lukaszewski
Wright State University

Brian Murray
University of Dallas

James H. Dulebohn
Michigan State University

ABSTRACT

People have long made invidious distinctions between individuals (e.g., the clean and the unclean, good and evil, black and white, sacred and profane, etc.) (Smith, 1995), and these distinctions affect the degree to which individuals experience prejudice, unfair discrimination, and oppression in organizations and society as a whole. Although there may be a number of reasons for these distinctions, we use several theories in this chapter

Forgotten Minorities in Organizations, pp. 1–37
Copyright © 2023 by Information Age Publishing
www.infoagepub.com
All rights of reproduction in any form reserved.

(e.g., social dominance theory, and cultural racism) to explain why people are motivated to divide individuals into dominant in-groups and subordinate out-groups (Durkheim, 1973; Sidanius et al., 1992; Sidanius & Pratto, 1999; Tajfel & Turner, 1979). For example, we review the basic tenets of social dominance and cultural racism theories and consider how they can be used to increase our understanding of the exclusion of out-group members or individuals we label "forgotten minorities." We also review the topics of the chapters included in this volume (e.g., autism, anxiety disorders, people with disabilities engaging in self-employment, adverse impact against people with disabilities, veterans, people with a criminal history, the working poor, considering socioeconomic status in organizational research, and Native Americans).

People have long made invidious distinctions between individuals (e.g., the clean and the unclean, good and evil, black and white, sacred and profane, etc.) (Smith, 1995), and these distinctions affect the degree to which individuals experience prejudice, unfair discrimination, and oppression in organizations and society as a whole. Although there may be a number of reasons for these distinctions, there are several theories (e.g., social identity theory, social dominance theory, and cultural racism) that explain why people are motivated to divide individuals into dominant in-groups and subordinate out-groups (Durkheim, 1973; Sidanius et al., 1992; Sidanius & Pratto, 1999; Tajfel & Turner, 1979). It merits noting that these theories are very similar, but we believe that social dominance theory (SDT) provides the most comprehensive explanation about why individuals are relegated to out-group status in organizations (Sidanius & Pratto, 1999). As a result, we review the tenets of social dominance theory, and consider how it can be used to increase our understanding of the exclusion of out-group members or individuals whom label "forgotten minorities."

SDT suggests that societies form group-based hierarchies in terms of a variety of human characteristics (e.g., race and ethnicity, gender, age), because these social hierarchies enable dominant in-group members to gain a disproportionate share of positive outcomes (e.g., power, monetary resources, good housing, good health), and ensure that out-groups receive a disparate share of negative outcomes. Even though the nature of group hierarchies varies across societies, SDT argues that these socially based group distinctions are universal throughout the world (Sidanius et al., 2004). Not surprisingly, the assignment of individuals to in-groups and out-groups has important implications for individuals, organizations, and society. For example, if individuals are assigned to an out-group, they are less likely to be employed, more likely to receive lower salary levels, and receive assignments to dead end jobs (Stone & Colella, 1996; Stone et al., 1992). As a result, these individuals may not have an opportunity to display their true talents and skills in organizations or enjoy a satisfying work life.

Further, the assignment of people to out-groups may result in the underutilization of talent or a "brain waste" in the workplace which can have a negative impact on the success rates of organizations. Interestingly, the COVID-19 pandemic and the "Great Resignation" caused massive layoffs in our society and motivated some individuals to rethink their long term employment goals. For instance, after the pandemic subsided many people decided to forgo new job opportunities in organizations and start their own businesses, retire early, or leave the workforce altogether (Klotz & Zimmerman, 2015). As a result, there has been an increased talent shortage, and this decrease in labor supply has had a negative impact on an organization's ability to hire skilled employees and achieve success. Further, if large numbers of employees decide to leave the workforce, our whole society may be negatively affected by lower tax revenues, higher costs associated with social services, and the loss of creativity or innovation. Further, our society may suffer in terms of social progress, which is the degree to which it meets basic human needs, enhances the wellbeing of people, or increases opportunities for all individuals (Abbott et al., 2011; Sen et al., 1997).

Given that group-based social hierarchies are pervasive in worldwide societies, and they are likely to have a negative impact on individuals, organizations, and societies, the primary purpose of this volume of Research in Human Research Management is to foster research on "forgotten minorities" or those who are members of groups that have been excluded from organizations and neglected by organizational research. In view of these arguments, this chapter (a) considers the effects of social dominance on the exclusion of out-groups or "forgotten minorities" in organizations, (b) presents a brief review of the existing organizational research on the exclusion and repudiation of out-group members (e.g., racial/ethnic minorities, women, older individuals), (c) offers directions for future research and practice on the exclusion of out-group members, and (d) provides an overview of the chapters included in this volume. It merits noting that chapters in this volume consider a number of "forgotten minorities" who have been disregarded in organizational research including adults with autism, those with mild autism, people with psychological or other types of disabilities, veterans, individuals who have a criminal history, the working poor, and Native Americans. One of the final chapters in the volume examines the importance of including individuals' socioeconomic status (SES) in organizational research.

HOW DOES SOCIAL DOMINANCE AFFECT THE EXCLUSION OF "FORGOTTEN MINORITIES?"

Social dominance theory (SDT) (Sidanius et al., 2004) suggests that societies form group-based hierarchies in terms of a variety of human characteristics (e.g., race or ethnicity, gender, age, religion) to ensure that dominant group members receive a disproportionate share of positive outcomes, and subordinate out-group members receive the majority of negative outcomes. The theory also predicts that there are individual differences in the motivation to achieve membership in high status or dominant in-groups and assign others to subordinate out-groups (Sidanius & Pratto, 1999). In the following sections we briefly describe social dominance theory and use the theory to explain why individuals are assigned to in-groups and out-groups in organizations. We also consider the effects of social dominance on the degree to which out-group members experience unfair discrimination, oppression, prejudice, and other negative outcomes in organizations.

According to SDT, some people in societies are motivated to create group-based hierarchies and assign individuals to in-groups and out-groups in order to receive the bulk of positive outcomes. The theory also predicts that cultural values and norms are used to legitimize and perpetuate these group-based hierarchies making it very difficult for an out-group member to overcome their assigned status (Sidanius & Pratto, 1999). One implication of this effect is that stereotypes of out-group members may be less likely to predict the exclusion of out-group members than the motivation to maintain dominance and control over outcomes. In addition, SDT indicates that group-based inequalities are maintained through three primary mechanisms: aggregated individual discrimination, aggregated institutional discrimination, and behavioral asymmetry (Sidanius et al., 1992). Aggregated individual discrimination is often defined as the simple, daily, and sometimes inconspicuous acts of discrimination that one individual exhibits against another (e.g., employer is friendlier to European-American than African American job applicants) (Sidanius et al., 1992). Aggregated institutional discrimination means that an institution adopts rules and practices that result in a disproportionate allocation of positive and negative outcomes across social status hierarchies (e.g., a law firm that only hires applicants from elite universities may exclude racial or ethnic minorities because they typically cannot afford to attend these universities) (Sidanius et al., 1992). Further, behavioral asymmetry suggests that dominant and subordinate groups maintain the status quo by ensuring that dominant groups remain on top and subordinate groups remain on the bottom (e.g., an African American partner in law firm is reluctant to recommend an African American job applicant because he/she fears the person will perform poorly and harm their reputation) (Sidanius et al., 1992).

SDT also proposes that widely held cultural ideologies (i.e., legitimizing myths) provide the moral justification for social hierarchies and conceal the privileges often experienced by dominant groups members (e.g., favoritism in hiring). Legitimizing myths typically include beliefs, stereotypes, and cultural ideologies that provide justification for the disproportional distribution of valued outcomes in a society (Sidanius & Pratto, 1999, p. 45). For example, stereotypes often legitimize hiring men over women because it is assumed that men are more intelligent, assertive, and capable than women. Similarly, stereotypes that racial and ethnic minorities have low levels of cognitive ability justify hiring whites for jobs over racial and ethnic minorities. Although these beliefs are largely false, they ensure that dominant group members remain at the top of organizations and society, and subordinate group members remain at the bottom. Stated differently, group-based hierarchies are based on cultural norms and values, and these norms and values serve as explanations for the assignment of individuals to in-groups and out-groups. Given that group-based hierarchies are based on cultural norms and values, they may not be the same across cultures. For instance, in Western European and U.S. cultures men typically have more power and status than women, but in some Native American cultures (e.g., Iroquois or Haudenosaunee tribes) clan mothers often have more power and standing than men (Onondaga Nation, 2022). Thus, group hierarchies are based on socially constructed myths that vary from culture to culture, and these myths serve as approval for assigning individuals to in-groups and out-groups.

Further, Sidanius and Pratto (1999) argued that legitimizing myths in a society perpetuate intergroup dominance and serve to enhance or attenuate social hierarchies (e.g., hierarchy-enhancing and hierarchy-attenuating legitimizing myths). Hierarchy-enhancing myths (e.g., racism or meritocracy) contribute to greater levels of group-based inequality, and some individuals are more likely to endorse hierarchy-enhancing myths, social dominance, and inequality than others. As a result, these people are motivated to perpetuate social hierarchies so that they can maintain control over positive outcomes (Sidanius & Pratto, 1999). Hierarchy-attenuating myths (e.g., egalitarianism, feminism) contribute to greater levels of group-based equality, and some people are more likely to endorse hierarchy attenuating ideologies than others (e.g., equality) (Sidanius & Pratto, 1999). SDT also proposes that the relative counterbalancing of hierarchy-enhancing and hierarchy-attenuating beliefs stabilize group-based inequality.

SDT and related theories (Tajfel & Turner, 1979) argue that people are motivated to favor in-groups or help in-group members because their values and beliefs are aligned with their own (Everett et al., 2015) and denigrate out-group members so that they receive negative outcomes (Everett et al., 2015). They also are likely to view in-group members as morally superior (e.g., the in-group is the most honest, trustworthy, and peaceful group) (Brewer, 1999) and view out-group members as immoral which leads to derogation and contempt against them. Considerable research has supported these arguments (Everett et al., 2015), but cultural racism theory adds one underlying process that may explain how in-group members justify denigrating out-group members and relegating negative out-groups to them (Balibar, 2008; Barker, 1981; Kusche & Barker, 2019; Taguieff, 2001). Cultural racism theory (Balibar, 2008) argues that dominant in-group members typically set the standards and norms in organizations, and compare out-group members' standards, norms, and behaviors to those requirements. If out-group members' behaviors and norms do not live up to the in-group's standards they are viewed as inferior or second rate (Balibar, 2008). For example, if the in-group standard indicates that people should be self-reliant or not depend on others, and out-group members use social services for food or housing then they will likely to be viewed as inferior and substandard. Thus, when out-group members are viewed as inferior or substandard human beings, they are more likely to experience prejudice and unfair discrimination in organizations than when they are not perceived as substandard (Balibar, 2008). Further, we believe that who sets the standards in organizations is an important determinant of unfair discrimination and exclusion of out-group members in organizations and should be added to SDT.

Further, SDT predicts that socially constructed group hierarchies consist of a hegemonic group (i.e., a group that has dominance or control over others) at the top, and negative reference groups at the bottom. Negative reference groups include those groups that are stigmatized in society (e.g., racial minorities, people with disabilities, LGBTQIA persons), and in-group members typically strive to distance themselves from these group members (Merton & Kitt, 1950). Hegemonic group members are more likely to hold high-status powerful social roles (e.g., in Western cultures men possess more power and are more likely to dominate others than women.). Likewise, members of negative reference groups are more likely to hold low status positions with little power and experience prejudice and unfair discrimination in organizations. People typically identify with their reference groups, and these groups guide their behaviors and attitudes and help them identify the appropriate social norms and values (Merton & Kitt, 1950).

In summary, SDT maintains that people in all societies are motivated to form group-based hierarchies in order to maintain the dominance of in-groups and ensure that they receive more positive outcomes than subordinate out-groups (Sidanius et al., 1992). The theory also suggests that these group-based hierarchies are based on cultural values and myths which legitimize and perpetuate inequalities between groups (e.g., women are less competent than men, African Americans have lower cognitive ability levels than European-Americans) (Sidanius & Pratto, 1999). Further, cultural racism theory suggests (Balibar, 2008), but SDT implies (Sidanius et al., 1992), that the dominant group sets the standards in these contexts and evaluates out-group members on the degree to which they live up to standards. If out-groups do not live up to standards, then they are viewed as inferior or substandard, and this judgment leads to prejudice, unfair discrimination, and exclusion in organizations (Balibar, 2008; Sidanius et al., 1992).

Further, we believe that establishing dominant in-groups and inferior out-groups is very dysfunctional in organizations and societies because the talents and skills of out-group members are not valued or fully utilized by society. Based on SDT, we contend that many out-group members have been excluded or marginalized in organizations because in-groups want to maintain dominance and control over valued outcomes. Although it is not explicit in SDT, the theory suggests that stereotypes may not be the primary determinant of unfair discrimination. Instead, the SDT implies that the motive to maintain dominance is one of the most important causes of unfair discrimination, and stereotypes or cultural values serve as the justification for assigning people to in-groups and out-groups. Even though this argument may be accurate, much of the organizational research has emphasized the effects of stereotypes and stigmas on job expectancies and employment-related decisions (Dipboye & Colella, 2005). Thus, we believe that the research should be expanded to consider other reasons for the exclusion of out-group members (e.g., social dominance, cultural racism). Further, the organizational research has focused on a limited subset of out-group members (African Americans, women, older workers), and we believe that research is needed to examine the work-related experiences of a much broader array of those who have been relegated to subordinate group status.

As a result, one of the primary purposes of the present chapter and this volume of Research in Human Resource Management is to consider the experiences of those that we label as "forgotten minorities," or those who have been relegated to out-group status and have been neglected by organizational research. Therefore, we consider the status of several forgotten minorities in organizations (e.g., adults with autism spectrum disorder, people with anxiety, veterans, those with a criminal history, the working poor, Native Americans). In order to meet these goals, we briefly review the existing research on the unfair treatment of three key out-groups in organizations (e.g., racial and ethnic minorities, women, and older workers).

Brief Review of Existing Research on Out-group Members in Organizations

Given the basic tenets of social dominance (Sidanius et al., 1992), it is clear that there are dominant in-groups and subordinate out-groups in the U.S. and other societies. In the United States, men with light colored skin, who are young, able-bodied, have a straight sexual orientation, and descend from ancestors who came from European countries are considered the dominant in-group. In contrast, women, racial or ethnic minorities, those who have a dark skin color, trace their ancestry to non-European countries (i.e., Africa, Latin America, Asia, or North America prior to European invasion), have a disability, or claim a LGBTQIA sexual orientation or gender identity are typically relegated to subordinate out-group status. Further, out-group members often experience prejudice and unfair discrimination in organizations. Thus, social scientists have long been concerned with enhancing social equality and increasing the inclusion and opportunities of out-group members in our society (Stone et al., 1992).

Although research in organizational behavior (OB), human resource management (HR), and industrial-organizational psychology has focused on unfair discrimination in organizations, much of the research has examined the work-related experiences of African Americans, women, and older workers (Hebl et al., 2020). However, in recent years, some research has examined the employment problems experienced by people with disabilities or those who state a LGBTQIA sexual orientation or gender identity, and a few other out-group members (e.g., people who share Islamic religious beliefs). However, the latter research has been very limited and has emphasized only subsets of racial or ethnic minorities (e.g., African Americans), people with disabilities (e.g., those who have physical disabilities), those who identify as LGBTQIA (e.g., gays and lesbians), and members of only a few religions (e.g., Muslims). Thus, we provide a brief overview of the existing research in the paragraphs that follow, and offer directions for future research.

Research on Racial/Ethnic Minorities

As just noted, White males who trace their ancestry to Europe are typically viewed as the dominant in-group in the U.S. and many other Western societies (Stone-Romero & Stone, 2002). As a result, people who trace their ancestry to Africa, Asia, or Latin America often are consigned to subordinate out-group status and are likely to face unfair discrimination and prejudice in organizational settings (Stone et al., 2020). Although there are many reasons for this distinction, one of the key reasons is that those who have European ancestry have lighter skin colors than those from other continents (e.g., Africa, Asia, Central and South America). Thus, individuals in the U.S. often are divided into hierarchical groups based on their skin color, and those individuals with brown or black skin color are relegated to out-groups.

To date, there has been considerable research on the exclusion of some racial or ethnic minorities (e.g., African Americans) in organizations, and this research has focused on unfair discrimination in terms of HR processes (e.g., selection, performance ratings.) (e.g., Cox & Nkomo, 1990). For instance, a 1985 meta-analysis on the effects of race on performance ratings found that blacks received lower evaluations in actual organizational settings than contrived settings (Kraiger & Ford, 1985). Similarly, a study by Ilgen and Yountz (1986) found that biases in performance ratings against African Americans were due to negative stereotypes about them. Other research by Sackett and DuBois (1991) found that Black ratees consistently received lower ratings than White ratees from both White and Black raters. However, a recent meta-analysis showed that there were still Black-White differences in performance ratings, but the differences were lower than in previous years (McKay & McDaniel, 2006). Further, the new meta-analysis revealed that several factors were responsible for these differences including rater bias, criterion type (cognitive vs. noncognitive), opportunity bias, and rating purpose. Likewise, results of a study by Stone-Romero et al. (2020) found that African Americans and Mexican Americans were rated lower and stereotyped more negatively than other racial and ethnic groups in the U.S. including Anglo-Americans, Native Americans, East Indian Americans, and Chinese Americans. These authors also found that Chinese Americans were rated higher than other racial/ethnic groups (e.g., Anglo-Americans, East Indian Americans, Hispanic Americans, and African Americans) in terms of competence, adjustment, cognitive ability, reliability, skills, and status levels. Thus, despite the passage of legislation, it appears that ethnic and racial minorities continue to be viewed as out-group members and receive lower ratings than dominant in-group members.

Although considerable research has focused on unfair discrimination and biases against African Americans in organization, relatively little research (e.g., Avery et al., 2008; Guerrero & Posthuma, 2014; Stone-Romero et al., 2020) has focused on members of other racial or ethnic groups (e.g., Hispanic Americans, Asian Americans), and to our knowledge no research has focused on biases against Native Americans in work settings. For example, a limited number of empirical studies and literature reviews have examined unfair discrimination against Hispanic Americans (e.g., Avery et al., 2008; Blancero et al., 2014; Del Campo et al., 2010; Foley et al., 2002; Guerrero & Posthuma, 2014; Hirsh & Lyons, 2010) or Asian Americans in organizations (e.g., Chou & Feagin, 2020; Gündemir et al., 2019; Leong & Grand, 2008; Min, 2002; Stone-Romero et al., 2020; Yu, 2020). However, the numbers of these racial and ethnic groups are increasingly dramatically in our society. For instance, taken together they now constitute 39.1% of the population compared to 60.1% of Whites European-Americans (U.S. Census

Bureau, 2020) and are expected to become the majority of the population (i.e., 55.7% compared to 44.3% of White European-Americans) by the year 2060 (U.S. Census Bureau, 2020). Thus, if we continue to exclude or treat racial and ethnic minorities poorly, we will have a significant shortage of labor in our country.

Given these changes in the demographics of the population, we believe that additional research is needed to understand the biases and unfair discrimination toward all racial or ethnic minorities in organizations so we can eliminate these problems and increase their inclusion. As noted above, most of the research in HR and OB has examined the effects of stereotypes, stigmas, rater bias, opportunity bias, and the nature of the performance criteria on unfair discrimination. However, little research has examined the degree to which in-group members' motivation to maintain dominance affects the exclusion of these groups in organizations (Umphress et al., 2007, 2008). Thus, we believe that future research should examine the extent to which social dominance is a key determinant of unfair treatment of racial and ethnic minorities. In addition, we believe that differences in cultural values may play an important role in the exclusion of out-group members because dominant group members set the standards and view other groups negatively if they do not live up to those standards (Balibar, 2008). Thus, future research is needed to examine the effects of these cultural value differences on prejudice and unfair discrimination against racial and ethnic minorities.

In addition, we believe that research is needed on the different racial and ethnic groups in our society because the stereotypes and attributions about these group members vary considerably. For instance, the research by Stone-Romero et al. (2020) found that attributions about Native Americans were less favorable than those about European-Americans, but the stereotypes of European-Americans were more negative than those about Chinese Americans. This research suggests that we may not be able to generalize about the bases for unfair discrimination of one out-group (e.g., Native Americans) from attributions made about others (e.g., Chinese Americans). Further the research by Stone-Romero and his colleagues suggests that all racial and ethnic minorities (e.g., Chinese Americans) may not be viewed more negatively than dominant in-group members (e.g., European-Americans). Thus, we need a better understanding of the reasons for the exclusion and unfair discrimination against varying racial and ethnic out-group members especially those who have not been considered by previous research (e.g., Middle Easterners, those from Australia or New Zealand, Filipino Americans, people from Columbia, Peru, Guatemala). It merits noting that researchers often cluster Hispanic or other group members (e.g., Asian-Americans) under one heading, but those from specific nations (e.g., Colombia, Peru, Cuba, Mexico) have very unique cultural values and attributes. As a result, we believe that research is needed to examine the factors that affect the exclusion and unfair treatment against all racial and ethnic out-group members in our society.

Research on Gender Discrimination

Today, women make up about 56% of the workforce and men constitute 44% of all workers in the United States (Bureau of Labor Statistic [BLS], 2021). However, women in the U.S. and many other nations are often relegated to out-group status and face obstacles to gaining access to jobs, equal compensation, and advancement opportunities (Hebl et al., 2020). In support of these arguments, a review of 15,465 studies on gender bias by Belingheri et al. (2021) found that women were consistently given lower levels of compensation than men even in the same jobs. Further, the results of the same research revealed that there are continuing biases against women in the hiring process, and high achieving men are more likely to be called back for an interview than high achieving women (Belingheri et al., 2021). In addition, there is a gender congruity bias that means that men are preferred over women for male-dominated jobs (e.g., manager), and women are preferred over men for female-dominated jobs (e.g., administrative assistant, nurse). It merits emphasis, however, that male dominated jobs (e.g., engineering, management) in Western societies typically have higher levels of status, power, and pay than female dominated jobs (e.g., administrative assistant, teacher).

One reason that women have often been treated unfairly in organizations is that, in the past, they had lower levels of education, less access to formal education, and were less likely to attend highly prestigious colleges or universities than men (Belingheri, 2021). However, women now make up the majority of students in colleges and universities and have greater access to highly prestigious colleges and universities so gender differences in educational levels may cease to exist in the near future (Hebl et al., 2020). Another reason that women experience unequal treatment in access to organizations is that they often choose gender congruent majors (e.g., humanities, social sciences) in college and have lower levels of digital skills than men (Hogue et al., 2019, Stone et al., 2017). As a result, they may lack the skills needed to gain access to high paying jobs in organizations (e.g., engineering, computer science) (Stone et al., 2020).

Once they are hired, women continue to experience unequal treatment in organizations and are often treated as if they are less competent than men, receive less support from leaders, and are less likely to be assigned to projects critical for promotion than men (Parker & Funk, 2017). Gender research has shown that one reason for this difference is that negative stereotypes have a major influence on employment decisions about women (e.g., women are often viewed as weak, passive, indecisive, dependent, devoted to family more than careers (Hosoda & Stone, 2000). However, recent research has shown that stereotypes about women are changing, and surveys have revealed that men and women are now perceived as similar in intelligence and competence levels (Hentschel et al., 2019; Pew Research Center, 2015). However, women continue to be held to higher and more restrictive standards in terms of promotions than men, and research shows that high performing women are still less likely to be promoted than high performing men (Belingheri et al., 2021).

Even though negative stereotypes about women are believed to be one of the key determinants of unfair discrimination against them, we also feel that the dominant in-group's (e.g., European-American males) motive to maintain dominance and control the receipt of positive outcomes may also play an important role in the process. Male dominant in-group members may be especially concerned that women will compete with them and take their jobs or promotions. As a result, they may strive to relegate women to low level jobs, prevent them from being included on high visibility projects, or preclude them from having a voice in the design or delivery of products (Hebl et al., 2020). As a result, it is not clear that stereotypes are the only reason that women are excluded in organizations. The motive to dominate them and control access to positive outcomes may also be a key determinant. As a result, we believe that additional research is needed to examine the degree to which motives to acquire social dominance, and the differences in women's values play a role in their exclusion in organizations. For example, many dominant in-group members may exclude women so that they can gain control over the most positive outcomes. They also may exclude women because women, on average, may have different value systems than men. For example, research by Schwartz and Rubel-Lifschitz (2009) found that women's value priorities included benevolence, altruism and social goals more than men, and men's value priorities emphasized power, achievement, and self-interest more than women. As a result, they may exclude women because they do not always live up to the dominant in-groups' values of power and achievement.

Research on Age Discrimination

In recent years the population of many industrialized countries has grown older, and the U.S. now has over 55.6 million people aged 65 or older (U.S. Census Bureau, 2020). Further, 10.6 million of those who are over 65 are still in the workforce, but it is expected that 42 million members of the baby boom generation (1946–1964) will retire in the next few years

(Cook, 2021; Fry, 2021). In fact, the COVID pandemic accelerated the retirement rate, and 2 million more workers retired earlier than expected during the past two years (Cook, 2021). Not surprisingly, the increased retirement rate has created a labor or skills shortage in our society, and members of the next generations (e.g., Generation X, Millennials, Generation Z) do not always have the experience and skills to make up for the deficiency (Cook, 2021). As a result, some estimates indicate that organizations are faced with a 6 million shortfall in skilled workers, and they face many challenges to filling their job vacancies (Cook, 2021).

Although we are experiencing a shortage of labor, organizations continue to unfairly discriminate and exclude talented older workers in organizations. For instance, nearly two-thirds of workers ages 55 to 64 report that their age has been a barrier to gaining access to jobs (Terrell, 2018), and a recent study using resumes of workers of various age groups found that the oldest applicants were more likely to experience unfair discrimination than younger or middle-aged applicants (Neumark et al., 2019). Thus, it may be that the dominant in-group in the U.S. (e.g., young and middle-aged individuals) may be motivated to exclude older workers so that they can gain access to positive outcomes (e.g., promotions and higher pay levels). One example of this phenomenon is that some millennials have argued that "baby boomers have antiquated beliefs and should get out of their way and let them make progress" (Valdez, 2017). Further, negative stereotypes about older workers often serve as the justifications for prejudice and unfair discrimination against them. In view of these problems, we provide a brief review of the research on unfair discrimination and biases against older workers in the employment process (e.g., hiring, training, performance appraisal) in the sections that follow.

Stereotypes of Older Workers. Although there may be a number of reasons for unfair discrimination against older workers in organizations, some researchers argue that negative stereotypes about them may be a key source of the problem (Truxillo et al., 2017). For example, research has shown consistently that older workers are negatively stereotyped as poor performers, resistant to change or new technologies, lacking in motivation to learn new skills, and incurring higher costs associated with higher compensation rates than their younger counterparts (Truxillo et al., 2017). In spite of these negative stereotypes, there are also a number of positive beliefs attributed to older workers including: they are reliable or dependable, more conscientious, less neurotic, more experienced, and exhibit more organizational citizenship behaviors than younger workers (Finkelstein et al., 2013; Truxillo et al., 2012). As might be expected there are also stereotypes of younger workers, and research has shown that they are not always viewed positively (Twenge, 2006). For example, they are often viewed as narcissistic, disloyal, entitled, job hoppers who are overly concerned with feedback (Twenge, 2006).

Even though the negative stereotypes of older workers are pervasive in our society, research has shown that these beliefs are generally unfounded, and most have not been thoroughly examined by research (Posthuma & Campion, 2009). Researchers found only one belief about older workers that has been supported by research (i.e., older workers have less desire to take part in developmental activities than younger workers) (Ng & Feldman, 2012). Further, based on models of social cognition (Brewer & Miller, 1984), it can be predicted that unfavorable stereotypes are likely to have a negative impact on job expectancies and employment decisions about older workers (Brewer & Miller, 1984). Thus, we review the effects of negative stereotypes on hiring, performance appraisal, and layoffs in the paragraphs that follow.

Unfair Discrimination in Hiring Process. A number of studies have examined the influence of negative stereotypes about older workers on hiring decisions, and the results of that research revealed that older workers are less likely to be hired than younger workers even though they have the same or greater qualifications (Rosen & Jerdee, 1976). Further, research has found that older applicants are more likely to experience shorter interviews, are less likely to be called back after interviews, and receive fewer job offers than their younger counterparts (Bendick et al., 1999). Research in Western nations also has highlighted that age-based stereotypes reduce the employability of older workers, and result in the characterizations of those over 45 as less adaptable, less creative and less flexible than their younger counterparts (Wilson et al., 2007).

Although we have no empirical support for our predictions, we believe that stereotype threat (i.e., the threat of being viewed through the lens of a negative stereotype, Steele & Aronson, 1995) associated with negative age stereotypes may have motivated older workers to leave the workforce after the COVID-19 pandemic (The Great Resignation). For example, it can be argued that many older workers were aware that age stereotypes serve as barriers to their employment, and they experienced stereotype threat when they were making decisions about pursuing new job opportunities. As a result, they decided to leave the workforce or retire early rather than seek new these opportunities. Taken together, the research just reviewed suggests that older workers continue to experience prejudice and barriers to employment based on unfounded negative stereotypes about their skills and abilities. Further, we believe that these negative stereotypes often result in stereotype threat among older workers, and this threat has a negative impact on their motivation to remain in the workforce. Although these arguments appear reasonable, additional research is needed to determine if stereotype threat affects older workers decisions to retire early.

Unfair Discrimination in Performance Appraisal and Layoffs. Research has shown consistently that employees' performance typically improves with age (Institute of Medicine, 2012) but decision makers still view older workers as poorer performers than younger ones (Truxillo et al., 2012). Further, results of research revealed that age biases often have a negative impact on subjective performance ratings (Waldman & Avolio, 1986) even though the results of meta-analyses indicated that there are few actual differences in the performance of older and younger workers (Ng & Feldman, 2008). In addition, studies have shown that when older workers are rated as poor performers, supervisors attribute the cause of their performance to stable factors (e.g., lack of ability) rather than unstable factors (e.g., lack of resources, time, or staff) that are beyond the person's control (Waldman & Avolio, 1986). Thus, there are negative stable attributions about the causes of older workers' poor performance, and research has shown that older workers are punished more severely for poor performance than their younger counterparts (Rupp et al., 2006).

Research also has revealed that older workers are more likely to be laid off from jobs than younger workers (Ng & Feldman, 2008). Reasons for these differences include that older employees are perceived to cost the organization more in salary and benefits, are viewed as having greater absenteeism, use more benefits, and need more training than younger workers (Ng & Feldman, 2008). However, studies have indicated that these beliefs are not accurate because older workers are not always more costly or need more training than younger workers (Ng & Feldman, 2008). Further, they actually have lower levels of absenteeism (Hedge et al., 2006), have fewer counterproductive behaviors, and exhibit more organizational citizenship behaviors than younger workers (Ng & Feldman, 2008). Taken together, the results of the research just noted indicated that unsubstantiated stereotypes about older workers have a negative impact on supervisory performance ratings and layoff decisions about them. Although most of the research on older workers has emphasized the effects of stereotypes on HR decisions, we believe that employment decisions about them may also be caused by social dominance. For instance, dominant young or middle aged in-group members may be motivated to exclude older workers so that they can access promotions, higher paying jobs, and control the receipt of positive outcomes. Although these arguments appear reasonable, we know of no research that has examined the effects of social dominance of in-group members on the marginalization of older workers. As a result, we believe that future research should examine this prediction.

In summary, our brief review of the research on racial or ethnic minorities, women, and older workers suggests that despite the passage of legislation each group continues to experience prejudice, unfair discrimination, and exclusion in organizational settings. Further, our review indicated that unfounded negative stereotypes about each group has a negative influence on (a) the degree to which they are perceived as qualified for jobs, (b) performance appraisals, and (c) layoff decisions about them. Even though most of the research on unfair discrimination has focused on stereotypes and stigmas (Dipboye & Colella, 2005), we argued that social dominance may also be a key reason that these out-groups are excluded in organizations. Thus, we believe that future research should focus on the degree to which in-group members' motives to maintain dominance in organizations, and differences in in-groups' and out-groups' cultural values affect unfair discrimination against these groups.

We also emphasized that the exclusion of a large percentage of our population in organizations means that we are underutilizing the many talents and skills that these individuals bring to the workforce. For instance, there are approximately 124 million people that are racial or ethnic minorities, 166.4 million women in our population, and approximately 42 million individuals who are between the ages of 55 and 64 (U.S. Census Bureau, 2020). Thus, if we continue to exclude these groups in organizations, then our society may not be able to compete effectively in the global marketplace. As a result, we believe that research should identify strategies that can be used to increase the inclusion of all individuals in our society and in organizations.

Forgotten Minorities

Although considerable research has focused on the exclusion of racial and ethnic minorities, women, and older workers in organizations, there are many other out-groups that have been largely ignored by our research (e.g., Native Americans, those with neurological or psychological disabilities, the working poor). Thus, one of the primary goals of this volume was to consider the reasons that "forgotten minorities" are dominated and excluded in organizations. We chose a number of distinct groups (e.g., adults with autism, those with anxiety disorders, Native Americans) because we have limited knowledge about how to attract, motivate, and retain them in organizations, and we wanted to foster research on strategies that might enhance their employment opportunities. In particular, this volume includes 11 chapters that focus on the following topics: the motives underlying the exclusion of forgotten minorities, adults with autism spectrum disorder (ASD), those with mild autism, individuals with anxiety disorders, people with disabilities seeking self-employment, and adverse impact against those with disabilities. The volume also consists of chapters on veterans, individuals with a criminal history, the working poor, Native Americans, and includes a chapter that considers the importance of studying individuals at all levels of socioeconomic status. In the paragraphs that follow, we provide a brief description of each of these chapters.

Motives for Dominating and Excluding Forgotten Minorities

The first chapter in this volume emphasizes that people have long made invidious distinctions between individuals (e.g., the clean and the unclean, good and evil, black and white, sacred and profane, etc.) (Smith, 1995), and these distinctions affect the degree to which individuals experience prejudice, unfair discrimination, and oppression in organizations and society. Although there may be a number of reasons for these distinctions, the authors use social dominance and cultural racism theory to explain why people are motivated to divide individuals into in-groups and out-groups and exclude them from organizations (Durkheim, 1973; Sidanius et al., 1992; Sidanius & Pratto, 1999; Tajfel & Turner, 1979). Further, the chapter reviews the basic tenets of social dominance theory and considers how it can be used to increase our understanding of the exclusion of "forgotten minorities" in organizations. The chapter also considers the predictions made by cultural racism theory (Balibar, 2008) which argues that dominant in-group members typically set the standards and norms in organizations, and compare out-group members' standards, norms, and behaviors to those requirements. If out-group members' behaviors and norms do not live up to the in-group's standards they are viewed as inferior or second rate (Balibar, 2008). For example, if the in-group standard indicates that people should be self-reliant, and out-group members use social services for food or housing then they are likely to be viewed as inferior and substandard. It follows that when out-group members are viewed as inferior or substandard human beings, they are more likely to experience prejudice and unfair discrimination in organizations than when they are not.

Adults With Autism Spectrum Disorder (ASD)

The second chapter in the volume is by Giannantonio, Hurley-Hanson, and Griffiths and is extremely interesting because it focuses on adults with neurological disabilities especially autism spectrum disorder (ASD). To our knowledge, very few articles in HR, OB, or industrial and organizational psychology have concentrated on this key group of people in our society (Hurley-Hanson et al., 2020). The Center for Disease Control (CDC) estimates that there are 5.4 million (2.21% of population) adults in the United States who have symptoms that fall along the autism spectrum (CDC,

2022). ASDs can be defined as a group of neurological or developmental disabilities that affect the person's social relations, communication, and behavioral challenges (National Institute of Mental Health [NIH], 2022a). Autism is known as a "spectrum" disorder because there are wide variations in the type and severity of symptoms people experience. For example, some people with ASD may have advanced conversation skills whereas others may be nonverbal, and some people with ASD need a lot of help in their daily lives, but others can work and live with little to no support. Further, people with ASD also vary in terms of their ability to listen to those who are talking, and may have trouble understanding another's point of view. They also differ in terms of their ability to adjust to social situations, and their ability to display facial expressions, movements, and gestures that correspond to what is being said in a conversation (NIH, 2022a).

Although the percentages vary, some estimates indicate that only 22% of adults with autism are employed, and a vast majority of those with autism are unemployed or have difficulties gaining access to jobs. Further, when they are employed, they are typically assigned to part-time, low-level jobs, or experience underemployment. This bias is unfortunate because jobs have an important impact on one's personal identity, and allow individuals to gain feelings of self-efficacy when they can use their skills and abilities to master tasks. In view of the employment problems experienced by adults with ASD, we argue, as do others, that adults with ASD may have a lower quality of life than those without the disorder (Giannantonio & Hurley-Hanson, 2022).

Despite these problems, little research in HR, OB, or industrial and organizational (I&O) psychology has focused on the employment challenges of those with ASD (e.g., Bruyere & Colella, 2022; Giannantonio et al., 2022; Hurley-Hanson et al., 2020). There has been research on advancing the employment of people with ASD in the fields of rehabilitation or vocational psychology, but most of those articles focus on specialized programs for those with the disorder (Migliore et al., 2014; Schaller & Yang, 2005). To our knowledge, research has not examined (a) the unique skills that people with ASD bring to the workforce, (b) the obstacles and barriers that affect their ability to access jobs, or (c) the strategies needed to facilitate the employment of these individuals. Interestingly, some research in rehabilitation psychology has shown that people with ASD have a number of skills that can add value to organizations including high levels of mathematical skills, memory, intense focus on a task, reliability, loyalty, honesty, punctuality, and attention to detail (e.g., Bury et al., 2019; Happè & Frith, 2010). Further, research has shown that some adults with autism have unique talents including high levels of creativity and musical and artistic abilities. In fact, a number of very successful people in Western societies were believed to have autism including Albert Einstein, Charles Darwin,

Emily Dickinson, Bill Gates, Michelangelo, Wolfgang Mozart, Ludwig Van Beethoven, Vincent Van Gogh, George Orwell, Elon Musk, and many others (ABA, 2022). Given that people with autism may have many talents and skills that they can bring to the workforce, we believe that the chapter on adults with ASD by Giannantonio, Hurley-Hanson, and Griffiths makes an important contribution to our literature, and offers interesting directions for future research on increasing the inclusion of adults with ASD.

Mild Autism

The third chapter is by Petrovski and concentrates on adults with mild autism which is another important group that has been neglected by research in HR, OB, and I&O psychology. Professionals in psychology and psychiatry used the term "Asperger's syndrome" to refer to mild autism until recently when the editors of the *Diagnostic and Statistical Manual-5* (DSM-5) eliminated the term and subsumed it under the overall ASD title. Although it is difficult to establish accurate estimates, some reports indicate that 1 in every 250 people in the U.S. has mild ASD (Asperger/Autism Network [AANE], 2020). Characteristics of mild ASD typically include poor social interactions, obsessive behaviors, odd speech patterns, limited facial expressions, and other unusual mannerisms (e.g., avoiding eye contact) (Cimera & Cowan, 2009; Howlin et al., 2005). For example, they may stand too close to others, talk incessantly about a single topic, avoid making eye contact when speaking, and are not always aware that others are not listening to them. Although estimates vary, some reports indicate that 75 to 85% of adults with mild autism do not hold full time jobs (Grandin, 1999). However, these individuals often have a wide array of unique talents and skills including average to very high intelligence, good verbal skills, rich vocabularies, ability to absorb and memorize large amounts of information, ability to think in virtual images, propensity to be self-motivated and work alone, and the ability to be an independent learner (Grandin, 1999). They may also have the ability to concentrate on work for long periods of time, be detail oriented, take an interest in arcane fields of knowledge, and exhibit high levels of honesty and fairness. (Grandin, 1999). When individuals with mild autism are employed, they often hold jobs in computer programming, accounting, photography, physics, mathematics, equipment design, car mechanics, and animal training (Grandin, 1999).

Given the many talents among those with mild autism, it is surprising that more of them are not employed. However, mild autism is not well understood in the workplace, and there are very few support systems for workers with mild autism or their supervisors. Further, many adults with mild autism have trouble fitting into the workplace and supervisors may not know how to work effectively with them. Thus, rehabilitation and vocational psychologists have argued that organizations should hire professionals to coach or train employees with mild autism, supervisors, coworkers on how to work together effectively (Grandin, 1999).

The chapter by Petrovski on mild autism focuses on the employment barriers faced by these individuals with mild autism. In particular, she concentrates on the personal, institutional, and social barriers existing in the job market, and considers how these barriers are created or perpetuated and establish an uneven playing field for these individuals. The author uses social identity theory (SIT) (Tajfel & Turner, 1986) and Goffman's (1963) concept of social stigma to propose a model that explains how stereotypes and stigmas contribute to hiring discrimination against individuals with mild autism. She also offers directions for future research and practice on how organizations can enhance the inclusion of these individuals in organizations.

People With Psychological Disabilities

The next chapter in the volume focuses on psychological (mental) disabilities or anxiety disorders. Individuals with psychological disabilities have often been overlooked in organizations, and almost forgotten in organizational research (Stone & Colella, 1996). Even though there is research on disabilities at work, in general (e.g., Beatty et al., 2018; Colella & Bruyere, 2011; Goldman et al. 2006; Stone & Colella, 1996) there have been relatively few articles on psychological disabilities in organizations (e.g., Follmer & Jones, 2018; Santuzzi et al., 2022). Despite the lack of research on these types of disabilities, mental illness, including anxiety and depression, are the most common illnesses worldwide, and are considered disabilities that greatly interfere with work activities (Americans with Disabilities Act [ADA], 1990). For example, the World Health Organization (WHO, 2017) estimates that approximately 264 million people in the world have anxiety disorders, and about 40 million people in the U.S. experience anxiety on a daily basis (Anxiety & Depression Association of America [ADAA], 2022). Anxiety is defined as a disorder that is characterized by constant worry and fear, and often includes generalized anxiety, phobias, obsessive-compulsive disorder, and panic disorder (NIH, 2022b).

People with anxiety disorders. Given the pervasiveness of anxiety disorders, the next chapter in the volume, authored by Mendoza, Mendiola, Mathys, Cheng, and King, focuses on individuals with excessive anxiety in organizations. Approximately, 4.3 million people with anxiety disorders are employed in the U.S. (Preidt, 2015), but they often face a host of challenges in the workplace including perceptions that their anxiety decreases performance and morale and increases fatigue and absenteeism rates. Anxiety disorders are considered mental health disorders that are often characterized by feelings of worry, anxiety, or fear that are strong enough to interfere with one's daily activities. Examples of anxiety disorders include panic attacks, obsessive-compulsive disorders, and stress that is out of proportion to the impact of the event (Noyes & Hoehn-Saric, 1998). Although these symptoms may not apply to all employees with anxiety, many organizations are reluctant to hire people with this disorder or offer them opportunities for training or advancement (Noyes & Hoehn-Saric, 1998). Further, 15% of the people who are unemployed in the U.S. report that they are not in the workforce because they experience mental illness especially anxiety (Goodkind, 2021).

Research has also shown that there are often stereotypes and stigmas associated with people who have anxiety disorders in the workplace (Stone & Colella, 1996), and employers often perceive that employees with anxiety disorders will have numerous cognitive and behavioral difficulties in the workplace (e.g., Erickson et al., 2009; Ivandic et al., 2017). First, when people are anxious at work, they may worry about things that they cannot control, and lose the ability to concentrate on the task at hand, formulate new ideas, or develop creative solutions to problems (Ivandic et al., 2017). Second, anxiety often makes individuals irritable and impatient, and when they are distressed, they become easily annoyed. As a result, they may have problems completing a project or interacting with coworkers; consequently, others may find that it is difficult to interact effectively with them (Erickson et al., 2009). Third, a person who is anxious is in a constant state of fight or flight may withdraw from responsibilities and colleagues. As a result, they may become disengaged, have increased absenteeism and feel distant or left out of work groups (Erickson et al., 2009). Fourth, anxiety can increase a person's fear of failure and their sense of dread which may result in feelings of being overwhelmed or paralyzed when attempting to complete a task. This fear of failure may also result in wasting time or procrastination which may prevent the person from achieving his or her work goals (Ivandic et al., 2017).

Even though it is typically thought that anxiety decreases work performance, some theory and research in psychology shows that a moderate amount of anxiety may have a positive effect on work performance. For instance, the Yerkes-Dodson (1908) law predicts that performance increases with physiological arousal or anxiety, but only up to a certain point (i.e., the inverted U model of arousal). When anxiety is too low or too high, performance decreases, but when arousal or anxiety is in the middle range performance increases. Recent research by Cheng and McCarthy (2018) provided support for these arguments and found that anxiety may direct attention to work tasks, and increase the extent to which individuals focus on tasks. Further, results of research by the same authors revealed that anxiety is often a key motivator, and stress can actually stimulate motivation and drive (Cheng & McCarthy, 2018) Thus, in contrast to employers' perceptions, moderate levels of anxiety may actually enhance employees' motivational and performance levels (Cheng & McCarthy 2018).

In an effort to address these issues, the chapter by Mendoza et al. (in this volume) considers the barriers and unfounded stereotypes experienced by people with anxiety disorders in the workplace. The authors argue that employees with anxiety are stigmatized, and their levels of anxiety are often inflated which makes it difficult for them to access and maintain employment. In addition, the pervasive stigma associated with mental illness can prevent employees from sharing their experiences, and preclude them from getting the help that they need. The chapter also provides an overview of anxiety disorders and uses the theory of workplace anxiety (Cheng & McCarthy, 2018) to discuss how it will impact performance and other work behaviors. The authors consider how the stigma associated with mental illness can exacerbate the negative effects of anxiety disorders at work, and highlight individual, ally (manager and coworker), and organizational interventions that can be used to reduce stigmas associated with anxiety disorders. They also offer directions for future research and practice on the topic.

People With Disabilities Seeking Self-Employment

Another very extremely interesting chapter in this volume is by Metzler and Moog. It focuses on the relations between disability, health, and the decision to enter or leave self-employment. To our knowledge, this study is the first research that assesses the extent to which self-employment depends on a person's disability or health status. It also used samples of employees from the German Socio-Economic Panel (SOEP) waves from 1994 to 2018. Results of their study revealed that disability status was not related to the decision to enter self-employment, but perceptions of health were related to that decision. These findings suggest that individuals who want to enter self-employment in Germany need to perceive that they are healthy before they start a new business. The results also revealed that there was a strong association between individuals' decision to leave self-employment and disability status, but there was a weak relation between decision to leave self-employment and health status. These findings imply that people with disabilities who want to be self-employed confront challenges to maintain their businesses because of their disability rather than the perceived quality of their health. We believe that this chapter makes an important contribution to the literature because it focuses on employment of decisions of those with disabilities and distinguishes disabilities from a person's overall health status.

Adverse Impact and Disability Status

The final chapter on people with disabilities in this volume is by Strah and Rupp. It examines the extent to which selection techniques have the potential for adverse impact for people with disabilities. This topic has not received a lot of attention in organizational research, but it is critical to understanding access to organizations among people with disabilities. The authors reviewed the legal research and case law on the adverse impact associated with HR practices for those with disabilities, and considered the potential for common selection tools (e.g., cognitive ability tests, interviews) to produce adverse impact against those with disabilities. For example, they argued that cognitive ability tests may have adverse impact on people with learning disabilities, and suggested that interviews are likely to have adverse impact on those with autism spectrum disorder because of their communication limitations. Then, they discussed the theoretical and practical issues associated with studying adverse impact against people with disabilities using two frameworks including the well-established accommodation framework and less-well-established (in terms of disability) disparate impact framework. The authors conclude their chapter by proposing an agenda for future research that includes potential steps for identifying disability-related adverse impact, ways to address adverse impact within selection contexts, and practical ways to build inclusive selection systems.

Additional Topics of "Forgotten Minorities"

The next set of chapters in this volume focuses on several groups that might be considered "forgotten minorities" including veterans, those who were previously incarcerated, those individuals who might be viewed as the working poor, and Native Americans. The final chapter in this volume considers the importance of considering socioeconomic status in HR, OB, and I&O psychology related research.

Veterans

The next chapter is by DiPietropolo, Ford, and Correa and concentrates on the degree to which hiring decisions about veterans are influenced by conscious, social and unconscious biases. This chapter is intriguing because it focuses on the conflicting stereotypes about military veterans (Stone et al., 2018; Stone & Stone, 2015). For instance, veterans are often stereotyped negatively and viewed as having mental health problems, including depression, post-traumatic stress disorder, unpredictable behaviors, and difficulties transitioning from military to civilian organizations (Schreger & Kimble, 2017). As a result, most research has shown that employers are less likely to hire veterans than nonveterans (Stone & Stone, 2015). However, recent surveys revealed that veterans may not always be perceived negatively, but may be viewed more positively today than in the past (Pew Research Center, 2019). These surveys indicated that the majority of people in the U.S. believe that veterans are more honorable, patriotic, hard-working, and disciplined than their civilian counterparts (Pew Research Center, 2019). In view of these inconsistent stereotypes about veterans, the authors conducted a study to examine the degree to which hiring managers were biased in favor of veterans. However, they argued that biases in favor of veterans are problematic because they may set veterans up for failure if they do not live up to the expectations of hiring managers.

They also reported the results of an empirical study that assessed the extent to which hiring managers' conscious, social, and unconscious biases favored veterans and influenced employment decisions about them. The results revealed that conscious and social biases were positively, not negatively, related to employment decisions about veterans. They also offered directions for future research and practice on biases that may affect the employment of veterans.

Individuals With a Criminal History

The eighth chapter in this volume is by Palmer Johnson and Jones Young and focuses on the employment difficulties faced by those with a criminal history. In the United States, about 70 million adults have a criminal history, and many of these individuals are racial or ethnic minorities (e.g., African Americans, Hispanic Americans, Native Americans.). For example, some estimates indicate that 38.3% of prison inmates are African American, 19% are Hispanic Americans, 1.4% Asian American, 2.5% Native Americans, and 33.7% are European-Americans (Prison Policy, 2010). Once these people have completed their prison sentences, they are faced with major obstacles gaining employment, and the unemployment rate of those who have been to prison is 27% compared to 6% in the overall population (Prison Policy, 2010). As a result, a criminal history is one of the most damaging stigmas in the employment process. This chapter deals with the challenges that individuals with a criminal history face when obtaining employment and presents strategies that might assist those individuals with reducing the stigma associated with previous criminal history. For example, the attainment of higher education has been shown to decrease the stigma associated with a criminal history (Moore et al., 2017).

The authors conducted 21 interviews with men and women who were recently released from prison, seeking paid employment, and had completed or were pursuing a bachelor's, master's, or doctoral degree. Their results revealed that the completion of higher education provided (a) awareness of structural barriers that increase visibility of a criminal history, (b) confidence to disclose one's criminal history, (c) ability to pursue a true-to-self provisional strategy, and d) readiness to pursue a highly skilled occupation. The authors conclude that higher education may be the "great equalizer" in terms of higher lifetime earnings and career advancement among those with a criminal history, and may help moderate negative perceptions about them. However, the authors contend that higher education may not always have a positive influence on those with a criminal history especially for racial and ethnic minorities or those from low SES backgrounds. Thus, the authors offer directions for future research on reducing the stigmas associated with a criminal history, and helping those with a history of incarceration gain employment. They also identify some specific practices that can be used to achieve these goals.

The Working Poor

The ninth chapter in this volume concentrated on the working poor and was authored by Williams and Heath. Even though the U.S. is one of the world's wealthiest nations, over 38 million citizens live at or below the poverty level, and 7 million of those people are a part of a group that are viewed as the working poor (BLS, 2018). The BLS defines the working poor as individuals who work at least 27 weeks in a year, but their income falls below the national poverty level (BLS, 2018). One study by the National Low Income Housing Coalition (Bravve et al., 2012) found that there are no congressional districts in the U.S. where a low-income worker (employed full time) could afford a two-bedroom apartment. Thus, the homeless rate in the country has accelerated in recent years, and some estimates indicate that every day over 552, 830 individuals are homeless in the United States (Stasha, 2022). This circumstance means that even though people are working full time they may live in persistent poverty in the United States. Moreover, living in poverty has a detrimental impact their self-identity, self-efficacy, and opportunities for the future (Leana et al., 2012). Interestingly, as of January 1, 2022, 30 states increased their minimum wage to a rate higher than the federal minimum wage ($7.25) ranging from $9.00 in Nebraska to $15.20 in Washington, D.C.). However,

15 states still adhere to the federal minimum wage, and 5 states have no minimum wage (Department of Labor, 2022).

Although the problems experienced by the working poor are pervasive in our society, relatively little research in HR, OB, or I&O psychology has focused on the experiences or strategies that might be used to enhance their self-efficacy and ensure that they have a high-quality working life (e.g., Leana et al., 2012). Thus, this chapter focused on two strategies that might be used to enhance the self-efficacy and increase job opportunities for the working poor. Based on Bandura's social cognitive theory (Bandura, 1989) the authors considered how (a) mentoring relationships, and (b) supervisory supportive feedback might enhance self-efficacy and career opportunities for the working poor. In addition, they proposed that if the working poor feel that they are members of an out-group in organizations, these perceptions will have a negative impact on their perceptions of self-efficacy, motivation, feelings of inclusion, and retention in organizational settings.

Although these arguments appear reasonable, the authors maintain that additional research is needed to examine the degree to which (a) mentoring, and (b) supportive feedback enhances the self-efficacy and decreases poverty among the working poor. They also identified several factors that might be used to enhance the self-efficacy of the working poor. For instance, they maintained that successful role models who have a working poor background, goal setting, training, and mastery experiences might have a positive effect on those who work full time, but still live in poverty.

Socioeconomic Status

The next chapter in this volume highlights the importance of including socioeconomic status (SES) as a key variable in organizational research, and was authored by Silver, Phetmisy, Fe-Kaji, Corrington, Ng, and Hebl. Socioeconomic status (SES) refers to the social standing of an individual or group of people, and reflects a combination of income, education, and occupational levels (American Psychological Association, 2020). Despite the fact that differences in SES have important implications for understanding the needs, motives and behaviors of individuals in organizations, relatively little research has included this variable in their research (Bergman & Jean, 2016). For example, employees who come from low SES backgrounds may have different role perceptions and work scripts than those from high SES backgrounds (Stone-Romero et al., 2003). As a result, these differences may affect job related attitudes and behaviors, and create interpersonal problems in organizations including intergroup conflict and communication difficulties.

In view of the importance of SES, the authors maintain that more research is needed that includes SES, and they present a model based on current research (ASA; Schneider, 1987) that breaks down the impact of SES in three separate stages of the employment cycle: attraction, selection, and attrition. For each stage, they consider both the perspective of the individual who may be low in SES (self) and how other organizational members (e.g., supervisors, coworkers, subordinates) perceive those who may be low in SES. They conclude that organizational scholars should include SES in their research and include employees from a wide array of SES backgrounds so that our research can reflect the experiences of organizational members across the SES spectrum. They also maintain that employees in management and leadership positions are over-represented in organizational research, and those from low SES backgrounds are often overlooked in our research. This interpretation of the phenomenon is relatively new. Considerable prior research between the 1950s and 1970s (Katz & Kahn, 1978) examined the effects of job enrichment on the attitudes and motivation of assembly workers (Hackman & Oldham, 1975), and other research assessed the factors that may enhance the lives of the hard core unemployed (Friedlander & Greenberg, 1971; Goodman & Salipante, 1973). The authors contend that research on SES in organizations should consider the unique stressors experienced by low SES individuals (e.g., childcare problems, difficulties with transportation), the differences in the meaning of work, and the impact of work on their self-perceptions and self-identity.

Native Americans

The final chapter in this volume is on Native Americans in organizations, and is by Stone, Lukaszewski, Canedo, and Contreras Krueger. Native people in the U.S. and the Americas experience numerous problems gaining and maintaining employment, and their employment problems exacerbate existing difficulties associated with poverty, food and housing insecurity, and alcohol or drug addiction (Reclaiming Native American Truth, 2018). We know of no other research in OB, HR, or I&O psychology on the challenges faced by Natives in the workplace. As a result, this chapter (a) presents a model of the factors thought to affect unfair discrimination against Natives in organizations, (b) reviews the existing theory and research on these issues, (c) offers hypotheses to facilitate research on the topic, and (d) presents practical strategies that might be used to decrease unfair discrimination and enhance the inclusion of Natives in organizations. The model presented in this chapter was based on theories of social cognition, social categorization, and cultural racism. It predicts that unfounded negative stereotypes about Natives are important determinants of employment decisions about them. Similarly, social categorization theory predicts that dominant group members (e.g., European Americans) denigrate out-group members (e.g., Natives) to boost their own self esteem (Turner et al., 1987). Further, the theory of cultural racism argues that dominant groups in a society (e.g., European-Americans in the United States) determine the values, standards, norms, and when a nondominant group's (e.g., Natives) cultural values do not live up to these cultural standards, they are viewed as inferior and experience unfair discrimination in organizations. The authors also present specific hypotheses to guide future research, and consider implications for future research and practice are considered.

CONCLUSION

In conclusion, we have assembled a very interesting set of chapters on forgotten minorities, those who have been excluded in organizations and forgotten in organizational research. It is our hope that these chapters will foster additional research on members of these important out-groups. Throughout this chapter, we argued that there may be multiple reasons that out-group members are treated unfairly or excluded from organizations. One key source of the problem is that they are stereotyped and stigmatized by organizational decision makers. However, another potential reason is that those who are in the dominant in-group are motivated to exclude out-group members so that they can obtain a disproportionate share of positive outcomes in organizations (Sidanius et al., 1992). Although social dominance may be an important motive for excluding out-group members, relatively little research in OB, HR, or I&O psychology has examined dominance as an important motive for denigrating and excluding forgotten minorities in organizations (e.g., Guimond et al., 2003; Simmons & Umphress, 2015; Umphress et al., 2008). Thus, we also hope that this research will broaden our explanations for the derogation and exclusion of out-group members in the workplace.

We also hope that the same research will help forgotten minorities increase their access to jobs, and offer organizations key strategies for decreasing unfair discrimination and increasing the inclusion of all members of our society.

REFERENCES

AANE [Asperger/Autism Network] (2022). *Asperger profiles: prevalence*. Retrieved March 1, 2022, from https://www.aane.org/prevalence/

ABA. (2022). *30 incredibly successful people on the autism spectrum*. Retrieved May 15, 2022, from https://www.abadegreeprograms.net/successful-people-on-the-autism-spectrum/

Abbott, P., Wallace, C., & Sapsford, R. (2011). Surviving the transformation: Social quality in Central Asia and the Caucuses. *Journal of Happiness Studies, 12*, 199–223. https://doi.org/10.1007/s10902-010-9187-9

ADA [Americans with Disabilities Act]. (1990). *Americans with disabilities.* Retrieved February 15, 2021, from https://www.dol.gov/general/topic/disability/ada

ADAA [Anxiety & Depression Association of America]. (2022). *Facts and statistics.* Retrieved April 1, 2022, from https://adaa.org/understanding-anxiety/facts-statistics

American Psychological Association. (2020). *Socioeconomic status.* Retrieved March 1, 2022, from https://www.apa.org/topics/socioeconomic-status/

Avery, D. R., McKay, P. F., & Wilson, D. C. (2008). What are the odds? How demographic similarity affects the prevalence of perceived employment discrimination. *Journal of Applied Psychology, 93*, 235–249. https://doi.org/10.1037/0021-9010.93.2.235

Balibar, É. (2008). Racism revisited: Sources, relevance, and aporias of a modern concept. *PMLA, 123*(5), 1630–1639. https://doi.org/10.1632/pmla.2008.123.5.1630

Bandura, A. (1989). Regulation of cognitive processes through perceived self-efficacy. *Developmental Psychology, 25*(5), 729. https://doi.org/10.1037/0012-1649.25.5.729

Barker, M. (1981). *The new racism: Conservatives and the ideology of the tribe.* Junction Books.

Beatty, J. E., Baldridge, D. A., Boehm, S., Kulkarni, M., & Colella, A. (2018). On the treatment of persons with disabilities in organizations: A review and research agenda. *Human Resource Management, 58*(2), 119–137. https://doi.org/10.1002/hrm.21940

Belingheri, P., Chiarello, F., Fronzetti Colladon, A., & Rovelli, P. (2021). *Twenty years of gender equality research: A scoping review based on a new semantic indicator.* Retrieved March 1, 2021, from https://journals.plos.org/plosone/article?id=10.1371/journal.pone.0256474

Bendick M., Jr., Brown, L. E., & Wall, K. (1999). No foot in the door: An experimental study of employment discrimination against older workers. *Journal of Aging & Social Policy, 10*, 5–23. https://doi.org/10.1300/J031v10n04_02

Bergman, M. E., & Jean, V. A. (2016). Where have all the "workers" gone? A critical analysis of the unrepresentativeness of our samples relative to the labor market in the industrial-organizational psychology literature. *Industrial and Organizational Psychology, 9*(1), 84–113. https://doi.org/10.1017/iop.2015.70

Blancero, D., Olivas Luján, M. R., & Stone, D. L. (2014). Introduction to Hispanic and Latin American work issues. *Journal of Managerial Psychology, 29*(6), 616–643.

BLS [Bureau of Labor Statistic]. (2018). *A profile of the working poor.* Retrieved October 15, 2021, from https://www.bls.gov/opub/reports/working-poor/2018/home.htm#:~:text=About%2038.1%20million%20people%2C%20or,to%20the%20U.S.%20Census%20Bureau

BLS [Bureau of Labor Statistics]. (2021). *Women in the labor force: A databook.* https://www.bls.gov/opub/reports/womens-databook/2020/home.htm#:~:text=In%202019%2C%2057.4%20percent%20of,of%2060.0%20percent%20in%201999.ce%)

Bravve, E., Bolton, M., Couch, L., & Crowley, S. (2012). *Out of reach.* Retrieved November 29, 2021, from http://nlihc.org/sites/default/files/oor/2012-OOR.pdf

Brewer, M. B. (1999). The psychology of prejudice: Ingroup love and outgroup hate? *Journal of Social Issues, 55*(3), 429–444. https://doi.org/10.1111/0022-4537.00126

Brewer, M. B., & Miller, N. (1984). Beyond the contact hypothesis: Theoretical perspectives on desegregation. In N. Miller & M. B. Brewer (Eds.), *Groups in contact: The psychology of desegregation* (pp. 281–302). Academic Press.

Bruyere, S. M., & Colella, A. (2022) *Neurodiversity in the workplace: An overview of interests, issues, and opportunities.* Routledge.

Bury, S. M., Jellett, R., Spoor, J. R., & Hedley, D. (2020). 'It defines who I am' or 'It's something I have': What language do Australian adults on the autism spectrum prefer? *Journal of Autism and Developmental Disorders*, 1–11. https://doi.org/10.1007/s10803-020-04425-3

CDC [Centers for Disease Control and Prevention]. (2022). *Autism spectrum disorder (ASD).* Retrieved January 5, 2022, from https://www.cdc.gov/ncbddd/autism/features/adults-living-with-autism-spectrum-disorder.html

Cheng, B. H., & McCarthy, J. M. (2018). Understanding the dark and bright sides of anxiety: A theory of workplace anxiety. *Journal of Applied Psychology, 103*(5), 537. https://doi.org/10.1037/apl0000266

Chou, R. S., & Feagin, J. R. (2020). From the myth of the model minority: Asian Americans facing racism. In J. Brueggemann (Ed.), *Inequality in the United States: A Reader* (pp. 224–242). Routledge.

Cimera, R. E., & Cowan, R. J. (2009). The costs of services and employment outcomes achieved by adults with autism in the US. *Autism, 13*(3), 285–302. https://doi.org/10.1177/1362361309103791

Colella, A., & Bruyère, S. M. (2011). Disability and employment: New directions for industrial and organizational psychology. In S. Zedeck (Ed.), *APA handbook of industrial and organizational psychology* (Vol. 1, pp. 473–503). American Psychological Association.

Cook, I. (2021). *Who is driving the great resignation?* Retrieved October 15, 2021, from https://hbr.org/2021/09/who-is-driving-the-great-resignation

Cox T., Jr., & Nkomo, S. M. (1990). Invisible men and women: A status report on race as a variable in organization behavior research. *Journal of Organizational Behavior, 11*, 419–431. https://doi.org/10.1002/job.4030110604

Del Campo, R. G., Rogers, K. M., & Jacobson, K. J. (2010). Psychological contract breach, perceived discrimination, and ethnic identification in Hispanic business professionals. *Journal of Managerial Issues, 22*, 220–238.

Department of Labor. (2022). *Consolidated minimum wage table.* Retrieved March 1, 2022, from https://www.dol.gov/agencies/whd/mw-consolidated

Dipboye, R. L., & Colella, A. (Eds.). (2013). *Discrimination at work: The psychological and organizational bases.* Psychology Press.

Durkheim, E. (1973). *On morality and society: Selected writings*. University of Chicago Press.

Erickson, S. R., Guthrie, S., VanEtten-Lee, M., Himle, J., Hoffman, J., Santos, S. F., Janeck, A. S., Zivin, K., & Abelson, J. L. (2009). Severity of anxiety and work-related outcomes of patients with anxiety disorders. *Depression and Anxiety*, *26*(12), 1165–1171. https://doi.org/10.1002/da.20624

Everett, J. A., Faber, N. S., & Crockett, M. (2015). Preferences and beliefs in in-group favoritism. *Frontiers in Behavioral Neuroscience*, *9*, 1–21. https://doi.org/10.3389/fnbeh.2015.00015

Finkelstein, L. M., Ryan, K. M., & King, E. B. (2013). What do the young (old) people think of me? Content and accuracy of age-based metastereotypes. *European Journal of Work and Organizational Psychology*, *22*(6), 633–657. https://doi.org/10.1080/1359432X.2012.673279

Foley, S., Kidder, D. L., & Powell, G. N. (2002). The perceived glass ceiling and justice perceptions: An investigation of Hispanic law associates. *Journal of Management*, *28*, 471–496. https://doi.org/10.1016/S0149-2063(02)00140-X

Follmer, K. B., & Jones, K. S. (2018). Mental illness in the workplace: An interdisciplinary review and organizational research agenda. *Journal of Management*, *44*(1), 325–351. https://doi.org/10.1177/0149206317741194

Friedlander, F., & Greenberg, S. (1971). Effect of job attitudes, training, and organization climate on performance of the hard-core unemployed. *Journal of Applied Psychology*, *55*(4), 287–295. https://doi.org/10.1037/h0031532

Fry, R. (2021). *Amid the pandemic, a rising share of older U.S. adults are now retired*. Retrieved January 5, 2022, from https://www.pewresearch.org/fact-tank/2021/11/04/amid-the-pandemic-a-rising-share-of-older-u-s-adults-are-now-retired/

Giannantonio, C. M., & A. E. Hurley-Hanson (2022). Recruitment strategies. In S. M. Bruyere & A. Colella (Eds.), *Neurodiversity in the workplace* (pp. 61–99). Routledge.

Goffman, E. (1963). *Stigma: Notes on the management of spoiled identity*. Prentice Hall.

Goldman, B. M., Gutek, B. A., Stein, J. H., & Lewis, K. (2006). Employment discrimination in organizations: Antecedents and consequences. *Journal of Management*, *32*(6), 786–830. https://doi.org/10.1177/0149206306293544

Goodkind, N. (2021, December 13). *15% of unemployed say they aren't working due to mental health problems*. Retrieved March 1, 2022, from https://fortune.com/2021/12/13/unemployment-mental-health-covid-pandemic/are not employed

Goodman, P. S., Salipante, P., & Paransky, H. (1973). Hiring, training, and retaining the hard-core unemployed: A selected review. *Journal of Applied Psychology*, *58*(1), 23. https://doi.org/10.1037/h0035403

Grandin T. (1999). *Choosing the right job for people with autism or Asperger's Syndrome*. Retrieved April 2, 2022, from https://www.iidc.indiana.edu/irca/articles/choosing-the-right-job-for-people-with-autism-or-aspergers-syndrome.html

Guerrero, L., & Posthuma, R. A. (2014). Perceptions and behaviors of Hispanic workers: A review. *Journal of Managerial Psychology*, *29*, 616–643. https://doi.org/10.1108/JMP-07-2012-0231

Guimond, S., Dambrun, M., Michinov, N., & Duarte, S. (2003). Does social dominance generate prejudice? Integrating individual and contextual determinants of intergroup cognitions. *Journal of Personality and Social Psychology, 84*(4), 697–721. https://doi.org/10.1037/0022-3514.84.4.697

Gündemir, S., Carton, A. M., & Homan, A. C. (2019). The impact of organizational performance on the emergence of Asian American leaders. *Journal of Applied Psychology, 104*(1), 107–122. https://doi.org/10.1037/apl0000347

Hackman, J. R., & Oldham, G. R. (1975). Development of the job diagnostic survey. *Journal of Applied Psychology, 60*(2), 159–170. https://doi.org/10.1037/h0076546

Happè F, & Frith U. (2010). *Autism and talent.* Oxford University Press.

Hebl, M., Cheng, S. K., & Ng, L. C. (2020). Modern discrimination in organizations. *Annual Review of Organizational Psychology and Organizational Behavior, 7,* 257–282. https://doi.org/10.1146/annurev-orgpsych-012119-044948

Hedge, J. W., Borman, W. C., & Lammlein, S. E. (2006). *The aging workforce: Realities, myths, and implications for organizations.* American Psychological Association.

Hentschel, T., Heilman, M. E., & Peus, C. V. (2019). The multiple dimensions of gender stereotypes: A current look at men's and women's characterizations of others and themselves. *Frontiers in Psychology, 10,* Article 11. https://doi.org/10.3389/fpsyg.2019.00011

Hirsh, E., & Lyons, C. J. (2010). Perceiving discrimination on the job: Legal consciousness, workplace context, and the construction of race discrimination. *Law & Society Review, 44,* 269-298. https://doi.org/10.1111/j.1540-5893.2010.00403.x

Hogue, M., Fox-Cardamone, L., & Knapp, D. E. (2019). Fit and congruency: How women and men self-select into gender-congruent jobs. *Journal of Personnel Psychology, 18*(3), 148–156. https://doi.org/10.1027/1866-5888/a000233

Hosoda, M., & Stone, D. L. (2000). Current gender stereotypes and their evaluative content. *Perceptual and Motor Skills, 90,* 1283–1294. https://doi.org/10.2466/pms.2000.90.3c.1283

Howlin, P., Alcock, J., & Burkin, C. (2005). An 8-year follow-up of a specialist supported employment service for high-ability adults with autism or Asperger syndrome. *Autism, 9*(5), 533–549. https://doi.org/10.1177/1362361305057871

Hurley-Hanson, A. E., Giannantonio, C. M., & Griffiths, A. J. (2020). *Autism in the workplace: Creating positive employment and career outcomes for generation A.* Palgrave Macmillan.

Ilgen, D. R., & Youtz, M. A. (1986). Factors affecting the evaluation and development of minorities in organizations. In K. Rowland & G. Ferris (Eds.), *Research in personnel and human resource management: A research annual* (pp. 307–337). JAI.

Institute of Medicine. (2012). *Aging and the macroeconomy: Long-term implications of an older population.* National Academic Press.

Ivandic, I., Kamenov, K., Rojas, D., Cerón, G., Nowak, D., & Sabariego, C. (2017). Determinants of work performance in workers with depression and anxiety: A cross-sectional study. *International Journal of Environmental Research and Public Health, 14*(5), 1–11. https://doi.org/10.3390/ijerph14050466

Katz, D., & Kahn, R. L. (1978). *The social psychology of organizations.* Wiley.

Klotz, A. C., & Zimmerman, R. D. (2015). On the turning away: an exploration of the employee resignation process. In M. R. Buckley, A. R. Wheeler, & J. R. B. Halbesleben (Eds.), *Research in personnel and human resources management* (Vol. 33, pp. 51–119). Emerald Group Publishing Limited.

Kraiger, K., & Ford, J. K. (1985). A meta-analysis of ratee race effects in performance ratings. *Journal of Applied Psychology, 70*, 56–65. https://doi.org/10.1037/0021-9010.70.1.56

Kusche, I., & Barker, J. L. (2019). Pathogens and immigrants: A critical appraisal of the behavioral immune system as an explanation of prejudice against ethnic out-groups. *Frontiers in Psychology, 10*(1), 1–9. https://doi.org/10.3389/fpsyg.2019.02412

Leana, C. R., Mittal, V., & Stiehl, E. (2012). Perspective: Organizational behavior and the working poor. *Organization Science, 23*(3), 888–906. https://doi.org/10.1287/orsc.1110.0672

Leong, F. T., & Grand, J. A. (2008). Career and work implications of the Model Minority Myth and other stereotypes for Asian Americans. In G. Li & L. Wang (Eds.), *Model Minority Myths revisited: An interdisciplinary approach to demystifying Asian American education experiences* (pp. 91–115). Information Age Publishing.

McKay, P. F., & McDaniel, M. A. (2006). A reexamination of black-white mean differences in work performance: More data, more moderators. *Journal of Applied Psychology, 9*, 538–554. https://doi.org/10.1037/0021-9010.91.3.538

Merton, R. K., & Kitt, A. S. (1950). Contributions to the theory of reference group behavior. In R. K. Merton and P. F. Lazarsfeld (Eds.), *Continuities in social research: Studies in the scope and method of The American Soldier* (pp. 40–105). Free Press.

Migliore, A., Butterworth, J., & Zalewska, A. (2014). Trends in vocational rehabilitation services and outcomes for youth with autism: 2006–2010. *Rehabilitation Counseling Bulletin, 57*, 80–89. https://doi.org/10.1177/0034355213493930

Min, P.G. (2002). *Second generation: Ethnic identity among Asian Americans.* AltaMira

Moore, K. E., Milam, K. C., Folk, J. B., & Tangney, J. P. (2017). *Self-stigma among criminal offenders: Risk and protective factors.* Retrieved February 5, 2022, from https://www.ncbi.nlm.nih.gov/pmc/articles/PMC6157751/

Neumark, D., Burn, I., & Button, P. (2019). Is it harder for older workers to find jobs? New and improved evidence from a field experiment. *Journal of Political Economy, 127*(2), 922–970. https://doi.org/http://www.journals.uchicago.edu/loi/jpe

Ng, T. W., & Feldman, D. C. (2008). The relationship of age to ten dimensions of job performance. *Journal of Applied Psychology, 93*, 392–423. https://doi.org/10.1037/0021-9010.93.2.392

Ng, T. W., & Feldman, D. C. (2012). Evaluating six common stereotypes about older workers with meta-analytical data. *Personnel Psychology, 65*, 821–858. https://doi.org/10.1111/peps.12003

NIH [National Institute of Mental Health]. (2022a). *Autism spectrum disorder.* Retrieved March 5, 2022, from https://www.nimh.nih.gov/health/topics/autism-spectrum-disorders-asd

NIH [National Institute of Mental Health] (2022b). *Anxiety disorders*. Retrieved March 7, 2022, from https://www.nimh.nih.gov/health/topics/anxiety-disorders

Noyes, R., Jr., & Hoehn-Saric, R. (1998). *The anxiety disorders*. Cambridge University Press. https://doi.org/10.1017/CBO9780511663222

Onondaga Nation. (2022). *Clan mothers*. Retrieved December 29, 2021, from https://www.onondaganation.org/government/clan-mothers/

Parker, K., & Funk, C. (2017). *Gender discrimination comes in many forms for today's working women*. Retrieved January 11, 2022, from http://www.pewresearch.org/fact-tank/2017/12/14/gender-discrimination-comes-in-many-forms-for-todays-working-women/

Pew Research Center. (2015). *Women and leadership: Public says women are equally qualified, but barriers persist*. Retrieved April 10, 2022, from https://www.pewresearch.org/social-trends/2015/01/14/women-and-leadership/

Pew Research Center. (2019). *Key findings about America's military veterans*. Retrieved April 2, 2022, from https://www.pewresearch.org/fact-tank/2019/11/07/key-findings-about-americas-military-veterans/

Posthuma, R. A., & Campion, M. A. (2009). Age stereotypes in the workplace: Common stereotypes, moderators, and future research directions. *Journal of Management, 35*, 158–188. https://doi.org/10.1177/0149206308318617

Preidt, R. (2015). *Over 4 million workers have anxiety disorders*. Retrieved March 2, 2022, from https://www.webmd.com/anxiety-panic/news/20150521/over-4-million-working-americans-suffer-from-anxiety-disorders#:~:text=Over%204%20Million%20Workers%20Have%20Anxiety%20Disorders&text=That%20number%20represents%203.7%20percent,experience%20overwhelming%20worry%20and%20fear.

Prison Policy. (2010). *U.S. incarceration rates by race and ethnicity, 2010*. Retrieved March 5, 2022, from https://www.prisonpolicy.org/graphs/raceinc.html?gclid=Cj0KCQjwvqeUBhCBARIsAOdt45a35lopUFNVfvH08aT3BIE3ommACPe70lLE10r3jkZ4Hnqw7S6NI3kaAsc1EALw_wcB

Reclaiming Native American Truth. (2018). *A project to dispel America's myths and misconceptions*. Retrieved March 1, 2021, from https://rnt.firstnations.org/

Rosen, B., & Jerdee, T. H. (1976). The influence of age stereotypes on managerial decisions. *Journal of Applied Psychology, 61*, 428–432. https://doi.org/10.1037/0021-9010.61.4.428

Rupp, D. E., Vodanovich, S. J., & Crede, M. (2006). Age bias in the workplace: The impact of ageism and causal attributions. *Journal of Applied Social Psychology, 36*, 1337–1364. https://doi.org/10.1111/j.0021-9029.2006.00062.x

Sackett, P. R., & DuBois, C. L. (1991). Rater-ratee race effects on performance evaluation: Challenging meta-analytic conclusions. *Journal of Applied Psychology, 76*, 873–877. https://doi.org/10.1037/0021-9010.76.6.87

Santuzzi, A. M., Martinez, J. J., & Keating, R. T. (2022). The benefits of inclusion for disability measurement in the workplace. *Equality, Diversity and Inclusion, 41*(3), 474–490. https://doi.org/10.1108/EDI-06-2020-0167

Schaller, J., & Yang, N. K. (2005). Competitive employment for people with autism: Correlates of successful closure in competitive and supported employment. *Rehabilitation Counseling Bulletin, 49*(1), 4–16. https://doi.org/10.1177/00343 552050490010201

Schneider, B. (1987). The people make the place. *Personnel Psychology, 40*(3), 437–453. https://doi.org/10.1111/j.1744-6570.1987.tb00609.x

Schreger, C., & Kimble, M. (2017). Assessing civilian perceptions of combat veterans: An IAT study. *Psychological Trauma: Theory, Research, Practice, and Policy, 9*(S1), 12–18. https://doi.org/10.1037/tra0000191

Schwartz, S. H., & Rubel-Lifschitz, T. (2009). Cross-national variation in the size of sex differences in values: effects of gender equality. *Journal of Personality and Social Psychology, 97*(1), 171–185. https://doi.org/10.1037/a0015546

Sen, A., Sen, M. A., Foster, J. E., Amartya, S., & Foster, J. E. (1997). *On economic inequality*. Oxford University Press.

Sidanius, J., Devereux, E., & Pratto, F. (1992). A comparison of symbolic racism theory and social dominance theory as explanations for racial policy attitudes. *The Journal of Social Psychology, 132*(3), 377–395. https://doi.org/10.10 80/00224545.1992.9924713

Sidanius, J., & Pratto, F. (1999). *Social dominance: An intergroup theory of social hierarchy and oppression*. Cambridge University Press.

Sidanius, J., Pratto, F., Van Laar, C., & Levin, S. (2004). Social dominance theory: Its agenda and method. *Political Psychology, 25*(6), 845–880. https://doi.org/10.1111/j.1467-9221.2004.00401.x

Simmons, A. L., & Umphress, E. E. (2015). The selection of leaders and social dominance orientation. *Journal of Management Development, 34*(10), 1211–1226. https://doi.org/10.1108/JMD-11-2014-0149

Smith, H. (1995). *The illustrated world's religions: A guide to our wisdom traditions*. Harper.

Stasha, S. (2022). *The state of homelessness in the US—2022*. Retrieved March 27, 2022, from https://policyadvice.net/insurance/insights/homelessness-statistics/#:~:text=2.,US%20is%20estimated%20at%20 552%2C830.&text=With%20around%20half%20a%20million,which%20 counts%20over%20327.2%20million.

Steele, C. M., & Aronson, J. (1995). Stereotype threat and the intellectual test performance of African Americans. *Journal of Personality and Social Psychology, 69*, 797–811. https://doi.org/10.1037//0022-3514.69.5.797

Stone, C. B., Lengnick-Hall, M., & Muldoon, J. (2018). Do stereotypes of veterans affect chances of employment? *The Psychologist-Manager Journal, 21*(1), 1–33. https://doi.org/10.1037/mgr0000068

Stone, C., & Stone, D. L. (2015). Factors affecting hiring decisions about veterans. *Human Resource Management Review, 25*(1), 68–79. https://doi.org/10.1016/j.hrmr.2014.06.003

Stone, D. L., & Colella, A. (1996). A model of factors affecting the treatment of disabled individuals in organizations. *Academy of Management Review, 21*, 352–401. https://doi.org/10.5465/AMR.1996.9605060216

Stone, D. L., Krueger, D., & Takach, S. (2017). Social issues associated with the Internet at work. In G. Hertel, D. L. Stone, R. D. Johnson, & J. Passmore (Eds.), *The psychology of the internet at work* (pp. 424–447). Wiley Blackwell.

Stone, D. L., Lukaszewski, K. M., Krueger, D. C., & Canedo, J. C. (2020). A model of factors thought to affect unfair discrimination against immigrants in organizations. In D. L. Stone, J. H. Dulebohn, & K. M. Lukaszewski (Eds.), *Research in Human Resource Management: Diversity and Inclusion in Organizations* (pp. 331–360). Information Age Publishing.

Stone, E. F., Stone, D. L., & Dipboye, R. L. (1992). Stigmas in organizations: Race, handicaps, and physical unattractiveness. *Advances in Psychology, 82*, 385–457. https://doi.org/10.1016/S0166-4115(08)62608-4

Stone-Romero, E. F., & Stone, D. L. (2002). Cross-cultural differences in responses to feedback: Implications for individual, group, and organizational effectiveness. *Research in Personnel and Human Resources Management, 21*, 275–331. https://doi.org/10.1016/S0742-7301(02)21007-5

Stone-Romero, E. F., Stone, D. L., Hartman, M., & Hosoda, M. (2020). Stereotypes of ethnic groups in terms of attributes relevant to work organizations: An experimental study. In D. L. Stone, J. H. Dulebohn, & K. M. Lukaszewski (Eds.), *Diversity and inclusion in organizations* (pp. 59–84). Information Age Publishing.

Stone-Romero, E. F., Stone, D. L., & Salas, E. (2003). The influence of culture on role conceptions and role behavior in organizations. *Applied Psychology, 52*(3), 328–362. https://doi.org/10.1111/1464-0597.00139

Taguieff, P. A. (2001). *The force of prejudice: On racism and its doubles* (Vol. 13). University of Minnesota Press.

Tajfel, H., & Turner, J. C. (1986). The social identity theory of intergroup behavior. In S. Worchel & W. Austin (Eds.), *Psychology of intergroup relations* (pp. 7–24). Nelson Hall.

Tajfel, H., & Turner, J. C. (1979). An integrative theory of intergroup conflict. In W. G. Austin, & S. Worchel (Eds.), *The social psychology of intergroup relations* (pp. 33–47). Brooks/Cole.

Terrell, K. (2018). *Age discrimination common in workplace, survey says.* Retrieved April 1, 2022, from https://www.aarp.org/work/age-discrimination/common-at-work/

Truxillo, D. M., Fraccaroli, F., Yaldiz, L. M., & Zaniboni, S. (2017). Age discrimination at work. In E. Parry and J. McCarthy (Eds.), *The Palgrave handbook of age diversity and work* (pp. 447–472). London.

Truxillo, D. M., McCune, E. A., Bertolino, M., & Fraccaroli, F. (2012). Perceptions of older versus younger workers in terms of big five facets, proactive personality, cognitive ability, and job performance. *Journal of Applied Social Psychology, 42*, 2607–2639. https://doi.org/10.1111/j.1559-1816.2012.00954.x

Turner, J. C., Hogg, M. A., Oakes, P. J., Reicher, S. D., & Wetherell, M. S. (1987). *Rediscovering the social group: A self-categorization theory.* Basil Blackwell.

Twenge, J. M. (2006). *Generation Me: Why today's young Americans are more confident, assertive, entitled--and more miserable than ever before.* Free Press.

Umphress, E. E., Simmons, A. L., Boswell, W. R., & Triana, M. D. C. (2008). Managing discrimination in selection: the influence of directives from an authority and social dominance orientation. *Journal of Applied Psychology*, *93*(5), 982–993. https://doi.org/10.1037/0021-9010.93.5.982

Umphress, E. E., Smith-Crowe, K., Brief, A. P., Dietz, J., & Watkins, M. B. (2007). When birds of a feather flock together and when they do not: status composition, social dominance orientation, and organizational attractiveness. *Journal of Applied Psychology*, *92*(2), 396 –409. https://doi.org/10.1037/0021-9010.92.2.396

U.S. Census Bureau. (2020). *Population by age*. Retrieved April 22, 2022, from https://www.census.gov/programs-surveys/acs/data/experimental-data/1-year.html

Valdez, O. (2017). *Get out of our way, baby boomers*. Retrieved March 22, 2022, from https://www.huffpost.com/entry/get-out-of-our-way-baby-boomers_b_586ad3 68e4b04d7df167d6bf

Waldman, D. A., & Avolio, B. J. (1986). A meta-analysis of age differences in job performance. *Journal of Applied Psychology*, *71*, 33–38. https://doi.org/10.1037/0021-9010.71.1.33

WHO [World Health Organization]. (2017). *Depression and other common mental disorders*. Retrieved March 15, 2022, from https://apps.who.int/iris/bitstream/handle/10665/254610/WHO-MSD-MER-2017.2-eng.pdf

Wilson, M., Parker, P., & Jordan, K. (2007). Age biases in employment: Impact of talent shortages and age on hiring. *University of Auckland Business Review*, *9*, 33–41.

Yerkes, R. M., & Dodson, J. D. (1908). The relation of strength of stimulus to rapidity of habit formation. *Journal of Comparative Neurology and Psychology*, *18*(5), 459–482. https://doi.org/10.1002/cne.920180503

Yu, H. H. (2020). Revisiting the bamboo ceiling: Perceptions from Asian Americans on experiencing workplace discrimination. *Asian American Journal of Psychology*, *11*, 158–167. https://doi.org/10.1037/aap0000193

CHAPTER 2

AUTISM SPECTRUM DISORDER AND GENERATION A

A Forgotten Minority in the Workplace

Cristina M. Giannantonio, Amy E. Hurley-Hanson, and Amy Jane Griffiths
Chapman University

ABSTRACT

This chapter will focus on the work experiences and career outcomes of young adults with ASD who are at risk of becoming forgotten minorities in organizations. While there is relatively little research on the careers of individuals with autism spectrum disorder (ASD), research suggests that their life and work outcomes are less favorable than those experienced by the general population (Griffiths et al., 2016). It is predicted that one-half million young adults with ASD will reach adulthood and enter the workforce during the current decade. The term *Generation A* refers to this incoming cohort of young adults who are likely to need support to successfully navigate the school-to-work transition (Hurley-Hanson et al., 2020). With Generation A poised to enter the workforce in unprecedented numbers, research is needed to help individuals, organizations, and society work together to create successful work experiences and career outcomes for these young adults and to prevent them from becoming forgotten minorities. Specific issues to be addressed in this chapter include the scope and importance of understanding how individuals with ASD, particularly members of Generation A, may become forgotten minorities; the role of functioning level, self-concept, disclosure, stigma, and image norms in preventing Generation A from becoming a forgotten minority;

Forgotten Minorities in Organizations, pp. 39–71
Copyright © 2023 by Information Age Publishing
www.infoagepub.com
All rights of reproduction in any form reserved.

suggestions for future research on forgotten minorities; and implications for human resource management policies and organizational practices.

The passage of several employment laws in the second half of the 20th century focused attention on the discrimination experienced by members of several protected classes. The Equal Pay Act of 1963 addressed pay inequality faced by women; Title VII of the Civil Rights Act of 1964 extended workplace protections based on Sex, Color, Race, Religion, and National Origin; the Age Discrimination in Employment Act of 1968 added age as a protected characteristic for individuals over the age of 40; and the Americans with Disabilities Act of 1991 added disabilities as a protected characteristic. While much work remains to be accomplished to achieve significant diversity and inclusion, these employment laws have helped to eradicate discrimination in the workplace for large numbers of individuals, have shaped organizations' diversity policies and programs, and have been the focus of volumes of research in the human resource management (HRM), organizational behavior, and careers literatures.

Although research on disabilities in organizations exists (Bell, 2006; Stone et al., 1992; Stone & Colella, 1996), most of this research has centered on race (Avery et al., 2018), gender (Hurley & Giannantonio, 1999; Joshi et al. 2015), and age (Truxillo et al., 2015). At the same time, it is important to note that less research has focused on individuals who may identify as members of out-groups who feel they have been forgotten by organizational diversity and inclusion efforts. These groups are often referred to as "forgotten minorities." Stone et al. (2020) have called for increased research on "forgotten minorities," the members of various out-groups who have received limited attention within organizations and organizational scholars.

While research on autism spectrum disorder (ASD) exists, most of this research has focused on young children, preschool and K–12 educational programs, and the causes of autism. Additionally, much ASD research has been limited to populations in the United States. While some research has focused on the school-to-work transition of young adults with ASD, it is important to note that less research has focused on the work experiences and career outcomes of individuals with ASD, suggesting that these individuals have become a forgotten minority in the workplace.

Additionally, research funding on ASD has primarily been directed toward understanding the underlying biology and risk factors contributing to autism, with far fewer research dollars being focused on programs to actually help individuals with ASD. According to the Interagency Autism Coordinating Committee's (IACC) 2018 report on funding for autism research in the United States, 61% of funding was spent on biology and risk factors while only 3% was spent on lifespan issues and 6% on services.

International research funding reveals a similar pattern, with 3% spent on lifespan issues and 5% on services in 2016.

The limited research attention on lifespan issues, in conjunction with limited research focusing on adults with ASD, may contribute to these individuals becoming forgotten minorities in the workplace. This chapter will specifically focus on the work experiences and career outcomes of young adults with ASD who are at risk of becoming forgotten minorities in organizations. It is predicted that one-half million young adults with autism spectrum disorder (ASD) will reach adulthood and enter the workforce during the current decade. Hurley-Hanson et al. (2020) introduced the term *Generation A* to refer to this incoming cohort of young adults who are likely to need support to navigate the school-to-work transition successfully. With Generation A poised to enter the workforce in unprecedented numbers, research is needed to help individuals, organizations, and society work together to create successful work experiences and career outcomes for these young adults and to prevent them from becoming forgotten minorities.

Several explanations have been offered as to the primary reasons why young adults with ASD have been forgotten by organizational researchers. Historically, the focus of virtually all human resource, organizational behavior, and careers research has been conducted on neurotypical individuals. Increased awareness of the advantages that neurodiverse individuals bring to the workplace (Austin & Pisano, 2017) may create an opportunity for research to be conducted on the issues faced by this largely forgotten outgroup. Additionally, previous research on young adults with ASD has largely been published in medical and educational journals, with far fewer studies being published in the premier "A level" human resource, organizational behavior, and careers journals.

One purpose of this chapter is to offer suggestions for how researchers can address these reasons. Specific issues to be addressed in this chapter include the scope and importance of understanding how individuals with ASD, particularly members of Generation A, may become forgotten minorities; the role of functioning level, self-concept, disclosure, stigma, and image norms in excluding forgotten minorities from the workplace; suggestions for future research on forgotten minorities; and implications for human resource management policies and organizational practices.

THE SCOPE AND IMPORTANCE OF UNDERSTANDING HOW INDIVIDUALS WITH ASD, PARTICULARLY MEMBERS OF GENERATION A, MAY BECOME FORGOTTEN MINORITIES

According to the Centers for Disease Control and Prevention (CDC), 1 in 54 children have ASD, and the presence of ASD is 4.3 times more common in boys (1 in 34) than in girls (1 in 144) (CDC, 2020). Autism Speaks (2019a) estimates that there are 3.5 million people with ASD in the United States. The number of people with ASD is estimated to be in the tens of millions worldwide. Although it is difficult to get exact numbers, it is estimated that 1% of the world's population has ASD (CDC, 2020; Grønborg et al., 2013; Malcolm-Smith et al., 2013).

According to Autism Speaks (2019b), "Autism Spectrum Disorder (ASD) and autism are both general terms for a group of complex disorders of brain development. These disorders are characterized, in varying degrees, by difficulties in social interaction, verbal and nonverbal communication, and repetitive behaviors." The World Health Organization (2013, p. 7) describes ASD as "neurodevelopmental impairments in communication and social interaction and unusual ways of perceiving and processing information." As such, individuals with ASD often have difficulty understanding others' thoughts, intentions, and emotions (Bruggink et al., 2016). Some individuals with ASD may have difficulty regulating their own emotions. These challenges may create transition and employment issues for young adults with ASD (Samson et al. 2012), not only as they enter the workplace but potentially throughout their work lives as their careers unfold.

The unemployment and underemployment rates for individuals with ASD remain staggeringly high compared to the general population (Baldwin et al. 2014; Nord et al., 2016; Scott et al., 2015). Unemployment statistics for adults with ASD reveal that 85% are unemployed and that 69% of them want to work (National Autistic Society, 2016). The unemployment rate for individuals with ASD is much higher than that of adults with other disabilities. Roux et al. (2017) found that 95% of individuals with a learning disability, 91% of individuals with a speech and language impairment, and 74% of individuals with an intellectual disability had held a job in their early 20s. Research has also shown that many individuals with ASD have never been members of the labor force (Cidav et al., 2012).

Additionally, unemployment rate measures typically do not consider underemployment, whereby an individual works fewer hours than they would like or is working in a job below their skill level. Research has shown that young adults with ASD are more likely to be underemployed (Baldwin et al., 2014; Nord et al., 2016; Scott et al., 2015), overeducated, and overqualified for their jobs. This means that their work may be beneath their capabilities (Baldwin et al., 2014).

Young adults with ASD have been found to work in a limited number of occupations (Roux et al., 2013). Even when individuals with ASD do work, employment outcomes for adults with ASD are lower than those for the general population (Jennes-Coussens et al., 2006; Taylor et al., 2015). Adults with ASD tend to be underpaid compared to their peers without ASD (Ballaban-Gil et al. 1996; Howlin et al, 2004; Roux et al., 2013).

Research suggests that individuals with ASD who secure employment also face significant challenges in maintaining employment (Baldwin et al., 2014; Lorenz & Heinitz, 2014; Roux et al., 2013). When they experience conflict or stress at work, adults with ASD may quit or miss work without prior notice (Richards, 2012). They also are more likely than their peers without ASD to change jobs frequently and, as a result, to experience higher levels of ongoing stress and financial concerns (Baldwin et al., 2014).

Shattuck et al. (2012) found that 35% of young adults with ASD have never held a job, been members of the labor force, nor attended educational programs after high school (Shattuck et al., 2012; Cidav et al., 2012). A study of 200 transition-age young adults with ASD found that 81% were unemployed (Gerhardt & Lanier, 2011). A small study of young adults with ASD and IQs above 50 found that only 11.76% were employed (Howlin et al. 2004). Other studies have found that approximately half of the young adults with ASD have worked for pay after high school (Roux et al., 2013). The same study also found that the odds of ever having a paid job were higher for those who were older, from higher-income households, or who had better conversational or functional skills (Roux et al., 2013).

The statistics for young adults are particularly troubling, as it is estimated that one-half-million individuals with ASD will reach adulthood in the current decade and will be poised to enter the workplace in unprecedented numbers. These numbers are staggering and suggest the need to examine this cohort's long-term employment, career, and life outcomes. Hurley-Hanson, et al. (2020) introduced the term *Generation A* to refer to this generational cohort of young adults with ASD.

It is important that individuals with ASD, particularly Generation A members, do not become forgotten minorities because there are numerous benefits associated with including them in organizations. Austin and Pisano (2017), in their much-cited *Harvard Business Review* article, detail the numerous advantages that neurodivergent individuals bring to the workplace. The authors suggest that neurodivergent applicants, particularly individuals with ASD, represent an enormous pool of untapped talent that could increase companies' productivity. With 40% of global corporations having trouble recruiting the talent they need (Manpower Group, 2018), these individuals represent a rich, yet heretofore, untapped segment of the labor force.

Researchers have identified several potential skill sets and common characteristics of neurodivergent individuals that may benefit organizations. Much of this research has focused on the skill sets of individuals with ASD. These skills include visual acuity, more deliberative decision making, increased attentional focus, logical thinking, an affinity for technology, as well as professional and occupational interests in science, technology, engineering, and math (STEM) fields (Crespi, 2016). STEM fields are of particular interest, as there is a growing need for a skilled workforce in these areas (U.S. Bureau of Labor Statistics, 2018). While there is a lot of emphasis on hiring neurodivergent individuals in the technology and software fields, it is important to remember that neurodivergent individuals may have interests and talents in all fields (Ovaska-Few, 2018). While neurodivergent individuals may appear to be an ideal fit for this segment of the labor market, it should be recognized that some individuals may experience challenges with other aspects of employment, such as job-required social interaction. Organizations must be cognizant of the challenges and barriers they face and acknowledge the possibility that some individuals may not be successful in certain positions.

There are numerous potential benefits to individuals, organizations, and society when individuals with ASD are able to obtain and maintain jobs. Employment can result in more positive life outcomes for individuals with ASD and their families and caregivers. Sustained employment and the ability to live independently have the potential to reduce the financial toll on society of caring for individuals with ASD. The movement of Generation A into the workplace offers numerous benefits for the organizations that employ them. In addition to filling the demand for skilled workers, financial and reputational benefits may accrue for organizations that hire individuals with ASD. These include tax incentives provided by the federal government and other economic advantages, as well as positive perceptions of the organization by applicants and others within the community.

There are individual, organizational, and societal costs when individuals with ASD remain unemployed. These include the financial, social, and psychological costs of unemployment for individuals with ASD, their families, and caregivers. Ganz (2007) estimated the lifetime lost productivity costs for individuals with ASD to be $2.52 million. The annual cost of lost productivity for individuals and their parents is estimated to be between $39,000 and $130,000 (Ganz, 2007). There are lost productivity costs for organizations facing labor and skills shortages that might be avoided by employing individuals with ASD. Finally, there are societal costs associated with supporting individuals with ASD who are unable to find and maintain employment. The cost to society of forgetting individuals with ASD and excluding them from employment is staggering. The total cost of ASD support services in the United States exceeds $236 billion annually (Buescher et al., 2014). This number is expected to rise to 1 trillion dollars by 2025 (Baldwin et al. 2014; Leigh & Du, 2015). Research suggests that the costs of supporting an individual with ASD may exceed $2 million throughout the individual's lifetime (Buescher et al., 2014).

Moreover, of relevance to this chapter is the potential for individuals with ASD, particularly Generation A, to become forgotten minorities in organizations and to receive limited research attention from management scholars. Several factors may explain the scant research on the work and career experiences of Generation A. First, ASD presents along a *spectrum*. This means that the functioning level of individuals with ASD may vary from very low to very high. Because of the spectrum's breadth, many variations in skill sets, and the presence of comorbidities, it is challenging to generalize research results across individuals with ASD.

Second is the issue of disclosure. Unlike physical disabilities, which are discernible and visibly perceived, individuals with invisible disabilities such as ASD have the choice of whether to disclose their disability or not. Fear of stigmatization and being perceived as an out-group member and other negative outcomes may result in some individuals with ASD choosing not to reveal their disability, rendering it difficult to include these individuals in research on ASD in the workplace.

A third reason Generation A is a forgotten minority is the relatively small sample size of these members who are currently in the workforce. Most members of Generation A have minimal work and career experiences. At this point in time, while some individuals are transitioning into organizations, other individuals are in the career exploration stage. These factors make it very difficult to study the career experiences of Generation A empirically. Early research on this issue has primarily consisted of anecdotal studies documenting the work and career experiences of high-profile individuals with ASD.

Research is needed to help individuals with ASD not be forgotten. Theoretical models may help to increase research in this area. A deeper understanding of the career experiences of individuals with ASD may help increase positive work outcomes for members of Generation A. The next section of the chapter presents a theoretical model that may explain how members of Generation A and individuals with ASD may be prevented from becoming forgotten minorities.

THEORETICAL MODEL

Stone and Colella's (1996) theoretical model examining the factors that affect the treatment of disabled individuals in organizations has driven much of the empirical research on the inclusion of disabled individuals in organizational settings. Several elements in their model may provide a framework for understanding how to prevent Generation A from becoming a forgotten minority. Their model also has implications for organizations that desire to generate a neurodiverse workforce. The factors identified in Stone and Colella's model are the person characteristics of both the individual with ASD and the observer, environmental factors, and organizational characteristics. While consideration of each element in their model is beyond the scope of this chapter, this section's focus will be to introduce those elements of the person characteristics components of the model that may be most salient for keeping Generation A from becoming a forgotten minority. The person characteristics examined in this chapter are relevant to both the individual with ASD and those who observe them, providing a theoretical framework for examining and understanding this issue. The person characteristics considered are functioning level, self-concept, disclosure, stigma, and image norms.

Functioning Level

Understanding individual differences among individuals with ASD is critically important. ASD presents across a broad spectrum of functioning levels. This has implications for the types of intellectual, emotional, and social skills that an individual may possess. In turn, this influences the types of jobs they are qualified for and that they will be able to obtain across their careers (Nicholas et al., 2014). Functioning level also has implications for the behaviors they may exhibit in the workplace and the level of support required in their personal and professional lives. Functioning level is also important for understanding observers' reactions to individuals with ASD. Recruiters, managers, and coworkers may not be familiar with the myriad ways that ASD may present itself in the workplace, may hold inaccurate stereotypes about individuals with ASD, and may ignore individual differences among those with ASD. It may be expected that many observers will have had limited experience working with individuals with ASD. Studies on contact with stigmatized individuals, along with education, have been found to have a large effect on attitudes and may help reduce stigma (Corrigan, 2012; Griffiths et al., 2014; Yamaguchi et al., 2013). Exposing individuals, organizations, and society to the benefits of employing individuals with autism may lead to more inclusive workplaces. These factors may contribute to some individuals with ASD becoming forgotten minorities in organizations.

There are no standard definitions for classifying functioning level across specific skills, nor does there appear to be a universal assessment instrument to identify career-focused skill sets for individuals with ASD. In 2014 the Virginia Commonwealth University and Rehabilitation Research and Training Center working with Autism Speaks, created a community-based functional skills assessment for transition-aged youth with ASD (Virginia Commonwealth University [VCU], 2014). A section of this assessment looks at career paths and employment. This assessment can be used for multiple age groups, and the assessment differs depending on the age group. Although there are not many ASD-specific assessments available, there are other skills-based assessments that can be used to identify individual interests, strengths, and struggles for individuals with ASD. The following are sample assessments, O*net (2019), Casey Life Skills (2017), PAIRIN (n.d.), Mind Tools (2019), and Reflect (Graduate Management Admission Council, 2014). There are also online resources, such as careeronestop. org, which offers assessments and toolkits to help match the assessment outcomes with potential jobs. The creation of valid and reliable ASD skills assessments would be beneficial to individuals with ASD and potential employers. It would facilitate the person-job match process both for individuals with ASD and the organizations that seek to employ them.

Understanding the role of functioning level in causing Generation A members to become forgotten minorities is particularly important. Research suggests that the school-to-work transition may be particularly challenging for young adults with ASD when they leave high school. Additionally, research has found that transition services are inadequate for this generational cohort (Griffiths et al., 2020). Federally mandated benefits end, and many services are no longer provided after leaving high school. This is referred to as "the services cliff" (Roux, 2015). It occurs when these individuals no longer have transition services to help them move into the workplace. Research is needed to determine if functioning level influences the effects of the services cliff on the job search and employment experiences of individuals with ASD. Anecdotal evidence suggests that more attention has been focused on high functioning individuals with ASD by both organizations and researchers, suggesting that low functioning individuals with ASD may be even more forgotten than individuals with moderate or high functioning ASD.

It is important to note the relationship between functioning levels and skills and abilities, as the former influences the latter, and the latter influences an individual's ability to successfully perform on a job. There are various ways in which employers can assess the skills and abilities of potential employees with ASD. First, as should be done with all applicants, candidates' skills should be assessed using job-related assessments that are appropriate for each job's requirements. Second, some required skills such as professional certificates or educational degrees would be listed on a candidate's resume and may be verified by contacting the granting institution. Third, organizations may work with nongovernmental organizations (NGOs) and Federal and State Departments of Rehabilitation, whose missions are to place individuals with ASD into jobs. These organizations and agencies often perform initial screenings of candidates, including assessing functional, social, and job skills. Additionally, they are responsible for communicating with prospective employers to obtain necessary job skills requirements, assessing their clients in these skill areas, and providing needed training in these areas.

Self-Concept

Examining how members of Generation A have become forgotten minorities also requires understanding the important role of the self-concept. Finding and maintaining employment is critical for adults with ASD to become engaged and active citizens who experience a positive quality of life and feelings of dignity and self-worth. The experience of working and developing a work identity—the process of defining who one is in relation to work—is a psychological process that is a crucial part of the experience of adulthood (Dutton et al., 2010; Kira & Balkin, 2014; Saayman & Crafford, 2011). Thus, occupational choices are one way in which we define ourselves.

Central to career development is Super's variable of the individual's self-concept (Super, 1957, 1963). Super (1957) defines the self-concept as "the individual's picture of himself" and "the constellation of self-attributes considered by the individual to be vocationally relevant" (Super, 1963, p. 20). Moreover,

> Super proposes the notion that people strive to implement their self-concept by choosing to enter the occupation seen as most likely to permit self-expression. Furthermore, Super suggests that the particular behaviors a person engages in to implement the self-concept vocationally are a function of the individual's stage of life development. (Osipow, 1983, p. 153)

In each of Super's stages of career development, there is an emphasis on forming, redefining, or maintaining the self-concept (Ornstein et al. 1989).

Super's career theory suggests that individuals choose occupations that allow them to play a role that is consistent with their self-concept. The self-concept includes the attributes one believes define oneself, such as abilities, personality traits, and values. Abilities may be broadly defined to include both physical and psychological characteristics. Individuals perceive themselves to possess several physical (e.g., "I am strong.") and psychological (e.g., "I am good with people.") abilities. Irrespective of accuracy, these perceptions may influence (and constrain) the number of occupations that are considered to allow for the implementation of the self-concept (Giannantonio & Hurley-Hanson, 2006).

Little is known about the self-concepts of individuals with ASD and how their perceptions of their abilities influence their choice of occupations. Additionally, little is known about the effects of not seeing individuals with disabilities successfully perform various occupations on the career aspirations and enactment of the self-concept of young adults with ASD. Career aspirations may become limited if it is believed that individuals with ASD cannot pursue certain occupations. Additionally, an individual's perceptions of their diagnosis are likely to influence their self-concept and their perceptions of their abilities to successfully engage in job search activities and gain employment. Understanding the role of the self-concept on career aspirations is particularly important for members of Generation A who are poised to enter the workforce in unprecedented numbers and who are at risk of becoming forgotten minorities.

Disclosure

Closely aligned with self-concept is the issue of disclosure and the role it may play in Generation A becoming a forgotten minority. Disclosure of neurodiversity in the workplace is a complex decision with personal, professional, and legal ramifications (Megrew, 2019). Individuals with ASD must consider and recognize the effects of disclosure on their coworkers and supervisors, as well as its implications for their own organizational work experiences. Research suggests that disclosure is a difficult decision for workers with ASD. Hedley et al. (2016) found that 100% of their participants with ASD struggled to decide whether to disclose their disability or not. Employees must consider that once they decide to disclose, the decision cannot be reversed (Brownlow et al., 2018). Unlike physical disabilities, which are discernible and visibly perceived, individuals with invisible disabilities such as ASD may choose not to disclose their disability. Some individuals may be concerned that disclosing a disability will alter their colleagues' perceptions of their knowledge, skills, and abilities and affect their professional credibility. In addition, neurodivergent individuals may be concerned that employers may misunderstand their diagnosis or may even discriminate against them because of it. Furthermore, individuals with ASD may be concerned that once they disclose, their persona becomes that of the "autistic" employee, and their interactions will be perceived through the lens of ASD. Fear of tokenism may create perceptions that they will have to work harder than neurotypical employees to prove that they can successfully perform on the job.

The decision not to disclose and conceal a diagnosis of ASD may result in a different set of issues for members of Generation A. Research suggests that one problem with concealment strategies is that subsequent disclosure of a health condition or disability may violate others' expectations and result in negative reactions (Ragins, 2008; Stone et al., 1986; Tagalakis et al., 1988). The research on concealment strategies indicates that their effectiveness may depend on the nature of the disability and the degree to which the disclosure is seen as voluntary (Stone et al., 1986; Tagalakis et al., 1988). Research has also found that there is an emotional cost associated with concealment strategies and that not being able to present one's authentic self in the workplace may create long-term emotional labor for some neurodivergent individuals (Brownlow et al., 2018).

Individuals with ASD who are successfully hired but who did not disclose during the recruitment process face the issue of whether or not to disclose once they are hired and the timing of the decision to disclose. Neurodivergent individuals who choose not to disclose their diagnosis may be misunderstood at work if they are perceived as not adhering to social norms, their behavior deviates from expected workplace behavior, or they violate social interaction rules. Neurodivergent employees may face isolation, rejection, harassment, bullying, and discrimination on the job if they do not disclose their diagnosis and their behaviors are interpreted as odd, quirky, or unfriendly.

Disclosure of neurodiverse disabilities may help individuals receive needed accommodations at work. If an individual discloses that they have ASD early in the hiring process, an organization may be able to provide them with alternative recruitment methods. Although disclosure may help individuals receive needed accommodations, once an employee discloses their disability, misunderstandings regarding the individual and their abilities may lead to stigmatization (Brownlow et al., 2018).

Stigma

Compounding the problem of disclosure in the workplace is the issue of stigma (von Schrader et al., 2014). Disclosure of a disability and specifically a diagnosis of ASD has been found to lead to stigmatization (Goffman, 1986; Johnson & Joshi, 2016; Myers, 2004). Stigma refers to attitudes and beliefs that lead people to reject, avoid, or fear those they perceive as different (Disabilities Rights California, 2018). Many researchers have relied on Goffman's (1963) definition, which states that stigma is an "attribute that is deeply discrediting" and that reduces the person "from a whole and usual person to a tainted, discounted one" (p. 3). Social stigma "is a belief held by a large faction of society in which persons with the stigmatized condition are less equal or are part of an inferior group" (Ahmedani, 2011, p. 4). In the workplace, social stigma may cause individuals with ASD to be perceived as inferior, resulting in barriers or unequal access to opportunities. It is important to note that stigma is a distinct concept, separate from prejudice and stereotyping, although these may factor into the process of stigmatization (Dovidio et al. 2001).

Stigmatization has been found to lead to a variety of negative consequences for individuals with ASD. These consequences include difficulties gaining employment, obtaining housing, accessing health care, maintaining relationships, and building self-esteem (Baumeister, & Leary, 1995;

Link & Phelan, 2001; Read & Harré, 2001). In organizations, the dominant group's attitudes and beliefs may lead to stigmatization (Link & Phelan, 2001). Dominant groups in organizations can stigmatize and exclude others because of the power they have. For an organization to "address the fundamental cause of stigma—it must either change the deeply held attitudes and beliefs of powerful groups that lead to labeling, stereotyping, setting apart, devaluing, and discriminating, or change circumstances so as to limit the power of such groups to make their cognitions the dominant ones" (Link & Phelan, 2007, p. 282).

Research has examined the relationship between ASD and stigma (Brownlow et al., 2018). Stigma may arise because the person belongs to a defined group (individuals with ASD), or they do not display the social and behavioral norms expected in the workplace. Stigma has been found to have a unique relationship with ASD because of three characteristics associated with a diagnosis of ASD. First, ASD is considered to be a hidden disability. This means that most people with ASD do not appear to have a disability. They may not be perceived as having a disability until they exhibit a behavior outside of the norm, which then leads to stigmatization. Second, some individuals may exhibit symptoms of ASD that involve socially unacceptable behaviors such as verbal and behavioral outbursts, being unaware of social conventions (e.g., speaking frankly), and violating personal space boundaries (Autism Speaks, 2018). Third, while individuals with ASD may appear to be physically able, they may suffer from an extremely pervasive disability (Gray, 1993) and may be unable to perform physical tasks due to dysgraphia and low muscle tone.

The stigma related to ASD is often more pronounced than the stigma associated with other disabilities in the workplace. This may be "due to the stereotypes and perceptions [which] can range from doubts about their diagnoses to unfair expectations of savant-like capabilities" (Neely & Hunter, 2014, p. 276). Individuals with ASD may face stigmatization due to misperceptions and stereotypes about ASD. The stigma of ASD may arise from preconceived stereotypes (described as labeling) or observation (described as behavioral effects). Butler and Gillis (2011) suggest that both of these sources of stigma may be associated with ASD. Research findings suggest that behavior has a more significant impact on stigma than labeling (Farina et al. 1973; Jones et al., 1984; Link et al. 1987).

The manifestations of the stigma that individuals with ASD may experience at work include being socially excluded, being ignored, being bullied, and not being given work assignments that they were capable of doing. In addition, individuals with ASD report not being supported at work (Cassidy, 2012). Although coworkers may be empathetic towards employees with ASD, they may stigmatize them as being members of a disabled group. They may stereotype them as not being able to work up to performance standards or as not being able to work with other employees. For example, an adult with ASD may enter the work setting without disclosing their disability. In that case, a stigmatizer may perceive any displayed differences as resulting from someone who is not adhering to social norms. Alternatively, a stigmatizer may recognize the behavioral manifestations of ASD and stigmatize an individual who has chosen not to disclose their diagnosis. Individuals with ASD who choose not to disclose their diagnosis may still experience stigmatization at work if their behavior falls outside the norms of expected workplace behavior, commonly expected social interaction rules, and image norms of the ideal worker.

Image Norms

Finally, image norms may play a role in explaining how neurodiverse individuals, particularly members of Generation A, become forgotten minorities. An image norm is a belief that individuals must present an image that is consistent with occupational, organizational, or industry standards in order to be hired or promoted (Giannantonio & Hurley-Hanson, 2006). There are two ways image norms may affect the employment experiences of Generation A. First, members of Generation A may perceive that they do not fit the image norm of the jobs, organizations, and industries they are interested in pursuing. Such image norms may be formed in the exploration stage of career development and likely arise from a child's interactions with individuals who hold various jobs, messages conveyed through print and broadcast media, and comments from family, friends, and teachers about the types of jobs the young adult is expected to pursue or is told to avoid because of their diagnosis. Image norms may be created at an early age through a child's interactions with individuals they observe performing specific jobs. The people who are seen holding these jobs strongly influences children's perceptions of the images associated with specific occupations. These perceptions may have long-lasting effects on occupational choice (Palladino Schultheiss et al., 2005). Children with ASD need to see people like them in various jobs and occupations that they encounter in their daily lives. If children with ASD do not see adults with ASD in various jobs, they may not believe that they can pursue these occupations for themselves.

Image norms may also arise from comments that family, friends, and teachers make. Relevant others may express their beliefs about the importance of image in certain occupations. As career aspirations are expressed, they may share their opinions about the child's likelihood of success in the chosen occupation. Research suggests that family members are important sources of information about the role of image in careers (Hensley Choate,

2005). Comments from family, friends, and teachers may become deeply ingrained and have long-lasting influences on the child's career. Research is needed to understand the impact of such comments on the career interests and aspirations of individuals with ASD. Children with ASD must not receive comments that discourage them from pursuing certain occupations due to their diagnosis. Equally important, young adults with ASD should not receive comments that stereotype them into believing that they should only work in occupations, companies, and industries that are traditionally suggested individuals with ASD pursue.

Image norms may also arise from messages conveyed by the media. Images of occupations, organizations, and even industries may be found on the internet, in print, and through broadcast media (Hartung et al., 2005). These visual images of jobs may serve to reinforce the occupational stereotypes held by children and young adults. In time, these descriptions of jobs may become the basis for occupational image norms. A study of junior high school students found that the younger they were, the more likely they were to be influenced by role models on television in terms of their anticipated career choices (King & Multan, 1996). Little is known about the effect of seeing characters with autism in film and television successfully performing various jobs (e.g., The Good Doctor) on the image norms of young adults. Interestingly, it has been suggested that the increase in medical school applications—the Dr. Fauci effect—may be partially attributed to public perceptions of the dedication and sacrifice of health care providers during the COVID-19 pandemic (Murphy, 2020).

In recent years, individuals with ASD have been featured in literature, television, and movies as major or supporting characters. Several books have exposed readers to characters with ASD and provided a glimpse into their thinking processes and how they interact with family, friends, and coworkers. Several television shows have featured main characters with ASD. Including characters with ASD in popular media may help reduce the stigma associated with ASD and create image norms that can change perceptions about the types of occupations that individuals with ASD can pursue. Such image norms may have long-lasting effects on an individual's career choices in later stages of career development.

Image norms also may be formed as young adults are exposed to formal sources of job information such as the *Occupational Information Network* (O*Net) and the *Occupational Outlook Handbook* (OOH) (Herr et al., 2004). The descriptions of occupations found in these formal sources are essential depictions of the world of work (Hartung, 1996). Such images may be particularly salient for young adults first entering the labor market who typically possess limited information about specific occupations. When disabilities are discussed in occupational information, they often conform with stereotypes about the type of occupations appropriate for those with disabilities. Little is known about the effects of formal occupational information on creating image norms that might influence the career choices of individuals with ASD, particularly members of Generation A.

Second, image norms held by employment decision-makers in organizations may cause Generation A to become forgotten. Organizational members may have image norms of the ideal worker for their company. If an individual with ASD does not fit that image, they may not be considered for a job. Companies' public relations materials (Gibson, 2004) may convey images about the organization's ideal worker. Image norms also may be conveyed to young adults during the recruiting process. Recruiters and other organizational representatives may not be experienced with interviewing individuals with ASD. They may misinterpret the interests and behaviors of the ASD candidate and perceive that they do not fit the company's image. This may be because the recruiter may hold image norms about the organization they work for and the job they are recruiting for, bringing these beliefs into the interview process. When a recruiter observes that an applicant does not fit the firm's image norm, they may begin to assign negative characteristics to that applicant. They may place them in categories with stereotyped beliefs and perhaps exclude them from the organization (Kurzban & Leary, 2001; Leary & Schreindorfer, 1998). If an applicant does not fit the image norm the recruiter perceives is necessary to succeed in that job and company, the applicant's lack of fit with the recruiter's image norm may lead to them not being hired and ultimately becoming forgotten.

DIRECTIONS FOR FUTURE RESEARCH

Future research is needed to investigate how the five distinct, yet related person factors identified above will enable individuals with ASD to have successful work experiences, achieve positive career outcomes, and avoid being forgotten in the workplace. Understanding the employment experiences of individuals with ASD, particularly members of Generation A, can provide several interesting research streams for human resource, organizational behavior, and careers scholars. While future research on these issues should be conducted at the individual, the organizational, and the societal level, the research questions presented in this chapter are primarily focused on the individual level. It is suggested that the research agenda for academics interested in understanding and improving the work experiences and career outcomes of individuals with ASD should consider the person characteristics identified in Stone and Collella's (1996) model with a particular emphasis on the role of functioning level, self-concept, disclosure, stigma, and image norms. This section of the chapter presents future research questions that are critical for advancing understanding the role of each of these variables in preventing individuals with ASD from becoming forgotten minorities. It is important to note that future research is also needed at the organizational and societal level in order to prevent members of Generation A from becoming forgotten minorities.

Functioning Level

Understanding individual differences in functioning level among individuals with ASD is critically important. ASD presents across a broad spectrum of functioning levels which impacts the career-focused skill sets individuals possess. Research is needed to develop and validate a standard assessment instrument for classifying the functioning levels of individuals with ASD. Most research on the employment of individuals with ASD has focused on high functioning individuals. A more complete understanding of autism in the workplace will be dependent on including individuals along additional points on the autism spectrum.

The large numbers of young adults comprising Generation A suggest that more research is needed to understand their school-to-work transition experiences. One critical research area is studying how functioning level influences the effects of the services cliff on the job search and employment experiences of individuals with ASD. This may provide insight into understanding the barriers to employment faced by individuals with ASD during each phase of the job search process. Finally, research should focus on identifying the types of professional and personal support needed by individuals at different functioning levels in order for individuals with ASD to be successful on the job.

Self-Concept

Understanding how members of Generation A have become forgotten minorities also requires understanding how the relationship between the self-concept and employment is actualized for individuals with ASD. Little is known about the role a diagnosis of ASD plays in shaping an individual's self-concept and how perceptions of their diagnosis influence their choice of occupations. These gaps provide careers researchers several areas for future study. Some research has focused on early career stage issues such as successfully engaging in job search activities and gaining employment. Additional research is needed which focuses on how the self-concepts of individuals with ASD may change as they progress through Super's (1957, 1963) stages of career development. The movement of Generation A into the workforce during the current decade provides researchers with the opportunity to engage in longitudinal studies of career aspirations and career progression for individuals with ASD and other neurodiverse diagnoses.

Disclosure

Disclosure of neurodiversity in the workplace is a complex decision, and individuals with ASD must consider the effects of disclosure on their coworkers and supervisors, as well as its implications for their own organizational work experiences. Disclosure and concealment have been examined in the broader context of the disabilities literature. Less is known about the factors that influence an individual's decision to disclose or to conceal a diagnosis of ASD in the workplace.

An emerging body of research has examined the effects of the timing of disclosure during the job search and hiring process versus disclosure post-hire. Research is needed to examine the implications of disclosure, as well as concealment, on the behaviors and attitudes of supervisors, coworkers, and other organizational stakeholders (e.g., customers and suppliers). Research is also needed that examines the long-term emotional costs associated with concealment strategies that prevent individuals with ASD from being able to present their authentic self in the workplace.

Stigma

Compounding the problem of disclosure in the workplace is the related issue of stigma and stigmatization. Social stigma may cause individuals with ASD to be perceived as inferior, resulting in barriers or unequal access to employment opportunities. Research is needed to understand whether the stigma of ASD arises from preconceived stereotypes (labeling) or observation (behavioral effects). For example, how do the norms of expected workplace behavior, commonly expected social interaction rules, and image norms of the ideal worker interact to stigmatize neurodiverse individuals? It is important to examine how stigmatization manifests itself in organizational settings despite the protection provided by employment legislation prohibiting discrimination, harassment, and bullying. Research is needed to assess the long-term effectiveness of diversity and inclusion efforts in mitigating stigma against neurodiverse individuals.

Image Norms

The image norms held by individuals with ASD, as well as those held by organizational members and stakeholders, may contribute to Generation A becoming a forgotten minority in the workplace. Future research is needed to understand the factors that influence the image norms individuals with ASD form about different occupations, organizations, and industries, as well as their perceptions of their ability to work in those jobs, companies, and sectors. Research is needed to assess whether seeing individuals with ASD perform various jobs (i.e., serve as role models) influences occupational choice. Similarly, how do visual images of occupations in print and broadcast media, characters with ASD portrayed in film and television successfully performing various jobs, and comments from family, friends, and teachers, influence the career decisions of young adults with ASD?

Future research must also consider how the image norms held by organizational stakeholders and other organizational representatives may contribute to Generation A becoming forgotten minorities. While the research on recruitment effects is well documented, little is known about the reactions to and inferences made by individuals with ASD during the recruiting process. Finally, research is needed which focuses on understanding whether recruiters' and other organizational representatives' inexperience with interviewing individuals with ASD may potentially prevent these individuals from progressing further in the hiring process.

While the research directions outlined above focus on each of the five-person characteristics discussed in this chapter, it should be noted that these factors are interrelated, and future research should be conducted using research designs that simultaneously examine their effects. Future research should also focus on studying all cohorts of individuals with ASD and move beyond anecdotal studies documenting the work and career experiences of high-profile individuals with ASD. It is also important that future research includes longitudinal studies that will capture the work experiences and career outcomes of Generation A across the life span. Finally, care should be taken that researchers focus on the questions that are important to individuals with ASD and that these individuals have a voice in setting future research agendas. This research has important implications for HRM practice and policies and will enable organizations to successfully create company policies and practices that allow for the successful employment of individuals with ASD.

IMPLICATIONS FOR PRACTICE

There are several implications for HRM practice if organizations desire to create successful work experiences and career outcomes for Generation A. In addition, a significant number of organization-level policy changes will have to be made to prevent Generation A from becoming a forgotten minority. HRM functions will need to undergo significant changes to improve the ability of organizations to successfully attract, motivate, and retain employees with ASD. Initially, the most important areas of HRM to consider will be job analysis and recruitment and selection. These will allow organizations to attract and select individuals with ASD into the organization. Subsequently, once these individuals become employees, changes to performance management, training and development, and compensation and benefits systems may also need to be made. Before making changes to specific HRM policies, organizations will need to prioritize their strategic initiatives to include hiring individuals with ASD.

Strategic Initiatives

As managers become aware of the changing demographics of the labor market, including the large number of Generation A members who will be seeking employment in the current decade, they will need to prioritize strategic initiatives directed at increasing the number of Generation A members in their workforce. Top management support for this type of initiative is critical to the success of these programs. Some organizations have already begun to develop initiatives to hire a neurodivergent workforce. A few of these organizations have joined together to share best practices for organizational initiatives aimed at hiring individuals with ASD. One example is the Autism@Work Roundtable. Industry leaders including Ernst & Young LLP, JP Morgan Chase & Co., Microsoft, SAP, Ford, IBM, Travelers Insurance, Fidelity Investments, Freddie Mac, and Cintas created this group to help organizations develop diversity initiatives to hire people with ASD. Their Autism@Work Playbook includes specific recommendations for recruiting, interviewing, training, and maintaining neurodivergent individuals' employment (ASHA Leader, 2019). It is important to note that many of the initiatives are in the high technology and STEM fields. While there is a lot of emphasis on hiring neurodivergent individuals in the technology and software fields, it is important to consider individual differences and that neurodivergent individuals may have interests and talents in all fields (Ovaska-Few, 2018). While neurodivergent individuals may appear to be an ideal fit for this segment of the labor market, it should be recognized that some individuals may experience challenges with other aspects of employment, such as job-required social interaction.

These strategic initiatives will need to be supported through thoughtful management of the organizational change process. Developing and implementing these types of initiatives involves company-wide changes across departments and throughout all organization levels. Consistent with other diversity and inclusion initiatives, change is needed in all areas of the organization in order for the program to be viable and sustainable. The HR functions of job analysis, recruitment and selection, performance management, training and development, and compensation and benefits will all need to be examined and adapted to increase the inclusion of people with ASD.

Job Analysis

The job analysis process is central to virtually all other components of an organization's Human Resource Management system. The data collected in job analysis becomes the foundation for the job descriptions and job specifications that are listed in job postings. Organizations need to look at the job postings they develop, the places they post current employment opportunities, and their effect on recruiting practices (Austin & Pisano, 2017). Central to recruitment is the issue of developing appropriately written job postings. Organizations need to identify the knowledge, skills, and abilities that are genuinely needed for job vacancies. This ensures that neurodivergent candidates do not inadvertently self-select themselves out of positions they are qualified for (Härtel et al. 2013). Job postings should include the specific skills necessary for the position. Job postings should use precise, literal language. Many businesses list similar criteria for all of their vacancies, but hiring managers should think critically about each position and only list what the job truly requires. Online job postings often list attributes that neurodivergent candidates may not identify with. The language used in the posting may deter certain groups of candidates from applying for the job (Collier & Zhang, 2016).

The Equal Employment Opportunity Commission (2015) suggests that job postings use inclusive language and state the company's commitment to equal hiring practices (e.g., This company is an equal opportunity employer. We encourage qualified applicants from diverse backgrounds and experiences, including those with ASD, to apply. Accommodations are available.). Businesses need to be clear in their job postings that they have neurodiversity policies in place and communicate that their organizational environment is supportive and inclusive. A diversity and inclusion statement should be included in the job posting stating willingness to discuss and provide accommodations (Chartered Institute of Personnel and Development, 2018).

Recruitment and Selection

Organizations must consider ways to adapt and modify their recruitment and selection practices so that individuals with ASD can gain entry into the workplace. There is concern that current hiring practices may create entry barriers for individuals with ASD (Hedley et al., 2016; Smith et al., 2014; Vogus & Lounds-Taylor, 2018). These include finding out where to look for job vacancies, finding help with the recruitment process, developing a realistic awareness of careers and the work environment, anxiety, lack of confidence in job search abilities, diminished motivation to persist in job search, and logistical challenges such as having access to transportation (Moss & Butts, 2019). If applicants are unable to move past initial screenings, they will not be able to "get their foot in the door" and secure employment.

It may be necessary to modify the recruitment interview so that recruiters do not negatively evaluate neurodivergent candidates whose verbal and nonverbal behaviors do not exhibit expected social conventions. Recruiters need training on how to interact with and fairly evaluate these individuals. It is essential that organizations provide accommodations to prospective neurodivergent employees throughout the recruitment process. They should also state that applicants should request accommodations for the interview if needed. The interview provides an opportunity for organizations to show their commitment to inclusivity (Giannantonio & Hurley-Hanson, 2021). Organizations should consider the emphasis that is placed on communication skills to determine the required level of competency for various jobs. Depending on the employment opportunity, these could include using online questionnaires, phone interviews, or having applicants develop a website or video showing their skills (Moss & Butts, 2019). Adapting and modifying an organization's recruitment policies will be essential to the successful implementation of diversity initiatives.

It is also important that organizations use selection methods that will both appropriately assess the knowledge, skills, and abilities required of open positions and provide opportunities for individuals with ASD to successfully perform on these assessments. It has been suggested that alternatives to traditional interviews be used when evaluating neurodivergent job applicants to allow them to demonstrate their skills. These may involve not emphasizing the applicants' paper resumes (Davis, 2017) and the use of video resumes (Ovaska-Few, 2018). SAP, a company well-known for hiring people with ASD, has an innovative interview process for applicants with ASD. They have applicants come to their office and work on LEGO Mindstorm projects that increase in difficulty as the day progresses. In the second half of the day, applicants participate in team projects. SAP uses a month-long screening process to help potential employees develop soft skills, such as teamwork and workplace etiquette (Nezich, 2017). Candidates are offered the option of walking while they talk during the interview.

Other companies have also modified the interview process as part of their hiring initiatives. Microsoft adjusted its interview process to better assess applicants with ASD. They bring in ten to twelve candidates to meet throughout four and a half days. Candidates partake in a variety of exercises, mock interviews with feedback, and final interviews with hiring managers (Eng, 2018). As of 2017, Ernst & Young LLP separates the interview process into different sections. Applicants first go through a phone interview. This is followed by assessments of online skills and critical thinking, which were designed specifically for their Center of Excellence of Neurodiversity. The next step is a video interview. They then conduct a "super week" where applicants participate in team-based simulations, work on interpersonal skills development, and are introduced to job roles. These are examples of how organizations may adapt their selection processes (e.g., traditional selection interviews, assessment centers, and probationary periods) that might more accurately assess prospective applicants with ASD.

Performance Management

The performance appraisal and management process will need to be assessed and modified to provide reliable and valid evaluations of employees with ASD. Is it important that all performance raters and evaluators understand the issues associated with the performance management of individuals with ASD. This is especially important when organizations utilize 360-degree performance management systems that employ self, peer, and customer ratings of employee performance in addition to ratings by the immediate supervisor or manager.

While performance feedback is important for all employees, how the performance feedback is delivered is especially important for employees with ASD. Research has found that immediate feedback was important and effective for individuals with disabilities (Barbetta et al., 1994). Managers need to be very clear and specific about required job tasks, expected performance standards, and deadlines for completing work tasks and projects. Organizations may consider putting performance expectations, work assignments, and deadlines in writing, which would be helpful for all employees, not only employees with ASD. Research suggests that for employees with ASD, it is important for leaders to clearly describe performance expectations and job duties, to provide clear instructions, and to maintain consistency in the workplace (Hagner & Cooney, 2005). It will be important for managers to identify the obstacles that might obstruct the performance of employees with ASD, especially if the individual with ASD is not aware of the obstacles and barriers hindering their performance.

An interesting stream of research has begun examining the effectiveness of covertly delivering feedback to individuals with ASD through earbud speakers. This way of delivering feedback is called covert audio coaching. A study by Bennett et al. (2010) found that covert audio coaching produced improvements in the participant's job skills and that the skills were maintained over time. Covert audio coaching has many similarities to side-by-side job coaching but may offer long-term advantages. One difficulty with side-by-side job coaching is how and when to reduce the presence of the coach from the workplace. "One advantage of covert audio coaching is that as an employee's performance improves, there are fewer verbal prompts from the coach. It may also be advantageous to have a process where employees with ASD start out with a side-by-side coach and eventually move to a covert audio coaching situation. One limitation of covert audio coaching is that it is only possible with individuals who have excellent attention and receptive language skills (Bennett et al., 2013).

Training and Development

Training and development may help employees with ASD understand their current job and what is required for advancement in the organization. The training of employees with ASD is a prime example of how organizations can collaborate with nonprofit and government agencies to help them develop training programs. For example, The Autism@Work Roundtable consults with other companies to help them with all aspects of the hiring process, including training. Their Playbook helps prospective employers with the training of neurodiverse individuals ("Playbook Helps Companies," 2019). Existing training and career development programs will need to be assessed, and new ones may need to be created for coworkers, team members, supervisors, managers, and leaders that will help inform other employees' perceptions about individuals with ASD, share effective communication strategies for providing them with developmental feedback, and develop efforts to create an inclusive work environment and organizational culture where all employees feel supported and valued. Such training may help to reduce the stigma experienced in the workplace by some individuals with ASD. For example, at SAP, there is a large effort to train current employees on the benefits of working with individuals with ASD and how they can help make the program successful (Holland, 2016).

Compensation and Benefits

The compensation and benefits package provided to employees with ASD will need to be examined to ensure that individuals with ASD are fairly compensated and receiving salaries and benefits that are appropriate to their knowledge, skills, and abilities, as well as being consistent with the compensation packages offered to neurotypical employees. The importance of pay for individuals' perceptions of self-worth, their ability to be self-sufficient, as well as its relationship to job satisfaction and equity perceptions, suggests the importance of this component of an organization's HRM system. Organizations need to assess whether their compensation and benefits packages are providing individuals with ASD what they need and want in order to remain motivated, perform at high levels, and remain with the organization.

If organizations desire to create successful work experiences and career outcomes for Generation A and wish to prevent Generation A from becoming a forgotten minority, Human Resource Management functions will need to make significant changes such as those outlined above. Successfully attracting, motivating, and retaining employees with ASD has long-term benefits for both organizations and members of Generation A. Research has long documented the financial and psychological benefits of having a job. Meaningful employment may give individuals with ASD the opportunity to support themselves and gain financial independence, which in turn has a positive effect on quality of life (Ross & Van Willigen, 1997) and general life satisfaction (Chiang et al., 2013; Hendricks, 2010; Mavranezouli et al., 2014).

In conclusion, there is much work to be done both by organizations and HRM researchers to prevent individuals with ASD, particularly members of Generation A, from becoming forgotten minorities in the workplace. There are many opportunities for academics to discover the answers to the research questions surrounding this important issue and which will provide guidance to organizations that are committed to employing individuals with ASD and ensuring that all employees are afforded the dignity and respect of meaningful work. Hopefully, these steps will prevent Generation A from becoming a forgotten minority in the workplace.

REFERENCES

Ahmedani B. K. (2011). Mental health stigma: Society, individuals, and the profession. *Journal of Social Work Values and Ethics*, 8(2), 41–416.

Austin, R., & Pisano, G. (2017, May–June). Neurodiversity as a competitive advantage. *Harvard Business Review*, 98–104.

Autism Speaks. (2018, August). *To disclose or not to disclose?* https://www.autismspeaks.org/tool-kit-excerpt/disclose-or-not-disclose

Autism Speaks. (2019a). *What is autism?* https://www.autismspeaks.org/what-autism

Autism Speaks. (2019b). *Employers & recruiters.* https://www.autismspeaks.org/employers-people-autism

Avery, D. R., Volpone, S. D., & Holmes IV, O. (2018). Racial discrimination in organizations. In A. J. Colella & E. B. King (Eds.), *Oxford library of psychology. The Oxford handbook of workplace discrimination* (pp. 89–109). Oxford University Press. https://doi.org/ 10.1093/oxfordhb/9780199363643.013.8

Baldwin, S., Costley, D., & Warren, A. (2014). Employment activities and experiences of adults with high-functioning Autism and Asperger's disorder. *Journal of Autism and Developmental Disorders, 44*(10), 2440–2449. https://doi.org/10.1007/s10803-014-2112-z

Ballaban-Gil, K. R., Rapin, I., Tuchman, R. & Shinnar, S. (1996). Longitudinal examination of the behavioral, language, and social changes in a population of adolescents and young adults with autistic disorder. *Pediatric Neurology, 15*(3), 217–223. https://doi.org/10.1016/S0887-8994(96)00219-6

Barbetta, P. M., Heward, W. L., Bradley, D. M., & Miller, A. D. (1994). Effects of immediate and delayed error correction on the acquisition and maintenance of sight words by students with developmental disabilities. *Journal of Applied Behavior Analysis, 27*(1), 177–178.

Baumeister, R. F. & Leary, M. R. (1995). The need to belong: Desire for interpersonal attachments as a fundamental human motivation. *Psychological Bulletin, 17*, 497–530. https://doi.org/10.1037/0033-2909.117.3.497

Bell, M. P. (2006). *Diversity in organizations*. Cengage South-Western.

Bennett, K., Brady, M. P., Scott, J., Dukes, C., & Frain, M. (2010). The effects of covert audio coaching on the job performance of supported employees. *Focus on Autism and Other Developmental Disabilities, 25*(3), 173–185. https://doi.org/10.1177/1088357610371636

Bennett, K .D., Ramasamy, R., & Honsberger, T. (2013). The effects of covert audio coaching on teaching clerical skills to adolescents with autism spectrum disorder. *Journal of Autism and Developmental Disorders, 43*(3), 585–593. https://doi.org/10.1007/s10803-012-1597-6

Brownlow, C., Werth, S., & Keefe, K. (2018). Autism spectrum disorder: Emotion work in the workplace. In S. Werth & C., Brownlow (Eds.), *Work and identity* (pp. 23–37). Palgrave Macmillian. https://doi.org/10.1007/978-3-319-73936-6_3

Bruggink, A., Huisman, S., Vuijk, R., Kraaij, V., & Garnefski, N. (2016). Cognitive emotion regulation, anxiety and depression in adults with autism spectrum disorder. *Research in Autism Spectrum Disorders, 22*, 34–44. https://doi.org/10.1016/j.rasd.2015.11.003

Buescher, A. V. S., Cidav, Z., Knapp, M., & Mandell, D. S. (2014). Costs of autism spectrum disorders in the United Kingdom and the United States. *JAMA Pediatrics, 168*, E1–E8. https://doi.org/10.1001/jamapediatrics.2014.210

Butler, R. C. & Gillis, J. M. (2011). The impact of labels and behaviors on the stigmatization of adults with Asperger's disorder. *Journal of Autism and Developmental Disorders, 41*(6), 741–749. https://doi.org/10.1007/s10803-010-1093-1099

Casey Life Skills. (2017). *Casey family programs*. https://caseylifeskills.secure.force.com

Cassidy, S. (2012, May 14). Autistic adults bullied and not supported at work, poll shows. *Independent*. https://www.independent.co.uk/news/uk/home-news/autistic-adults-bullied-and-not-supported-at-work-poll-shows-7743517.html

Centers for Disease Control and Prevention [CDC]. (2020). Data & statistics on autism spectrum disorder. https://www.cdc.gov/ncbddd/autism/data.html

Chiang, H. M., Cheung, Y. K., & Tsai, L. Y. (2013). Factors associated with participation in employment for high school leavers with autism. *Journal of Autism and Developmental Disorders, 43*, 1832–1842.

Cidav, Z., Marcus, S. C., & Mandell, D. S. (2012). Implications of childhood autism for parental employment and earnings. *Pediatrics, 129*(4), 617–623. https://doi.org/10.1542/peds.2011-2700

Chartered Institute of Personnel and Development. (2018). *Neurodiversity at work.* https://www.cipd.co.uk/Images/neurodiversity-at-work_2018_tcm18-37852.pdf

Corrigan, P. W. (2012). Where is the evidence supporting public service announcements to eliminate mental illness stigma? *Psychiatric Services, 63*(1), 79–82.

Collier, D., & Zhang, C. (2016). Can we reduce bias in the recruiting process and broaden/diversify pools of candidates by using different types of words/styles in job descriptions? Cornell University, Digital Collections @ ILR. http://digitalcommons.ilr.cornell.edu/student/140

Crespi, B.J. (2016). Autism as a disorder of high intelligence. *Frontiers in Neuroscience. 10*(300). https://doi.org/10.3389/fnins.2016.00300

Davis, G. P. (2017, March 17). Diversity is not enough. Inclusion is the key. *Higher Education Today.* https://www.higheredtoday.org/2017/03/17/diversity-not-enough-inclusion-key/

Disabilities Rights California. (2020, December). *Principles: The stigma of mental health and violence.* https://www.disabilityrightsca.org/legislation/principles-the-stigma-of-mental-health-and-violence

Dovidio, J. F., Major, B., & Crocker, J. (2001). Stigma: Introduction and overview. In T. F. Heatherton, R. E. Kleck, M. R. Hebl, & J. G. Hull (Eds.), *The social psychology of stigma* (pp. 1–28), Guilford Press

Dutton, J. E., Roberts, L. M., & Bednar, J. (2010). Pathways for positive identity construction at work: Four types of positive identity and the building of social resources. *The Academy of Management Review, 35*(2), 265–293. https://doi.org/10.5465/AMR.2010.48463334

Eng, D. (2018). *Where autistic worker thrive.* Fortune. https://fortune.com/2018/06/24/where-autistic-workers-thrive/

Equal Employment Opportunity Commission [EEOC]. (2015, February 3). *Recruiting, hiring, retaining, and promoting people with disabilities: A resource guide for employers.* https://www.eeoc.gov/eeoc/interagency/upload/employing_people_with_disabilities_toolkit_february_3_2015_v4-2.pdf

Farina, A., Felner, R. D., & Boudreau, L. (1973). Reactions of workers to male and female mental patient job applicants. *Journal of Consulting and Clinical Psychology, 41*, 363–372. https://doi.org/10.1037/h0035329

Ganz, M.L. (2007). The lifetime distribution of the incremental societal costs of autism. *Archives of Pediatrics and Adolescent Medicine. 161*(4), 343–349. https://doi.org/10.1001/archpedi.161.4.343

Gerhardt, P. F., & Lainer, I. (2011). Addressing the needs of adolescents and adults with autism: A crisis on the horizon. *Journal of Contemporary Psychotherapy, 41*(1), 37–45. https://doi.org/10.1007/s10879-010-9160-2

Giannantonio, C.M., & Hurley-Hanson, A.E. (2006). Applying image norms across super's career development stages. *Career Development Quarterly, 54*, 318–330. https://doi.org/10.1002/j.2161-0045.2006.tb00197.x

Giannantonio, C. M., & Hurley-Hanson, A. E. (in press). Recruitment strategies: Generating a neurodiverse workforce. *Neurodiversity in the Workplace.*

Gibson, D. E. (2004). Role models in career development: New directions for theory and research. *Journal of Vocational Behavior, 65*, 134–156. https://doi.org/10.1016/S0001-8791(03)00051-4

Goffman, E. (1986). *Stigma: Notes on the management of spoiled identity.* Simon & Schuster.

Goffman, E. (1963). *Stigma: Notes on the management of spoiled identity.* Prentice-Hall.

Graduate Management Admission Council. (2014). *Reflect.* https://www.gmac.com/

Gray, D. E. (1993). Perceptions of stigma: The parents of autistic children. *Sociology of Health & Illness, 15*, 102–120. https://doi.org/10.1111/1467-9566.ep11343802

Griffiths, A. J., Giannantonio, C. M., Hurley-Hanson, A. E., & Cardinal, D. N. (2016). Autism in the workplace: Assessing the transition needs of young adults with autism spectrum disorder. *Journal of Business and Management, 22*, 5–22.

Griffiths, A. J., Hanson, A. H., Giannantonio, C. M., Mathur S. K., Hyde, K., & Linstead, E. (2020). Developing employment environments where individuals with ASD thrive: Using machine learning to explore employer policies and practices. *Brain Sciences. 10*(9), 632–654. https://doi.org/10.3390/brainsci10090632

Griffiths, K. M., Carron-Arthur, B., Parsons, A., & Reid, R. (2014). Effectiveness of programs for reducing the stigma associated with mental disorders. A meta-analysis of randomized controlled trials. *World Psychiatry, 13*(2), 161–175.

Grønborg, T. K., Schendel, D. E., & Parner, E. T. (2013). Recurrence of autism spectrum disorders in full- and half-siblings and trends over time: A population-based cohort study. *JAMA Pediatrics. 167*(10), 947–953. https://doi.org/10.1001/jamapediatrics.2013.2259

Hagner, D., & Cooney, B. F. (2005). "I Do That for Everybody": Supervising employees with autism. *Focus on Autism and Other Developmental Disabilities, 20*, 91–97.

Härtel, H., Härtel, G. F. & Trumble, R. (2013). IDADA: The individual difference approach to assessing and developing diversity awareness. *Journal of Management & Organization, 19*(1), 60–74. https://doi.org/10.1017/jmo.2013.4

Hartung, P. J. (1996). Work illustrated: Attending to visual images in career information materials. *Career Development Quarterly, 44*, 234–241. https://doi.org/10.1002/j.2161-0045.1996.tb00254.x

Hartung, P. J., Porfeli, E. J., & Vondracek, F. W. (2005). Child vocational development: A review and reconsideration. *Journal of Vocational Behavior, 66*(3), 385–419. https://doi.org/10.1016/j.jvb.2004.05.006

Hedley, D. H., Uljarevic, M., Cameron, L., Dissanayake, C., Halder, S., & Richdale, A. (2017). Employment programs and interventions targeting adults with autism spectrum disorder: A systematic review of the literature. *Autism, 21*(8). https://doi.org/10.1177/1362361316661855

Hendricks, D. (2010). Employment and adults with autism spectrum disorders: Challenges and strategies for success. *Journal of Vocational Rehabilitation, 32*, 125–134. https://doi.org/10.3233/JVR-2010-0502

Hensley Choate, L. (2005). Toward a theoretical model of women's body image resilience. *Journal of Counseling and Development, 83*(3), 320–330. https://doi.org/10.1002/j.1556-6678.2005.tb00350.x

Herr, E. L., Cramer, S. H., & Niles, S. G. (2004). *Career guidance and counseling through the lifespan* (6th ed.). Pearson.

Holland, R. (2016, July 11). *The benefits of recruiting employees with autism spectrum disorder.* Forbes,. https://www.forbes.com/sites/hbsworkingknowledge/2016/07/11/the-benefits-of-recruiting-employees-with-autism-spectrum-disorder/#368dc83840a2

Howlin, P., Goode, S., Hutton, J., & Rutter, M. (2004). Adult outcome for children with autism. *Journal of Child Psychology and Psychiatry, 45*(2), 212–229. https://doi.org/10.1111/j.1469-7610.2004.00215.x

Hurley, A. E., & Giannantonio, C. M. (1999). Career attainment for women and minorities: The interactive effects of age, gender, and race. *Women in Management Review, 14*(1), 4–13. https://doi.org/10.1108/09649429910255447

Hurley-Hanson, A. E, & Giannantonio, C. M. (2017). LMX and autism. In T. A. Scandura & E. Mourino (Eds.), *Effective working relationships in leading diversity in the 21st century* (pp. 281–301). Information Age Publishing.

Hurley-Hanson, A. E., Giannantonio, C. M., & Griffiths, A. J. (2020). *Autism in the workplace. creating positive outcomes for Generation A.* Palgrave Macmillan. https://doi.org/10.1007/978-3-030-29049-8

Interagency Autism Coordinating Committee (IACC). (2018). *United States data 2018.* U.S. Department of Health and Human Services. https://iacc.hhs.gov/funding/data/subcategories/?fy=2018

Jennes-Coussens, M., Magill-Evans, J., & Koning, C. (2006). The quality of life of young men with Asperger syndrome: A brief report. *Autism, 10*(4), 403–414. https://doi.org/10.1177/1362361306064432

Johnson, T. D., & Joshi, A. (2016). Dark clouds or silver linings? A stigma threat perspective on the implications of an autism diagnosis for workplace well-being. *Journal of Applied Psychology, 101*(3), 430–449. https://doi.org/10.1037/apl0000058

Jones, E. E., Farina, A., Hastorf, A. H., Markus, H., Miller, D. T., &Scott, R. (1984). *Social stigma: The psychology of marked relationships.* W. H. Freeman.

Joshi, A., Neely, B., Emrich, C., Griffiths, D., & George, G. (2015). Gender research in AMJ: An overview of five decades of empirical research and calls to action: Thematic issue on gender in management research. *The Academy of Management Journal, 58*(5), 1459–1475. https://doi.org/10.5465/amj.2015.4011

King, M. M., & Multan, K. D. (1996). The effects of television role models on the career aspirations of African American junior high school students. *Journal of Career Development, 23*(2), 111–125. https://doi.org/10.1177/089484539602300202

Kira, M., & Balkin, D. B. (2014). Interactions between work and identities: Thriving, withering, or redefining the self. *Human Resource Management Review, 24*(2), 131–143. https://doi.org/10.1016/j.hrmr.2013.10.001

Kurzban, R., & Leary, M. R. (2001). Evolutionary origins of stigmatization: The functions of social exclusion. *Psychological Bulletin, 127*(2), 187–208. https://doi.org/10.1037/0033-2909.127.2.187

Leary, M. R., & Schreindorfer, L. S. (1998). The stigmatization of HIV and AIDS: Rubbing salt in the wound. In V. J. Derlega & A. P. Barbee (Eds.), *HIV and social interaction* (pp. 12–29). SAGE.

Leigh, J. P., & Du, J. (2015). Brief report: Forecasting the economic burden of autism in 2015 and 2025 in the United States. *Journal of Autism and Developmental Disorders, 45*(12), 4135–4139. https://doi.org/10.1007/s10803-015-2521-7

Link, B. G., & Phelan, J. C. (2001). Conceptualizing stigma. *Annual Review Sociology, 27*, 363–385. https://doi.org/10.1146/annurev.soc.27.1.363

Link, B. G., & Phelan, J. C. (2007). Conceptualizing stigma. In E. J. Clarke & D. H. Kelly (Eds.), *Deviant Behavior* (pp. 264–287). Macmillan.

Link, B. G., Cullen, F. T., Frank, J., & Wozniak, J. F. (1987). The social rejection of former mental patients: Understanding why labels matter. *The American Journal of Sociology, 92*(6), 1461–1500. https://doi.org/10.1086/228672

Lorenz, T., & Heinitz, K. (2014). Aspergers–different, not less: Occupational strengths and job interests of individuals with Asperger's syndrome. *PLOS One, 9*(6). https://doi.org/e100358

Malcolm-Smith, S., Hoogenhout, M., Ing, N., Thomas, K. G., & de Vries, P. (2013). Autism spectrum disorders—Global challenges and local opportunities. *Journal of Child and Adolescent Mental Health, 25*(1), 1–5. https://doi.org/10.2989/17280583.2013.767804

ManpowerGroup. (2018). *Solving the talent shortage.* https://go.manpowergroup.com/talent-shortage-2018

Mavranezouli, I., Megnin-Viggars, O., Cheema, N., Howlin, P., Baron-Cohen, S., & Pilling, S. (2014). The cost-effectiveness of supported employment for adults with autism in the United Kingdom. *Autism, 18*, 975–984.

Megrew, L. E. (2019). *Neurodiversity and the organizational interview process: A phenomenological study of adult high-functioning autistics* (Publication No. 27542600) [Doctoral dissertation, Grand Canyon University]. ProQuest Dissertations and Theses Global. https://login.libproxy.chapman.edu/login?url=https://search-proquest-com.libproxy.chapman.edu/docview/2321034834?accountid=10051

Mind Tools. (2019). *SMART Goals: How to make your goals achievable.* https://www.mindtools.com/pages/article/get-started.htm

Moss, H., & Butts, L. (2019, July 19). Workplace challenges for women with autism, with Marcie Ciampi, M.Ed. (No. 68) [Audio podcast episode]. In *Spectrumly Speaking.* https://www.differentbrains.org/workplace-challenges-for-women-with-autism-with-marcie-ciampi-m-ed-samantha-craft-spectrumly-speaking-ep-68/

Myers, K. R. (2004). Coming out: Considering the closet of illness. *Journal of Medical Humanities. 25*(4), 255–270. https://doi.org/10.1007/s10912-004-4832-0

National Autistic Society. (2016). *About the campaign.* www.autism.org.uk

Neely, B. H., & Hunter, S. T. (2014). In a discussion on invisible disabilities, let us not lose sight of employees on the autism spectrum. *Industrial and Organizational Psychology, 7*(2), 274–277. https://doi.org/10.1111/iops.12148

Nezich, H. (2017). *More companies hiring employees with autism*. Diversability. https://diverseabilitymagazine.com/2017/07/companies-hiring-employees-autism/

Nicholas, D. B., Attridge, M., Zwaigenbaum, L., & Clarke, M. (2015). Vocational support approaches in autism spectrum disorder: A synthesis review of the literature. *Autism. 19*(2), 235–245. https://doi.org/10.1177/1362361313516548

Nord, D. K., Stancliffe, R. J., Nye-Legerman, K., & Hewitt, A. S. (2016). Employment in the community for people with and without autism: A comparative analysis. *Research in Autism Spectrum Disorders, 24*, 11–16. https://doi.org/10.1016/j.rasd.2015.12.013

O*Net Resource Center. (2019). *O*NET® career exploration tools*. https://www.onetcenter.org/tools.html

Ornstein, S., Cron, W., & Slocum, J. (1989). Life stage versus career stage: A comparative test of the theories of Levinson and Super. *Journal of Organizational Behavior, 10*, 117–133. https://doi.org/10.1002/job.4030100203

Osipow, S. H. (1983). *Theories of career development*. Prentice-Hall.

Ovaska-Few, S. (2018, January 1). Promoting neurodiversity: A pilot program at EY recruits workers with autism. *Journal of Accountancy*. https://www.journalofaccountancy.com/issues/2018/jan/ey-pilot-program-workers-with-autism.html

PAIRIN. (n.d.). *Soft skills assessment*. https://www.pairin.com/products/essential-skill-tools/

Palladino Schultheiss, D. E., Palma, T. V., & Manzi, A. J. (2005). Career development in middle childhood: a qualitative inquiry. *Career Development Quarterly, 53*, 246–262. https://doi.org/10.1002/j.2161-0045.2005.tb00994.x

Playbook helps companies hire people with ASD. (2019). *The ASHA Leader, 24*(5). https://doi.org/10.1044/leader.NIB4.24052019.13

Ragins, B. R. (2008). Disclosure disconnect: Antecedents and consequences of disclosing invisible stigmas across life domains. *Academy of Management Review, 33*(1), 194–215. https://doi.org/10.2307/20159383

Read, J., & Harré, N. (2001). The role of biological and genetic causal beliefs in the stigmatization of "mental patients'. *Journal of Mental Health, 10*(2), 223–235. https://doi.org/10.1080/09638230123129

Richards, J. (2012). Examining the exclusion of employees with Asperger syndrome from the workplace. *Personnel Review, 41*(5), 630–646. https://doi.org/10.1108/00483481211249148

Ross, C. E., & Van Willigen, M. (1997). Education and the subjective quality of life. *Journal of Health and Social Behavior, 38*(3), 275-297. https://doi.org/10.2307/2955371.

Roux, A. (2015, August 31). *Falling off the services cliff.* Drexel University Life Course Outcomes Research Program Blog. http://drexel.edu/autismoutcomes/blog/overview/2015/August/falling-off-the-services-cliff/

Roux, A., Rast, J., Anderson, K., & Shattuck, P. (2017). *National autism indicators report developmental disability services and outcomes in adulthood*. Life Course Outcomes Research Program, A. J. Drexel Autism Institute, Drexel University. https://drexel.edu/autismoutcomes/publications-and-reports/publications/National-Autism-Indicators-Report-Developmental-Disability-Services-and-Outcomes-in-Adulthood/

Roux, A. M., Shattuck, P. T., Cooper, B. P., Anderson, K. A., Wagner, M., & Narendorf, S. C. (2013). Postsecondary employment experiences among young adults with an Autism Spectrum Disorder RH: Employment in young adults with autism. *Journal of the American Academy of Child & Adolescent Psychiatry, 52*(9), 931–939. https://doi.org/10.1016/j.jaac.2013.05.019

Saayman, T., & Crafford, A. (2011). Negotiating work identity. *Journal of Industrial Psychology, 37*(1), 1–21. https://doi.org/10.4102/sajip.v37i1.963

Samson, A. C., Huber, O., & Gross, J. J. (2012). Emotional reactivity and regulation in adults with autism spectrum disorders. *Emotion, 12,* 659–665. https://doi.org/10.1037/a0027975

Scott, M., Falkmer, M., Girdler, S., & Falkmer, T. (2015). Viewpoints on factors for successful employment for adults with autism spectrum disorder. *PLOS ONE, 10*(10), e0139281. https://doi.org/10.1371/journal.pone.0143674

Shattuck, P. T., Narendorf, S. C., Cooper, B., Sterzing, P. R., Wagner, M., & Taylor, J. L. (2012). Postsecondary education and employment among youth with an autism spectrum disorder. *Pediatrics, 129*(6), 1042–1049. https://doi.org/10.1542/peds.2011-2864

Smith, M. J., Ginger, E. J., Wright, K., Wright, M. A., Taylor, J. L., Humm, L. B., Olsen, D. E., Bell, M. B., & Fleming, M. F. (2014). Virtual reality job interview training in adults with autism spectrum disorder. *Journal of Autism and Developmental Disorders, 44,* 2450–2463. https://doi.org/10.1007/s10803-014-2113-y

Stone, D. L., & Colella, A. (1996). A model of factors affecting the treatment of disabled individuals in organizations. *Academy of Management Review, 21*(2), 352–401.

Stone, D. L., Dulebohn, J. H., & Lukaszewski, K. M. (2020). *Diversity and inclusion in organizations.* Information Age Publishing.

Stone, E. F., Shetzer, L., & Eggleston, S. (1986). *Effect of handicap type, handicap revelation mode, and interviewee ratings of applicant suitability* [Paper presentation]. The annual meeting of the Academy of Management, Chicago, Illinois.

Stone, E. F., Stone, D. L., & Dipboye, R. (1992). Stigmas in organizations: Race, handicaps, and physical unattractiveness. In K. Kelley (Ed.), *Issues, theory and research in industrial and organizational psychology* (pp. 385–457). Elsevier.

Super, D. E. (1957). *Psychology of careers.* Harper & Row.

Super, D. E. (1963). The definition and measurement of early career behavior: A first formulation. *The Personnel and Guidance Journal, 41*(9), 775–780. https://doi.org/10.1002/j.2164-4918.1963.tb02394.x

Tagalakis, V., Amsel, R., & Fichten, C. S. (1988). Job interview strategies for people with a visible disability. *Journal of Applied Psychology, 18,* 520–532.

Taylor, J. L., Henninger, N. A., & Mailick, M. R. (2015). Longitudinal patterns of employment and postsecondary education for adults with autism and average-range IQ. *Autism, 19*(7), 785–793. https://doi.org/10.1177/1362361315585643

Truxillo, D., & Cadiz, D., & Hammer, L. (2015). Supporting the aging workforce: A research review and recommendations for workplace intervention research. *Annual Review of Organizational Psychology and Organizational Behavior, 2,* 51–381.

U.S. Bureau of Labor Statistics (2018). *Monthly labor review*. https://www.bls.gov/opub/mlr/2018/home.htm

Virginia Commonwealth University. (2014). *Community based functional skills assessment for transition aged youth with autism spectrum disorder*. http://www.vcuautismcenter.org/documents/FinalCommunityAssessment711141.pdf

Vogus, T., & Lounds-Taylor, J. (2018). Flipping the script: Bringing an organizational perspective to the study of autism at work. *Autism, 22*(5), 514–516. https://doi.org/10.1177/1362361318776103

von Schrader, S., Malzer, V., & Bruyère, S. (2014). Perspectives on disability disclosure: The importance of employer practices and workplace climate. *Employees Responsibilities and Rights Journal, 26*, 237–255. https://doi.org/10.1007/s10672-013-9227-9

World Health Organization. (2013). *Autism spectrum disorders and other developmental disorders: From raising awareness to building capacity*.

Yamaguchi, S., Wu, S.I., Biswas, M., Yate, M., Aoki, Y., Barley, E. A., & Thornicroft, G. (2013). Effects of short-term interventions to reduce mental health-related stigma in university or college students: A systematic review. *Journal of Nervous and Mental Disease, 201*(6), 490–503.

CHAPTER 3

FORGOTTEN MINORITIES AT WORK

Marginalization of Jobseekers With Mild Autism

Daniela Petrovski
York University

ABSTRACT

The number of people diagnosed with autism has been on the rise since the 1990s (CDC Press Release, 2020; Taylor et al., 2012; Roux et al., 2013) and roughly half of them are unemployed which results in financial cost for communities and psychological hardship for themselves (Cimera & Cowan, 2009; Howlin et al., 2005). In this conceptual chapter, I focus on the employment barriers faced by a particular type of individuals on the autism spectrum disorders (ASD), namely, individuals with mild autism (previously referred to as Asperger's syndrome). In particular, I examine the related personal, institutional, and social barriers existing in the job market, and elucidate, how these barriers are created and perpetuated to establish an uneven playing field for ASD-affected jobseekers relative to their neurotypical counterparts. In doing so, I draw on social identity theory (SIT; Tajfel & Turner, 1986) and Goffman's (1963) concept of social stigma to propose a model that explains how stereotypes and stigma contribute to hiring discrimination against individuals with mild autism. Lastly, I offer recommendations on how

Forgotten Minorities in Organizations, pp. 73–103
Copyright © 2023 by Information Age Publishing
www.infoagepub.com
All rights of reproduction in any form reserved.

organizations can address this problem by putting interventions in place to reintegrate overlooked minorities of this sort back into the workforce.

Although the term "minority" literally implies a small number of people in a certain group, it is frequently associated with underrepresented groups in organizations or structures of power and privilege (Bell, 2012; Dworkin & Dworkin, 1999). For example, in many places, women outnumber men population-wise, but men occupy most of the positions of power, status, and earn higher salaries (Moyser, 2017). This is because dominant groups (such as males or neurotypicals for example) tend to occupy dominant positions in society and impose their characterization of required qualities for occupying such space, thus excluding their nondominant counterparts (Bell, 2012). One of the nondominant groups (sometimes referred to as a "forgotten minority") comprises people on the autism spectrum disorder (ASD) especially people with mild autism who are often very skillful and talented.

The number of people diagnosed with autism has been on the rise since the 1990s (CDC Press Release, 2020; Taylor et al., 2012; Roux et al., 2013) and roughly half of them are unemployed, which results in high financial cost to society as well as psychological hardship for themselves and their families (Cimera & Cowan, 2009; Howlin et al., 2005). This includes mildly autistic individuals,[1] (previously diagnosed as Asperger's syndrome) even though they can be quite skillful and have no intellectual disabilities whatsoever (Taylor & Seltzer, 2011). As a matter of fact, many of them have unique skills and abilities that organizations can benefit from (Shattuck et al., 2012).

Although there is a fair amount of research on autism, the focus has been primarily on children, with very little theoretical and empirical work done on the employment outcomes related to adults on the ASD (Taylor et al., 2012). This is surprising given that the unemployment rate among this group is at an all-time high (Pesce, 2019). Indeed, merely about 14% of individuals with autism across educational backgrounds and age groups in the U.S. are gainfully employed (Roux et al., 2013). Further, the employment rate of individuals with autism in the U.S. is the lowest among jobseekers with disabilities (Whittenburg et al., 2019).

Taken together, these statistics suggest a troubling trend in which individuals on the autism spectrum are at a grave disadvantage in the labor market compared to their neurotypical counterparts. This brings to the fore multiple questions related to the barriers to job finding success that exist for this seemingly "forgotten minority" group in the labor market. Yet, limited attention has been devoted to show how the stigmatization associated with mental disorders such as autism produce barriers in the labor market that can serve to further alienate an already marginalized group.

Hence, there is a great need for more research on transition barriers from school to work, exclusion at work, negative stereotypes, discrimination, and sensory environments (e.g., Annabi & Locke, 2019; Austin & Pisano, 2017; Baldwin & Costley, 2016; Maroto & Pettinicchio, 2015). In addition, human resources management (HRM) professionals will benefit from insights of how to improve workplace acceptance and inclusion of autistic individuals.

The purpose of this chapter, therefore, is to address some of these issues. Specifically, I argue that personal, institutional, and societal barriers operating in the job market are establishing an uneven playing field for jobseekers with mild autism relative to their neurotypical counterparts. To my knowledge, there is no organizational research on the exclusion or inclusion in hiring of autistic jobseekers. Drawing insights from social identity theory (SIT; Tajfel & Turner, 1986) and Goffman's (1963) concept of social stigma I propose a model that explains how stereotypes and stigma contribute to discrimination in hiring against individuals with mild autism which barriers give rise to systemic inequality in the labor market. Lastly, I offer recommendations on how organizations can address this problem by putting interventions in place to reintegrate these forgotten minorities into the workforce.

LITERATURE REVIEW

Autism Spectrum Disorders, Terms, and Description of Mild Autism

According to the Centers for Disease Control and Prevention (CDC) there is no cure for autism, but there are treatments to help reduce symptoms and to improve their ability to function in the community. However, advocates and autistic individuals have developed distinct cultures with some seeking cure and others advocating for acceptance and accommodation instead of cure (Silverman, 2008). The individuals diagnosed with Asperger's syndrome are usually advocating for their acceptance (Silverman, 2008). The terms high functioning autism and Asperger's syndrome have been used interchangeably (although there are some small differences) to talk about persons with mild autism (Cooper & Allely, 2017). The term autism was coined by Eugen Bleule in 1911 and the terms Asperger's emerged around 1940s when was popularized by Leo Kanner and Hans Asperger as separate from autism (Heifetz, 2019; Silverman, 2012; Thomas & Boellstorff, 2017). The diagnosis of ASD as one spectrum with different degrees of autism was identified in 2013 with the new *Diagnostic and Statistical Manual of Mental Disorders* (*DSM*) -5 that replaced the DSM-4 where there were four different diagnosis for the autism spectrum: autistic disorder, Asperger's disorder, childhood disintegrative disorder, and pervasive developmental disorder not otherwise specified (PDD-NOS or atypical autism) (Cooper & Allely, 2017; Heifetz, 2019; Thomas & Boellstorff, 2017).

People often talk about low and high functioning autism to differentiate among the ASD's which has created issues in terms of its meaning and the misconception that high functioning may not need help and that low functioning are not able to perform work or learn (den Houting, 2019; Thomas & Boellstorff, 2017). The difference between the two is considered in terms of intelligence such that high functioning autism (IQ of 70 and above) have normal language development while the severity of language development varies among the others on the spectrum (Perkins et al., 2010). However, lack of language abilities is not necessarily lack of thinking ability (Thomas & Boellstorff, 2017) and it could be rather lack of proper resources and understanding of these individuals that makes observers to misjudge them. With the new DSM-5 there are three broad groups of autism for the purpose of recommending treatments and those are mild,[2] intermediate, and severe.

Autism spectrum disorders are referred as "pervasive, developmental, neurological conditions which adversely impact behavior in three key domains: social interaction, verbal and nonverbal communication, and obsessive and/or stereotyped patterns of behavior" (Perkins et al., 2010, p. 1239). The perceived adversity in social interaction comes mostly from lack of emotional imitation (or facial expressions) and the inability to understand metaphors (Perkins et al., 2010). Adverse behaviors are considered the repetitive behaviors they do to soothe themselves, following rigid schedules, and lack of regulation in terms of specific sensory stimuli/environments (Buckley, 2017; Gurney et al., 2003). According to the DSM-5 manual, they show hyper- or hyporeactivity to sensory inputs such as to sound/noise, smell, light, or touch (e.g., they might appear indifferent to temperature, avoid specific sounds and smells, or be fascinated with lights). In other words, they express over or under-sensitivity to certain light, sound, smell, taste, or touch. The repetitive behaviors may include movements such as flapping a hand or rocking, and ritualistic behaviors may include eating the same type of foods, having dressing rituals, sitting at the same spot, playing with the same toys, and so on.

The similarity among all ASD's is that they have strong interests in certain subjects, great attention to details, perform best when following routines, and sensitivity to certain sensory stimuli (Perkins et al., 2010). Also, it is important to note that every autistic individual is different and that there is a large variation in terms of skills and needs as well as fluctuations of competences and capabilities within a person over time (den Houting, 2019). One of the observable differences between non-autistic and autistic persons is the function of mimicking emotions (perceived as empathy) which involves imitating others' expressions and language (Perkins et al., 2010). This does not mean they lack empathy but that they may express it differently (Buckley, 2017). The inability to imitate others is considered a deficit because it makes them different from the dominant group (Rogers et al., 1996; Perkins et al., 2010).

The individuals with mild autism may exhibit fairly normal communication but have difficulty "recognizing higher-order mental states from faces" such as flirting for example although they are able to recognize basic emotions such as happiness (Adolphs et al., 2001, p. 232). For example, they have difficulty interpreting others' intentions, emotions, and opinions or predicting what people may do next if it is not explicitly communicated to them (Attwood, 2007; Perkins et al., 2010). This in turn causes them to take verbal communication literally and speak in a direct and very truthful way (Buckley, 2017). Neurotypicals, on the other hand, can recognize deception and manipulation in others as they possess and use those capabilities themselves.

Some researchers have attempted to explain this ability to detect deception using the theory of the mind saying that is an evolutionary protection from deception so that people can make inferences about the others' (dishonest) perceptions, goals, beliefs, and expectations based on their own (dishonest) mental schemas (Baron-Cohen, 1995; Gallese & Goldman, 1998). The idea is that being self-aware of one's own deceptions can help people guess other people's deceptions (Gallese & Goldman, 1998). However, another explanation declares that damage of amygdala functioning can result in some autistic individuals being unable to decode facial expressions such as trustworthiness and fear (Adolphs et al., 1998; Adolphs et al., 2001; Baron-Cohen et al., 2000). That being said, individuals with mild autism are still able to make proper social judgments from verbal expressions. Thus, clear, explicit, and verbal communication in addition to visual presentation (or facial expression) is necessary for them to understand visual meaning of social information (Adolphs et al., 2001).

Some autistic people are known as autistic savages or geniuses showing amazing talents and abilities to memorize (Treffert, 2009). A famous example is the character Raymond Babbitt from the movie *Rain Man* based on a real person (although he was somewhat represented differently in the movie) whose abilities included memorizing over 6,000 books, having complete knowledge of geography, music, literature, history, sports and other areas among other talents (Peek & Hanson 2008; Treffert, 2009). There is a consideration that about 1 in 10 individuals on the ASD have some savant skills (Heifetz, 2019) as well as that about 50% of the people exhibiting savant syndrome are autistic while the others have some other brain injury or a disorder (Treffert, 2009). Many autistic savants have shown extraordinary memory, music and arithmetical ability, precise timekeeping skill, and spatial orientation (Treffert, 2009).

Autistic Individuals and Unemployment

ASD is viewed as a cognitive impairment under the Americans with Disabilities Act (ADA). The ADA, which is established by the U.S. Government of Labor, prohibits discrimination and promotes equal employment opportunity for persons with disabilities. Yet, the employment outcomes of autistic jobseekers are staggeringly low even with the Disability Employment Incentive Act in the U.S., which offers tremendous tax credit for employers who hire people with disabilities. Canada has recently included the Accessible Canada Act to incentivize the hiring of people on the autism spectrum. Autistic individuals have more difficulty finding a job, have fewer working hours, make less money, and rarely have benefits (Pesce, 2019). This situation is similar in many developed countries such as Australia, United Kingdom, and Canada (Dudley et al., 2015; Scott et al., 2019). For example, in Australia the employment of autistic individuals is 62% while the national employment is 95% (Australian Bureau of Statistics, 2013; Baldwin & Costley, 2016). These statistics include people with mild autism, and it is estimated that about 50% of the people diagnosed with autism are high functioning (Christensen et al., 2016). Recent statistics suggest that 85% of college graduates with mild autism cannot find a job compared with just 4.5% of their neurotypical counterparts (Pesce, 2019). Furthermore, about one third of autistic adults without intellectual disability are neither employed nor engaged in higher education (Taylor & Seltzer, 2011). These numbers may be higher because females are usually not diagnosed until later in adulthood (Baldwin & Costley, 2016) since the diagnostic criteria are largely based on the male autism expressions (Suckle, 2021). Even among the employed adults with mild autism, many do not receive adequate support at work to do their jobs well (Beardon & Edmonds, 2007). Only about one third of the employed females with mild autism had some support at work for their autism spectrum disorders in Australia (Baldwin & Costley, 2016). These statistics are telling and point to a worrisome trend in which individuals with autism encounter great difficulty in the labor market.

Additionally, the financial costs of autism services run into billions of dollars annually. For example, the cost of autism over the lifespan is estimated to be $2.4 million for a person who is severely impacted and $1.4 million for a person without intellectual impairment (Autism Society, 2019). Taken together, these employment barriers are not only creating a heavy financial burden for families of autistic individuals but also contributing to a lower quality of life for unemployed ASD jobseekers (Cimera & Cowan, 2009). Unemployment also brings psychological costs for unemployed ASD job-seekers including social isolation, low self-esteem, lower quality of life, and other mental health issues (Cimera & Cowan, 2009; Taylor & Hodapp, 2012; Vogeley et al., 2013).

Based on this literature review, I have created a model with propositions to explain theoretically the fewer job offers (high unemployment rate) for autistic individuals and more specifically to understand the personal and systemic barriers that autistic individuals face when looking for a job. The practical implication of it is to raise awareness about autism and propose some solutions to eliminate these barriers. Figure 3.1 shows a model of personal and institutional barriers in hiring (receiving fewer job offers) for individuals with mild autism. The model is explained in more details in the following sections.

THEORETICAL OVERVIEW AND PROPOSITIONS

I draw on social identity theory (Tajfel & Turner, 1986), and social stigma (Goffman, 1963) to offer an explanation to the complexity in under-standing the personal, organizational, and societal processes involved in marginalization of job seekers with mild autism. Social identity theory (Tajfel & Turner, 1986) explains how individuals' self-concepts come from the perceived memberships in their social groups and from the significance they attach to these groups. Individuals' identification to those groups affects and guide their internal processes and external behaviors. Social identity theory explains that individuals' self esteem relates to the group they identify positively with and tend to give more resources to that group to

Figure 3.1

Model of Personal and Institutional Barriers in Hiring for Individuals With Mild Autism. Personal Barriers

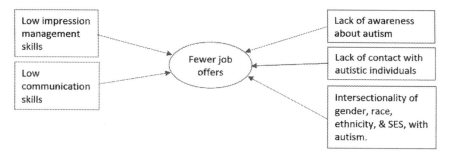

preserve it. For example, in an experiment Billig and Tajfel (1973) showed how participants allocated more resources to their in-group members comparing to the out-groups even though they were chosen only by a flip of a coin to be part of their group. The participants had no information about their in-group members except that they were in a same group. Similar behavior happened in Jane Elliot's famous blue and brown eyes exercise on April 5, 1968 (the day after Martin Luther King was assassinated) when she tried to show her third-grade students how discrimination feels and works in society (Anthony, 2009; Elliot, 2019). Elliot split her class in two groups (blue eyes and brown eyes) and told them the blue eyes students were superior to the brown eyes children only to tell them the next day she made a mistake and that it was the people with brown eyes who were superior. This superficial distinction made the children to group themselves as per their eye colour and to mistreat the other children.

Tajfel and Turner (1986) differentiated between personal and social identity; the personal identity is rare because people in general are cognitively lazy and tend to define others based on social categories rather than based on individual characteristics. Relying on their knowledge of social cognition (how the brain works in terms of creating categorizations), Tajfel and Turner argued that people categorize themselves and others to make meaning of the social world. When these categories are salient, the distinction of "us and them" emerges. More specifically, people assign positive characteristics to their groups to preserve and enhance their self esteem and exaggerate the similarities within their group while exaggerating the differences with other groups. People tend to group themselves and others in various social categories such as religious orientation, gender, age, ethnicity, and so on (Tajfel & Turner, 1986).

The social identity comes from the perception of belonging to a certain group which identification of self and others is "relational and comparative" (Tajfel & Turner, 1986, p. 16). This social identification comes from the perception of self as psychologically entangled with the group and the behavior and emotions are a by-product of it (Tajfel & Turner, 1986). Individuals look at the behaviors of the in-group members and tend to behave in a same or similar way. "Striving for a positive social identity, group members are motivated to think and act in ways that achieve or maintain a positive distinctiveness between one's own group and relevant outgroups" (Hornsey, 2008, p. 207). This is the progression that leads people to ostracise and derogate out-group members, especially if individuals perceive themselves to be in a favorable group (Brewer & Miller, 1984). When an individual finds themself in an unpopular or low status group, they may try to leave the group, focus on a characteristic that make their group look better, or try to increase their status (Hornsey, 2008; Tajfel & Turner, 1979).

This competitive process for establishing different forms of positive group distinctiveness creates depersonalization of out-group members (Brewer & Miller, 1984), especially for dominant groups, who often act entitled to express freely their depersonalization of minority groups (Bell, 2012; Dworkin & Dworkin, 1999). This in-group favoritism can lead to allocation of resources to their members (Billig & Tajfel, 1973), such as job offers to the neurotypicals at the expense of those perceived as out-group (e.g., neurodivergent people) and with that further perpetuating the power of the dominant group and inequalities in a community. A portion of social identity theory aligns with Dworkin and Dworkin's (1999) group aware-ness of out-groups (as nondominant out-group members) which explains that those who experience judgemental or disapproving treatment by oth-ers become aware of it. This reduces the self-esteem of the nondominant members and may reduce their motivation to apply for jobs. Reduced self esteem and internalized hopelessness is part of the self-stigma concept that explains how low self-esteem and low self-efficacy reduces the efforts to search for a job or even make efforts to live independently (Corrigan et al., 2014).

This overgeneralization of characteristics, attitudes, and behavior of a large group leads to stereotyping of the whole group, which is often a basis for discrimination (Bell, 2012; Cox, 1994). Stereotypes are over-generalizations and prejudiced characterizations of a whole group of people based on only one or few characteristics (Bell, 2012; Cummings et al., 2013). For example, people with mild autism are not all the same (homogenous group), but people may make inferences for all individuals with that diagnosis based on knowing only one person with mild autism. More specifically, stereotypes are cognitive schemas or shortcuts about a whole group of people that are most often negative and incorrect (Stangl et al., 2019). Stereotypes affect prejudice (attitudes) or prejudgment, which means making irrational judgments before knowing someone well, usu-ally with a negative connotation (Bell, 2012; Cummings et al., 2013). In other words, stereotyping is categorizing people (putting them in groups) based on very few characteristics and this can create negative attitudes or prejudice against them. Stereotyping and prejudice further affect stigma, which is a social process that leads to devaluation and discrediting others (Goffman, 1963). Stigmatized individuals are judged to have undesirable characteristics for specific social contexts (Crocker et al., 1998). Some of the stigmas about people with mental illness are that they may be danger-ous, unpredictable, and incompetent to have a good job (Angermeyer & Dietrich, 2006; Corrigan et al., 2014).

Corrigan et al. (2014) developed a matrix of four types of stigma: public stigma, self-stigma; label avoidance, and structural stigma. "Public stigma occurs when the general population endorses stereotypes and decides to discriminate against people labeled mentally ill" which leads to discrimination in hiring, discrimination in renting/housing, and substandard medical care (Corrigan et al., 2014, p. 43). Self-stigma includes internalized negative attitudes and beliefs such as low self-esteem and low self-efficacy and this reduces the efforts for job searching or for living independently (Corrigan et al., 2014). Label avoidance is the perception of public disrespect that causes individuals to avoid seeking care in order to evade being labeled, and structural stigma are stereotypes embedded in the institutional practices which lead to loss of opportunities for people with mental illness as well as for the organizations (Corrigan et al., 2014). Regardless of the type, all stigmas have damaging effect on stigmatized individuals. For example, "[s]tigma impacts care seeking at personal, provider, and system levels" and also impacts negatively employment opportunities, housing, and social life for stigmatized individuals and their families (Corrigan et al., 2014, p. 43). Stigma also affects individuals with mild autism because some of their behaviors affected by autism are visible and perceived as abnormal (Gray, 2002; Staniland & Byrne, 2013).

Personal Factors Affecting the Exclusion of People With Mild Autism

Adults with mild autism face many challenges in terms of finding and maintaining a job. First, the language and behavioral skills of individuals with mild autism differ from their neurotypical counterparts (Howlin et al., 2005). For example, their literal way of communicating with colleagues and recruiters presents a difficulty to find and maintain a competitive job (Jacob et al., 2015; Rogge & Janssen, 2019). In addition to having difficulty interpreting other people's facial expressions (Adolphs et al., 2001), autistic individuals own facial expressions may be misaligned with the meaning they intend to convey in a normal social exchange with recruiters (Buckley, 2017). Additionally, they are less likely to boast about themselves or try to appeal to others about their abilities and accomplishments (Izuma et al., 2011), which is part of impression management practice that neurotypical individuals generally engage in during an interview. Research suggests that impression management is an important skill for a fruitful life in general and for job finding success in particular (Luo et al., 2017; van Hooft et al., 2020). Since autistic individuals do not engage in impression management, which includes nonverbal communication, eye gaze and facial expressions (Kuzmanovic et al., 2011; Vogeley et al., 2013), they are less likely to succeed at a job interview. The proposition following this review is:

Proposition 1: Low level of impression management skills leads to fewer job offers for individuals with mild autism.

Some other reasons for high unemployment might involve lack of transition services and supports to help students with mild autism to "successfully transition into meaningful employment experiences during and after high school" (Lee & Carter, 2012, p. 989). Many scholars have emphasized the need for quality transition programs for individuals with mild autism that can help them with employability skills (Hendricks & Wehman, 2009; Lee & Carter, 2012; Moxon & Gates, 2001). The secondary education focuses mainly on school achievement without providing any work preparation or experience (Lee & Carter, 2012) and after high school they are left on their own to figure out how to succeed (Howlin et al., 2005). Also, employers look for good interpersonal skills in job applicants, which put individuals with mild autism at a disadvantage (Carter & Wehby, 2003) because dealing with the social demands of so many people such as recruiters, interviewers, social contacts, coworkers, supervisors, and the job search process itself is challenging and overwhelming (Higgins et al., 2008; Lee & Carter, 2012).

Finding a job is already a challenge but finding a good fit or good job match for the individuals with mild autism is a greater challenge, which can make a big difference in maintaining the job and progressing or not (Hawkins, 2004; Higgins et al., 2008; Hurlbutt & Chalmers, 2004). Some jobs that mandate quick processing of demands such as cashier, cook, or a waiter might not be well suited for them (Stankova & Trajkovski, 2010). Good job fit includes matching their strengths, interests, and needs with the job essential tasks (Lee & Carter, 2012). While autistic individuals may have many skills and talents (sometimes referred as their special interests) that come from their ability to focus on tasks, they are not aware how to articulate these in terms of transferable skills and use them for work. Even when they get a job, they are often overqualified for their jobs, which makes many of them experience boredom at work (Baldwin et al., 2014). They have expressed boredom at work as one of the worst things in their work experiences, which implies that there is often a lack of fit or matching the job with their skills and interests (Baldwin et al., 2014). This is probably because they are not often accepted where they could fit, thus they must settle for the places they get accepted. One of the reasons for it is their lack of training in expressing properly their strength, skills, abilities, and interests as work related transferable skills. Another reason could be lack of intervention services and support programs to help them articulate these in interviews and with that to find the most suitable jobs. Individuals with mild autism are often overqualified for the jobs they hold, meaning their educational level exceeds the requirements for the job (Baldwin et al., 2014). The negative outcomes of over qualification are earning less than they should, more job changes and career movements because of their boredom and dissatisfaction at work, and depression (Alpin et al., 1998; Baldwin et al., 2014; Bracke et al., 2013). Other communication challenges may involve understanding complex job applications and answering certain interview questions (Baldwin et al., 2014; Beardon & Edmonds, 2007; Hillier et al. 2007; Robertson, 2010). Thus, individuals with mild autism get fewer job offers because they are unsure and unaware of how to articulate their talents, skills, and abilities at job applications and job interviews. Therefore:

> **Proposition 2:** Lack of communication skills especially in expressing their employability skills leads to fewer job offers for individuals with mild autism.

Knowing the employment challenges individuals with mild autism face creates a need for organizations and communities to engage in greater awareness and empathy and create training programs and support to help them transition into the labor market, not only for economic reasons but for their well-being (Taylor et al., 2012). Yet, there is no research (to my knowledge) on the job search experiences and careers of autistic jobseekers. This shows a gap and presents a need for more organizational research to examine the barriers of finding and maintaining employment for autistic people. Understanding these challenges can inform organizational practices, specifically around crafting policies and guidelines to minimize, if not completely eradicate labor market barriers and create a more favorable experience for all individuals with ASD, but especially for individuals with mild autism, who have the intelligence to perform many jobs.

Thus far, I have explored some of the individual variables impacting the employment experiences of individuals with mild autism. Now, I turn my attention to factors outside the individual. That is, factors embedded within institutional and social structures that affect autistic individuals' employment success. At a systems level, we need to consider the negative effects of stereotyping, stigmatizing, and discriminating, which affect individuals in this group in a negative way both in gaining employment and thriving at work. Stereotypical beliefs along with stigma (negative judgments) can lead to intentional and unintentional discriminatory practices (Earnshaw et al., 2020; Stangl et al., 2019).

System Factors Affecting the Exclusion of People With Mild Autism

The social identity involves social comparison which results in a desire for positive in-group distinctiveness and depersonalization of out-group members (Brewer & Miller, 1984), especially by the dominant group. In this case the dominant group are the neurotypical people (versus the neurodivergent) who hold positions of power and make rules and decisions about job descriptions, recruitment, selection, and hiring. Not surprisingly, "the rules of the game" of this dominant group are un/intentionally excluding their out-group members or nondominant group, such as the neurodivergent individuals from participating in the labour market. Social exclusion affects people negatively causing depression and suicidal ideation among most people, but this is even more pronounced among autistic people (Hedley et al., 2018; Jones et al., 2021). The discrimination against autistic people in organizations is real and obvious to the autistic and non-autistic adults (Jones et al., 2021).

Discrimination affects individuals negatively, but also organizations. Having in mind the benefits from hiring diverse workers (e.g., Bell, 2012; Cox, 1994), organizations have a lot to lose on a long run. "In a job-related context, stereotyping can prevent individuals who would be capable, committed workers from being hired, promoted, or trained" (Bell, 2012, p. 43). Discrimination is rooted in stereotyping and stigma. Stereotypes entail overgeneralizations and, with that, expectations of certain manners and behaviors by some groups which are often judged negatively (e.g., Corrigan et al., 2014). Autistic individuals are expected to have challenges interacting with customers, coworkers, and superiors in terms of participating in small talks, professional mannerisms, language, and dressing up, among others (Hawkins, 2004; Higgins et al., 2008; Hurlbutt & Chalmers, 2004). This is because the world of work is not as diverse as the natural world/population to be accustomed to variety of mannerisms, expressions, and dressing up. Furthermore, lack of knowledge and awareness of autism may lead to stereotyping, which is often inaccurate (based on movies, gossip, or one example). One of the main obstacles of job finding for people with autism is certain ritualistic behaviors that they display because of which they are negatively stereotyped and not because of the lack of skills they possess or their job performances (Howlin, & Moss, 2012; Hurlbutt & Chalmers, 2004). For example, repetitive flapping hands, rocking, arranging objects in a specific order, and following routines (Boyd et al., 2012).

Stereotyping and prejudice create stigma (especially for people with mental health issues), which is a devaluation and discrediting of others (Goffman, 1963). The two types of stigma—public and structural—explain that the stigma is entrenched in the organizational practices such as recruitment and selection of job candidates, which are structured in a way that excludes people with mental health disorders (Corrigan et al., 2014). Stigma affects individuals with mild autism even more than other mental health issues because of the visibility of their oddly defined behaviors (Gray, 2002; Staniland & Byrne, 2013). This is most likely because of lack of awareness about autism and lack of understanding for individuals with mild autism by hiring committees since autistic individuals do not show any cognitive impairment and are able to succeed at school (where they feel accepted) (Ferraioli & Harris, 2011). Therefore, it is necessary for organizations to not only recognize negative stereotypes but also work to eliminate stigma associated with autism (Campbell, 2006; Staniland & Byrne, 2013). As noted earlier, autistic individuals have a higher rate of unemployment than other disability groups (Roux et al., 2013) and this is partly due to the negative judgments and lack of knowledge about autism (Howlin & Moss, 2012). Therefore, the proposition derived from this literature review is:

Proposition 3: Lack of awareness and knowledge about autism leads to stereotyping, stigma, and fewer job offers.

According to the social identity theory people are more accepting of differences or heterogeneity in their in-group than in the out-group members. In-group members are seen as a homogenous, with similar attitudes and behaviors (Bell, 2012). This is most likely due to higher intensity of interactions with the in-group versus the out-group members (Bell, 2012; Brewer & Miller, 1984). Even similar expressions and behaviors displayed by both groups are usually judged as negative by the non-dominant groups comparing to the dominant groups (Dworkin & Dworkin, 1999). For example, assertiveness in females is perceived as negative or aggressive and normal in males (Dworkin & Dworkin, 1999).

Although research and governments have pointed out the benefits of hiring a diverse workforce, in-group favoritism in hiring still exists, as evident in the unemployed groups. This is not because they lack skills and abilities, but more likely because of prejudice in hiring and not getting opportunities to show their skills and abilities. For example, individuals with mild autism often have extraordinary abilities in perception and attention, which can help them gain expertise in areas such as processing, computing, engineering and mathematics, design, and so on (Plaisted Grant & Davis, 2009), but they are among the disability groups with the highest unemployment rates (Whittenburg et al., 2019). They need acceptance and psychological support to develop those abilities as well as opportunities to show them (Plaisted Grant & Davis, 2009).

Since prejudice and discrimination can be explained with SIT and more specifically with social categorization (which is one of the main elements in SIT), some researchers have tried to find solutions for reducing discrimination by offering an opposing process such as decategorization (Brewer & Miller, 1984) and the contact hypothesis (Allport, 1954; Cook, 1978). The process of decategorization includes differentiation (pointing out on the distinctiveness of the members within a category) and personalization (self-other comparison on an individual level that crosses the group boundaries). More specifically, differentiation happens when an individual learns unique information about out-group members, making the categorization into smaller subgroups; this can lead to a different response as oppose to looking at them under a broad category (Brewer & Miller, 1984). Personalization encourages contact between different groups with the goals of reducing the focus on category-based information and increasing the personalized information exchange about each other (Brewer & Miller, 1984). The purpose of the process of decategorization "is not simply to redistribute members of different social categories but to promote intergroup acceptance and to reduce the role that category membership plays in creating barriers to individual social mobility and to the development of positive interpersonal relationships" (Brewer & Miller, 1984, p. 287). Put simply, the goal is to decategorize the broad categorizations that generate in-group positive bias and out-group depersonalization. The discrimination will be reduced with increased contact and exchange of personal information between different group members.

Similarly, the contact hypothesis explains that positive interpersonal contact can reduce prejudice between the different group members (Allport, 1954). The contact should be long enough and with authentic information so the members can learn about their similarities because short and casual contact may have the opposite effect (Allport, 1954; Rademaker et al., 2020). The contact hypothesis has been tested and shown to reduce prejudice among students toward their peers with disabilities (MacMillan et al., 2014). Based on this, it is possible that one of the reasons for prejudice and fewer job offers for people with mild autism is the lack of contact between the neurotypical people and neurodiverse people. Based on this theory, lack of contact is connected with lack of opportunities for decategorization, which reduces discrimination for out-group members. Therefore:

Proposition 4: Lack of contact between neurotypical recruiters and people with mild autism leads to prejudice and fewer job offers.

Having work is important for anyone, but it is even therapeutic for people on the autism spectrum (Cimera & Cowan, 2009; Taylor & Hodapp, 2012; Vogeley et al., 2013). However, the high unemployment rate shows prejudice and discrimination in hiring against these people. This is despite the incentives established by the Disability Employment Incentive Act in the U.S. and the Accessible Canada Act (in Canada) that include incentives for hiring people on the autism spectrum. Adding the existing prejudice towards certain identity attributes such as gender, race, low socioeconomic status, and ethnicity to the discrimination of autistic individuals, it can make life even more difficult for them. This is explained in Stone and

Colella's (1996) seminal model that describes how stereotypes and discrimination of disabled individuals is affected by combination of factors that include personal characteristics (attributes of the disabled person and of the observer), organizational characteristics [technology, policies and practices, norms and values, and legislation (the Americans with Disabilities Act)]. Stereotyping is also affected by the attributes of the observers, which include demographic characteristics, personality, and previous contact with a disabled person (Stone & Colella, 1996).

Among the personal attributes of the disabled individuals, Stone and Colella (1996) include the nature of the disability (aesthetics, perceived danger to others, short or long-term course of disability, concealability, and disruptiveness), previous performance level, gender, race, interpersonal style, and status. These "are thought to influence the categorization of the disabled person, the inferences made about the individual's job-related attributes, performance expectancies, and the subsequent treatment of the person in the organization" (Stone & Colella, 1996, p. 361). Observers often rely on the nature of the disability to categorize disabled individuals (physical disabilities, mentally ill, sensory impairments, learning disabilities, neurological conditions, and addictions), which categorizations lead to different stereotyping and work-related expectations (Stone & Colella, 1996).

According to the SIT, people describe themselves and others based on social categories such as religious orientation, gender, age, ethnicity, status, and so on (Tajfel & Turner, 1986). Since we live in a capitalistic and competitive world, people engage in comparison, which is part of any competition, and this motivates them to see their in-group members in a positive light (to preserve their self-esteem and to win the competition), while perceiving the out-groups in a negative light. People engage in social comparisons which motivate them to see themselves in favorable light while perceiving the out-group members as less favorable (Brewer & Miller, 1984; Tajfel & Turner, 1986). Liking a certain group more is not by itself negative but coupled with power and allocation of resources it becomes discrimination and creates inequality. The in-group favoritism along with receiving resources in institutions and society allow some groups with certain categories to become dominant in society (Bell, 2012; Dworkin & Dworkin, 1999). Some examples of dominant group categories are White males and neurotypicals as they hold the highest number of decision-making positions, which perpetuates their dominance in society and leads to inequalities and high unemployment rates for nondominant groups in a community.

The stereotyping that comes from categorization is usually against the out-group members or the nondominant groups. Stereotypes still affect people with various disabilities as they are often perceived as less desirable employees than those without disability (Stone & Colella, 1996). Adding gender, race, low status, and ethnicity, can cause some individuals to experience double discrimination (Stone & Colella, 1996) in receiving job offers. This means that women and racial minorities with a disability (such as autism) may be disadvantaged even more than other individuals with one disability (Stone & Colella, 1996). Previous research has shown that gender prejudice adds on disability prejudice increasing discrimination of women with disabilities (Gunderson & Lee, 2016). In social interactions, women are judged harsher than men (Baldwin & Costley, 2016). Similarly, "racial minorities with disabilities are likely to experience dual sources of discrimination" (Stone & Colella, 1996, p. 368).

Stone and Colella's (1996) framework on factors affecting the discrimination of persons with disabilities talks about the importance of intersectionality of gender, race, interpersonal style, and social status as these factors increase the experienced discrimination. The intersectionality of multiple attributes affecting discrimination is rarely studied despite the need for diversity and inclusion in organizations (Stone & Colella, 1996). Sociologists have pointed out that diversity is advertised on companies' websites but is not so evident in practice since there are still inequalities at work and communities (Embrick, 2011). Organizations should be concerned with changing the male dominance and contribute to equal opportunities for underrepresented groups at work (Embrick, 2011). In that regard, academics have called for a broader look at inequalities by including intersectionality of various attributes that contribute to it when studying these issues in organizations (e.g., Duffy et al., 2016; Gillborn, 2015). Intersectionality discusses how various characteristics such as race, gender, and other are interrelated in a social context (Gillborn, 2015). The proposition that follows this literature review is:

Proposition 5: The intersectionality of the historically prejudiced social categories such as women, racialized minorities, and low socioeconomic status with mild autism leads to fewer job offers for these individuals because of stereotypes and prejudice.

Neurodiversity Perspective: A Remedy for Inclusion

As a response to the damaging effects of stigmatization, some scholars have emphasized the need for anti-stigma interventions (e.g., Chan et al., 2009; Gray, 2002; Staniland & Byrne, 2013). These interventions are rooted in the anti-stigma literature on mental health, which include awareness, contact or inclusion, and some combination of these (Chan et al., 2009; Staniland & Byrne, 2013). The goal of anti-stigma interventions is to create awareness and provide a mechanism for changing the negative attitudes and behavioral intentions about mental health issues and disorders (Chan et al., 2009; Staniland & Byrne, 2013). One of the most successful elements from these interventions is positive personal contact with autistic individuals or with other mental health disorders (Chan et al., 2009; Staniland & Byrne, 2013). However, although these programs are effective in improving attitudes and behaviors towards autistic individuals to some level, they do not change the behavioral intentions, which means more needs to be done to address the issue of inclusion of autistic individuals (Staniland & Byrne, 2013).

Another response to inclusion is the neurodiversity movement that refers to autistic individuals as people who think differently and with unique abilities and skills (or differently abled) (Silberman, 2017). The notion of viewing autistic individuals as differently wired is based on biodiversity as beneficial and required in nature. The term came from a communication between the journalist Harvey Blume and sociologist Judy Singer in the 1990s while discussing in an online forum for autistic people (Silberman, 2017). Harvey Blume used the word neurological plurality and Judy Singer narrowed it to neurodiversity, implying neurological connections that are very diverse among all people (Silberman, 2017). While disability is usually perceived as a deficit of some physical, cognitive, or emotional features, neurodiversity is presented as a social model of disability which means that disability for autistic people comes from the environments that are unreceptive towards them and not so much from their autism (den Houting, 2019). The neurodiversity movement was led by autistic neurodivergent individuals and started as a protest of viewing autistic individuals only in terms of their pathologies while ignoring the positive side such as their unique abilities (den Houting, 2019; Silberman, 2017). Because of the movement, positive changes have come in terms of viewing neurodivergent people in a more positive light with more support and strength-based interventions instead of focusing only on normalization (den Houting, 2019).

Aligning with the neurodiversity perspective, the view of deficit and difficulties of responding in a direct and straightforward manner has become desirable characteristics of honesty, competence, accuracy, reliability, low absenteeism, and uninterested in "office drama" (Hillier et al. 2007; Muller et al., 2003). Speaking in a direct, straightforward, and truthful manner is a lot more valuable and beneficial for an organization (Austin & Pisano, 2017; Buckley, 2017) than engaging in deceptive impression management. The lack of mimicking emotions and behavior such as imitating others (Perkins et al., 2010) is actually a strength to respond in an authentic and honest way (Baron-Cohen et al., 2000; Gallese & Goldman, 1998). Adjusting the workplace to accommodate autistic individuals is therefore only a small cost to get all these benefits of reliable and honest employees.

Provided there is a supportive environment, adults with mild autism can fit in a variety of occupations including fast-paced work (initially considered unsuitable for autistic individuals) such as sales, creative arts, and military (Baldwin et al., 2014; Muller et al., 2003). Some of the jobs in which adults on the autism spectrum can do well are those that require "visual thinking, systematic information processing or precise technical abilities (e.g., architect, librarian, computer programmer)" (Baldwin et al., 2014, p. 2441). Supportive environments do not only hire neurodivergent people, they provide the conditions for them to feel accepted for who they are and to thrive at work. Some of these conditions include but are not limited to appreciating people on the autism spectrum (or inclusive atmosphere), providing the opportunities for autistic people to express their strengths, and opportunities for growth (Baldwin et al., 2014). However, not many autistic individuals are receiving adequate support in successful transitioning from school to work (Baldwin et al., 2014; Beardon & Edmonds, 2007). There have been criticisms that the neurodiversity paradigm or movement may have resulted in individuals with mild autism to have lower support needs and therefore not provided adequate support.

Theoretical and Practical Implications

The literature on autism identifies factors that both hinder and facilitate the employment of ASD individuals, including interventions (e.g., job-specific skills and training) and support programs (e.g., accommodation and coaching) to enhance employment for this population (e.g., Austin & Pisano, 2017; Chen et al., 2015; Krzeminska et al., 2019; Remington & Pellicano, 2018; Scott et al., 2019; Waisman-Nitzan, 2018). Some of the research deals with autism in the workplace, especially around positive work identity (McIntosh, 2016), person-organization fit (Pence & Svyantek, 2016), work behaviors (Coetzer, 2016), and the transition needs and experiences of young adults entering the workplace (Griffiths et al., 2016). Other studies have addressed themselves to exploring strategies that organizations can use to accommodate employees on the autism spectrum disorder (Seitz & Smith, 2016; Waisman-Nitzan et al., 2018), including the roles and responsibilities of HRM in creating a more inclusive environment for autistic individuals (Markel & Elia, 2016). However, no research has studied the personal, institutional, and social barriers operating in the job market for individuals with mild autism. This chapter is a theoretical attempt to add to the literature on stereotyping, stigma, and discrimination by showing how the stigmatization associated with autism produces barriers in the labor market for autistic individuals. It also adds to our understanding of social identity theory (Tajfel & Turner, 1986) and Goffman's (1963) social stigma by focusing on a group not studied before such as autistic individuals.

The autism spectrum disorders are under the Disability Discrimination Act, which is protected against discrimination at work. This means that employers can be held legally accountable if they do not make reasonable accommodation to include these individuals (Cooper & Allely, 2017). Therefore, employers ought to adjust their recruitment and selection practices to accommodate the uniqueness of these individuals instead of discriminating against them for their differences (Sumner & Brown, 2015). Most of the people with autism have developed extraordinary knowledge in different fields and have skills and capabilities that can be adjusted to the demands of many workplaces (Shattuck et al., 2012).

One important element in succeeding at work for autistic individuals is matching jobs with their skills, in addition to helping them with employability skills (Mawhood & Howlin, 1999) such as writing resumes, interview skills, and interpersonal communication, as well as knowledge and understanding by employers for their disorders. Academics have emphasized the benefits from transition programs from school-to-work, and for support and training programs (e.g., Hillier et al., 2007; Howlin et al., 2005; Lee & Carter, 2012). One suggestion to create useful transition program is the collaboration between autistic individuals, their families, educational and vocational counsellors, and employers (Lee & Carter, 2012). They can all take part at different stages starting with the preparation for work during high school to starting work and during adjustment at work (Lee & Carter, 2012). This can be an opportunity for communities to connect and work together and come up with better solutions that will in turn create resilient and happier communities.

Educational counselors can provide assessment of skills, interests, strengths, and needs while vocational professionals can provide ideas of what jobs are out there for those strengths and interests, where to find more career related information, and teach them how to search for jobs, write a resume, and answer interview questions (Lee & Carter, 2012). In addition, training intervention in improving communication and, more specifically, on asking the right questions to initiate conversations and improve social skills can improve the job search outcomes and organizational socialization process of ASD individuals (Palmen et al., 2008). These skills can be taught quickly to individuals with mild autism by using procedures with generalization strategies (Palmen et al., 2008). Also, work skills, or more specifically, task engagement skill can be taught using simulation-based training that includes clear procedures, generalization strategies, and practice (Palmen & Didden, 2012). The employment skills programs cost money but, in the long run, the benefits will outweigh the costs by helping autistic individuals gain employment and have a better quality of life as well as reducing societal costs through paying taxes and claiming less benefits (Howlin et al., 2005).

Regarding anti-stigma initiatives, researchers have proposed three kinds of information delivery for non-autistic children: (1) emphasizing the similarity between autistic students and their peers, (2) emphasizing that autism is a fact of life and not a choice, and (3) providing guidance on how to communicate with autistic individuals (Campbell, 2006; Staniland & Byrne, 2013). Some firms are also beginning to explore initiatives to offer autistic students work experiences and internships to enhance their job finding success (Carrero et al., 2019; Remington & Pellicano, 2018). Especially significant in recent discussions is the idea that some autistic individuals possess special talents that can improve organizational competitiveness (Austin & Pisano, 2017) especially in the area of information technology (Annabi & Locke, 2019). Increasing the contact and communication between neurodivergent and non-autistic individuals at work can increase understanding for them and reduce the stereotyping and stigma, which may also spill over to the community. The practical implications for HR professionals align with the acceptance perspective of autistic advocates (versus the cure perspective) which in this case involve: raising awareness about autism, increase hiring of autistic individuals, and providing accommodations for them.

Future Research Directions

Based on the high rate of unemployment and underemployment of autistic individuals, it appears that current HRM practices (recruitment, selection, training, and compensation) are inadequately designed or tailored to properly evaluate ASD job applicants' skills, knowledge, and abilities. Individuals with mild autism do not exhibit cognitive and language impairment and they have many strengths, skills, and interests which can act as a competitive advantage for organizations. However, their ritualistic behaviors and social interaction difficulties become a barrier to their employment success. Future research should explore ways in which HRM practices can be better tailored to cater to this group of individuals. More specifically, researchers could look at better ways of interviewing to eliminate some of the inherent biases in how ASD candidates are evaluated both in their verbal and nonverbal expressions.

In addition, researchers can explore different employment transition programs in order to find the best programs and services to enhance job finding success and employment outcomes at work. For example, scholars can investigate appropriate ways to conduct interviews, how to properly assess resumes of disability groups, and more specifically how to evaluate the skills of autistic individuals. Future research should also investigate how to implement anti-stigma programs in the workplace to raise awareness and understanding of autistic individuals. Since previous research on anti-stigma interventions has shown that they help in attitude changes but not a change in behavioral intentions, this is another area for future research (Staniland & Byrne, 2013). It is beneficial to know the effects of the interventions in the short and the longer term. Finally, longitudinal research is needed to know the variables that can predict long-term success at work and the possibility for growth and advancements within a career. From the perspective of autistic individuals, it is valuable to know how and when the right moment is to disclose a diagnosis to an employer.

CONCLUSION

The job search experiences of individuals with mild autism are characterized by various individual, institutional, and societal barriers, and established systems of employment practices that put them at grave disadvantage compared to their neurotypical counterparts. Some of the main issues include difficulty finding suitable employment, a lack of person-job fit, and lack of acceptance and socialization in the workplace. The stigmas associated with negative attitudes towards people that are different from the dominant group, such as the neurotypicals, make individuals with mild autism isolated and excluded from work and social life. Neurodiversity as anti-stigma movement has been helpful, but there is still more to be done to reduce the stigma and make the workplace more inclusive for autistic individuals so they can fit. To address these challenges, I suggest that organizations and society put interventions in place to reintegrate these individuals into the workforce. Some of these include employment services, training opportunities, resume writing, coaching, employment counseling, and interview preparation sessions to increase employment offers for these individuals. This research is intended to advocate for more support in order to enhance the labor market experiences of autistic individuals. I also hope to raise awareness that can stimulate a conversation in favor of creating a more level playing field for autistic jobseekers.

REFERENCES

Adolphs, R., Tranel, D., & Damasio, A. R. (1998). The human amygdala in social judgment. *Nature (London)*, *393*(6684), 470–474. https://doi.org/10.1038/30982
Adolphs, R., Sears, L., & Piven, J. (2001). Abnormal processing of social information from faces in autism. *Journal of Cognitive Neuroscience*, *13*, 232–240. https://doi.org/10.1162/089892901564289

Allport, G. W. (1954). *The nature of prejudice*. Addison-Wesley.

Alpin, C., Shackleton, J. R., & Walsh, S. (1998). Over- and under-education in the UK graduate labour market. *Studies in Higher Education, 23*(1), 17–34. https://doi.org/10.1080/03075079812331380462

Angermeyer, M. C., & Dietrich, S. (2006). Public beliefs about and attitudes towards people with mental illness: A review of population studies. *Acta Psychiatrica Scandinavica, 113*, 163–179. https://doi.org/10.1111/j.1600-0447.2005.00699.x

Annabi, H., & Locke, J. (2019). A theoretical framework for investigating the context for creating employment success in information technology for individuals with autism. *Journal of Management & Organization, 25*, 499–515. https://doi.org/10.1017/jmo.2018.79

Anthony, A. (2009). *Jane Elliott, the American schoolmarm who would rid us of our racism*. The Guardian. https://www.theguardian.com/culture/2009/oct/18/racism-psychology-jane-elliott-4

Attwood, T. (2007). *The complete guide to Asperger's syndrome*. Jessica Kingsley.

Austin, R. D., & Pisano, G. P. (2017). Neurodiversity as a competitive advantage. *Harvard Business Review, 95*, 96–103.

Australian Bureau of Statistics. (2013). Labour force. Cat. no. 6202.0, January. Canberra, ACT, Australia.

Autism Society. (2019). https://www.autism-society.org/what-is/facts-and-statistics/

Baldwin, S., & Costley, D. (2016). The experiences and needs of female adults with high-functioning autism spectrum disorder. *Autism, 20*(4), 483–495. https://doi.org/10.1177/1362361315590805

Baldwin, S., Costley, D., & Warren, A. (2014). Employment activities and experiences of adults with high-functioning autism and Asperger's disorder. *Journal of Autism and Developmental Disorders, 44*(10), 2440–2449. https://doi.org/10.1007/s10803-014-2112-z

Baron-Cohen, S. (1995). *Mindblindness: An essay on autism and theory of mind*. MIT Press. https://doi.org/10.7551/mitpress/4635.001.0001

Baron-Cohen, S., Ring, H. A., Bullmore, E. T., Wheelwright, S., Ashwin, C., & Williams, S. C. R. (2000). The amygdala theory of autism. *Neuroscience and Biobehavioral Reviews, 24*, 355–364. https://doi.org/10.1016/S0149-7634(00)00011-7

Beardon, L., & Edmonds, G. (2007). *ASPECT consultancy report: A national report on the needs of adults with Asperger syndrome*. The Autism Centre, Sheffield Hallam University.

Bell, M. (2012). *Diversity in organizations* (2nd ed.). South-Western College.

Billig, M., & Tajfel, H. (1973). Social categorization and similarity in intergroup behaviour. *European Journal of Social Psychology, 3*(1), 27–52. https://doi.org/10.1002/ejsp.2420030103

Boyd, B. A., McDonough, S. G., & Bodfish, J. W. (2012). Evidence-based behavioral interventions for repetitive behaviors in autism. *Journal of Autism and Developmental Disorders, 42*(6), 1236–1248. https://doi.org/10.1007/s10803-011-1284-z

Bracke, P., Pattyn, E., & von dem Knesebeck, O. (2013). Overeducation and depressive symptoms: Diminishing mental health returns to education. *Sociology of Heath and Illness, 35*(8), 1242–1259. https://doi.org/10.1111/1467-9566.12039

Brewer, M. B., & Miller, N. (1984). Beyond the contact hypothesis: Theoretical perspectives on desegregation. In N. Miller & M. Brewer (Eds.), *Groups in conflict: A psychology of desegregation* (pp. 281–302). Academic.

Buckley, C. (2017). Autism in adults. *InnovAiT, 10*(6), 319–326. https://doi.org/10.1177/1755738016683410

Campbell, J. M. (2006). Changing children's attitudes toward autism: A process of persuasive communication. *Journal of Developmental and Physical Disabilities, 18*, 251–272. https://doi.org/10.1007/s10882-006-9015-7

Carrero, J., Krzeminska, A., & Härtel, C. E. J. (2019). The DXC technology work experience program: disability-inclusive recruitment and selection in action. *Journal of Management & Organization, 25*, 535–542. https://doi.org/10.1017/jmo.2019.23

Carter, E. W., & Wehby, J. H. (2003). Job performance of transition-age youth with emotional and behavioral disorders. *Exceptional Children, 69*, 449–465. https://doi.org/10.1177/001440290306900404

CDC Press Release. (2020). https://www.autism-society.org/releases/cdc-releases-new-prevalence-rates-of-people-with-autism-spectrum-disorder/

Chan, J. N., Mak, W. S., & Law, L. C. (2009). Combining education and video-based contact to reduce stigma of mental illness: "The Same or Not the Same" anti-stigma program for secondary schools in Hong Kong. *Social Science and Medicine, 68*, 1521–1526. https://doi.org/10.1016/j.socscimed.2009.02.016

Chen, J., Leader, L., Sung, G., & Leahy, C. (2015). Trends in employment for individuals with autism spectrum disorder: A review of the research literature. *Review Journal of Autism and Developmental Disorders, 2*, 115–127. https://doi.org/10.1007/s40489-014-0041-6

Christensen, D. L., Baio, J., Van Naarden Braun, K., Bilder, D., Charles, J., Constantino, J. N., Daniels, J., Durkin, M. S., Fitzgerald, R. T., Kurzius-Spencer, M., Lee, L.-C., Pettygrove, S., Robinson, C., Schulz, E., Wells, C., Wingate, M. S., Zahorodny, W., & Yeargin-Allsopp, M. (2016). Prevalence and characteristics of autism spectrum disorder among children aged 8 years—Autism and developmental disabilities monitoring network, 11 sites, United States, 2012. *MMWR. Surveillance Summaries, 65*(3), 1–23. https://doi.org/10.15585/mmwr.ss6503a1

Cimera, R., & Cowan, R. (2009). The costs of services and employment outcomes achieved by adults with autism in the US. *Autism, 13*(3), 285–302. https://doi.org/10.1177/1362361309103791

Coetzer, G. H. (2016). Researching autism spectrum disorder in the workplace: Lessons learned from researching the relationship between adult attention deficit disorder and organizational behavior. *Journal of Business and Management, 22*, 39 – 70.

Cook, S. W. (1978). Interpersonal and attitudinal outcomes in cooperating interracial groups. *Journal of Research & Development in Education, 12*(1), 97–113.

Cooper, P., & Allely, C. (2017). You can't judge book by its cover: Evolving professional responsibilities, liabilities and judgecraft when party has Asperger's syndrome. *Northern Ireland Legal Quarterly, 68*(1), 35–58.

Corrigan, P., Druss, B., & Perlick, D. (2014). The impact of mental illness stigma on seeking and participating in mental health care. *Psychological Science in the Public Interest, 15*(2), 37–70. https://doi.org/10.1177/1529100614531398

Cox, T. (1994). *Cultural diversity in organizations: Theory, research & practice*. Barrett-Koehler.

Crocker, J., Major, B., & Steele, C. (1998). Social stigma. In S. Fiske, D. Gilbert, & G. Lindzey (Eds.), *Handbook of social psychology* (Vol. 2, pp. 504–553). McGraw Hill.

Cummings, J. R., Lucas, S. M., & Druss, B. G. (2013). Addressing public stigma and disparities among persons with mental illness: The role of federal policy. *American Journal of Public Health, 103*(5), 781–785. https://doi.org/10.2105/AJPH.2013.301224

den Houting, J. (2019). Neurodiversity: An insider's perspective. *Autism: The International Journal of Research and Practice, 23*(2), 271–273. https://doi.org/10.1177/1362361318820762

Dudley, C., Nicholas, D. B., & Zwicker, J. D. (2015). What do we know about improving employment outcomes for individuals with autism spectrum disorder? *University of Calgary SPP Research Papers, 8*, 1–35.

Duffy, R., Blustein, D., Diemer, M., & Autin, K. (2016). The psychology of working theory. *Journal of Counseling Psychology, 63*(2), 127–148. https://doi.org/10.1037/cou0000140

Dworkin, A. G., & Dworkin, R. J. (1999). *The minority report: an introduction to racial, ethnic, and gender relations* (3rd ed.). Harcourt Barce College Publishers.

Earnshaw, V., Brousseau, N., Hill, E., Kalichman, S., Eaton, L., & Fox, A. (2020). anticipated stigma, stereotypes, and COVID-19 testing. *Stigma and Health (Washington, D.C.), 5*(4), 390–393. https://doi.org/10.1037/sah0000255

Elliot, J. (2019). *The Blue Eyes & Brown Eyes Exercise*. https://janeelliott.com/

Embrick, D. G. (2011). The diversity ideology in the business world: A new oppression for a new age. *Critical Sociology, 37*, 541–556.

Ferraioli, S. J., & Harris, S. L. (2011). Effective educational inclusion of students on the autism spectrum. *Journal of Contemporary Psychotherapy, 41*, 19–28. https://doi.org/10.1007/s10879-010-9156-y

Gallese, V., & Goldman, A. (1998). Mirror neurons and the simulation theory of mind-reading. *Trends in Cognitive Sciences, 2*(12), 493–501. https://doi.org/10.1016/S1364-6613(98)01262-5

Gillborn, D. (2015). Intersectionality, critical race theory, and the primacy of racism: Race, class, gender, and disability in education. *Qualitative Inquiry, 21*(3), 277–287. https://doi.org/10.1177/1077800414557827

Goffman, E. (1963). *Stigma: Notes on the management of spoiled identity*. Prentice Hall.

Gray, D. E. (2002). 'Everybody just freezes. Everybody is just embarrassed': Felt and enacted stigma among parents of children with high functioning autism. *Sociology of Health & Illness, 24*, 734–749. https://doi.org/10.1111/1467-9566.00316

Griffiths, A. J., Giannantonio, C. M., Hurley-Hanson, A. E., & Cardinal, D. N. (2016). Autism in the workplace: Assessing the transition needs of young adults with autism spectrum disorder. *Journal of Business and Management*, *22*, 5–22.

Gunderson, M., & Lee, B. Y. (2016). Pay discrimination against persons with disabilities: Canadian evidence from PALS. *International Journal of Human Resource Management*, *27*(14), 1531–1549. https://doi.org/10.1080/09585192.2015.1 072106

Gurney, J., Fritz, M., Ness, K., Sievers, P., Newschaffer, C., & Shapiro, E. (2003). Analysis of prevalence trends of autism spectrum disorder in Minnesota (Archives of Pediatrics & Adolescent Medicine). JAMA, *The Journal of the American Medical Association*, *290*(14). https://doi.org/10.1001/archpedi.157.7.622

Hawkins, G. (2004). *How to find work that works for people with Asperger syndrome.* Jessica Kingsley.

Hedley, D., Uljarević, M., Foley, K. R., Richdale, A., & Trollor, J. (2018). Risk and protective factors underlying depression and suicidal ideation in autism spectrum disorder. *Depression and Anxiety*, *35*(7), 648–657. https://doi.org/10.1002/da.22759.

Heifetz, M. (2019). Autism spectrum disorder (ASD) in Canada. In *The Canadian Encyclopedia*. https://www.thecanadianencyclopedia.ca/en/article/autism-spectrum-disorder-asd-in-canada

Hendricks, D. R., & Wehman, P. (2009). Transition from school to adulthood for youth with autism spectrum disorders. *Focus on Autism and Other Developmental Disabilities*, *24*, 77–88. https://doi.org/10.1177/1088357608329827

Higgins, K. K., Koch, L. C., Boughfman, E. M., & Vierstra, C. (2008). School-to-work transition and Asperger syndrome. *Work: A Journal of Prevention, Assessment and Rehabilitation*, *31*, 291–298.

Hillier, A., Campbell, H., Mastriani, K., Vreeburg Izzo, M., KoolTucker, A. K., Cherry, L., & Beversforf, D. Q. (2007). Two-year evaluation of a vocational support program for adults on the autism spectrum. *Career Development for Exceptional Individuals*, *30*(1), 35–47. https://doi.org/10.1177/088572880703 00010501

Hornsey, M. J. (2008). Social identity theory and self-categorization theory: A historical review. *Social and Personality Psychology Compass*, *2*(1), 204–222. https://doi.org/10.1111/j.1751-9004.2007.00066.x

Howlin, P., & Moss, P. (2012). Adults with autism spectrum disorders. *The Canadian Journal of Psychiatry*, *57*(5), 275–283. https://doi.org/10.1177/070674371205700502

Howlin, P., Alcock, J., & Burkin, C. (2005). An 8 year follow-up of a specialist supported employment service for high-ability adults with autism or Asperger syndrome, *Autism 9*(5), 533–549. https://doi.org/10.1177/1362361305057871

Hurlbutt, K., & Chalmers, L. (2004). Employment and adults with Asperger syndrome. *Focus on Autism and Other Developmental Disabilities*, *19*, 215–222. https://doi.org/10.1177/10883576040190040301

Izuma, K., Matsumoto, K., Camerer, C. F., & Adolphs, R. (2011). Insensitivity to social reputation in autism. *Proceedings of the National Academy of Sciences*, *108*(42), 17302–17307. https://doi.org/10.1073/pnas.1107038108

Jacob, A., Scott, M., Falkmer, M., & Falkmer, T. (2015). The costs and benefits of employing an adult with autism spectrum disorder: A systematic review. *PLoS ONE, 10*(10), e0139896. https://doi.org/10.1371/journal.pone.0139896

Jones, S. C., Gordon, C. S., Akram, M., Murphy, N., & Sharkie, F. (2021). Inclusion, exclusion and isolation of autistic people: Community attitudes and autistic people's experiences. *Journal of Autism and Developmental Disorders*. https://doi.org/10.1007/s10803-021-04998-7

Kenny, L., Hattersley, C., Molins, B., Buckley, C., Povey, C., & Pellicano, E. (2016). Which terms should be used to describe autism? Perspectives from the UK autism community. *Autism: The International Journal of Research and Practice, 20*(4), 442–462. https://doi.org/10.1177/1362361315588200

Krzeminska, A., Austin, R. D., Bruyère, S. M., & Hedley, D. (2019). Special issue: The advantages and challenges of neurodiversity employment in organizations. *Journal of Management and Organization, 25*, 453–463. https://doi.org/10.1017/jmo.2019.58

Kuzmanovic, B., Schilbach, L., Lehnhardt, F., Bente, G., & Vogeley, K. (2011). A matter of words: Impact of verbal and nonverbal information on impression formation in high-functioning autism. *Research in Autism Spectrum Disorders, 5*(1), 604–613. https://doi.org/10.1016/j.rasd.2010.07.005

Lee, G., & Carter, E. (2012). Preparing Transition-Age Students with High-Functioning Autism Spectrum Disorders for Meaningful Work. *Psychology in the Schools, 49*(10), 988–1000. https://doi.org/10.1002/pits.21651

Luo, Q., Ma, Y., Bhatt, M., Read Montague, P., & Feng, J. (2017). The functional architecture of the brain underlies strategic deception in impression management. *Frontiers in Human Neuroscience, 11*, 513–513. https://doi.org/10.3389/fnhum.2017.00513

MacMillan, M., Tarrant, M., Abraham, C., & Morris, C. (2014). The association between children's contact with people with disabilities and their attitudes towards disability: a systematic review. *Developmental Medicine and Child Neurology, 56*(6), 529–546. https://doi.org/10.1111/dmcn.12326

Markel, K. S., & Elia, B. (2016). How human resource management can best support employees with autism: Future directions for research and practice. *Journal of Business and Management, 22*, 71–86.

Maroto, M., & Pettinicchio, D. (2015). Twenty-five years after the ADA: Situating disability in America's system of stratification. *Disability Studies Quarterly, 35*, 3. https://doi.org/10.18061/dsq.v35i3.4927

Mawhood, L., & Howlin, P. (1999). The outcome of a supported employment scheme for high-functioning adults with autism or Asperger syndrome. *Autism, 3*, 229–254. doi:10.1177/1362361399003003003.

McIntosh, C. K. (2016). Asperger's syndrome and the development of a positive work identity. *Journal of Business and Management, 22*, 87–102.

Moxon, L., & Gates, D. (2001). Children with autism: Supporting the transition to adulthood. *Educational and Child Psychology, 18*, 28–40.

Moyser, M. (2017). Chapter "Women and Paid Work" in *Women in Canada: A gender-based statistical report*. http://www.statcan.gc.ca/pub/89-503-x/2015001/article/14694-eng.pdf

Muller, E., Schuler, A., Burton, B., & Yates, G. B. (2003). Meeting the vocational support needs of individuals with Asperger syndrome and other autism spectrum disabilities. *Journal of Vocational Rehabilitation, 18*, 163–175.

Palmen, A., & Didden, R. (2012). Task engagement in young adults with high-functioning autism spectrum disorders: Generalization effects of behavioral skills training. *Research in Autism Spectrum Disorders, 6*, 1377–1388. doi:10.1016/j.rasd.2012.05

Palmen, A., Didden, H., & Arts, M. (2008). Improving question asking in high-functioning adolescents with autism spectrum disorders—Effectiveness of small-group training. *Autism: the International Journal of Research and Practice, 12*(1), 83–98. https://doi.org/10.1177/1362361307085265

Peek F., & Hanson L.L. (2008). *The life and message of the real rain man.* Dude.

Pencene, S., & Svyantek, D. J. (2016). Person-organization fit and autism in the workplace. *Journal of Business and Management, 22*, 117–134.

Perkins, T., Stokes, M., McGillivray, J., & Bittar, R. (2010). Mirror neuron dysfunction in autism spectrum disorders (Report). *Journal of Clinical Neuroscience, 17*(10). https://doi.org/10.1016/j.jocn.2010.01.026

Pesce, N. L. (2019). *Most college grads with autism can't find jobs.* https://www.marketwatch.com/story/most-college-grads-with-autism-cant-find-jobs-this-group-is-fixing-that-2017-04-10-5881421

Plaisted Grant, K., & Davis, G. (2009). Perception and apperception in autism: rejecting the inverse assumption. *Philosophical Transactions. Biological Sciences, 364*(1522), 1393–1398. https://doi.org/10.1098/rstb.2009.0001

Rademaker, F., de Boer, A., Kupers, E., & Minnaert, A. (2020). Applying the contact theory in inclusive education: A systematic review on the impact of contact and information on the social participation of students with disabilities. *Frontiers in Education (Lausanne), 5*. https://doi.org/10.3389/feduc.2020.602414

Remington, A., & Pellicano, E. (2018). 'Sometimes you just need someone to take a chance on you': An internship programme for autistic graduates at Deutsche Bank, UK. *Journal of Management & Organization, 25*, 516–534. https://doi.org/10.1017/jmo.2018.66

Robertson, S. M. (2010). Neurodiversity, quality of life, and autistic adults: Shifting research and professional focuses onto real-life challenges. *Disability Studies Quarterly, 30*(1). http://dsq-sds.org/article/view/1069/1234

Rogers, S., Bennetto, L., Mcevoy, R., & Pennington, B. (1996). Imitation and pantomime in high-functioning adolescents with autism spectrum disorders. *Child Development, 67*(5), 2060–2073. https://doi.org/10.2307/1131609

Rogge, N., & Janssen, J. (2019). The economic costs of autism spectrum disorder: A literature review. *Journal of Autism and Developmental Disorders, 49*(7), 2873–2900. https://doi.org/10.1007/s10803-019-04014-z

Roux, A., Shattuck, P., Cooper, B., Anderson, K., Wagner, M., & Narendorf, S. (2013). Postsecondary employment experiences among young adults with an autism spectrum disorder. *Journal of the American Academy of Child & Adolescent Psychiatry, 52*(9), 931–939. https://doi.org/10.1016/j.jaac.2013.05.019

Scott, M., Milbourn, B., Falkmer, M., Black M., Bolte, S., Halladay, A., Lerner, M., Taylor, J. L., & Girdler, S. (2019). Factors impacting employment for people with autism spectrum disorder: A scoping review. *Autism, 23*, 869–901. https://doi.org/10.1177/1362361318787789

Seitz, S. R., & Smith, S. A. (2016). Working toward neurodiversity: How organizations and leaders can accommodate for autism spectrum disorder. *Journal of Business and Management, 22*, 135–151.

Shattuck, P., Roux, A., Hudson, L., Taylor, J., Maenner, M., & Trani, J. (2012). Review of Services for Adults with an Autism Spectrum Disorder. *The Canadian Journal of Psychiatry, 57*(5), 284–291. https://doi.org/10.1177/070674371205700503

Silberman, S. (2017). Beyond "Deficit-Based" thinking in autism research: Comment on "Implications of the idea of neurodiversity for understanding the origins of developmental disorders" by Nobuo Masataka. *Physics of Life Reviews, 20*, 119–121. https://doi.org/10.1016/j.plrev.2017.01.022

Silverman, C. (2008). Fieldwork on another planet: social science perspectives on the autism spectrum. *BioSocieties. 3*(3), 325–341. https://doi.org/10.1017/S1745855208006236.

Silverman, C. (2012). *Understanding autism: Parents, doctors, and the history of a disorder*. Princeton University Press.

Stangl, A. L., Earnshaw, V. A., Logie, C. H., van Brakel, W., Simbayi, L. C., Barré, I., & Dovidio, J. F. (2019). The health stigma and discrimination framework: A global, crosscutting framework to inform research, intervention development, and policy on health-related stigmas. *BMC Medicine, 17*, 31. http://dx.doi.org/10.1186/s12916-019-1271-3

Staniland, J.J., & Byrne, M. K. (2013). The effects of a multi-component higher-functioning autism anti-stigma program on adolescent boys. *J Autism Dev Disord 43*, 2816–2829. https://doi.org/10.1007/s10803-013-1829-4

Stankova, T., & Trajkovski, V. (2010). Attitudes and opinions of employers, employees and parents about the employment of people with autism in the Republic of Macedonia. *Journal of Special Education and Rehabilitation, 11*(3), 16–29.

Stone, D. L., & Colella, A. (1996). a model of factors affecting the treatment of disabled individuals in organizations. *The Academy of Management Review, 21*(2), 352–401. https://doi.org/10.2307/258666

Suckle, E. K. (2021). DSM-5 and challenges to female autism identification. *J Autism Dev Disord, 51*, 754–759. https://doi.org/10.1007/s10803-020-04574-5

Sumner, K., & Brown, T. (2015). Neurodiversity and human resource management: Employer challenges for applicants and employees with learning disabilities. *The Psychologist Manager Journal, 18*(2), 77–85. https://doi.org/10.1037/mgr0000031

Tajfel, H., & Turner, J. C. (1979). An integrative theory of intergroup conflict. In W. G. Austin & S. Worchel (Eds.), *The social psychology of intergroup relations* (pp. 33–47). Brooks/Cole.

Tajfel, H., & Turner, J. C. (1986) The social identity theory of intergroup behavior. In S. Worchel & W. G. Austin (Eds.), *Psychology of intergroup relations* (2nd ed., pp. 7–24). Nelson-Hall.

Tan, C. (2018). "I'm a normal autistic person, not an abnormal neurotypical": Autism Spectrum Disorder diagnosis as biographical illumination. *Social Science & Medicine, 197,* 161–167. https://doi.org/10.1016/j.socscimed.2017.12.008

Taylor, J. L., & Hodapp, R. M. (2012). Doing nothing: Adults with disabilities with no daily activities and their siblings. *American Journal on Intellectual and Developmental Disabilities, 117*(1), 67–79. https://doi.org/10.1352/1944-7558-117.1.67

Taylor, J. L., & Seltzer, M. M. (2011). Employment and post-secondary educational activities for young adults with autism spectrum disorders during the transition to adulthood. *Journal of Autism and Developmental Disorders, 41,* 566–574. https://doi.org/10.1007/s10803-010-1070-3

Taylor, J., McPheeters, M., Sathe, N., Dove, D., Veenstra-VanderWeele, J., & Warren, Z. (2012). A systematic review of vocational interventions for young adults with autism spectrum disorders. (Report). *Pediatrics, 130*(3), 531–538. https://doi.org/10.1542/peds.2012-0682

Thomas, H., & Boellstorff, T. (2017). Beyond the spectrum: Rethinking autism. *Disability Studies Quarterly, 37*(1). https://doi.org/10.18061/dsq.v37i1.5375

Treffert, D. A. (2009). The savant syndrome: an extraordinary condition. A synopsis: Past, present, future. *Philosophical transactions of the Royal Society of London. Series B, Biological sciences, 364*(1522), 1351–1357. https://doi.org/10.1098/rstb.2008.0326

van Hooft, E. A. J., Kammeyer-Mueller, J. D., Wanberg, C. R., Kanfer, R., & Basbug, G. (2020). Job search and employment success: A quantitative review and future research agenda. *Journal of Applied Psychology.* Advance online publication. https://doi.org/10.1037/apl0000675

Vogeley, K., Kirchner, J., Gawronski, A., Elst, L., & Dziobek, I. (2013). Toward the development of a supported employment program for individuals with high-functioning autism in Germany. *European Archives of Psychiatry and Clinical Neuroscience, 263*(2), 197–203. https://doi.org/10.1007/s00406-013-0455-7

Waisman-Nitzan, M., Gal, E., & Schreuer, N. (2018). Employers' perspectives regarding reasonable accommodations for employees with autism spectrum disorder. *Journal of Management & Organization, 25,* 481–498. https://doi.org/10.1017/jmo.2018.59

Whittenburg, H. N., Cimera, R. E., & Thoma, C. A. (2019). Comparing employment outcomes of young adults with autism: does postsecondary educational experience matter? *Journal of Postsecondary Education and Disability, 32*(2), 159–172.

NOTES

1. The term "autistic individual" will be hereinafter used to refer to individuals on the ASD spectrum which represents identity-first language as opposed to individual with autism which is person-first language because it is not something that can be removed from the person and it is their preferred term (Kenny et al., 2016; Tan, 2018). Many of them are comfortable with person-first but most seem to prefer the identity-first language (Kenny et al., 2016).

2. Since the term Asperger's syndrome is no longer in use and the division on high and low functioning is perceived misleading, I will use the term mild autism to talk about autistic individuals that previously had been diagnosed with Asperger's or high functioning autism.

CHAPTER 4

"I'M ANXIOUS BUT I DON'T HAVE ANXIETY!"

How Stigma Exacerbates the Effect of Anxiety Disorders in the Workplace

Eli Mendoza, Sara Mendiola, Lindsay Mathys, Shannon K. Cheng, and Eden B. King
Rice University

ABSTRACT

Anxiety disorders are the most common mental illness in the world, and as the world becomes increasingly stressful, the number of people looking for help with anxiety continues to increase. However, many barriers to honest conversations surrounding anxiety disorders persist, including in the workplace. Everyday anxiety and anxiety disorders are often conflated, potentially making it harder for employees with anxiety disorders to voice their experiences or believe their experiences are serious enough to be addressed. This continued stigma surrounding mental illness can prevent employees with anxiety disorders from getting the help that they need. In this chapter, we give an overview of anxiety disorders and how they can impact employee performance, building from Cheng and McCarthy's (2018) theory of workplace anxiety. We also discuss how mental illness stigma can exacerbate the negative effects of anxiety disorders at work, and highlight individual, ally (manager and coworker), and organizational level interventions that have been

Forgotten Minorities in Organizations, pp. 105–134
Copyright © 2023 by Information Age Publishing
www.infoagepub.com
All rights of reproduction in any form reserved.

researched to treat anxiety disorders and/or reduce stigma. Future research and practical implications are also discussed.

Anxiety disorders are the most common mental illness around the world and in the United States, impacting around 284 million people worldwide and about 40 million U.S. adults each year (Anxiety and Depression Association of America [ADAA], n.d.; Ritchie & Roser, 2018). This is close to 20% of the U.S. adult population, and about 34% of these cases are moderate and 23% are severe (National Institute of Mental Health [NIMH], 2017). In addition, as the world becomes increasingly stressful, the number of people looking for help with anxiety continues to increase. For example, amidst the COVID-19 pandemic, over 300,000 people took Mental Health America's anxiety screener from January to September 2020, a 93% increase from the previous year (Mental Health America, 2020). Workplaces are also beginning to place higher concern on employee well-being and understanding the importance of addressing mental health in the workplace (Agovino, 2019; Pfeffer & Williams, 2020).

However, as these conversations increase, it is also important to understand barriers to honest conversations and significant progress surrounding mental health in the workplace. For example, with respect to anxiety disorders, people often conflate everyday anxiety and anxiety disorders (Levine, 2010), which may hinder conversations on how to best address anxiety disorders in the workplace. Everyday anxiety is a common response of nervousness, uneasiness, and tension to stressful situations, such as paying the bills, having a difficult conversation, giving a presentation, or taking an exam. This response is derived from our biological fight-or-flight response to external threats, which helps us survive in dangerous situations (e.g., encountering a bear on a hike, driving on an icy road)—our heart pumps faster to get blood to our muscles and lungs, our breathing intensifies, and we become more alert (Nash-Wright, 2011). However, if this response is prolonged, we can also start to experience irritability, fatigue, muscle tension, digestive troubles, difficulty sleeping, and avoidance behavior (American Psychological Association, 2020; American Psychiatric Association, 2017), as it is hard for the mind and body to be on high alert for an extended period of time.

In contrast, anxiety disorders involve consistent and excessive fear or worry that causes significant distress and interferes with daily life (American Psychiatric Association, 2017). With everyday anxiety, feelings of nervousness, uneasiness, and tension are proportional to the stress of the situation; in addition, people who experience everyday anxiety are usually able to control or reduce these feelings relatively easily. People who have anxiety disorders have a harder time distinguishing between what is a "real" threat versus not, and as such, the anxiety they experience is more intense, longer in duration, and harder to control—leading to a much more significant impact on people's everyday lives.

Why are these distinctions important? Because everyday anxiety is so common, it is possible that employees with anxiety disorders may have a harder time voicing their experiences or start to think that their experiences do not need to be addressed—because they perceive that others are dealing with similar issues. In 2006, ADAA conducted a Workplace Stress and Anxiety Disorders Survey, where they found that 40% of respondents experienced persistent stress or excessive anxiety in their daily lives, although only 9% had been diagnosed with an anxiety disorder. It is possible that some of the respondents had undiagnosed anxiety disorders; however, it is also noteworthy that 40% of respondents agreed that "persistent stress and/or excessive anxiety are a normal part of life," and only a fourth of those diagnosed with an anxiety disorder had told their employers about their condition (ADAA, 2006). This is in line with broader statistics of how, even though anxiety disorders are highly treatable, less than 40% of individuals with anxiety disorders actually receive treatment (ADAA, n.d.). As a result, increasing mental health awareness needs to be approached thoughtfully— if employers simply normalize the experience of stress and anxiety at work, without taking into consideration the stigmatization of mental illnesses, as well as the professional and personal consequences of disclosing a mental illness, employees dealing with mental illness still may not feel comfortable getting the help they need to reach their full potential at work.

The prevalence of anxiety disorders also highlights the importance and impact of addressing these concerns. Untreated anxiety disorders can result in over $4 billion in indirect workplace costs in the United States (Kuhl, 2017), as well as greater absenteeism and reduced productivity (Harder et al., 2014; Hendriks et al., 2014; Plaisier et al., 2010). Looking beyond the United States, the World Health Organization recently reported that untreated depression and anxiety will result in a global cost of $925 billion by 2030 (Luxton, 2016). However, both depression and anxiety are highly treatable, and although scaling up treatment for depression and anxiety would cost $147 billion over the next 15 years, it would yield a $399 billion return on investment via improved workforce participation (Luxton, 2016). As a result, it is imperative that employees with anxiety and other mental disorders feel comfortable getting the treatment they need, which involves organization not only providing access to the treatment, but also reducing the stigma and consequences of disclosing a mental illness at work. For example, in the Workplace Stress and Anxiety Disorders Survey, participants with anxiety disorders mentioned multiple barriers to talking openly about their anxiety disorders at work, including fears that their boss would interpret it as a lack of interest or unwillingness to do their work, that it would affect promotion opportunities, and that it would go in their file

(ADAA, 2006). Because of how prevalent anxiety is, individuals with anxiety disorders may be even more reluctant to speak up because they do not want others to think that they cannot keep up—that is, if everyone else has anxiety, they may feel that they should be able to handle their anxiety as well.

To better understand how anxiety disorders can impact employee experiences and performance, as well as the role that stigma plays, we have three objectives in this chapter. First, we will give an overview of what anxiety disorders are and how they can impact employee performance, building from Cheng and McCarthy's (2018) theory of workplace anxiety. Then, we will discuss the stigma that continues to surround mental illness, as well as how it applies to anxiety disorders and exacerbates the negative effects of anxiety disorders at work. We will then highlight individual, ally (manager and coworker), and organizational level interventions that have been researched to treat anxiety disorders and/or reduce mental illness stigma and discuss future research and practical implications. We contribute to the literature by integrating research on anxiety disorders, stigma, and performance management across multiple different fields, including clinical psychology, industrial-organizational psychology, social psychology, and human resource management. We also hope to provide managers and coworkers with greater awareness and understanding of anxiety and anxiety disorders, in order to better support all employees' mental health at work.

WHAT ARE ANXIETY DISORDERS, AND HOW DO THEY IMPACT WORK?

In the *Diagnostic and Statistical Manual of Mental Disorders* (DSM-5), anxiety disorders are classified as conditions characterized by anxiety, fear, and avoidance. In addition, the DSM-5 notes that, among the most prevalent psychiatric diagnoses, anxiety disorders can be particularly difficult to diagnose, due to how anxiety, fear, and avoidance are normal and adaptive responses to stressful situations (American Psychiatric Association, 2013). As a result, when people have mild symptoms, it may be hard to determine whether they have an anxiety disorder or are experiencing everyday anxiety. In general, in order for someone to be diagnosed with an anxiety disorder, the symptoms they are experiencing should be excessive or beyond what would be appropriate for the situation or the person's age. Additionally, the symptoms should be hindering the person's ability to function normally on a day-to-day basis (American Psychiatric Association, 2017). Similar to any other mental illness, if untreated, anxiety disorders can significantly impact employees' work experience and their ability to perform (Harder et al., 2014). However, if treated and managed appropriately, to the point where individuals with anxiety disorders experience levels of anxiety that are not excessive, there can also be positive effects of their anxiety on workplace performance.

Common Anxiety Disorders and How They Show Up at Work

Anxiety disorders can come in many different forms, the most common in the U.S. being specific phobia (impacting 7–9% of U.S. adults), social anxiety disorder (7%), panic disorder (2–3%), agoraphobia (2%), and generalized anxiety disorder (2%; American Psychiatric Association, 2017). Specific phobias are characterized by an excessive and persistent fear of a specific object, situation, or activity that is generally not harmful (e.g., spiders, flying). Another example that is defined as its own category in the DSM-5 is agoraphobia, which is characterized by the fear of being in situations where escape might be difficult or where help might not be available if something goes wrong (e.g., using public transportation, being in enclosed spaces, standing in line or being in a crowd; American Psychiatric Association, 2017). This can have significant consequences for employees, if their job requires them to be in different situations they may not feel comfortable in, and in general, agoraphobia can significantly limit a person's mobility and everyday life. Another phobia that is particularly relevant is workplace phobia, which is the fear of approaching or even thinking of the workplace (Muschalla & Linden, 2009, 2014). While this fear is often accompanied by comorbid anxiety diagnoses, those with workplace phobia have noteworthy avoidance tendencies, as demonstrated by the high levels of sick leave reported, even more so than that of other anxiety disorders (Haines et al., 2002; Muschalla & Linden, 2009).

Social anxiety disorder (SAD), previously called social phobia, is characterized by significant anxiety and discomfort about being embarrassed or rejected in interpersonal or social situations (e.g., meeting new people, eating/drinking in public, public speaking; American Psychiatric Association, 2017). Because many jobs require some degree of social interaction, this can pose a significant challenge to employees with SAD (Moitra et al., 2011). Research has shown how employees with SAD are less productive and have more absences than their counterparts without SAD (Kessler, 2003; Kessler et al., 2005; Wittchen et al., 1999). Additionally, the social anxiety and fears of employees with SAD may lead them to reject promotions, resulting in lower hourly wages and sometimes even higher rates of unemployment (Wittchen et al., 1999).

Panic disorders are characterized by recurrent panic attacks, which are periods of overwhelming physical and psychological distress. During these attacks, individuals can experience a combination of several different symptoms, including (but not limited to) rapid heart rate, sweating, trembling, shortness of breath, chest pain, dizziness or light-headiness, numbness, chills or hot flashes, and nausea or abdominal pains (American Psychiatric Association, 2017). Unfortunately, individuals with panic disorders are often unable to pinpoint exactly what triggers their panic attacks (Roy-Byrne et al., 2006). As a result, it is possible for panic attacks to occur at work, leading to a decrease in the individual's productivity, an increase in sick leave, and an increased use of primary care and other healthcare providers (Roy-Byrne et al., 2006; Pignone et al., 2002).

Generalized anxiety disorder (GAD) is described as consistent, heightened anxiety and worry, as well as an increased tension from excessive vigilance. It can also be accompanied by other common somatic symptoms, such as feeling restless or on edge, fatigue, difficulty concentrating, muscle tension, or problems sleeping (American Psychiatric Association, 2017; Wittchen, 2002). GAD has a high rate of comorbidity with other mental health conditions, such as major depressive disorder, yet GAD alone can also be responsible for significant workplace impairment (Hoffman et al., 2008; Wittchen, 2002). Employees with GAD often experience reduced productivity, as well as increased disability or sick leave and higher rates of visits to healthcare providers (Hoffman et al., 2008; Wittchen, 2002).

However, it is important to note that providing accommodations to employees with anxiety disorders can significantly improve their workplace experiences and ability to perform. Accommodations, such as services from an employee assistance program (EAP), reduced work hours, modified job duties, access to a peer support group, changing to a different job, getting a job coach, working from home, modifying methods for instruction and feedback, and extended job training, have been demonstrated to improve productivity, reduce absenteeism, and have better long-term benefits for many workers with anxiety disorders, such as being less likely to still have their disorder after one year (Bolo et al., 2013; Cooper & Cartwright, 1994). Unfortunately, many employees with anxiety disorders do not receive the accommodations they need—for example, only about 30% had received accommodations from their employers (Wang et al., 2011). Not receiving appropriate accommodations can be due to multiple factors, including a lack of disclosure from the employee (often due to stigma or not wanting to be a burden; Brohan et al., 2012; Santuzzi et al., 2014) or a lack of knowledge about what accommodations could be provided (both from the employee and employer perspective; Schultz et al., 2011). However, reasonable accommodations are legally required by the Americans with Disabilities Act (1990) and can help make anxiety disorders much more manageable at work.

The Bright Side of Anxiety at Work

In fact, appropriately managing anxiety disorders at work can help these employees instead potentially gain some of the positive effects anxiety can have on workplace performance (Cheng & McCarthy, 2018). The theory of workplace anxiety (TWA; Cheng & McCarthy, 2018) highlights both the "bright" and "dark" sides of workplace anxiety, which is defined as "feelings of nervousness, uneasiness, and tension about job-related performance" (Cheng & McCarthy, 2018, p. 537; Linden & Muschalla, 2007). The negative effects of workplace anxiety can include poorer job performance, an increase in distractibility or misinterpretations of others' actions, and even dishonest workplace behaviors (due to increased threat perception (Cheng & McCarthy, 2018). However, workplace anxiety can have positive effects as well. For example, a moderate amount of anxiety can serve a motivating function that helps improve job performance, such as by increasing attentiveness, monitoring of oneself and others, and sensitivity to feedback (Elliot & McGregor, 1999; Eysenck & Derakshan, 2011). The TWA sheds light on the processes and boundary conditions leading to these differential effects and why it is important to consider workplace anxiety's complexity, recognizing its positive effects in addition to the negative.

Although the TWA examines the effects of workplace anxiety, and not anxiety disorders, we believe that it is still a helpful model to highlight the potential strengths individuals with anxiety disorders can bring to the workplace. Oftentimes, we primarily focus on the negative effects of mental illness in the workplace, advocating for better mental health awareness in order to reduce the cost of mental illness in the workplace; however, there are fewer conversations about the positive traits, attributes, or perspectives that individuals with different mental illnesses can bring to the workplace (e.g., how individuals with depression can make better complex sequential decisions; von Helversen et al., 2011). Although excessive worrying or nervousness can be harmful in life and at work, having some anxiety or well-managed anxiety disorders may be able to help improve job performance via increased self-regulatory processing. For example, when looking at discrete job performance episodes, the TWA proposes that moderate levels of situational anxiety (i.e., the anxiety one feels about a particular job performance episode) can facilitate job performance by increasing arousal and self-monitoring, helping motivate employees to achieve the task at hand (Cheng & McCarthy, 2018).

It is important to still take into consideration how anxiety can negatively impact job performance, which the TWA suggests occurs through cognitive interference for episodic performance. Cognitive interference is the "tendency to spend a disproportionate amount of cognitive processing ruminating on task-irrelevant, or off-task thoughts" (Cheng & McCarthy, 2018, p. 548), which can disrupt concentration and override productive actions (Sarason et al., 1996). In addition, too much cognitive interference can make it harder to engage in the helpful self-regulatory processing that anxiety can provide (Cheng & McCarthy, 2018). Individuals with untreated anxiety disorders likely experience more cognitive interference, which can help explain the overall negative effect of anxiety disorders on job performance. However, this also emphasizes the importance of appropriately managing anxiety disorders and allowing these employees to get the treatment and accommodations they need—as this will allow them to reduce their cognitive interference and improve their job performance.

The TWA also discusses the effects of dispositional workplace anxiety (i.e., the anxiety one feels in general about job performance) on typical job performance, which is an employee's performance over time or multiple performance episodes. Over time, the excessive worry and tension that employees with anxiety disorders experience, as well as efforts to combat cognitive interference that occurs daily, can lead to emotional exhaustion, which can have a significant negative impact on employee well-being and performance. However, typical job performance can also be positively impacted by the long-term self-regulatory processing and more careful and deliberate mindsets associated with anxiety (Cheng & McCarthy, 2018). Employees with moderate levels of anxiety approach challenging goals with increased effort and persistence, and work to avoid negative outcomes by developing action plans (Norem & Chang, 2002).

Untreated anxiety disorders likely heighten both dispositional and situational workplace anxiety - exacerbating the negative effects of cognitive interference on episodic job performance and emotional exhaustion on typical job performance and hindering the benefits of both short- and long-term self-regulatory processing that anxiety can provide. As such, in this chapter, we adapt Cheng and McCarthy's (2018) TWA to look at the effect of anxiety disorders on job performance more broadly, in order to also incorporate the effects of stigma and interventions at the individual, ally, and organizational levels (see Figure 4.1). Anxiety disorders also differ from everyday anxiety in that, even when anxiety disorders are appropriately managed, employees with anxiety disorders may still have moderate levels of anxiety—compared to employees with everyday anxiety, who likely have a lower baseline of anxiety. However, this moderate level of anxiety has the potential to create positive effects on job performance, via healthy levels of cognitive interference and emotional exhaustion, as well as improved self-regulatory processing.

Figure 4.1

Proposed Model

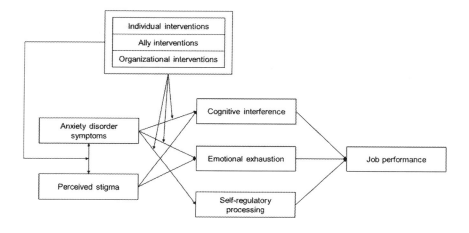

WHAT ROLE DOES STIGMA PLAY?

Defining Stigma

Stigma is classically defined by Erving Goffman (1963) as attribute(s) that are deeply discrediting, reducing a person from "whole and usual" to a "tainted, discounted one." Stigma is socially and culturally derived, and society's definitions of who is stigmatized versus who is not can shape how we view ourselves and interact with others (Crocker et al., 1998; Jones et al., 1984). For example, non-stigmatized individuals typically desire social distance from stigmatized individuals (Link et al., 1999), which can lead to ostracism and isolation of those with a stigmatized identity.

Jones and colleagues (1984) defined six dimensions to describe the most important distinctions of stigma. These dimensions include: (1) concealability, the degree to which the target's stigma is known; (2) course of the mark, the extent to which the target's stigma increases, decreases, or remains consistent across time; (3) disruptiveness, or the degree to which the target's stigma significantly influences work and social interactions; (4) aesthetics, or how the stigma impacts the target's appearance; (5) origin, or the time since the target has had the stigma; and (6) peril, or the amount of danger the target's stigma poses to others.

Mental Illness Stigma

Mental illness remains one of the most highly stigmatized conditions in society, and its stigma has three main characteristics: legitimacy, fluctuations, and dangerousness (Follmer & Jones, 2018). These characteristics tie in well with Jones et al.'s (1984) dimensions of concealability, course of the mark, disruptiveness, and peril. Mental illness is commonly perceived as less *legitimate* than physical disorders or other conditions, particularly since they often are not visible manifestations. Another factor that ties into legitimacy is perceived responsibility—for example, research has shown that people are more supportive and view individuals better if they believed the person's condition was due to a cause outside of their control (e.g., brain chemistry, bad background, trauma), compared to if they thought the condition was within their control (e.g., laziness, drug use; Corrigan et al., 2003; Corrigan et al., 2007). The *fluctuations* that individuals with mental illness experience can also undermine the legitimacy of their conditions; an individual with mental illness may be able to adequately work on some days but experience significant impairment on others (Follmer & Jones, 2018). These attitudes inherently affect how others view employees with mental illness, and what accommodations they are willing to provide these employees.

Even if the legitimacy and fluctuations of an individual's mental illness are accepted, the stigma of instability and *dangerousness* can remain prevalent. Understanding that mental illness is a real and serious psychological condition does not necessarily eliminate stigma and discrimination; although mental health awareness continues to grow in organizations, individuals with mental illness still face more negative hiring outcomes and performance expectations (Ren et al., 2008; Shankar et al., 2014). It is clear that mental illness stigma harms personal outcomes as well, as stigma and discrimination has also created obstacles for developing and maintaining social relationships, keeping housing, and achieving long-term goals (Corrigan et al., 2007; Santuzzi et al., 2014). The stigma surrounding mental illness is incredibly pervasive, and research has demonstrated how even mental health professionals can still hold negative beliefs about mental illness (Ahmedani, 2011). This stigma can also easily be internalized by individuals with mental illness (known as self-stigma), leading people to avoid seeking treatment or even acknowledging that they have a mental illness (Clement et al., 2015; Eisenberg et al., 2009; Henderson et al., 2012).

Anxiety Disorder Stigma and the Impact on Employees With Anxiety Disorders

Regarding stigma around anxiety disorders, although many of the attributes of general mental illness stigma apply, different disorders have specific stigma attributes as well. For example, although many mental ill-nesses are viewed with a *weak-not-sick* perception (i.e., mental illnesses are a personal weakness, not a real medical problem), these perceptions have been more commonly associated with anxiety and depressive disorders (Anderson et al., 2015; Curcio & Corboy, 2020; Griffiths et al., 2011). A recent review of anxiety disorders and stigma also highlighted how the mis-identification of anxiety disorders as not real mental disorders can lead to others dismissing anxiety disorders or blaming symptoms, such as for SAD, on personal attributes like shyness, introversion, or awkwardness (Curcio & Corboy, 2020; Davidson, 2005). It is important to note that individuals with anxiety disorders actually seem to be less inclined to engage in self-stigmatization than any other mental disorder group, and it is suggested that the negative public perceptions of anxiety disorders (e.g., *weak-not-sick* perceptions) are a stronger driver of the attitudes and behaviors of indi-viduals with anxiety disorders, rather than their own personal views about their conditions (Curcio & Corboy, 2020; Evans-Lacko et al., 2012).

For example, this public stigma can impact how much employees with anxiety disorders decide to share with others about their condition. Because anxiety disorders, like many mental illnesses, can be categorized as an "invisible" disability (i.e., symptoms are not readily visible), individuals with anxiety disorders may be motivated to try to conceal their conditions—in order to avoid the social and professional costs of disclosure (Brohan et al., 2012; Santuzzi et al., 2014). Research has demonstrated how employees with anxiety disorders may fear lower expectations, harassment, social exclusion, or ignorance surrounding the seriousness of their conditions from coworkers or managers (ADAA, 2006; Pilling et al., 2013; Schrader et al., 2013). These fears are not unfounded—in addition to negative attitudes stemming from stigma, coworkers can negatively perceive the accommodations employees with anxiety disorders may receive. Cowork-ers can interpret these adaptations as preferential treatment, especially if the disclosure was confidential and/or coworkers are unable to connect the accommodations to the condition (Schrader et al., 2013; Santuzzi et al., 2014; MacDonald-Wilson et al., 2010). These perceptions of unfair treat-ment may be especially relevant for conditions like anxiety disorders that often are not perceived as real or serious conditions.

However, concealing an anxiety disorder prevents these employees from getting accommodations that may help their performance and well-being; in addition, it can increase stress and exacerbate symptoms (Santuzzi et al., 2014). The decision whether or not to disclose an invisible condition can be very cognitively taxing in itself (Lindsay et al., 2019; Smart & Wegner, 1999). For example, since the nature of the invisible disabilities are often imperceptible, disclosing can be perceived as suspicious or illegitimate, placing individuals in the position where they must defend or prove their own condition (Santuzzi et al., 2014; Schrader et al., 2013). The timing in which one decides to disclose an invisible disability can also add complexities. Disclosure of an invisible disability during the hiring process leads to concerns about potential discrimination and being rejected from a position (Santuzzi et al., 2014); however, waiting to disclose until one is employed can not only be viewed as sneaky or untrustworthy, but could also result in a deprivation from or lack of necessary accommodations, as well as worse performance reviews (Santuzzi et al., 2014).

As a result, when employees with anxiety disorders are thinking about if and when to disclose their conditions, as well as trying to understand how others may perceive them, they can experience additional cognitive interference—on top of the cognitive interference their anxiety disorders already create for them. Disclosure decisions are tough enough, without preexisting conditions of excessive worrying and fear. In addition, regularly thinking about the stigma of one's identity and managing how one interacts with others can exacerbate feelings of emotional exhaustion over time. Lastly, being aware of and concerned about anxiety disorder stigma can actually negatively impact anxiety disorder symptoms, and research has also shown how worse symptomatology is related to increased perceived stigma (Curcio & Corboy, 2020; Pyne et al., 2004)—highlighting a potential reciprocal relationship between the two. See Figure 4.1 for the proposed relationships between perceived stigma and cognitive interference, emotional exhaustion, and anxiety disorder symptoms.

However, there are many ways that stigma surrounding anxiety disorders can be combated (Rüsch et al., 2005). For example, at the interpersonal level, perceptions of anxiety stigma can change based on levels of exposure to anxiety. People with more exposure to anxiety disorders, either from a personal diagnosis or knowing someone with an anxiety disorder, are less likely to have personal stigma against people with anxiety disorders (Batterham et al., 2013). Education on anxiety disorders can also help lessen the social stigma (Szeto & Dobson, 2010). In the next section, we will discuss more interventions aimed at not only addressing anxiety disorder stigma, but also reducing anxiety disorder symptoms and creating work environments that can allow employees with anxiety disorders to truly thrive.

WHAT INTERVENTIONS HELP ADDRESS ANXIETY DISORDER SYMPTOMS AND STIGMA?

Taking action to combat the stigma surrounding anxiety disorders and maintaining a supportive, productive work environment can and should occur within all levels of an organization including the individual, manager and coworker, and the broader organizational levels (Follmer & Jones, 2018; Martin et al., 2016). Creating an informed and inclusive workplace allows employees with different kinds of mental disorders to feel more secure; it also builds greater health, well-being, personal enjoyment, devotion, and loyalty from all employees (Battams et al., 2014; Locke et al., 2015; Santuzzi et al., 2014; Schrader et al., 2013). At the individual-level, employees with anxiety disorders can seek treatment, educate themselves on anxiety disorders, and learn healthy coping mechanisms to decrease anxiety and improve overall health (Mayo-Wilson et al., 2014; Locke et al., 2015). It is also extremely important that managers and coworkers act as mental illness allies, educating themselves via mental health training to reduce the stigma surrounding anxiety disorders, and ensuring. that all employees feel supported (Battams et al., 2014; Dimoff et al., 2016; Mac-Donald-Wilson et al., 2010). Lastly, anxiety disorders should be addressed at the organizational level through implementing a corporate education and training system, as well as adjusting the structure of the workplace to feel more inclusive and increasing available resources (Cooper & Cartwright, 1994; Joyce et al., 2016; Naveen, 2017; Szeto & Dobson, 2010). We propose these multilevel interventions as moderators that help temper the negative effects of anxiety disorders on cognitive interference and emotional exhaustion, while allowing individuals with anxiety disorders to better manage their symptoms and gain the positive benefits of anxiety (i.e., increased self-regulatory processing). We also propose that these interventions will serve as a moderator in the relationship between anxiety disorder symptoms and stigma, helping reduce the negative impact of each on the other (see Figure 4.1).

Individual Interventions

There are several strategies that can be adopted on the individual level to reduce personal anxiety disorder symptoms within the workplace. Some anxiety disorders, such as SAD, can be treated with cognitive behavioral therapy (CBT), an interactive form of psychotherapy (Mayo-Wilson et al., 2014). CBT is recommended as the most effective form of treatment for anxiety disorders, alongside pharmacological treatment, including selective serotonin reuptake inhibitors (SSRIs) and benzodiazepines (Mayo-Wilson et al., 2014; Nash-Wright, 2011; Pilling et al., 2013). Some research has indicated that a combination of psychotherapeutic and pharmacological treatment could be the best way to treat anxiety disorders; however, further research is needed in this area (Nash-Wright, 2011; Gonçalves & Byrne, 2012).

Considering the high cost of CBT and medication for anxiety, more cost-effective approaches, such as self-help interventions, have been recommended to overcome financial barriers to treatment (Lewis et al., 2012). While not as effective as traditional therapy or professional help, self-help is still considered more constructive than complete lack of treatment (Lewis et al., 2012). Additionally, several individual-level coping strategies provide a simple opportunity to help reduce anxiety (Locke et al., 2015). Adopting healthier daily living habits by improving sleep quality, increasing physical activity, decreasing potential triggering activities (e.g., caffeine consumption, smoking), and introducing mindfulness practice can lower stress and reduce some anxiety (Locke et al., 2015).

Employees with anxiety disorders also have the opportunity to more openly discuss their mental illnesses in the workplace, which can help increase visibility and awareness in the workplace about anxiety disorders, as well as let other individuals who may have anxiety disorders know that they are not alone (Nittrouer et al., 2014). However, it is very important to note that, due to the continued stigma and discrimination surrounding anxiety disorders and other mental illnesses in the workplace, this may not be a strategy employees feel able to engage in without repercussions. It is also imperative to emphasize that the burden of reducing stigma and discrimination should never be placed on the individuals who are experiencing marginalization—rather, others should also join in the fight and actively support and advocate for change.

Ally Interventions

Allies are commonly defined as "a person who is a member of the 'dominant' or 'majority' group who works to end oppression in his or her personal and professional life through his or her support of, and as an advocate with and for, the oppressed population" (Evans & Wall, 1991, p. 195). Ally behaviors can include both support and advocacy (Sabat et al., 2014). Supportive behaviors include providing psychological and/or tangible resources for individuals; for invisible disabilities, such as anxiety disorders, these behaviors can include receiving disclosures with empathy and understanding and providing social support (Sabat et al., 2014). In contrast, advocacy behaviors involve more outward displays of support, and for invisible disabilities, these could include educating peers, advocating for workplace accommodations, confronting instances of prejudice, and calling for better organizational policies (Sabat et al., 2014). Within organizations, both coworkers and managers can engage in support and advocacy behaviors for employees with anxiety disorders. It is important to note that, in Follmer and Jones's (2018) review on mental illness in the workplace, they specifically highlighted the important role of mental illness allies, while also pointing out the significant dearth of research on these allies and how they can most effectively support employees with mental illnesses.

However, research has demonstrated some ways in which coworkers and managers can better support mental health in the workplace. For example, coworkers can educate themselves, and differentiate accurate information from the media's often biased and distorted portrayal of mental illnesses (Evans et al., 2005). After becoming more self-aware, coworkers can help raise others' awareness and even examine company policies and practices, determining whether they are fully inclusive of employees with mental illnesses and other disabilities (Evans et al., 2005). Allies, particularly those in positions of leadership, can also use their platform to advocate for changes in policies and practices (Evans et al., 2005).

Because of their unique position and relationship with employees, managers have additional ways that they can provide support for employees with anxiety disorders. For example, managers can often serve as gatekeepers for whether or not employees with anxiety disorders or other mental illnesses receive the accommodations they need. If employees do not feel comfortable enough disclosing their conditions to their managers, they will continue to suffer in silence. Employees with invisible stigmatized identities often use anticipated reactions from others, as well as prior experiences of disclosing to others, to inform their disclosure decisions (Law et al., 2011; Ragins, 2008). As such, it is important that managers create an environment in which employees with anxiety disorders feel that their disclosures will be accepted and taken seriously, especially considering the *weak-not-sick* perceptions of anxiety disorders. Managers can help by being proactive about engaging in mental health training, getting informed about different mental illnesses and what accommodations they can provide. Managers should also proactively let employees know what accommodations are available if there is a need, how to request an accommodation, and the resources and support available to employees. When employees are dealing with a mental illness, such as anxiety disorders, trying to figure out employee rights and available resources can be overwhelming, so this is one particular area that managers could step up as allies.

Organizational Interventions

Organizational strategies are important in creating widespread positive effects for employee well-being, and in this section, these strategies are organized into two different types: educational and structural. Educational strategies are focused on educating employees about anxiety disorders, and structural strategies are focused on how workplace policies and practices can help reduce unnecessary stress or make anxiety disorder treatment more accessible. By putting these into practice, organizations can help improve the health, efficiency, and participation of all employees, both with and without anxiety disorders.

Educational Strategies

Organizations can help reduce mental illness stigma by providing trainings that help employees understand what mental illness looks like in the workplace. These trainings can also teach how to help those with mental illnesses and how employees who may need help can get it themselves. Both the Beyond Blue program and the Mental Health First Aid program have resulted in increased knowledge about mental illness, as well as increased confidence in helping coworkers who may be struggling with mental illnesses (Szeto & Dobson, 2010). Participants in the Mental Health First Aid program also reported feeling more comfortable conversing with and being friends with people with mental illnesses (Szeto & Dobson, 2010). Overall, stigma-reducing educational training programs like Beyond Blue and Mental Health First Aid can create more welcoming and less hostile work environments for those experiencing mental illnesses like anxiety disorders.

These trainings can also signal to employees with mental illness that their organization cares about their well-being, helping reduce self-stigma and increase help-seeking behaviors. Again, this is particularly important for anxiety disorders because people often see anxiety as very commonplace, and these types of trainings can help employees with anxiety disorders see that (1) their conditions are legitimate, and (2) their organization will take it seriously and help them get the accommodations and/or support they need. This helps the organization as well, because treating employees with mental illness helps reduce the cost and length of disability claims, and improves employee productivity (Szeto & Dobson, 2010).

Structural Strategies

Changing certain aspects of workplace structures can also create a more positive environment for employees with anxiety disorders by reducing unnecessary job demands and stress (e.g., role ambiguity, work overload, time pressure; Beehr & O'Driscoll, 2002). For example, setting clear expectations, such as increasing clarity of job expectations and roles in the workplace, can help reduce anxiety stemming from confusion or vague tasks (Naveen, 2017). Organizations can also increase employees' feelings of control by allowing for flexible work hours or adding a self-scheduling system for shifts, which have been shown to help reduce anxiety and depression symptomatology (Joyce et al., 2016). In addition, organizations can implement a regular employee survey to help identify common stressors. They then can convene a group with decision-making power and resources, as well as diverse perspectives, to help problem-solve how to address these stressors (Graveling et al., 2008). Structural strategies may sound intimidating or cost-intensive; however, there are often many changes that just require some additional thought and intention and can have a significant impact on employee experiences (Cooper & Cartwright, 1994).

Organizations should also make sure that employees know about and have easy access to different mental health resources. Many organizations provide these services through EAPs, which can include general well-being resources, such as stress management classes and physical activity and health programs, as well as specific resources for employees with anxiety disorders, such as counseling, CBT, and medication (Cooper & Cartwright, 1994; Joyce et al., 2016; Wagner et al., 2016). Increasing accessibility through the availability and promotion of EAPs within the organization can help reduce the stigma of these resources and lead to significant improvements in employee mental health (Sun et al., 2013). Managers and leaders can also further help promote these resources by regularly discussing them with their employees, and even sharing their personal experiences with using some of the resources.

DISCUSSION

The goals of the current chapter were to (a) distinguish anxiety disorders from everyday anxiety and highlight how anxiety disorders, as well as the stigma surrounding anxiety disorders, can impact employee experiences and performance, and (b) provide an overview of individual, ally, and organizational level interventions that can help mitigate some of the negative effects of anxiety disorders and stigma. To that end, we have integrated research across multiple different fields, including clinical psychology, industrial-organizational psychology, social psychology, and human resource management, to describe a model of anxiety disorders in the workplace (adapted from the TWA; Cheng & McCarthy, 2018). Now we will explore the implications of this work for research and practice, providing a few prioritized research questions.

Future Research Directions and Implications

One of the first value-adds in examining anxiety disorders in the workplace would be to engage in longitudinal research (Follmer & Jones, 2018).

Because anxiety disorders can often be conflated with everyday anxiety, it is important to have research that highlights how the duration and intensity of anxiety disorders is different and needs to be taken seriously. This would be best highlighted through longitudinal research, as opposed to cross-sectional research, as there may be acute instances of everyday anxiety that may look similar to the experience of someone with an anxiety disorder. For example, an employee with an anxiety disorder may be able to perform well in short bursts, perhaps even motivated by the anxiety they feel; however, over time, the consistent worry and tension may create an unsustainable level of arousal, resulting in poorer overall performance. This leads to our first research question:

> **Research Question 1:** How might anxiety disorders and everyday anxiety show up differently, both short- and long-term, in how they impact cognitive interference, emotional exhaustion, self-regulatory processing, and consequently, job performance?

Another area for future research is better understanding how stigma and other barriers might impact engagement in the proposed individual, ally, and organization-level interventions for anxiety disorders. Talking about mental health and providing mental health support is not a new endeavor for organizations (e.g., Elkin & Rosch, 1990; Walsh, 1982); however, the stigma surrounding mental illness persists, and many employees with different mental illnesses continue to worry about the social and professional consequences if they disclose their conditions (Brohan et al., 2012). This prevents these employees from getting the help and support they truly need, even if it is available to them. Similar research in the work-life literature demonstrates how, even when support is made available (e.g., maternity/paternity leave, flexible work practices), employees may not always take advantage of them, due to factors such as stigma, fear of professional consequences, or financial need (Grose, 2020; Hideg et al., 2018; Leslie et al., 2012). Because many organizations already have existing policies and practices that support employee mental health, it is important to .continue researching barriers to their full effectiveness, using a multilevel approach (e.g., individual-level barriers, lack of support from managers and coworkers, poor organizational culture or incentives).

Relatedly, there needs to be additional research on how people can better serve as mental illness allies. Specifically for anxiety disorders and the pervasive *weak-not-sick* stigma, as well as the regular conflation with everyday anxiety, it is important to examine how managers and coworkers may be able to help address these harmful perceptions and messaging. In addition, because many employees with anxiety disorders and other mental illnesses do not disclose their conditions to others, allies may need to provide more proactive and general allyship, as allies may not be aware of who is in direct need of their support and advocacy. There has been limited research on how mental illness allies can be the most effective, and if there are behaviors that can actually be harmful—for example, recent conversations about allyship have raised concerns about the use of the term "ally" and how it can be used as a self-serving label of support without meaningful action (Carlson et al., 2019). With respect to anxiety disorders and other mental illnesses, it is possible that employees may feel that their managers and coworkers are superficially supportive of mental health in the workplace, but would still view or treat them differently if they were to disclose their conditions. It is important to understand how managers and coworkers can both more effectively serve as allies, and what gaps still exist in allowing employees with mental illnesses to feel fully supported in the workplace. This leads to our second research question:

Research Question 2: How might allies more effectively create supportive interpersonal and structural environments for employees with anxiety disorders that reduce barriers to mental health resources and improve their work experience and performance?

There are three additional research directions that can help examine the generalizability of the proposed model. First, anxiety disorders are highly comorbid with other mental illnesses (Kaufman & Charney, 2000), and it would be interesting to explore how other mental illnesses (e.g., depressive disorders) may impact the proposed relationships or how they may operate through different mechanisms. Different mental illnesses can also be perceived and stigmatized differently (e.g., individuals with schizophrenia are more likely to be perceived as dangerous compared to individuals with depressive or anxiety disorders; Angermeyer & Matschinger, 2003), which can impact how strongly employees experience perceived stigma.

In addition to potentially experiencing more than one mental illness, every employee with an anxiety disorder also holds multiple other identities. The idea of intersectionality looks at the meaning and implications of simultaneous membership in multiple social identity groups (Crenshaw, 1989), proposing that inequities related to one identity (e.g., gender) can interrelate with inequities related to another identity (e.g., race). If employees with anxiety disorders are also part of another stigmatized group (e.g., racial minority, LGBTQ+), this can add another layer of concern regarding how they might be perceived or treated. For example, minority stress models have demonstrated having a marginalized identity in the workplace (e.g., with respect to race, gender, sexual orientation) can create additional stressors that can impact mental health outcomes (Meyer, 2003). In addition, employees with marginalized identities are often held to higher performance standards and offered less forgiveness when they make mistakes (e.g., Rosette & Livingston, 2012). As a result, future research should examine how intersectionality with other identities can impact employee experiences and outcomes.

Lastly, another factor that can impact employee experiences and outcomes is the culture in which they are embedded. This chapter primarily focused on the U.S. and other Western contexts; however, it is important to understand how other cultures might perceive and address anxiety disorders and other mental illnesses differently. For example, Curcio and Corboy's (2020) review of stigma and anxiety disorders found that cultural differences played a role in the relationship between stigma and help-seeking behaviors, such that those from Asian cultures had less favorable attitudes toward those seeking treatment for anxiety disorders. This is in line with other research highlighting higher levels of mental illness stigma in Asian cultures (Cheon & Chiao, 2012), and how different cultural values (e.g., saving face; Kramer et al., 2002) and understanding (e.g., viewing mental health symptoms as somatic rather than psychological; Li & Browne, 2000) can impact how anxiety disorders and other mental illnesses should be addressed. As such, future research on how to best address anxiety disorders in the workplace should take into consideration cultural factors that may influence the effectiveness of different interventions, which would help further understanding on how to modify the interventions accordingly. This is particularly important as organizations become more global, and employees can come from multiple different countries and cultures. This leads to our third research question:

> **Research Question 3:** How might research continue to create a more holistic understanding of employees with anxiety disorders, incorporating both internal and external factors, such as comorbidity with other mental illnesses, intersectionality with other identities, and different cultural contexts?

Practical Implications for Human Resource Management and Organizations

There are also multiple practical implications for human resource management and organizations regarding anxiety disorders and mental illness more generally. When implementing the individual, ally, and organizational-level interventions above, there are three considerations that we want to additionally highlight: open conversations, implementation attributes, and organizational culture. First, because anxiety disorders can often be conflated with everyday anxiety, it is important for organizations and people leaders to have open conversations and intentionally inform their employees of the distinction between everyday anxiety and potential anxiety disorders, while also reminding them that anxiety disorders are legitimate, and that the organization has resources to help employees with anxiety disorders. They should also combat the idea that "persistent stress and/or excessive anxiety are a normal part of life" (ADAA, 2006) and provide employees with resources if they feel that they are experiencing stress and anxiety that is detrimental to their well-being and performance. Lastly, they should acknowledge the stigma that still exists surrounding anxiety disorders and other mental illnesses, and how concerns about the social and professional consequences of disclosing a mental illness are not unfounded. They should also start conversations on how they will work to combat these concerns (e.g., mental illness education for all employees, antidiscrimination policies, de-biasing trainings for performance evaluations).

Second, it is important to pay attention to different implementation attributes; for example, Ryan and Kossek (2008) examined how the implementation of work-life policies impacted whether or not these policies broke down barriers to inclusiveness or actually created new ones. For employees with anxiety disorders, there is the opportunity for them to work with their employer to identify potential cost-effective accommodations; the Job Accommodation Network even provides information about specific disabilities and suggested accommodations broken down by limitation and work-related function (Job Accommodation Network, n.d.). However, if managers do not proactively provide resources and information to their employees, employees may not know these opportunities exist or feel encouraged to utilize these resources.

When providing resources and information, it is also important for managers to emphasize that they will work together with the employee to find a solution that works for them. For example, they could work with employees to conduct a behavior analysis to identify what kind of work conditions would allow the employee to be able to maximize important job behaviors (Hantula & Reilly, 1996). It is also important for managers to educate themselves on how to prevent accommodations from negatively impacting the employees' professional outcomes. For example, if an employee worked flexible or reduced hours or were to take disability leave, would that impact their performance evaluations or opportunities for promotion? Employees also often worry about the social backlash they may face if they receive accommodations (Santuzzi et al., 2014), and research has examined different ways to minimize this backlash by increasing perceptions of procedural justice (Colella et al., 2004). As such, managers should work with employees to come up with an implementation plan that addresses their potential concerns.

Lastly, organizational culture can have a significant impact on how employees with anxiety disorders will perceive or plan to address their conditions. For example, organizational and manager messaging may emphasize concern for mental health and employee well-being; however, if the organization is still primarily driven by a high productivity culture (Bellezza et al., 2017) or continues to uphold the "ideal worker norm" (i.e., the expectation that employees should prioritize work over all other parts of their lives; Davies & Frink, 2014), this may exacerbate *weak-not-sick* perceptions of anxiety disorders. Even if managers and coworkers are supportive, these cultural norms could push employees with anxiety disorders to feel as if their anxiety is not serious enough to be addressed, or that they need to keep working at the same rate to keep up with others. It is important for organizations to reflect on potential mismatches between their purported values of caring about mental health and how employees actually feel, and consider how broader organizational culture and practices (e.g., work incentives, performance evaluations) may be hindering true progress towards a mentally healthy workplace.

CONCLUSION

The ideas offered here suggest that, although mental health awareness is increasing in organizations, mental illness stigma continues to persist—even with more common mental illnesses like anxiety disorders. In fact, the prevalence of anxiety disorders can be additionally challenging for employees who experience it, as society can often view everyday anxiety and stress as normal—diminishing the legitimacy of the experiences of those with anxiety disorders. We discuss the impact of anxiety disorders and stigma at work, as well as how individuals, allies, and organizations can help. This chapter also has implications for how we continue to address the stigma and impact of mental illness at work more broadly, which will take an intentional, effortful, and multilevel approach—but one that is very much worth continuing to discuss, both for the organizations and the employees within them.

REFERENCES

Agovino, T. (2019). *Mental illness and the workplace*. Society of Human Resource Management. https://www.shrm.org/hr-today/news/all-things-work/pages/mental-illness-and-the-workplace.aspx

Ahmedani, B. K. (2011). Mental health stigma: Society, individuals, and the profession. *Journal of Social Work Values and Ethics*, *8*(2), 4–16. https://www.ncbi.nlm.nih.gov/pmc/articles/PMC3248273/

American Psychological Association. (2020, September). *What's the difference between stress and anxiety.* https://www.apa.org/topics/stress/anxiety-difference

American Psychiatric Association. (2013). *Diagnostic and statistical manual of mental disorders* (5th ed.). https://doi.org/10.1176/appi.books.9780890425596

American Psychiatric Association. (2017, January). *What are anxiety disorders?* https://www.psychiatry.org/patients-families/anxiety-disorders/what-are-anxiety-disorders

Americans With Disabilities Act of 1990, 42 U.S.C. § 12101 *et seq.* (1990).

Anderson, K. N., Jeon, A. B., Blenner, J. A., Wiener, R. L., & Hope, D. A. (2015). How people evaluate others with social anxiety disorder: A comparison to depression and general mental illness stigma. *American Journal of Orthopsychiatry, 85*(2), 131–138. https://doi.org/10.1037/ort0000046

Angermeyer, M. C., & Matschinger, H. (2003). The stigma of mental illness: Effects of labelling on public attitudes towards people with mental disorder. *Acta Psychiatrica Scandinavica, 108,* 304–309. http://dx.doi.org/10.1034/j.1600-0447.2003.00150.x

Anxiety and Depression Association of America. (2006). *Highlights: Workplace stress and anxiety disorders survey.* https://adaa.org/workplace-stress-anxiety-disorders-survey

Anxiety and Depression Association of America. (n.d.). *Facts and statistics.* https://adaa.org/understanding-anxiety/facts-statistics

Battams, S., Roche, A. M., Fischer, J. A., Lee, N. K., Cameron, J., & Kostadinov, V. (2014). Workplace risk factors for anxiety and depression in male-dominated industries: A systematic review. *Health Psychology and Behavioral Medicine: An Open Access Journal, 2*(1), 983–1008. https://doi.org/10.1080/21642850.2014.954579

Batterham, P. J., Griffiths, K. M., Barney, L. J., & Parsons, A. (2013). Predictors of generalized anxiety disorder stigma. *Psychiatry Research, 206*(2–3), 282–286. https://doi.org/10.1016/j.psychres.2012.11.018

Beehr, T. A., & O'Driscoll, M. P. (2002). Organizationally targeted interventions aimed at reducing workplace stress. In J. C. Thomas & M. Hersen (Eds.), *Handbook of mental health in the workplace* (pp. 103–119). SAGE.

Bellezza, S., Paharia, N., & Keinan, A. (2017). Conspicuous consumption of time: When busyness and lack of leisure time become a status symbol. *Journal of Consumer Research, 44*(1), 118–138. https://doi.org/10.1093/jcr/ucw076

Bolo, C., Sareen, J., Patten, S., Schmitz, N., Currie, S., & Wang, J. (2013). Receiving workplace mental Health accommodations and the outcome of mental disorders in employees with a depressive and/or anxiety disorder. *Journal of Occupational and Environmental Medicine, 55*(11), 1293–1299. https://doi.org/10.1097/jom.0b013e31829fd065

Brohan, E., Henderson, C., Wheat, K., Malcolm, E., Clement, S., Barley, E. A., Slade, M., & Thornicroft, G. (2012). Systematic review of beliefs, behaviours and influencing factors associated with disclosure of a mental health problem in the workplace. *BMC Psychiatry, 12*(1), 1–14. https://doi.org/10.1186/1471-244X-12-11

Carlson, J., Leek, C., Casey, E., Tolman, R., & Allen, C. (2019). What's in a name? A synthesis of "allyship" elements from academic and activist literature. *Journal of Family Violence, 1*–10. https://doi.org/10.1007/s10896-019-00073-z

Cheng, B. H., & McCarthy, J. M. (2018). Understanding the dark and bright sides of anxiety: A theory of workplace anxiety. *Journal of Applied Psychology, 103*(5), 537–560. https://doi.org/10.1037/apl0000266.

Cheon, B. K., & Chiao, J. Y. (2012). Cultural variation in implicit mental illness stigma. *Journal of Cross-Cultural Psychology, 43*(7), 1058–1062. https://doi.org/10.1177%2F0022022112455457

Clement, S., Schauman, O., Graham, T., Maggioni, F., Evans-Lacko, S., Bezborodovs, N., Morgan, C., Rüsch, N., Brown, J. S. L., & Thornicroft, G. (2015). What is the impact of mental health-related stigma on help-seeking? A systematic review of quantitative and qualitative studies. *Psychological Medicine, 45*(1), 11–27. https://doi.org/10.1017/S0033291714000129

Colella, A., Paetzold, R., & Belliveau, M. A. (2004). Factors affecting coworkers' procedural justice inferences of the workplace accommodations of employees with disabilities. *Personnel Psychology, 57*(1), 1–23. https://doi.org/10.1111/j.1744-6570.2004.tb02482.x

Cooper, C. L., & Cartwright, S. (1994). Healthy mind; healthy organization—A proactive approach to occupational stress. *Human Relations, 47*(4), 455–471. https://doi.org/10.1177/001872679404700405

Corrigan, P. W., Larson, J. E., & Kuwabara, S. A. (2007). Mental illness stigma and the fundamental components of supported employment. *Rehabilitation Psychology, 52*(4), 451–457. https://doi.org/10.1037/0090-5550.52.4.451

Corrigan, P., Markowitz, F. E., Watson, A., Rowan, D., & Kubiak, M. A. (2003). An attribution model of public discrimination towards persons with mental illness. *Journal of Health and Social Behavior, 44*, 162–179. https://doi.org/10.2307/1519806

Corrigan, P. W., Mittal, D., Reaves, C. M., Haynes, T. F., Han, X., Morris, S., & Sullivan, G. (2014). Mental health stigma and primary health care decisions. *Psychiatry Research, 218*(1-2), 35–38. https://doi.org/10.1016/j.psychres.2014.04.028

Crenshaw, K. (1989). Demarginalizing the intersection of race and sex: A black feminist critique of antidiscrimination doctrine, feminist theory and antiracist politics. *University of Chicago Legal Forum, 1*(8), 139–168.

Crocker, J., Major, B., & Steele, C. (1998). Social stigma: The psychology of marked relationships. *The Handbook of Social Psychology, 2*, 504–553.

Curcio, C., & Corboy, D. (2020). Stigma and anxiety disorders: A systematic review. *Stigma and Health, 5*(2), 125–137. http://dx.doi.org/10.1037/sah0000183

Davidson, J. (2005). Contesting stigma and contested emotions: Personal experience and public perception of specific phobias. *Social Science & Medicine, 61*(10), 2155–2164. http://dx.doi.org/10.1016/j.socscimed.2005.04.030

Davies, A. R., & Frink, B. D. (2014). The origins of the ideal worker: The separation of work and home in the United States from the market revolution to 1950. *Work and Occupations, 41*(1), 18–39. https://doi.org/10.1177/0730888413515893

Dimoff, J. K., Kelloway, E. K., & Burnstein, M. D. (2016). Mental health awareness training (MHAT): The development and evaluation of an intervention for workplace leaders. *International Journal of Stress Management, 23*(2), 167–189. https://doi.org/10.1037/a0039479

Eisenberg, D., Downs, M. F., Golberstein, E., & Zivin, K. (2009). Stigma and help seeking for mental health among college students. *Medical Care Research and Review, 66*(5), 522–541. https://doi.org/10.1177/1077558709335173

Elkin, A. J., & Rosch, P. J. (1990). Promoting mental health at the workplace: The prevention side of stress management. *Occupational Medicine, 5*(4), 739–754.

Elliot, A. J., & McGregor, H. A. (1999). Test anxiety and the hierarchical model of approach and avoidance achievement motivation. *Journal of Personality and Social Psychology, 76*(4), 628–644. https://doi.org/10.1037/0022-3514.76.4.628.

Evans, N. J., Assadi, J. L., & Herriott, T. K. (2005). Encouraging the development of disability allies. *New Directions for Student Services, 110*, 67–79. https://doi.org/10.1002/ss.166

Evans, N. J., & Wall, V. A. (1991). *Beyond tolerance: gays, lesbians, and bisexuals on campus.* American College Personnel Association.

Evans-Lacko, S., Brohan, E., Mojtabai, R., & Thornicroft, G. (2012). Association between public views of mental illness and self-stigma among individuals with mental illness in 14 European countries. *Psychological Medicine, 42*, 1741–1752. http://dx.doi.org/10.1017/S0033291711002558

Eysenck, M. W., & Derakshan, N. (2011). New perspectives in attentional control theory. *Personality and Individual Differences, 50*(7), 955–960. https://doi.org/10.1016/j.paid.2010.08.019

Follmer, K. B., & Jones, K. S. (2018). Mental illness in the workplace: An interdisciplinary review and organizational research agenda. *Journal of Management, 44*(1), 325–351. https://doi.org/10.1177/0149206317741194

Goffman, E. (1963). *Stigma: Notes on the management of a spoiled identity.* Prentice-Hall.

Gonçalves, D. C., & Byrne, G. J. (2012). Interventions for generalized anxiety disorder in older adults: Systematic review and meta-analysis. *Journal of Anxiety Disorders, 26*(1), 1–11. https://doi.org10.1016/j.janxdis.2011.08.010

Graveling, R. A., Crawford, J. O., Cowie, H., Amati, C., & Vohra, S. (2008). *A review of workplace interventions that promote mental wellbeing in the workplace.* Institute of Occupational Medicine.

Griffiths, K. M., Batterham, P. J., Barney, L., & Parsons, A. (2011). The generalised anxiety stigma scale (GASS): Psychometric properties in a community sample. *BMC Psychiatry 11*(1), 1–9. https://doi.org/10.1186/1471-244X-11-184

Grose, J. (2020). *Why dads don't take parental leave.* The New York Times. https://www.nytimes.com/2020/02/19/parenting/why-dads-dont-take-parental-leave.html

Haines, J., Williams, C. L., & Carson, J. M. (2002). Workplace phobia: psychological and psychophysiological mechanisms. *International Journal of Stress Management, 9*(3), 129–145. https://doi.org/10.1023/A:1015518030340

Harder, H. G., Wagner, S., & Rash, J. (2014). *Mental illness in the workplace: Psychological disability management.* Routledge.

Hantula, D. A., & Reilly, N. A. (1996). Reasonable accommodation for employees with mental disabilities: A mandate for effective supervision? *Behavioral Sciences & the Law, 14*(1), 107–120. http://dx.doi.org/10.1002/(SICI)1099-0798(199624)14:1%3C107::AID-BSL221%3E3.0.CO;2-6

Henderson, C., Evans-Lacko, S., & Thornicroft, G. (2013). Mental illness stigma, help seeking, and public health programs. *American Journal of Public Health, 103*(5), 777–780. https://doi.org/10.2105/ajph.2012.301056

Hendriks, S. M., Spijker, J., Licht, C. M. M., Beekman, A. T. F., Hardeveld, F., de Graaf, R., Batelaan, N. M., Penninx, B. W. J. H. (2014). Disability in anxiety disorders. *Journal of Affective Disorders, 166*, 227–233. https://doi.org/10.1016/j.jad.2014.05.006

Hideg, I., Krstic, A., Trau, R. N. C., & Zarina, T. (2018). The unintended consequences of maternity leaves: How agency interventions mitigate the negative effects of longer legislated maternity leaves. *Journal of Applied Psychology, 103*(10), 1155–1164. https://doi.org/10.1037/apl0000327

Hoffman, D. L., Dukes, E. M., & Wittchen, H. (2008). Human and economic burden of generalized anxiety disorder. *Depression and Anxiety, 25*(1), 72–90. https://doi.org/10.1002/da.20257

Job Accommodation Network (n.d.). *Anxiety disorder.* https://askjan.org/disabilities/Anxiety-Disorder.cfm

Jones, E. E., Farina, A., Hastorf, A. H., Markus, H., Miller, D. T., & Scott, R. A. (1984). *Social stigma: The psychology of marked relationships.* Freeman.

Joyce, S., Modini, M., Christensen, H., Mykletun, A., Bryant, R., Mitchell, P., & Harvey, S. (2016). Workplace interventions for common mental disorders: A systematic meta-review. *Psychological Medicine, 46*(4), 683–697. https://doi.org/10.1017/S0033291715002408

Kaufman, J., & Charney, D. (2000). Comorbidity of mood and anxiety disorders. *Depression and Anxiety, 12*(1), 69–76. https://doi.org/10.1002/1520-6394(2000)12:1+%3C69::AID-DA9%3E3.0.CO;2-K

Kessler, R. C. (2003). The impairments caused by social phobia in the general population: Implications for intervention. *Acta Psychiatrica Scandinavica Supplementum, 108*(417), 19–27. https://doi.org/10.1034/j.1600-0447.108.s417.2.x

Kessler, R. C., Berglund, P., Demler, O., Jin, R., Merikangas, K. R., & Walters, E. E. (2005). Lifetime prevalence and age-of-onset distributions of DSM-IV disorders in the national comorbidity survey replication. *Arch Gen Psychiatry, 62*(6), 593–602. https://doi.org/10.1001/archpsyc.62.6.593

Kramer, E. J., Kwong, K., Lee, E., & Chung, H. (2002). Cultural factors influencing the mental health of Asian Americans. *Western Journal of Medicine, 176*(4), 227–231.

Kuhl, E. A. (2017). *Anxiety disorders: Why they matter and what employers can do.* Center for Workplace Mental Health. http://workplacementalhealth.org/News-Events/News-Listing/Anxiety-Disorders-Why-They-Matter

Law, C. L., Martinez, L. R., Ruggs, E. N., Hebl, M. R., & Akers, E. (2011). Transparency in the workplace: How the experiences of transsexual employees can be improved. *Journal of Vocational Behavior, 79*(3), 710–723. https://doi.org/10.1016/j.jvb.2011.03.018

Leslie, L. M., Manchester, C. F., Park, T.-Y., & Mehng, S. A. (2012). Flexible work practices: A source of career premiums or penalties? *Academy of Management Journal, 55*(6), 1407–1428. https://doi.org/10.5465/amj.2010.0651

Levine, I. S. (2010, September). Mind matters: Anxiety in the workplace. *American Association for the Advancement of Science.* https://www.sciencemag.org/careers/2010/09/mind-matters-anxiety-workplace

Lewis, C., Pearce, J., & Bisson, J. (2012). Efficacy, cost-effectiveness and acceptability of self-help interventions for anxiety disorders: Systematic review. *British Journal of Psychiatry, 200*(1), 15–21. https://doi.org/10.1192/bjp.bp.110.084756

Li, H., & Browne, A. (2000). Defining mental illness and accessing mental health services: Perspectives of Asian Canadians. *Canadian Journal of Community Mental Health, 19*(1), 143–160.

Linden, M., & Muschalla, B. (2007). Anxiety disorders and workplace-related anxieties. *Journal of Anxiety Disorders, 21*(3), 467–474. https://doi.org/10.1016/j.janxdis.2006.06.006

Lindsay, S., Osten, V., Rezai, M., & Bui, S. (2019). Disclosure and workplace accommodations for people with autism: A systematic review. *Disability and Rehabilitation,* 1–14. https://doi.org/10.1080/09638288.2019.1635658

Link, B. G., Phelan, J. C., Bresnahan, M., Stueve, A., & Pescosolido, B. A. (1999). Public conceptions of mental illness: labels, causes, dangerousness, and social distance. *American Journal of Public Health, 89*(9), 1328–1333. https://doi.org/10.2105/ajph.89.9.1328

Locke, A. B., Kirst, N., & Schultz, C. G. (2015). Diagnosis and Management of Generalized Anxiety Disorder and Panic Disorder in Adults. *American Family Physician, 91*(9), 617–624. https://www.aafp.org/afp/2015/0501/p617.html

Luxton, E. (2016, April). *This is the surprisingly large economic dividend from investing in better mental health.* World Economic Forum. https://www.weforum.org/agenda/2016/04/treating-depression-is-good-for-the-global-economy/

MacDonald-Wilson, K. L., Russinova, Z., Rogers, E. S., Lin, C. H., Ferguson, T., Dong, S., & Macdonald, M. K. (2010). Disclosure of mental health disabilities in the workplace. *Work Accommodation and Retention in Mental Health,* 191–217. https://doi.org/10.1007/978-1-4419-0428-7_10

Martin, A., Karanika-Murray, M., Biron, C., & Sanderson, K. (2016). The psychosocial work environment, employee mental health and organizational interventions: Improving research and practice by taking a multilevel approach. *Stress and Health, 32*(3), 201–215. https://doi.org/10.1002/smi.2593

Mayo-Wilson, E., Dias, S., Mavranezouli, I., Kew, K., Clark, D. M., Ades, A. E., & Pilling, S. (2014). Psychological and pharmacological interventions for social anxiety disorder in adults: A systematic review and network meta-analysis. *The Lancet Psychiatry, 1*(5), 368–376. https://doi.org/10.1016/s2215-0366(14)70329-3

Mental Health America. (2020). *The state of mental health in America.* https://www.mhanational.org/issues/state-mental-health-america

Meyer, I. H. (2003). Prejudice, social stress, and mental health in lesbian, gay, and bisexual populations: Conceptual issues and research evidence. *Psychological Bulletin, 129*(5), 674–697.

Moitra, E., Beard, C., Weisberg, R. B., & Keller, M. B. (2011). Occupational impairment and social anxiety disorder in a sample of primary care patients. *Journal of Affective Disorders, 130*(1–2), 209–212. https://doi.org/10.1016/j.jad.2010.09.024

Muschalla, B., & Linden, M. (2009). Workplace phobia—A first explorative study on its relation to established anxiety disorders, sick leave, and work-directed treatment. *Psychology, Health & Medicine, 14*(5), 591–605. https://doi.org/10.1080/13548500903207398

Muschalla, B., & Linden, M. (2014). Workplace phobia, workplace problems, and work ability among primary care patients with chronic mental disorders. *The Journal of the American Board of Family Medicine, 27*(4), 486–494. https://doi.org/10.3122/jabfm.2014.04.130308

Nash-Wright, J. (2011). Dealing with anxiety disorders in the workplace: Importance of early intervention when anxiety leads to absence from work. *Professional Case Management, 16*(2), 55–59. https://doi.org/10.1097/NCM.0b013e3181f50919

National Institute of Mental Health. (2017, November). *Any anxiety disorder.* https://www.nimh.nih.gov/health/statistics/any-anxiety-disorder.shtml

Naveen, R. (2017). Mental health in the workplace: World Mental Health Day 2017. *Indian Journal of Occupational and Environmental Medicine, 21*(3), 99–100. https://doi.org/10.4103/ijoem.IJOEM_148_17

Nittrouer, C. L., Trump, R. C., O'Brien, K. R., & Hebl, M. (2014). Stand up and be counted: In the long run, disclosing helps all. *Industrial and Organizational Psychology, 7*(2), 235–241. https://doi.org/10.1111/iops.12139

Norem, J. K., & Chang, E. C. (2002). The positive psychology of negative thinking. *Journal of Clinical Psychology, 58*(9), 993–1001. https://doi.org/10.1002/jclp.10094

Pfeffer, J., & Williams, L. (2020). *Mental health in the workplace: The coming revolution.* McKinsey. https://www.mckinsey.com/industries/healthcare-systems-and-services/our-insights/mental-health-in-the-workplace-the-coming-revolution

Pignone, M. P., Gaynes, B. N., Rushton, J. L., Burchell, C. M., Orleans, C. T., Mulrow, C. D., & Lohr, K. N. (2002). Screening for depression in adults: A summary of the evidence for the U.S. preventive services task force. *Annals of Internal Medicine, 136*(10), 765–776. https://doi.org/10.7326/0003-4819-136-10-200205210-00013

Pilling, S., Mayo-Wilson, E., Mavranezouli, I., Kew, K., Taylor, C., & Clark, D. M. (2013). Recognition, assessment and treatment of social anxiety disorder: Summary of NICE guidance. *BMJ, 346*(7910). https://doi.org/10.1136/bmj.f2541

Plaisier, I., Beekman, A. T. F., De Graaf, R., Smit, J. H., Van Dyck, R., & Penninx, B. W. J. H. (2010). Work functioning in persons with depressive and anxiety disorders: The role of specific psychopathological characteristics. *Journal of Affective Disorders, 125*(1–3), 198–206. https://doi.org/10.1016/j.jad.2010.01.072

Pyne, J. M., Kuc, E. J., Schroeder, P. J., Fortney, J. C., Edlund, M., & Sullivan, G. (2004). Relationship between perceived stigma and depression severity. *The Journal of Nervous and Mental Disease, 192*(4), 278–283.

Ragins, B. R. (2008). Disclosure disconnects: Antecedents and consequences of disclosing invisible stigmas across life domains. *Academy of Management Review, 33*(1), 194–215. https://doi.org/10.5465/amr.2008.27752724

Ren, L. R., Paetzold, R. L., & Colella, A. (2008). A meta-analysis of experimental studies on the effects of disability on human resource judgments. *Human Resource Management Review, 18*(3), 191–203. https://doi.org/10.1097/01.nmd.0000120886.39886.a3.

Ritchie, H., & Roser, M. (2018). Mental health. *Our World in Data.* https://ourworldindata.org/mental-health

Rosette, A. S., & Livingston, R. W. (2012). Failure is not an option for Black women: Effects of organizational performance on leaders with single versus dual-subordinate identities. *Journal of Experimental Social Psychology, 48*(5), 1162–1167

Roy-Byrne, P. P., Craske, M. G., & Stein, M. B. (2006). Panic disorder. *The Lancet, 368*(9540), 1023–1032. https://doi.org/10.1016/s0140-6736(06)69418-x

Rüsch, N., Angermeyer, M. C., & Corrigan, P. W. (2005). Mental illness stigma: Concepts, consequences, and initiatives to reduce stigma. *European Psychiatry, 20*(8), 529–539. https://doi.org/10.1016/j.eurpsy.2005.04.004

Ryan, A. M., & Kossek, E. E. (2008). Work-life policy implementation: Breaking down or creating barriers to inclusiveness? *Human Resource Management, 47*(2), 295–310.

Sabat, I. E., Lindsey, A. P., Membere, A., Anderson, A., Ahmad, A., King, E., & Bolunmez, B. (2014). Invisible disabilities: Unique strategies for workplace allies. *Industrial and Organizational Psychology, 7*(2), 259–265. https://doi.org/10.1111/iops.12145

Santuzzi, A. M., Waltz, P. R., Finkelstein, L. M., & Rupp, D. E. (2014). Invisible disabilities: Unique challenges for employees and organizations. *Industrial and Organizational Psychology, 7*(2), 204–219. https://doi.org/10.1111/iops.12134

Sarason, I. G., Pierce, G. R., & Sarason, B. R. (1996). Domains of cognitive interference. In I. B. Weiner (Ed.), *Personality and clinical psychology series* (pp. 139–152). Lawrence Erlbaum.

Schrader, S. V., Malzer, V., & Bruyère, S. (2013). Perspectives on disability disclosure: The importance of employer practices and workplace climate. *Employee Responsibilities and Rights Journal, 26*(4), 237–255. https://doi.org10.1007/s10672-013-9227-9

Schultz, I. Z., Duplassie, D., Hanson, D. B., & Winter, A. (2011). Systemic barriers and facilitators to job accommodations in mental health: experts' consensus. In I. Schultz & E. Rogers (Eds.), *Work accommodation and retention in mental health* (pp. 353–372). Springer. https://doi.org/10.1007/978-1-4419-0428-7_19

Shankar, J., Liu, L., Nicholas, D., Warren, S. Lai, D., Tan, S., Zulla, R., Couture, J., & Sears, A (2014). Employers' perspectives on hiring and accommodating workers with mental illness. *SAGE Open, 4*(3). https://doi.org/10.1177/2158244014547880

Smart, L., & Wegner, D. M. (1999). Covering up what can't be seen: Concealable stigma and mental control. *Journal of Personality and Social Psychology, 77*(3), 474–486. https://doi.org/10.1037/0022-3514.77.3.474

Sun, J., Buys, N., & Wang, X. (2013). Effectiveness of a workplace-based intervention program to promote mental health among employees in privately owned enterprises in China. *Population Health Management, 16*(6), 406–414. https://doi.org10.1089/pop.2012.0113

Szeto, A. C., & Dobson, K. S. (2010). Reducing the stigma of mental disorders at work: A review of current workplace anti-stigma intervention programs. *Applied and Preventive Psychology, 14*(1–4), 41–56. https://doi.org/10.1016/j.appsy.2011.11.002.

von Helversen, B., Wilke, A., Johnson, T., Schmid, G., & Klapp, B. (2011). Performance benefits of depression: Sequential decision making in a healthy sample and a clinically depressed sample. *Journal of Abnormal Psychology, 120*(4), 962–968. https://doi.org/10.1037/a0023238

Wagner, S., Koehn, C., White, M., Harder, H., Schultz, I., Williams-Whitt, K., Warje, O., Dionne, C. E., Koehoorn, M., Pasca, R., Hsu, V., McGuire, L., Schulz, W., Kube, D., & Wright, M. D. (2016). Mental health interventions in the workplace and work outcomes: A best-evidence synthesis of systematic reviews. *The International Journal of Occupational and Environmental Medicine, 7*(1), 1–14. https://doi.org/10.15171/ijoem.2016.607

Walsh, D. C. (1982). Employee assistance programs. *The Milbank Memorial Fund Quarterly: Health and Society, 60*(3), 492–517.

Wang, J., Patten, S., Currie, S., Sareen, J., & Schmitz, N. (2011). Perceived needs for and use of workplace accommodations by individuals with a depressive and/or anxiety disorder. *Journal of Occupational and Environmental Medicine, 53*(11), 1268–1272. https://doi.org/10.1097/JOM.0b013e31822cfd82

Wittchen, H. U. (2002). Generalized anxiety disorder: prevalence, burden, and cost to society. *Depression and Anxiety, 16*(4), 162–171. https://doi.org/10.1002/da.10065

Wittchen, H., Fuetsch, M., Sonntag, H., Müller, N., & Liebowitz, M. (1999). Disability and quality of life in pure and comorbid social phobia—findings from a controlled study. *European Psychiatry, 14*(3), 118–131. https://doi.org/10.1016/s0924-9338(99)80729-9

CHAPTER 5

THE ASSOCIATION OF DISABILITY AND HEALTH SELF-PERCEPTION TO ENTERING AND LEAVING SELF-EMPLOYMENT

Christoph A. Metzler
German Economic Institute

Petra M. Moog
Siegen University

ABSTRACT

Using data from the German Socio-Economic Panel (SOEP) waves from 1994 to 2018, this study analyzes the relationship of disability and health status with the likelihood that 25- to 64-year-old individuals in Germany enter, maintain, or leave self-employment. The variable of "disability" is based on medical examinations by professionals, whereas the measurement of the quality of an individuals' health and their satisfaction is based on self-assessments. Although in common sense health and official disability status might seem similar, from a theoretical and medical perspective, they are discrete constructs and thus, the relationship of each variable to self-employment differs by a considerable amount. Logistic regressions in this

Forgotten Minorities in Organizations, pp. 135–176
Copyright © 2023 by Information Age Publishing
www.infoagepub.com
All rights of reproduction in any form reserved.

study illustrate how the process of entering self-employment is not significantly associated with the disability status of an individual, but rather to his or her health characteristics. These results indicate that individuals aiming to enter self-employment in Germany need a certain amount of health capital to start a business. In contrast, a regression analysis demonstrates a strong link between individuals leaving self-employment and disability status, with a relatively slight impact of health characteristics. These results imply that disabled self-employed individuals in Germany confront challenges to maintain their business, not due to the quality of their health, but rather from other contextual factors. This study contributes to the discussion of the two concepts—health and disability—and delivers insights regarding how future research should separately analyze these concepts, which display different empirical effects regarding self-employment.

Being self-employed offers a variety of personal advantages. In most European countries, self-employed individuals are more satisfied with their working life compared to individuals who are traditionally employed (Schneck, 2014). Marginalized individuals in the labor market, such as people with disabilities, often report less job satisfaction than individuals who do not belong to marginal groups (Pagán & Malo, 2009). This discrepancy could trigger individuals to choose self-employment to balance their lives better. Thus, self-employment could be a rational occupational choice (Lazear, 1998). From a static perspective, based on trend data, Metzler et al. (2021) found a significant negative connection between an existing disability and the likelihood of a person being self-employed in Germany. The authors argue that this link might be caused by specific compensations for disabled individuals provided by the German federal government, such as extended job protections to remain employed. Such compensation could also play a role in the process of entering self-employment and leaving it.

Another factor potentially influencing the intention to become and stay self-employed as a disabled individual could be health status. García-Gómez et al. (2010) postulated that research on health is needed to create effective labor market strategies that avoid the negative effects disability benefits can cause on employment. Disability and health are often mixed in empirical research, but it is critical to distinguish health from disability as two different concepts (Shandra, 2018). A permanent loss in performance due to failing health is a requirement for a disability (Altman, 2014; Jones & Saloniki, 2021). However, for disabled people, their daily life issues are influenced not only by health but also by issues of social participation (Shandra, 2018). To disentangle the discrete effects of disability and health, it is necessary to obtain deeper insight. This strategy embraces the following issues: (a) to understand the effect of using solely the measure "disability" as a binary distinction for individuals being either disabled or not (Altman, 2014) and (b) that the official definition of disability neglects a variety of health problems (Haan & Myck, 2009). Thus, in addition to analyzing disability, it is necessary to understand the role of health in the entrepreneurial journey (starting, staying, leaving) (Shepherd & Patzelt, 2017; Torrès & Thurik, 2019). Currently, health and disability status are either analyzed as separate concepts concerning their influences on the decisions of individuals in the process of becoming, staying, or leaving self-employed, or the two aspects are treated as synonyms, which is incorrect. This study sheds light on both aspects in parallel, using an occupational choice approach (Lazear, 2004, 2005). By doing so, the chapter contributes to the current research discussion in the following ways:

a. it shows the specific impact of a disability on the decision of individuals to start, stay or quit being self-employed;
b. it provides insights into the specific relation of health status and the decision of individuals to start, stay or quit being self-employed; and finally,
c. the two effects are tested jointly to deliver insights into whether both concepts could be used as a single variable (because they create the same outcomes) or if future research should clearly separate the two concepts to produce more precise results.

Thus, the main contribution of this work to entrepreneurship and occupational choice research is that we use a special innovative approach via a single dataset drawn from the German Socio-Economic Panel (SOEP) to deliver results for all research questions related to the concepts of health and disability. We offer a consistent review and analysis of the German situation, avoiding problems related to heterogeneous data (Simoes et al., 2015). Moreover, we enrich the discussion regarding research on the context of disability, delivering new insights through a comparative analysis of the triggering or hindering context factors specific to Germany and largely absent from other international contexts (García-Gómez et al., 2010; Pagán-Rodríguez, 2012b). Finally, we deliver new insights regarding health as a variable related to entering, staying in, or leaving self-employment. Thus, we effectively combine and discuss former results that have used a limited focus to evaluate one entrepreneurship status and its connection to health and/or disability (Fossen & König, 2017; Hessels et al., 2018).

To generate results and insights regarding these issues, the chapter is structured as follows: First, the relations between either disability or health and self-employment are discussed and illustrated, and other related factors are identified in a thorough literature review. Based on this discussion, the research questions with relevant hypotheses are precisely defined. With our data, we test, first, the impact of disability or health as well as the combined impact of both on self-employment in general (employment status). Second, the chapter includes an empirical analysis of the relation of disability and health characteristics with the likelihood of an individual in Germany entering self-employment. Finally, the likelihood of leaving self-employment in relation to the health and disability conditions of individuals is tested. These analyses deliver innovative results and are discussed thoroughly in the context of the current research on this topic. The chapter concludes with a summary of its results, a description of the limitations of the analyses and some ideas for future research.

THE PHENOMENA OF SELF-EMPLOYMENT, DISABILITY, AND HEALTH

This chapter highlights the situation of self-employed individuals in Germany and illustrates factors associated with their decision to enter, stay, or leave self-employment. "Self-employment" is chosen as a specific term related to the broader concept of "entrepreneurship." Self-employment is a term closely related to the German term Mittelstand, which is a segment of critical, small- and medium-sized, traditionally family-owned, companies that are central to Germany's economic success (Welter et al., 2015). Accordingly, this study's dataset offers empirically reliable, representative data for this group (TNS Infratest Sozialforschung, 2015). The SOEP is our source for individual data regarding German entrepreneurs who, in contrast to employed managers, own and run a company (Berthold & Neumann, 2008).

Before starting the discussion on the relation of being disabled or of differentiated health status with starting, maintaining, or leaving self-employment, we explain the important concept(s) the chapter addresses; particularly, the occupational choice of German individuals who are either disabled or in an inadequate health status. According to occupational choice theory, individuals decide to enter, stay, or leave a job due to specific factors. These factors, such as working conditions, wages, or levels of independence, might make a job attractive (Lazear, 2005; Van Praag & Cramer, 2001; Segal et al., 2005; Simoes et al., 2015). Accordingly, the assumption in this chapter is that being disabled or experiencing health conditions affects this decision: it might make self-employment more or less appealing (Doyel, 2002; Pagán-Rodríguez, 2012a; Shaheen, 2016; Shepherd & Patzelt, 2017). To better understand disability and health status, both concepts are explained below.

Disability Status in Germany

In Germany, a disability status is associated with certain benefits individuals might obtain to further their participation in the labor market *as employees*. This status is not granted by self-identification but by an official German health agency (Kock, 2004). Individuals must document their individual disability restrictions, for example, through medical examinations, and apply at an official institution. These documented restrictions, in combination with obstacles in the German system, limit the possibilities for disabled persons to participate in society and the labor market. Depending on the underlying conditions, the status "being disabled" can be given temporarily or permanently and to varying degrees, such as 30, 50, or 100%; the purported "grade of disability." The issued degree of disability is based on restrictions individuals face in their daily life due to insufficient health (FMLS, 2020). The official benefits accessible through from federal law increase with the grade of disability, which starts at 20 and increases to 100% (Kock, 2004). Part of these benefits are more relevant for employed workers, for example, increased job-loss protection for an employee, fewer working hours, special working equipment, additional paid vacation, and so forth.

Concerning self-employment, disabled individuals can apply for a specific grant or loan, but no other specific benefits are available (Kock, 2004; FMLS, 2020). Metzler et al. (2021) argued that these existing benefits structures in Germany are more beneficial for dependent workers. This could create negative incentives for disabled individuals to avoid self-employment. Empirical studies based on self-assessments of disability, such as Pagán's (2009), have neglected this central feature of the German context and hence were unable to provide robust or significant results.

The German definition of disability is based on equal participation in society and differs from the definition found in the United States. The U.S. definition of disability, in most official surveys, is based on an individual's restrictions from participating in work activities. Monetary supplements are regular supporting measures for the most severely affected persons (Burkhauser et al., 2003). Additionally, in the U.S., specific support for disabled self-employed individuals is still developing (Office of Disability Employment Policy, 2013). In Germany, obtaining monetary support based on one's limited ability to work is possible, but it is not identical to the status of being disabled (FMLS, 2020). The focus of the German supporting measures is on the (re)integration of a disabled individual into employment, especially into dependent employment. Therefore, the present article aims to closely examine the current quantitative situation of German disabled individuals who choose to enter, stay in, or leave self-employment.

Health and Disability Status

Haan and Myck (2009) proposed that disability status has a more permanent influence than health status on individuals' quality of life and decisions, but they also argued that both statuses often interact or become entangled. According to SOEP data, more individuals in Germany with a severe disability state that they have an insufficient health status than nondisabled individuals (Jansen & Metzler, 2019). Thus, the onset of a disability has a strong negative impact on health satisfaction, especially immediately after an individual becomes disabled. Individuals are at least moderately able to adjust their health satisfaction after some years of living with a disability. However, disability and health status do not seem to offer information about the similar experiences of disabled individuals in society or about their labor market access (Pagán-Rodríguez, 2012b). These differences might be related to (a) deviations between the image of oneself as unhealthy or disabled and the image from an outside perspective. In general, people more easily observe a physical disability and typically have only certain types of disability in mind, in contrast to certain health conditions, such as depression, which are not observable; thus, people might regard these individuals as healthy and nondisabled. (b) Individuals might be caught in an egocentric bias, causing them to overvalue their own perception (Ross & Sicoly, 1979). The healthy individuals of a society could associate negative attributes with the characteristics of deviating from a perceived physical or mental norm and stigmatize individuals who do not fit that schema (e.g., Campbell, 2009; Susman, 1994) and thus do not fit into a job or a society, for example. Therefore, a societally perceived norm regarding self-employment (powerful, highly energetic people) might exclude individuals who report diminishing health or a disability. Kašperová and Kitching (2014) postulated that self-employed persons are generally described as able-bodied. Varieties in their health do not seem to exist. In the following section, the chapter delves deeper into this subject to disentangle health and disability issues and shed some light on the continuum of disability and health issues.

Health and Human Capital

The association of human capital with the intentions to engage in self-employment and succeed is well researched. Moog (2002), for example, used a sample of 910 startups in Germany to analyze the connection of the human capital endowment of an individual to his or her likelihood of succeeding as a founder. Unger et al. (2011) also demonstrated this through a broad meta-analysis. However, no information on the health or disability status of founders has been mentioned in those or most other human capital-related studies.

In contrast to this absent empirical approach, in human capital theory, health is regarded as part of the resources a person has control over from birth and can invest in over his or her lifetime. Health is regarded as a subcategory of human capital (Becker, 2007). Due to aging, the health of an individual diminishes, but it can also be increased via individual investments, for example, by spending money on medical care or exercising. Therefore, health is not viewed as exogenous or as a fixed variable (Grossman, 1972) if individuals have the resources to invest in it or exist in a context allowing them to do so.

Mushkin (1962) did not regard health as a factor that is independent of the actual conditions found in a labor market. Therefore, a certain level of health can be a precondition for participating in a labor market. Health may also be related to the productivity of an individual (Mushkin, 1962) and, thus, make it easier for one to keep a job or be successful at it. Therefore, Hatak and Zhou (2021) linked the health of the self-employed person to the human capital he or she needs to achieve success. Thus, it seems reasonable to analyze health as a factor associated with the likelihood of individuals to stay in self-employment in general and, additionally, to enter and exit this occupational status.

Health and Self-Employment

In summary, the health of self-employed individuals remains a sparsely regarded topic, according to Torrès and Thurik (2019). The authors suggested two explanations for this. First, academic research in the past has looked primarily at the health of employees. Second, illness as a sign of weakness has not fit the dominant narrative regarding self-employment. Concerning the process of engaging in self-employment, the role of health is also rather understudied and rarely discussed as a research topic (Simoes et al., 2015); the first indications that sound health is positively related to the intention to begin self-employment can be found in a study by Razgallah et al. (2017) in France, performing a quantitative analysis with 212 participants from organizations for the disabled, showing that this relation is even stronger for females than males. For Germany, the results of Fossen and König (2017) illustrate a similar link during the process of choosing to enter self-employment. Individuals who change their occupational status from employment to self-employment in Germany are significantly less likely than people who maintain their occupational status to report a poor health status.

Becoming self-employed might also have a positive effect on the health of an individual, as Nikolova (2019) illustrated with an empirical analysis of SOEP data; indeed, individuals who switch from unemployment to self-employment have reported increases in their mental, but not their physical, well-being. In contrast, individuals switching from an employed position to a self-employed position report advantages in both health categories. Moreover, the results of a study by Stephan and Roesler (2010) show significant health differentials for German self-employed individuals compared to individuals active in dependent work. Stephan and Roesler used data from the representative German National Health Survey cohort in 1998 and conducted an multivariate analysis. Data for somatic diseases were created using self-assessments of individuals and external validations by trained physicians, whereas data for mental diseases were accumulated via clinical interviews performed by medical professionals. In both cases, self-employed individuals were less likely to be affected by any health issues.

Empirical studies from other countries show varying results. Among a sample of older Americans, a positive health differential for the self-employed compared to the employed can be found in the study of Rietveld et al. (2015), and in Gonçalves and Martins (2018) among a representative Portuguese sample. In contrast, a recent study by Bencsik and Chuluun (2021), based on more than 600,000 cases from the U.S., concludes that self-employed individuals self-report states of lower physical health and more health problems than employed persons.

Concerning individuals who leave self-employment, limited data are available. Pagán-Rodríguez (2012a) analyzed the association of disability with self-employment, based on two waves of European Share datasets. He found that older individuals with a disability status leave self-employment more often, typically within a three-year period. The author used a question of the SHARE dataset that summarized long-term "health problems," "disabilities," "illnesses" and "infirmities" as a single variable (Pagán-Rodríguez, 2012a, p. 84). However, no specific result for Germany is available as of yet. For depression as a singular illness, Hessels et al. (2018) show, with Australian data, a positive connection between worsening depression and leaving self-employment. The authors linked the consequences of depression to a possible decrease in physical strength of individuals and, thereby, to a decreased health status in general.

To conclude this section, the extant results differ regarding context and individual background, but more research has to be undertaken for each status:—beginning self-employment, being self-employed and leaving self-employment—in relation to health and disability issues.

Health and the German Context

The overall mixed results of current research can be partly explained by different datasets, measures, and research designs (Simoes et al., 2015). Different contexts could also be a factor, as self-assessment of health could potentially differ between ethnic groups (Giuntella & Mazzonna, 2015).

However, the first studies showed that the relations of self-reported health and objective health indicators are significantly and strongly connected. Thus, self-reported health seems to be a valid predictor for actual health status. This argument holds true regarding, for example, one's body mass index or measured grip strength (Kalwij & Vermeulen (2008) based on the SHARE dataset). Authors have shown that the difference in participation in the labor market between individuals reporting sound health and individuals reporting poor health, ceteris paribus, was 28.8% for males and 11.8% for females in Germany. Objective health indicators were added to show that these results were robust. Working with SOEP waves from 1990 to 2013, Kühn et al. (2019) demonstrated the same correlation, even when controlling for demographics, regions, and time periods. Goldberg et al. (2001) analyzed a French sample of middle-aged men and women in 1991 and 1996 to affirm the validity of self-reported health issues. Therefore, self-reported health seems to be a valid predictor of the chances of labor market participation by individuals in Germany due to their actual health conditions and, therefore, an important factor in our study.

Health and Disability and Demographic Variables

Health characteristics may also be related to other demographic variables. Grossman (1972, p. 225) identified the level of education of an individual as the most important "environmental variable" to determine one's ability to produce health capital. In a literature review of prior and contemporary theoretical and empirical studies on the link between mental health and education, Graeber (2017) identified two possible mechanisms by which both concepts might influence each other. First, individuals might have different resources to spend on their individual health production (e.g., having personal contacts with doctors or being able to afford costs for medical care) due to their position in society, which is based on their education. Second, behavioral changes in an individual might be based on knowledge gained through education, facilitating adaptations in his or her lifestyle to avoid harmful effects on health. A formal qualification that partly determines the position of an individual within a society can be the result of the investment of an individual in his or her human capital (Becker, 1962). This interconnection reinforces the importance of regarding health not only as a medical condition but also as a part of human capital (Becker, 2007).

Comparing SOEP data with regional labor market information drawn from the INKAR dataset (German Federal Office for Building and Regional Planning), Giuntella and Mazzonna (2015) analyzed differences in the health of natives and migrants. Upon arrival in Germany, migrant males are healthier than their native counterparts, but their health deteriorates rapidly in the following years. The authors linked this effect to the high physical demands found in blue collar jobs in which migrants are highly and disproportionately employed. The authors further described disability as an outcome of health. Their descriptive statistics indicated that migrant women are, on average, less likely to be disabled and less likely to face severe health limitations than their native peers. No significant differences could be found for their male counterparts.

Studies have further indicated that married people are healthier with respect to their self-reported health (Rohrer et al., 2008) and other objective health indicators, such as lower cortisol levels than individuals who are divorced or never married (Chin et al., 2017). The influence of sex is also relevant. Males are more likely to be disabled than females in Germany (Statistisches Bundesamt, 2018) but males also self-report higher satisfaction with their health (Kühn et al., 2019). Research on self-employment has predominantly stated that females are less likely to be self-employed than males. An often-mentioned cause for this phenomenon is a difference in risk attitude between the sexes (Wagner, 2007). These conclusions demonstrate that it is important to control for these aspects to deliver clearer insights into the impact of health status and disability on labor market participation, especially on self-employment.

Health, Disability, and Risk

Individuals with insufficient health could potentially be more risk averse. Schurer (2015) used the SOEP to compare several self-reported diseases and illustrate that individuals who suffer from depression in all age groups are more risk averse than people without. The risk aversion of individuals and its effect on their likelihood of choosing self-employment and staying in the profession have been the subject of a variety of studies. Caliendo et al. (2009) compared individuals participating in the SOEP survey in 2004 and 2005. For the whole sample, as well as for a subgroup of individuals who left regular employment for self-employment, the results show that individuals reporting lower risk aversion are more likely to become self-employed. Brachert et al. (2020) identify how higher tendencies toward risk taking are reported by individuals entering self-employment but not by employed or unemployed people. Therefore, individuals are even more likely to take risks after their transition into self-employment.

Health, Disability, and Satisfaction

A prior study with SOEP data by Brenke (2015) indicated that in 2013, self-employed individuals showed slightly higher job satisfaction than employed individuals. Similar levels of job satisfaction in Germany have been stable for a long period of time. Using data from the European Social Survey, Schneck (2014) also noted that self-employed individuals have more job satisfaction than their employed peers in Germany. However, no information on "disability status" or on "self-assessed health" can be found in these studies. Analyzing data from the European Household, Panel Pagán and Malo (2009) stated that disabled males and females demonstrate a higher mean of overall pleasure with their work than their nondisabled peers. The authors further showed that stable tenure and job security are highly correlated with job satisfaction among disabled individuals. However, this study was limited by the fact that its data originated from Spain; a country where the agreements of German social partners, naturally, do not apply and the available types of compensation for disabled individuals may differ. Moreover, the authors defined disability based on "chronic physical or mental health" challenges and "illnesses" (Pagán & Malo, 2009, p. 57), thereby mixing the concepts of "health" and "disability." Torrès and Thurik (2019) argued that the positive and negative relation of self-employment and satisfaction to health may change during different stages of a business. The SOEP dataset, however, has few to no indicators that describe the nature of a business, or the risks and opportunities self-employed individuals confront. Job satisfaction, therefore, might function as a latent variable when measuring this context.

Concerning Germany, Stephan and Roesler (2010) conclude that self-employed report significantly higher life satisfaction than their employed peers: In contrast to the U.S. where the outcome is reversed, as Bencsik and Chuluun (2021) state that Europeans face a more benevolent context with respect to the benefits provided by a state. Furthermore, in Germany, sound health is positively linked to life satisfaction of self-employed individuals (Hatak & Zhou, 2021) rather than to the onset of a disability (Infurna & Wiest, 2016).

Wrapping all this up and given the discussed line of reasoning and argument, results, and previous outcomes in this research field, six research questions must be addressed:

Research Question 1: Are disability or health characteristics, as separate concepts, significantly associated with the occupational status of individuals in Germany, whether they are self-employed or not?

Research Question 2: Are disability or health characteristics, as joined concepts, significantly associated with the occupational status of individuals in Germany, whether they are self-employed or not?

Research Question 3: Are disability or health characteristics, as separate concepts, significantly associated with whether individuals in Germany start self-employment?

Research Question 4: Are disability or health characteristics, as combined aspects, significantly associated with the occupational status of individuals in Germany who become self-employed?

Research Question 5: Here, we ask whether disability or health characteristics of individuals in Germany, as separate concepts, are significantly associated with leaving self-employment.

Research Question 6: Finally, we aim to investigate whether disability or health characteristics of individuals in Germany, as combined aspects, are significantly related to the occupational status of individuals who leave self-employment.

HYPOTHESES REGARDING THE IMPACT OF DISABILITY OR HEALTH ON SELF-EMPLOYMENT

The literature review has provided an initial overview of the connection between health, disability and self-employment and illustrated the relevant demographics to be controlled for. As shown, in several empirical studies (Giuntella & Mazzonna, 2015; Pagán & Malo, 2009; Pagán-Rodríguez, 2012a), "health" and "disability" are often measured as subcategories of one another, delivering either mixed, often inconsistent, or even contradictory results. Our six former mentioned research questions are based on this analysis. Thus, in this study, both concepts of disability and health are examined via separate items to test the impact of each concept, ceteris paribus, on the likelihood of individuals entering, staying in, or leaving self-employment. First, this approach is tested via separate models for disability and health status and, second, via a combined model, based on the following hypotheses.

To test the potential effects of disability and health on starting, staying in or leaving entrepreneurial activity in separate models, first, the following hypotheses are developed. Following Metzler et al. (2021), the first two hypotheses are testing the relationship of diversity and health separately on the likelihood to be self-employed:

Hyopthesis (1a): A more positive disability status is more likely to be negatively related to the likelihood of being and remaining self-employed in Germany.

And following especially the study of Stephan and Roesler (2010), the next hypothesis is dealing with the potential impact of health:

Hypothesis (1b): A more negative health status is more likely to be negatively related to the likelihood of being and remaining self-employed in Germany.

As discussed above, and due to the extant mixed results we showed in the literature analysis beforehand, the next hypothesis tests for the combined effect:

Hypothesis 2: A combination of health and disability issues might have a lesser or no significant effect on the likelihood of being and remaining self-employed in Germany.

The following hypotheses are strongly related to the study of Fossen and König (2017), now focusing on the likelihood of becoming self-employed:

Hypothesis (3a): A more positive disability status of an individual will deliver a more significant negative effect on one's likelihood of entering self-employment; and

Hypothesis (3b): A more negative health status of an individual will deliver a stronger negative effect on one's likelihood of becoming self-employed.

Again, following the first ideas and insights of Fossen and König (2017), we postulate the following hypothesis dealing with the combined effect of health and disability on becoming self-employed:

Hypothesis (4): A combination of a more negative health and a more positive disability status, will more likely generate a negative effect on the likelihood of an individual entering self-employment.

Based on the discussion above regarding the issues pushing individuals out of self-employment, and especially referring on the initial results of Pagán-Rodríguez (2012a), the next hypotheses are focusing on the effect of health and disability on leaving self-employment:

Hypothesis (5a): A more positive disability status will deliver more likely an increase of the likelihood that an individual leaves self-employment; and

Hypothesis (5b): A more negative health status of an individual will deliver more likely a significantly increase and effect on his or her likelihood of leaving self-employment.

Thus, formally we present as following the final

Hypothesis (6): A combination of a negative health and a positive disability status of an individual, will deliver a stronger effect on the likelihood of an individual leaving self-employment.

EMPIRICAL STUDY DESIGN: OPERATIONALIZATION AND METHODOLOGY

To ascertain the answers to and some possible insights from our research questions and hypotheses, the requirements of our dataset include a variety of aspects related to the status of an individual in the German labor market and individual demographics. Additionally, the dataset needs to offer information on the health and disability status of individuals. To further evaluate individual status changes, panel data are required for repeated measurements over longer periods. The data should also be representative of the German working population. The SOEP fulfills these methodological requirements. Indeed, in 2013, the SOEP was used for the first official report on the daily life of individuals with health restrictions and their overall participation in German society (FMLS, 2014). The SOEP offers data for western German households from 1984 to 2018 and for eastern households, after the unification, from 1990 to 2018. Thus, the SOEP dataset can be considered representative of Germany (DIW Berlin, 2016; Wagner et al., 2007). Individuals in the age spectrum of 25 to 64 years are included in the analysis to incorporate the German workforce. The relevant dataset is maintained by the German Institute for Economic Research (Berlin), and data can be freely accessed by researchers employed by universities or private and public research institutions (see https://www.diw.de/en/diw_01.c.601584.en/data_access.html).

To compare the effects of and relations among the different independent variables with those of the dependent variables and, therefore, generate answers to the research questions, the selected time span encompasses the relevant information available within the dataset for each independent and dependent variable. Thus, this study looks at the SOEP waves from 1994 to

2018. Table 5.1 offers an overview of the distribution of available cases that is found in a specific SOEP wave for each dependent variable of interest.

Table 5.1

Available Cases of Self-Employed Individuals With Health Restrictions

	Having a grade of disability of at least 30	Possessing a self-assessed deficient quality of health	Individuals with below average satisfaction with health
Self-employed	964	3,051	3,268
Nonself-employed	17,286	38,291	38,009
Going to enter self-employment	116	319	337
Not going to enter self-employment	12,940	28,609	28,803
Going to leave self-employment	108	318	290
Not going to leave self-employment	628	2,028	2,255

Note: Own calculation with SOEP waves from 1994 to 2018, nonweighted, only individuals between 25 and 64 years.

Operationalization of the Dependent Variables of Interest

We aim to answer whether disability or health issues might affect the participation of individuals in self-employment (entering, staying, and leaving). The SOEP offers the variable of "Being self-employed" to answer questions regarding participants employment in a given year; for example, "What is your current occupational status?" (TNS Infratest Sozialforschung, 2015, p. 53). There are five comprehensive categories of answers: "Self-employed," "Blue-collar worker," "White-collar worker," "Civil servant" and "Apprentice/trainee/intern." In each category, various further answers are available to specify an occupation; three out of four sub-answers available in the category of "self-employed" are summarized for this study: "Self-employed farmers," "Freelance professional/Self-employed academic" and "Other self-employed." Individuals who select "Family member working for self-employed relative" (TNS Infratest Sozialforschung, 2015, p. 53) are not considered self-employed; they are not responsible for the decisions and terms of their own business. Individuals in any other categories are summarized as "not self-employed." Thus, these variables measure the current status of self-employment (Brenke, 2015; Caliendo et al., 2014). The variable of entering self-employment (Fossen & König, 2017; Nikolova, 2019) entails a status change to self-employment that indicates an individual either has another occupation or is unemployed in the current period or changes his or her status to being self-employed one year later. Individuals who are either in retirement or are currently not participating in the labor market in the current period are excluded. This is done to sharpen the analysis and exclude unusual cases.

The variable of leaving self-employment (Caliendo et al., 2010; Nikolova et al., 2020) entails a status change that indicates an individual is self-employed in the current period and changes his or her status to dependent work, unemployment, retirement or pursuing no gainful occupation one year later. This broad approach is used to include older individuals, who might use self-employment as a bridge to continue being active in the labor market before entering retirement, in the analysis (Pagán-Rodríguez, 2012a).

Operationalization of the Independent Variables of Interest

Regarding health, the SOEP offers two self-assessment measurements for the health of an individual. The quality of health (Fossen & König, 2017; Haan & Myck, 2009) is measured by the question of "How would you describe your current health?" (TNS Infratest Sozialforschung, 2015, p. 65). Five answers are possible: "Bad," "poor," "satisfactory," "good" and "very good." Individuals stating that their current health is bad or poor are categorized as possessing "deficient health." Individuals stating that their current health is satisfactory are categorized as possessing "average health." Individuals stating that their current health is good or very good are categorized as possessing "sound health." Satisfaction with health (Kühn et al., 2019; Ravesteijn et al., 2013) is measured by the question of "How satisfied are you with your health?" (TNS Infratest Sozialforschung, 2015, p. 41), on a scale from zero, indicating "completely dissatisfied," to 10, indicating "completely satisfied."

Regarding being disabled/medical definition (Fossen & König, 2017; Giuntella & Mazzonna, 2015), this variable is measured by the question of "Have you been officially assessed as being severely disabled ... or partially incapable of work ... for medical reasons?" (TNS Infratest Sozialforschung, 2015, p. 65). A follow-up question asks participants to specify their degree of disability or reduction in earning capacity.

Control Variables Concerning Demographics

To generate nonbiased results in the best possible way, the data include commonly accepted and tested control variables that are likely linked to self-employment. These variables are as follows: "Sex" (for relevance see Jones & Latreille, 2011; Pagán, 2009), which the SOEP defines according to biological gender, whereby respondents can choose male or female. "Being married" (Chin et al., 2017; Rohrer et al., 2008) entails that individuals state whether they are married or participate in a registered same-sex partnership in one category by indicating yes. Individuals who are single, divorced or widowed indicate no in a second category. For "Having children under 16" (Joona, 2017; Patrick et al., 2016), participants are asked to state the year of birth of each child. The variable of "Formal qualification" (Metzler et al., 2021) is measured by the question of "What type of a degree/certificate/diploma did you obtain?" (TNS Infratest Sozialforschung, 2015, p. 46), which has a variety of possible answers. Two categories are summarized for the present study: first, a category encompassing all individuals who either obtain a vocational degree (e.g., by finishing an apprenticeship in the German dual education system) or an academic degree (e.g., by obtaining a master's degree at a university); and second, a category for all individuals who do not have a degree. Due to the small number of people with severe disabilities who obtain an academic degree and the high number within this group who have no formal qualification in Germany (Metzler, 2013), no further distinction between academic and vocational degree is made.

The variable "Migration background" (Giuntella & Mazzonna, 2015; Struminskaya, 2011) is measured by two questions (TNS Infratest Sozialforschung, 2015, p. 71):

1. "Have you had German citizenship since birth, or did you acquire it at a later date?"
2. "Were both of your parents born in Germany?"

A distinction between two categories is used, that is, individuals with a migration background who did not move to Germany and individuals with a migration background who did.

The "Age" (Kautonen et al., 2014; Kühn et al., 2019) of an individual is used as a control variable. No individuals younger than 25 years are analyzed in this study, as these individuals might still be in the early phases of building a career. No individuals older than 64 years are analyzed to exclude individuals who do not face the choice of being employed or unemployed and are more likely to be receiving a pension and to potentially work part time. "Place of residence" (Kühn et al., 2019) refers to the federal state within Germany ("Bundesland") where individuals live and is used as a control variable. As in Metzler et al. (2021), no separate subanalysis on a regional level can be conducted due to an insufficient number of available cases.

The following control variables concern attitude: "Satisfaction with life" (Hatak & Zhou, 2021) "Satisfaction with job" (Pagán & Malo, 2009) and "Satisfaction with leisure time" (Van der Zwan et al., 2018). All of these variables are measured on a scale between 0, indicating "completely dissatisfied" and 10, indicating "completely satisfied." "Readiness to assume risk" (Brachert et al., 2020, Caliendo et al., 2009) is a variable measured by the question of "Are you generally a person who is willing to take risks or do you try to avoid taking risks?" (TNS Infratest Sozialforschung, 2015, p. 42), on a scale of zero, indicating "risk averse," to 10, indicating "fully prepared to take risks." Table 5.6 shows the pairwise correlation between the independent variables and the control variables; additionally, information about the significance level for each pair is provided.

RESULTS REGARDING THE RELATIONSHIP OF DISABILITY, HEALTH, AND SELF-EMPLOYMENT

To provide some initial insights, in this section we offer a short descriptive analysis of the health and disability status of self-employed individuals. To illustrate the German context of individuals who are self-employed, as well as those entering and leaving self-employment, Table 5.2 lists the percentage of individuals in all available SOEP waves who are in different states of self-employment and disabled with a grade of at least 30, who possess deficient health or who are below average health. The results for leaving and entering self-employment show the values of an individual in the year before his or her transition.

The descriptive weighted analyses indicate that there is a different distribution of disability and health characteristics for each group. Self-employed individuals report a lower percentage of disability as well as a lower percentage of a deficient quality of or a below average satisfaction with health than employed individuals. Individuals entering self-employment are less likely to be disabled and less likely to have a deficient quality of or a below average satisfaction with health than individuals who are not entering self-employment. Individuals leaving self-employment are more likely to have a disability, a deficient quality or a below average satisfaction with health than individuals who are not leaving self-employment. Employed individuals have the highest rates of disability, deficient quality, and below average satisfaction with health across all studied groups. The descriptive results provide initial implications and indicate that the state of

Table 5.2

Characteristics Concerning Disability and Health

	Disabled	Possessing a self-assessed deficient quality of health	Individuals with below average satisfaction with health
Self-employed	3.67%	10.76%	12.04%
Nonself-employed	6.95%	13.55%	14.11%
Going to enter self-employment	4.02%	10.76%	12.68%
Not going to enter self-employment	6.60%	12.88%	13.54%
Going to leave self-employment	3.78%	13.30%	13.47%
Not going to leave self-employment	3.38%	9.79%	11.42%

Note: Own calculation with SOEP waves from 1994 to 2018, weighted, only individuals between 25 and 64 years, in relation to the number of individuals found in each group.

disability and health might be linked being self-employed or the process of joining or leaving self-employment.

In the following multivariate logistic regression analyses, four models are executed to better address the research questions regarding whether disability status and/or health characteristics have a significant negative or positive effect on the status of individuals who belong to a certain occupational group, as our hypotheses mention. The time span and the independent and control variables used, remain the same, but the dependent variable changes in each analysis. Similar to Metzler et al. (2021), odds ratios are used to illustrate the results of the logistic regression analyses. Hence, a value of less than one indicates a negative, a value of one equals a neutral and a value higher than one signals a positive relation (Szumilas, 2010). In the first step, an individual's current status of being self-employed is used as the dependent variable.

The Link of Health and Disability to the Status of Being Self-Employed

The regression models in Table 5.3 show that being disabled in Model A (OR = 0.48), having a deficient quality of health in Model B (OR =

0.70), and having a below average satisfaction with health in Model C (OR = 0.73), ceteris paribus, are significantly negatively related, at a 1% level between 1994 and 2018, to individuals' chance of being currently self-employed. Concerning quality of health in Model B, simply stating an average quality of health is significantly related to a lower chance of being self-employed as occupational status than to sound health (OR = 0.78). The same holds true for individuals in Model C with an average satisfaction with health compared to individuals with a high satisfaction (OR = 0.81). In the combined model, D, the significant negative links for being disabled (OR = 0.51) and having deficient health (OR = 0.81) hold true. Here, there is no significance for the association of below average satisfaction with health. Given that the official status of being disabled via medical examinations grants unique compensation for an individual while the status of having poor health via self-assessment does not, this result is not surprising.

Based on the consistent results from both respective models, the first research question can be answered: people with disabilities or deficient health are significantly less likely to be self-employed in the studied time-frame than people without a disability or people with sound health. Our Hypotheses 1a, and 1b hold true in both cases, testing this relation. For the hypothesis of the second research question (2a) there is no support in our results, as the negative links are constant in Model D. Therefore, it is likely that disability status has a unique connection to the status of being self-employed that is distinct from the health status of an individual, for example, by offering an individual unique compensation to help him or her participate in a labor market, as Metzler et al. (2021) postulated.

With respect to personal demographic characteristics, females are significantly less likely to be self-employed than their male counterparts, at a 1% level in all models. This result is in line with most research on occupational choice regarding self-employment (Welter et al., 2019). Individuals with high satisfaction with their work are more likely to be self-employed than people with moderate or below average work satisfaction. This result is consistent with prior empirical research by Benz and Frey (2008) on the situation in Germany and 22 other countries. Van der Zwan et al. (2018) described how self-employed individuals in Germany gain job satisfaction at the cost of losing satisfaction with their spare time. Finally, individuals with a high tendency to take risks are more likely to be self-employed than people with a moderate or a below average tendency, at a 1% level. Brachert et al. (2020) conclude that self-employment may strengthen risk-taking tendencies. Concerning personal characteristics, a constant significant negative link of having no children under 16 years, at a 5% level, to the likelihood of entering self-employment is found in all four models. Similar to this result, Joona (2017) observed a higher transition rate into

Table 5.3

The Influence of Disability and Self-Assessed Health on Being Self-Employed

	Model A: Disability	Model B: Quality of health	Model C: Satisfaction with health	Model D: Combined model
Independent variables of interest:				
Being disabled	0.48***(0.06)	-	-	0.51***(0.07)
Quality of health (reference category: sound health):				
Average quality of health	-	0.78***(0.04)	-	0.84***(0.04)
Deficient health	-	0.70***(0.05)	-	0.81***(0.06)
Satisfaction with health (reference category: high satisfaction):				
Average satisfaction with health	-	-	0.81***(0.04)	0.91*(0.05)
Below average satisfaction with health	-	-	0.73***(0.06)	0.92(0.07)
Personal characteristics:				
Having a formal qualification	1.39**(0.20)	1.39**(0.20)	1.41**(0.16)	1.37**(0.19)
Gender	0.68***(0.05)	0.69***(0.05)	0.69***(0.05)	0.69***(0.05)
No children under 16 years	0.82***(0.05)	0.83***(0.05)	0.83***(0.05)	0.83***(0.05)
Being married	0.87*(0.07)	0.89(0.07)	0.89(0.07)	0.88*(0.07)
Migration background (no personal experience)	0.74**(0.09)	0.74**(0.09)	0.73**(0.09)	0.74**(0.09)
Migration background (personal experience)	0.87(0.09)	0.88(0.09)	0.87(0.09)	0.87(0.09)
Age	1.04***(0.00)	1.04***(0.00)	1.04***(0.00)	1.04***(0.00)

(Table continued on next page)

Table 5.3 (Continued)

The Influence of Disability and Self-Assessed Health on Being Self-Employed

	Model A: Disability	Model B: Quality of health	Model C: Satisfaction with health	Model D: Combined model
		Attitude:		
Being satisfied with life (reference category: high satisfaction)				
Average satisfaction with life	1.03*(0.05)	1.09*(0.05)	1.08 (0.05)	1.10**(0.05)
Below average satisfaction with life	1.21**(0.11)	1.31***(0.11)	1.27***(0.11)	1.34***(0.11)
Being satisfied with work (reference category: high satisfaction)				
Average satisfaction with work	0.72***(0.03)	0.73***(0.03)	0.74***(0.03)	0.74***(0.03)
Below average satisfaction with work	0.56***(0.05)	0.56***(0.05)	0.56***(0.05)	0.56***(0.05)
Being satisfied with leisure time (reference category: high satisfaction)				
Average satisfaction with leisure time	1.28***(0.06)	1.31***(0.07)	1.32***(0.07)	1.31***(0.06)
Below average satisfaction with leisure time	2.47***(0.17)	2.57***(0.18)	2.59***(0.18)	2.57***(0.17)
Readiness to assume risk:				
Average risk friendly:	0.55***(0.03)	0.55***(0.03)	0.55***(0.03)	0.55***(0.03)
Below average risk friendly:	0.37***(0.03)	0.37***(0.03)	0.37***(0.03)	0.38***(0.03)
Further controls: Place of residence				
R^2	0.06	0.06	0.06	0.06
Prob > chi2	0.00	0.00	0.00	0.00

Note: Dependent variable: Being self-employed (yes = 1/no = 0), only employed persons between 25–64 years. Own calculation with SOEP 1994 to 2018 data, Logistic regression with Odds Ratios, *** Significant at 1% level, ** Significant at 5% level, * Significant at 10% level, weighted, clustered standard errors in brackets.

self-employment among females in Sweden for individuals having children than individuals having no children. Below-average satisfaction with leisure time also has a significant positive connection, at a 1% level, to the status of entering self-employment. Caliendo et al. (2009) and Brachert et al. (2020) found similar results with respect to risk attitudes. Leisure and work satisfaction are both related to life satisfaction. To increase either type of satisfaction, an individual has to invest time through hours spent on work or hours spent on leisure. Self-employment is associated with high job satisfaction (Van der Zwan et al., 2018). The scale of individuals with an initially high satisfaction with leisure time and low satisfaction with their work might balance over time, but the same could not hold true for individuals with an initially low satisfaction in both aspects. Therefore, they might be rather inclined to enter self-employment.

Therefore, our study is in line with several other studies regarding control variable outcomes, underlining the representative outcome of our main results for disability and health issues. In conclusion, the first three models show that using either disability status or health status as the main independent variable of interest has a strong impact on being self-employed, delivering robust results when working with the two concepts.

The Link of Health and Disability to the Status of Entering Self-Employment

In the following regression analyses, the state of entering self-employment during the following SOEP yearly period is used as the dependent variable. A disability is, ceteris paribus, not significantly linked to the likelihood of an individual entering self-employment in the following period (Model A). Having an average quality of health (OR = 0.83) or having deficient health (OR = 0.79) is significantly associated with a lower chance of entering self-employment in the following period than having sound health, at the 5% level (Model B). Finally, stating an average satisfaction with health (OR = 0.79) or a below average satisfaction with health (OR = 0.76) is linked to a lower chance of entering self-employment in the following period on a one and, respectively, a 5% level.

In the combined regression analysis (Model D), the direction of the odds ratios concerning health holds true, but only one result concerning average satisfaction with health stays significant at a 5% level. Therefore, Hypothesis 3a and the Hypothesis 4 are not endorsed, as no significant link of disability to the status of entering self-employment is found in the compiled models. In contrast, Hypothesis 3b holds true, as insufficient health turns out to be a significant negative predictor for entering self-employment.

The direction of the relationship of most of these variables with entering and being self-employed stays the same. As an exception, the direction of the result of satisfaction with work differs: A low satisfaction with work is significantly positively linked to entering self-employment in the following period. This result agrees with Van der Zwan et al.'s (2018) findings that individuals who switch to self-employment initially experience an increase in job satisfaction (see Table 5.4).

Table 5.4

The Influence of Disability and Self-Assessed Health on Entering Self-Employment

	Model A: Disability	Model B: Quality of health	Model C: Satisfaction with health	Model D: Combined model
Independent variables of interest:				
Being disabled	0.80(0.14)	-	-	0.85(0.15)
Quality of health (reference category: sound health):				
Average quality of health	-	0.83**(0.06)	-	0.91(0.08)
Deficient health	-	0.79**(0.09)	-	0.90(0.12)
Satisfaction with health (reference category: high satisfaction):				
Average satisfaction with health	-	-	0.79***(0.06)	0.83**(0.07)
Below average satisfaction with health	-	-	0.76**(0.09)	0.83(0.12)
Personal characteristics:				
Having a formal qualification	1.10(0.15)	1.09(0.15)	1.09(0.15)	1.08(0.14)
Gender	1.04(0.07)	1.05(0.07)	1.05(0.07)	1.04(0.07)
No children under 16 years	0.87*(0.07)	0.86*(0.07)	0.86*(0.07)	0.87*(0.07)

(Table continued on next page)

Table 5.4 (Continued)

The Influence of Disability and Self-Assessed Health on Entering Self-Employment

	Model A: Disability	Model B: Quality of health	Model C: Satisfaction with health	Model D: Combined model
Personal characteristics:				
Being married	0.99(0.08)	1.00(0.08)	1.00(0.08)	1.00(0.08)
Migration background (no personal experience)	1.26(0.18)	1.26(0.18)	1.25(0.18)	1.25(0.18)
Migration background (personal experience)	1.22**(0.12)	1.22*(0.12)	1.21*(0.12)	1.21(0.12)
Age	1.00(0.00)	1.00(0.00)	1.00(0.00)	1.00(0.00)
Attitude:				
Being satisfied with life (reference category: high satisfaction)				
Average satisfaction with life	0.97(0.07)	1.01(0.08)	1.03(0.08)	1.04(0.08)
Below average satisfaction with life	1.13(0.16)	1.23(0.18)	1.23(0.18)	1.24(0.18)
Being satisfied with work (reference category: high satisfaction)				
Average satisfaction with work	0.92(0.07)	0.93(0.07)	0.95(0.07)	0.95(0.07)
Below average satisfaction with work	1.31**(0.14)	1.35***(0.15)	1.37***(0.15)	1.38***(0.15)
Being satisfied with leisure time (reference category: high satisfaction)				
Average satisfaction with leisure time	0.99(0.07)	1.01(0.08)	1.02(0.08)	1.02(0.08)

(Table continued on next page)

Table 5.4 (Continued)

The Influence of Disability and Self-Assessed Health on Entering Self-Employment

	Model A: Disability	Model B: Quality of health	Model C: Satisfaction with health	Model D: Combined model
Being satisfied with leisure time (reference category: high satisfaction)				
Below average satisfaction with leisure time	1.39***(0.14)	1.42***(0.14)	1.44***(0.14)	1.45***(0.14)
Readiness to assume risk:				
Average risk friendly:	0.57***(0.05)	0.58***(0.05)	0.58***(0.05)	0.58***(0.05)
Below average risk friendly:	0.39***(0.04)	0.39***(0.04)	0.39***(0.04)	0.39***(0.04)
Further controls: Place of residence				
R^2	0.02	0.02	0.02	0.02
Prob > chi2	0.00	0.00	0.00	0.00

Note: Dependent variable: Entering self-employment (yes=1/no=0), only employed persons between 25–64 years. Own calculation with SOEP 1994 to 2018 data, Logistic regression with Odds Ratios, *** Significant at 1% level, ** Significant at 5% level, * Significant at 10% level, clustered standard errors in brackets.

The Link of Health and Disability to the Status of Leaving Self-Employment

In the third and final regression analyses, the state of leaving self-employment in the following period of the SOEP yearly panel is used as the dependent variable. Declaring a disability has, ceteris paribus, a positive connection, at a 1% level (OR = 2.15), to the likelihood of an individual leaving self-employment in the following period (Model A). Having deficient health (OR = 1.25) is significantly associated with a higher chance of leaving self-employment in the following period than having sound health, but the result is only significant at a 10% level (Model B). An average satisfaction with health or a below average satisfaction with health are not more significantly linked to the chance of leaving self-employment in the following period than possessing a high satisfaction with health (Model C). In the combined regression analysis (Model D), the direction, strength, and significance of the odds ratio for disability hold true, indicating that there is a unique connection of disability to the status of leaving self-employment. A consistent significant result for deficient health, at the 10% level, is also found. In conclusion, Hypothesis 5a holds true, while Hypothesis 5b is only partially supported by the results. Certain effects on the likelihood of leaving self-employment can be established, therefore the Hypothesis 6 is not backed up by the results.

Regarding demographics, a variety of significant results can be found. Individuals possessing a migration background and females are significantly more likely to leave self-employment than their counterparts. Joona (2010) calculated a similar result when comparing a subgroup of non-Western immigrants in Sweden to natives. She found differences in individuals' motives to join self-employment and their business sectors as possible explanations for this disparity. Regarding gender, Hsu et al. (2016) suggested that females are more likely than males to have intentions to leave self-employment if a conflict interfering with the balance of their work and family life exists. Having no children under 16 years living in a household significantly decreases the chance of leaving self-employment. This result differs from that of Millán et al. (2012), who found no significant association of dependent children in a household with the likelihood of exiting self-employment.

A significant negative link of having a formal qualification to leaving self-employment holds true for all four models. A positive association of formal human capital with survival in self-employment in a European context was also described in the study by Millán et al. (2012). However, in contrast to the present study, these authors based their analysis only on the highest achieved academic certificate. Regarding attitude, the results of satisfaction with work and satisfaction with leisure time are significant at a 1% level. Their direction is reversed when compared to the analyses of being self-employed given in Table 5.3. As higher job satisfaction is a typical benefit of being self-employed (Benz & Frey, 2008), it seems logical that individuals lacking this experience would leave self-employment. In contrast, being less satisfied with one's amount of spare time might be a typical cost of self-employment (Van der Zwan et al., 2018) and, therefore, would be accepted by those wishing to continue the profession. Overall, the results of the control variables in all models are consistent with the current literature, strengthening the robustness of our analyses (see Table 5.5).

Table 5.5

The Influence of Disability and Self-Assessed Health on Leaving Self-Employment

	Model A: Disability	Model B: Quality of health	Model C: Satisfaction with health	Model D: Combined model
Independent variables of interest:				
Being disabled	2.15***(0.38)	-	-	2.12***(0.39)
Quality of health (reference category: sound health):				
Average quality of health	-	0.95(0.08)	-	0.91(0.09)
Deficient health	-	1.25*(0.14)	-	1.28*(0.19)
Satisfaction with health (reference category: high satisfaction):				
Average satisfaction with health	-	-	1.10(0.08)	1.10(0.10)
Below average satisfaction with health	-	-	1.01(0.12)	0.81(0.13)
Personal characteristics:				
Having a formal qualification	0.62***(0.09)	0.62***(0.09)	0.62***(0.09)	0.62***(0.09)
Gender	1.79***(0.14)	1.78***(0.14)	1.79***(0.14)	1.79***(0.14)
No children under 16 years	0.85*(0.07)	0.86*(0.07)	0.86*(0.07)	0.85*(0.07)
Being married	0.95(0.08)	0.96(0.08)	0.96(0.08)	0.96(0.08)
Migration background (no personal experience)	1.57***(0.26)	1.56***(0.26)	1.56***(0.26)	1.57***(0.26)
Migration background (personal experience)	1.32**(0.15)	1.31**(0.15)	1.32**(0.15)	1.31**(0.15)
Age	0.96***(0.00)	0.97***(0.00)	0.97***(0.00)	0.96***(0.00)

(Table continued on next page)

Table 5.5 (Continued)

The Influence of Disability and Self-Assessed Health on Leaving Self-Employment

	Model A: Disability	Model B: Quality of health	Model C: Satisfaction with health	Model D: Combined model
Attitude:				
Being satisfied with life (reference category: high satisfaction)				
Average satisfaction with life	1.10(0.09)	1.08(0.10)	1.08(0.09)	1.07(0.09)
Below average satisfaction with life	1.48***(0.21)	1.43***(0.21)	1.43**(0.21)	1.49***(0.22)
Being satisfied with work (reference category: high satisfaction)				
Average satisfaction with work	1.47***(0.12)	1.47***(0.12)	1.47***(0.12	1.47***(0.12)
Below average satisfaction with work	2.70***(0.32)	2.66***(0.31)	2.66***(0.31)	2.76***(0.33)
Being satisfied with leisure time (reference category: high satisfaction)				
Average satisfaction with leisure time	0.79***(0.06)	0.79***(0.06)	0.79***(0.06)	0.79***(0.07)
Below average satisfaction with leisure time	0.63***(0.06)	0.63***(0.06)	0.63***(0.06)	0.63***(0.06)
Readiness to assume risk:				
Average risk friendly:	0.81**(0.07)	0.81**(0.07)	0.80**(0.07)	0.81**(0.08)
Below average risk friendly:	0.89(0.09)	0.89(0.09)	0.88(0.09)	0.89(0.09)
Further controls: Place of residence				
R^2	0.06	0.05	0.05	0.06
Prob > chi2	0.00	0.00	0.00	0.00

Note: Dependent variable: Leaving self-employment (yes= 1/no=0), only employed persons between 25–64 years. Own calculation with SOEP 1994 to 2018 data, Logistic regression with Odds Ratios, *** Significant at 1% level, ** Significant at 5% level, * Significant at 10% level, clustered standard errors in brackets.

Table 5.6

Pairwise Correlation Between Independent and Dependent Variables Used in the Regression Analyses

Variable	Being disabled	Quality of health	Satisfaction with health	Having a formal qualification	Sex	Children under 16 years	Being married	Migration background (no personal experience)	Migration background (personal experience)	Age
Being disabled	1									
Quality of health	0.31***	1								
Satisfaction with health	0.27***	0.70***	1							
Having a formal qualification	-0.04***	-0.08***	-0.05***	1						
Sex	-0.027***	0.04***	0.01***	-0.06***	1					
Children under 16 years	0.15***	0.12***	0.11***	0.06***	-0.30***	1				
Being married	-0.01***	0.02***	0.01***	-0.04***	-0.02***	-0.17***	1			
Migration background (no personal experience)	-0.03***	-0.03***	-0.04***	-0.03 ***	0.01**	-0.04***	-0.05***	1		

(Table continued on next page)

Table 5.6 (Continued)

Pairwise Correlation Between Independent and Dependent Variables Used in the Regression Analyses

Variable	Being disabled	Quality of health	Satisfaction with health	Having a formal qualification	Sex	Children under 16 years	Being married	Migration background (no personal experience)	Migration background (personal experience)	Age
Migration background (personal experience)	-0.03***	0.00	-0.02***	-0.39***	-0.01***	-0.12***	0.12***	-0.11***	1	
Age	0.23***	0.25***	0.22***	0.02***	-0.02***	0.36***	0.22***	-0.15***	-0.08***	1
Place of residence	0.00**	0.02***	0.02***	0.04***	0.00	0.02***	-0.00	-0.05***	-0.09***	0.02***
Being satisfied with life	0.13***	0.37***	0.42***	-0.04***	-0.02***	0.08***	-0.09***	-0.02***	-0.01***	0.05***
Being satisfied with work	0.07***	0.27***	0.35***	-0.03***	-0.00	0.04***	-0.03***	-0.01***	-0.01***	0.03***
Being satisfied with leisure time	-0.04***	0.13***	0.19***	-0.0	-0.01***	-0.12***	-0.00	0.02***	0.03***	-0.12***
Readiness to assume risk	0.03***	0.07***	0.08***	-0.01**	0.02***	0.05***	-0.03***	-0.00	-0.01***	0.07***

(Table continued on next page)

165

Table 5.6 (Continued)

Pairwise Correlation Between Independent and Dependent Variables Used in the Regression Analyses

	Place of residence	Being satisfied with life	Being satisfied with work	Being satisfied with leisure time	Readiness to assume risk
Place of residence	1				
Being satisfied with life	0.04***	1			
Being satisfied with work	0.02***	0.39***	1		
Being satisfied with leisure time	0.01***	0.28***	0.29***	1	
Readiness to assume risk	-0.02***	0.08***	0.06***	0.02***	1

Note: Own calculation with SOEP waves from 1994 to 2018, nonweighted, only individuals between 25 and 64 years, *** Significant at the 1% level, ** Significant at the 5% level, * Significant at the 10% level.

166

DISCUSSION

It is evident that, for the period of 1994 to 2018, disabled individuals in Germany are significantly less likely to be self-employed and more likely to leave self-employment than individuals lacking this status. In contrast, the process of entering self-employment does not seem to be linked to disability but rather to quality and satisfaction with health. Whereas insufficient health characteristics are also significantly negatively related to the likelihood of an individual being self-employed, this likelihood's association with an individual leaving self-employment is weak and restricted to the quality of health.

Therefore, health and disability seem to have a different relation to occupational choice regarding self-employment during different stages. The variables are not interchangeable. This is one of our main contributions to the research discussion.

The results of Metzler et al. (2021) suggesting that a specific negative link of disability to the chance of an individual being self-employed might be related to the relevant compensation available for certain grades of disability are supported. Health, on the other hand, cannot be merely regarded as a subtheme of disability. In a literature review, Simoes et al. (2015) concluded that the decisions of individuals with inadequate health regarding whether to enter self-employment might also be influenced by health-related benefits provided by the state that are more tailored to traditional employment than to self-employment. This is a useful explanation for the connection of "disability" to self-employment, but health seems to have an additional connection, as compensation in Germany is not provided based on a self-assessment of individual health. A negative association of disability status with the likelihood of being self-employed is rather unique to the German context, since self-employment is higher within the subgroup of disabled individuals in many other countries (e.g., Pagán, 2009; Renko et al., 2015). An empirically weaker but similar argument can be made for the negative relation of poor health to entering self-employment (Shepherd & Patzelt, 2017). Concerning entrepreneurial exits, our results enhance the results of Pagán-Rodriguez (2012a), who did not distinguish between disability and health.

The present study, therefore, offers a novel contribution to current research on self-employment; the concepts of "disability" and "health" are defined in the research background and empirically tested through independent and joined regression models concerning the occupational choice of disabled German individuals. "Disability" and "health" should be considered both related and discrete concepts on a theoretical level, while the distinction between them must be made on an empirical level—at least for the German context. These results are in line with the theoretical arguments of García-Gómez et al. (2010), Pagán-Rodríguez (2012b) and Shandra (2018), yet they contrast with several current empirical approaches (e.g., Giuntella & Mazzonna, 2015; Pagán & Malo, 2009; Pagán-Rodríguez, 2012a) but agree with Fossen and König (2017).

Concerning a possible distinctive relation of quality of and satisfaction with health to self-employment, little can be said. Both variables are highly intercorrelated. In two out of three regression models, both variables have similar results concerning direction: quality of health proves to be a more significant predictor for being self-employed and leaving self-employment; in contrast, satisfaction with health seems to be the more important factor with respect to entering self-employment. Here, a few comparisons to other research can be made. Fossen and König (2017) also found a negative link between the quality of health and the chance of entering entrepreneurship in Germany, but they did not use health satisfaction as an alternative or combinable variable. In contrast, Nikolova (2019) evaluated health satisfaction as an outcome of changes in self-employment but did not include quality of health as a separate variable. Hence, more research is needed to look for possible distinctive links.

The results in the current analysis indicate that individuals reporting below average satisfaction with their work are more likely to enter self-employment, strengthening the argument that disadvantaged individuals may indeed find a more satisfying working life through self-employment (Doyel, 2002). However, again, other results concerning satisfaction with life itself or leisure time paint a more ambiguous picture of self-employment, that is, as a potential neutralizer of societal marginalization.

Finally, the results at hand may offer implications for (nascent) entrepreneurs. Individuals aiming to enter entrepreneurship should look out for their health and invest in it long-term. As the first years in entrepreneurial activity are potentially stressful (Dahl et al., 2010), organizing time slots each week for fitness or relaxation could help to maintain health. Health programs targeting (nascent) self-employed individuals, for example, courses aimed at learning relaxation techniques, could help disabled and nondisabled self-employed individuals start and maintain their own business, although more research on the roles of stress and health in entrepreneurship is needed (Shepherd & Patzelt, 2017). Online support groups could also be a low-threshold method to enable discussions of (mental) health problems with other founders.

However, even the best prevention might not be sufficient to keep away serious illnesses. Employed individuals with health problems can more easily use extended sick leave. In contrast, such a step might seriously endanger a self-employed (Gonçalves & Martins, 2018). However, avoiding medical treatment might cause even more severe health problems in the future or lead to occupational burnout (Stephan & Roesler, 2010).

Our research indicates that self-employed individuals should visit a doctor despite the additional costs; a disability is primarily caused by long-term illness, which might endanger an entrepreneurial career. Additionally, entrepreneurs at a certain risk of developing a serious illness (e.g., due to genetic disposition) should plan in advance and develop strategies to cope with challenges of adapting to their disability. They might benefit from speaking to disabled entrepreneurs with similar conditions, who could act as mentors (Parker Harris et al., 2013). A vital part of this process is connected to being honest with oneself, friends, and family. Given that entrepreneurs were not seen as vulnerable in the past (Torrès & Thurik, 2019), a display of vulnerability might cause anxiety for entrepreneurs. More research is needed to examine the adaptation process.

CONCLUSIONS, LIMITATIONS, AND FURTHER RESEARCH

This study's analyses are limited by several restrictions that are briefly discussed below. This chapter extends existing quantitative research by using regression analyses with varying definitions of disability and health. This method rests on the assumption that an effect can be distinguished, ceteris paribus, using a similar set of variables for all individuals. However, the occupational choice of an older, disabled and ethnically German male might be influenced by factors that have no bearing on the decision of a young disabled female with a migration background. Therefore, additional qualitative studies for subgroups might offer further insights. Concerning qualitative studies, it might also be worthwhile to look at the situation of self-employed individuals who have a chronic illness or disability with either permanent or temporary effects on their health. The SOEP measures the quality and satisfaction with health at one point within a given year, but individuals with certain illnesses might experience different incidences over the course of that year. Furthermore, it would be interesting to investigate how self-employed individuals with insufficient health react in a crisis; to take Torrès and Thurik (2019) idea into consideration to discern whether self-employment itself might be linked to health, and whether this might change over time.

There are also alternative quantitative approaches to using SOEP data. Defining "Health x Disability" as an interaction term could potentially determine a combined association with occupational choices of disabled individuals who exceed the singular result of these variables. With respect to changes concerning disability and/or health status of an individual, further quantitative analyses might be helpful. An event history analysis could illustrate whether a self-assessment of health of self-employed individuals declines below a certain threshold value within a predetermined period. Alternatively, the number of "surviving" self-employed individuals with a disability within a predetermined period could be analyzed. A limitation of both approaches is the relatively small number of available cases (Table 5.1). This study's analyses use the SOEP dataset and, therefore, offer a typical set of moderation and control variables concerning the demographics and attitudes of individuals. However, other datasets might be available in the future that could provide further insights. For example, the SOEP dataset offers few to no data on self-employment activity itself, for example, annual turnover or acquired customers. A business-centered analysis could offer additional information that might help researchers understand individual decisions to maintain or leave self-employment. Another methodological challenge is the notion that the poor health of an individual could be the result of a certain type of employment and not a potential cause for choosing and maintaining a certain type of employment. A poor health status could also lead to the recognition of how an individual becomes disabled. Building on an SOEP analysis of the 1984 to 2009 waves, Ravesteijn et al. (2013) argued that high job-related physical demands and low job control (primarily found in blue-collar jobs) lower the self-reported health of individuals in Germany. The effect is stronger on older subgroups.

No information describing the cause of the disability of an individual is available in the SOEP. Looking at official statistics, in 2009, 2011, 2013, and 2015, less than 2% of all recognized, severely disabled individuals in Germany stated that the cause of their disability was either a work accident or a vocational disease (Statistisches Bundesamt, 2018). Therefore, identifying a direct causal effect of either being employed or self-employed on the likelihood of being disabled seems unlikely for the vast majority of cases. As mentioned above, health can be influenced by investments (Becker, 2007; Grossman, 1972). Thus, it would be of great interest to obtain insights into how self-employed and non-self-employed individuals address these investments in their health capital through treatments, disease prevention, organizing adequate work-life balances, and so forth, and how different existing schedules might influence whether individuals enter or leave self-employment.

These limitations aside, the current study delivers new insights into how health and disability, as separate concepts, influence an individual's decision to become, stay and no longer be self-employed. These understandings are at once innovative and fruitful contributions to the research on occupational choice regarding self-employment decision-making and important factors for further research on the roles of disability and health effects in the labor market.

REFERENCES

Altman, B. A. (2014). Another perspective: Capturing the working-age population with disabilities in survey measures. *Journal of Disability Policy Studies, 25*(3) 146–153.

Becker, G. S. (1962). Investment in human capital: A theoretical analysis. *Journal of Political Economy, 70*(5, Part 2), 9–49. https://doi.org/10.1086/258724

Becker, G. S. (2007). Health as human capital: Synthesis and extensions. *Oxford Economic Papers, 59*(3), 379–410. https://doi.org/10.1093/oep/gpm020

Bencsik, P., & Chuluun, T. (2021). Comparative well-being of the self-employed and paid employees in the USA. *Small Business Economics, 56*(1), 355–384. https://doi.org/10.1007/s11187-019-00221-1

Benz, M., & Frey B. S. (2008). The value of doing what you like: Evidence from the self-employed in 23 countries. *Journal of Economic Behavior & Organization, 68*(3-4), 445–455. https://doi.org/10.1016/j.jebo.2006.10.014

Berthold, N., & Neumann, M. (2008). The motivation of entrepreneurs: Are employed managers and self-employed owners different? *Intereconomics, 43*(4), 236–244. https://doi.org/10.1007/s10272-008-0256-9

Brachert, M., Hyll, W., & Sadrieh A. (2020). Entry into self-employment and individuals' risk-taking propensities. *Small Business Economics, 55*(4), 1057–1074. https://doi.org/10.1007/s11187-019-00173-6

Brenke, K. (2015). The vast majority of employees in Germany are satisfied with their jobs. *DIW Economic Bulletin, 5*(32/33), 429–436. DIW Berlin website. https://www.diw.de/documents/publikationen/73/diw_01.c.512472.de/diw_econ_bull_2015-32-1.pdf

Burkhauser, R. V., Houtenville, A. J., & Wittenburg, D. C. (2003). A user's guide to current statistics on the employment of people with disabilities. In D. C. Stapleton & R. V. Burkhauser (Eds.), *The decline in employment of people with disabilities: A policy puzzle* (pp. 23–85). W.E. Upjohn Institute for Employment Research.

Caliendo, M., Fossen, F., & Kritikos, A. (2009). Risk attitudes of nascent entrepreneurs - New evidence from an experimentally validated survey. *Small Business Economics, 32*(2), 153–167. https://doi.org/10.1007/s11187-007-9078-6

Caliendo, M., Fossen, F., & Kritikos, A. (2010). The impact of risk attitudes on entrepreneurial survival. *Journal of Economic Behavior & Organization, 76*(1), 45–63, https://doi.org/10.1016/j.jebo.2010.02.012

Caliendo, M., Fossen, F., & Kritikos, A. S. (2014). Personality characteristics and the decisions to become and stay self-employed. *Small Business Economics, 42*(4), 787–814. https://doi.org/10.1007/s11187-013-9514-8

Campbell, F. K. (2009). *Contours of ableism: The production of disability and abledness.* Palgrave Macmillan.

Chin, B., Murphy, M. L. M., Janicki-Deverts, D., & Cohen, S. (2017). Marital status as a predictor of diurnal salivary cortisol levels and slopes in a community sample of healthy adults. *Psychoneuroendocrinology, 78*, 68–75. https://doi.org/10.1016/j.psyneuen.2017.01.016

Dahl, M., Nielsen, J., & Mojtabai, R. (2010). The effects of becoming an entrepreneur on the use of psychotropics among entrepreneurs and their spouses. *Scandinavian Journal of Public Health, 38*(8), 857–863. https://doi.org/10.1177/1403494810375490

DIW Berlin. (2016). *Introduction to the socio-economic panel.* https://www.diw.de/documents/dokumentenarchiv/17/diw_01.c.551838.de/soep_introduction_2016.pdf

Doyel, A. W. (2002). A realistic perspective of risk in self-employment for people with disabilities. *Journal of Vocational Rehabilitation, 17*(2), 115–124. https://content.iospress.com/articles/journal-of-vocational-rehabilitation/jvr00151

FMLS—Federal Ministry of Labor and Social Affairs. (2014). *Federal Government Report on Participation with regard to the circumstances of persons with impairments participation – impairment – disability.* https://www.bmas.de/SharedDocs/Downloads/DE/Publikationen/a125-13-e-teilhabebericht-2013-englisch.pdf;jsessionid=151FFFD0E8E40A088C5A70ADDA09370F.delivery1-replication?__blob=publicationFile&v=1

FMLS—Federal Ministry of Labor and Social Affairs. (2020). *Social security at a glance 2020.* https://www.bmas.de/EN/Services/Publications/a998-social-security-at-a-glance.html

Fossen, F., & König, J. (2017). Public health insurance, individual health, and entry into self-employment. *Small Business Economics, 49*(3), 647–669. https://doi.org/10.1007/s11187-017-9843-0

García-Gómez, P., Jones, A. M., & Rice, N. (2010). Health effects on labour market exits and entries. *Labor Economics, 17*(1), 62–76. https://doi.org/10.1016/j.labeco.2009.04.004

Giuntella, O., & Mazzonna, F. (2015). Do immigrants improve the health of natives? *Journal of Health Economics, 43*, 140–153. https://doi.org/10.1016/j.jhealeco.2015.06.006

Goldberg, P., Guéguen, A., Schmaus, A., Nakache, J.-P., & Goldberg, M. (2001). Longitudinal study of associations between perceived health status and self-reported diseases in the French Gazel cohort. *Journal of Epidemiol and Community Health, 55*(4), 233–238. http://dx.doi.org/10.1136/jech.55.4.233

Gonçalves, J., & Martins, P. (2018). The effect of self-employment on health: Evidence from longitudinal social security data. *IZA Discussion Paper Series, 11305*, 1–24. http://ftp.iza.org/dp11305.pdf

Graeber, D. (2017). Does more education protect against mental health problems? *DIW Roundup Politik im Fokus, 113*, 1–10. DIW website: https://www.diw.de/de/diw_01.c.565260.de/presse/diw_roundup/does_more_education_protect_against_mental_health_problems.html

Grossman, M. (1972). On the concept of health capital and the demand for health. *Journal of Political Economy, 80*(2), 223–255. https://www.jstor.org/stable/1830580

Haan, P., & Myck, M. (2009). Dynamics of health and labor market risks. *Journal of Health Economics, 28*(6), 1116–1125. https://doi.org/10.1016/j.jhealeco.2009.09.001

Hatak, I., & Zhou, H. (2021). Health as human capital in entrepreneurship: Individual, extension, and substitution effects on entrepreneurial success. *Entrepreneurship Theory and Practice*, *45*(1), 18–42. https://doi.org/10.1177/1042258719867559

Hessels, J., Rietveld, C., Thurik, R., & Van der Zwan, P. (2018). Depression and entrepreneurial exit. *Academy of Management Perspectives*, *32*(3), 323–339. https://doi.org/10.5465/amp.2016.0183

Hsu, D. K., Wiklund J., Anderson S. E., & Coffey B. S. (2016). Entrepreneurial exit intentions and the business-family interface. *Journal of Business Venturing*, *31*(6), 613–627. https://doi.org/10.1016/j.jbusvent.2016.08.001

Infurna, F., & Wiest, M. (2016). The effect of disability onset across the adult life span. *The Journals of Gerontology, Series B: Psychological Sciences*, *73*(5), 755–766. https://doi.org/10.1093/geronb/gbw055

Jansen, A., & Metzler, C. A. (2019, June). *Anforderungen an Fachpraktiker- und Werkerberufe in Zeiten der Digitalisierung* [Requirements within professions for people with disabilites in times of digitization]. 20. Hochschultage Berufliche Bildung, Siegen, North Rhine-Westphalia. https://www.berufsbildung.nrw. de/cms/upload/hochschultage-bk/2019beitraege/ft04_JansenMetzler_anforderungen-fachpraktikerberufe.pdf

Jones, M., & Latreille, P. (2011). Disability and self-employment: Evidence for the UK. Applied Economics, *43*(27), 4161–4178. https://doi.org/10.1080/00036 846.2010.489816

Jones, M., & Salonaki, E.-C. (2021). Exploring the relationship between impairment and disability in Great Britain: Evidence from the life opportunities survey. *Journal of Policy and Disability Studies*. Advance online publication. https://doi. org/10.1177/10442073211021532

Joona, P. A. (2010). Exits from Self-Employment: Is there a native-immigrant difference in Sweden?. *International Migration Review*, *10*(3), 539–559. https:// doi.org/10.1111/j.1747-7379.2010.00817.x

Joona, P. A. (2017). Are mothers of young children more likely to be self-employed? The case of Sweden. *Review of Economics of the Household*, *15*(1), 307–333. https://doi.org/10.1007/s11150-016-9349-6

Kalwij, A., & Vermeulen, F. (2008). Health and labour force participation in older people in Europe: What do objective health indicators add to the analysis? *Health Economics*, *17*(5), 619–638. https://doi.org/10.1002/hec.1285

Kašperová, E., & Kitching, J. (2014). Embodying entrepreneurial identity. *International Journal of Entrepreneurial Behaviour and Research*, *20*(5), 438–452. https://doi.org/10.1108/IJEBR-07-2013-0108

Kautonen, T., Down, S., & Minniti, M. (2014). Ageing and entrepreneurial preferences. *Small Business Economics*, *42*(3), 579–594. https://doi.org/10.1007/ s11187-013-9489-5

Kock, M. (2004). Disability law in Germany: An overview of employment, education and access rights. *German Law Journal*, *5*(11). 1373–1392. https://doi. org/10.1017/S2071832200013286

Kühn, M., Dudel, C., Vogt, T., & Oksuzyan, A. (2019). Trends in gender differences in health and mortality at working ages among West and East Germans. *SSM-Population Health*, *7*, 1–10. https://doi.org/10.1016/j.ssmph.2018.100326

Lazear, E. P. (1998). *Personnel economics for managers*. Wiley.

Lazear, E. P. (2004). Balanced skills and entrepreneurship. *American Economic Review*, *94*(2), 208–211. https://doi.org/10.1257/0002828041301425

Lazear, E.P (2005). Entrepreneurship. *Journal of Labor Economics*, *23*(4), 649–680. https://doi.org/10.1086/491605

Metzler, C. A. (2013). Eine Chance für Behinderte. *IWD*, *2*(39), 8. https://www.iwd. de/artikel/eine-chance-fuer-behinderte-101308/

Metzler, C. A., Moog, P., & Audretsch, D. B. (2021). *The missing entrepreneurs*. Paper handed in to JBV, under review.

Millán J. M., Congregado, E., & Román, C. (2012). Determinants of self-employment survival in Europe. *Small Business Economics*, *38*(2), 231–258. https://doi.org/10.1007/s11187-010-9260-0

Moog, P. (2002). Human capital and its influence on entrepreneurial success. *Historische Sozialforschung*, *27*(4), 157–180. https://nbn-resolving.org/ urn:nbn:de:0168-ssoar-33954

Mushkin, S. (1962). Health as an investment. *Journal of Political Economy*, *70*(5), 129–157. https://doi.org/10.1086/258730

Nikolova, M. (2019). Switching to self-employment can be good for your health. *Journal of Business Venturing*, *34*(4), 664–691. https://doi.org/10.1016/j. jbusvent.2018.09.001

Nikolova, M., Nikolaev, B., & Popova, O. (2020). The perceived well-being and health costs of exiting self-employment. *Small Business Economics*. Advanced online publication. https://doi.org/10.1007/s11187-020-00374-4

Office of Disability Employment Policy. (2013). *Self-employment for people with disabilities*. https://www.dol.gov/sites/dolgov/files/odep/pdf/2014startup.pdf

Pagán, R. (2009). Self-employment among people with disabilities: Evidence for Europe. *Disability & Society*, *24*(2), 217–229. https://doi. org/10.1080/09687590802652504

Pagán, R., & Malo, M. (2009). Job satisfaction and disability: Lower expectations about jobs or a matter of health?. *Spanish Economic Review*, *11*(1) 51–74, https://doi.org/10.1007/s10108-008-9043-9

Pagán-Rodríguez, R. (2012a). Transitions to and from self-employment among older people with disabilities in Europe. *Journal of Disability Policy Studies*, *23*(2), 82–93. https://doi.org/10.1177/1044207311422232 https://doi. org/10.1177/1044207311422232

Pagán-Rodríguez, R. (2012b). Longitudinal analysis of the domains of satisfaction before and after disability: Evidence from the German Socio-Economic Panel. *Social Indicators Research*, *108*, 365–385. https://doi.org/10.1007/s11205-011-9889-3

Parker Harris, S., Renko, M., & Caldwell, K. (2013). Accessing social entrepreneurship: Perspectives of people with disabilities and key stakeholders. *Journal of Vocational Rehabilitation*, *38*(1), 35–48. https://doi.org/10.3233/JVR-120619

Patrick, C., Stephens, H., & Weinstein, A. (2016). Where are all the self-employed women? Push and pull factors influencing female labor market decisions. *Small Business Economics*, *46*(3), 365–390. https://doi.org/10.1007/s11187-015-9697-2

Ravesteijn, B., Van Kippersluis, H., & Van Doorslaer, E. (2013). The wear and tear on health: What is the role of occupation?. *SOEPpapers on Multidisciplinary Panel Data Research, 618*, 1–31. https://papers.ssrn.com/sol3/papers.cfm?abstract_id=2424673

Razgallah, M., Maalaoui, A., Carsrud, A., Brännback M., & Germon, R. (2017, October 1–3). *Fostering entrepreneurial intentions in disabled men and women: Investigating the roles of alertness and perceived health* [Paper presentation]. Diana International Conference, Kansas City, Missouri, United States of America.

Renko, M., Parker Harris, S., & Caldwell, K. (2015). Entrepreneurial entry by people with disabilities. *International Small Business Journal: Researching Entrepreneurship, 34*(5), 555–578. https://doi.org/10.1177/0266242615579112

Rietveld, C. A., Van Kippersluis, H., & Thurik, A. R. (2015). Self-employment and health: Barriers or benefits?. *Health Economics, 24*(10), 1302–1313. https://doi.org/10.1002/hec.3087

Rohrer, J. E., Bernard, M. E., Zhang, Y., Rasmussen, N., & Woroncow, H. (2008): Marital status, feeling depressed and self-rated health in rural female primary care patients. *Journal of Evaluation in Clinical Practice, 14*(2), 214–217. https://doi.org/ 10.1111/j.1365-2753.2007.00835.x

Ross, M., & Sicoly, F. (1979). Egocentric biases in availability and attribution. *Journal of Personality and Social Psychology, 37*(3), 322–336. https://doi.org/10.1037/0022-3514.37.3.322

Schneck, S. (2014). Why the self-employed are happier: Evidence from 25 European countries. *Journal of Business Research, 67*(6), 1043–1048. https://doi.org/10.1016/j.jbusres.2013.06.008

Schurer, S. (2015). Lifecycle patterns in the socioeconomic gradient of risk preferences. *Journal of Economic Behavior & Organization, 119*, 482–495. https://doi.org/10.1016/j.jebo.2015.09.024

Segal, G., Borgia, D., & Schoenfeld, J. (2005). The motivation to become an entrepreneur. *Int.J of Entrepreneurial Behaviour&Research, 11*(1), 42–57. https://doi.org/10.1108/13552550510580834

Shaheen, G. (2016). "Inclusive Entrepreneurship": A process for improving self-employment for people with disabilities. *Journal of Policy Practice, 15*(1–2), 58– 81. https://doi.org/10.1080/15588742.2016.1109963

Shandra, C. (2018). Disability as inequality: Social disparities, health disparities, and participation in daily activities. *Social Forces, 97*(1), 157–192. https://doi.org/10.1093/sf/soy031

Shepherd, D. A., & Patzelt, H. (2017). *Trailblazing in entrepreneurship*. Palgrave Macmillan

Simoes, N., Crespo, N., & Moreira, S. B. (2015). Individual determinants of self-employment entry: What do we really know?. *Journal of Economic Surveys, 30*(4), 783–806. https://doi.org/10.1111/joes.12111

Statistisches Bundesamt. (2018). *Statistik der schwerbehinderten Menschen 2017* [Statistics of severely disabled people 2017]. https://www.destatis.de/DE/Themen/Gesellschaft-Umwelt/Gesundheit/Behinderte-Menschen/Publikationen/Downloads-Behinderte-Menschen/sozial-schwerbehinderte -kb-5227101179004.pdf?__blob=publicationFile

Stephan, U., & Roesler, U. (2010). Health of entrepreneurs vs. employees in a national representative sample. *Journal of Occupational & Organisational Psychology*, *83*(3), 717–738. https://doi.org/10.1348/096317909X472067

Struminskaya, B. (2011). Selbstständigkeit von Personen mit Migrationshintergrund in Deutschland. Ursachen ethnischer Unternehmung [Self-employment of people with a migration background in Germany. Causes of ethnic enterprise]. *SOEP Papers on Multidisciplinary Panel Data Research*, *418*, 1–27.

Susman, J. (1994). Disability, stigma and deviance. *Social Science & Medicine*, *38*(1), 15–22.

Szumilas, M. (2010). Explaining odds ratios. *Journal of the Canadian Academy of Child and Adolescent*, *19*(3), 227–229. https://www.ncbi.nlm.nih.gov/pmc/articles/PMC2938757/

TNS Infratest Sozialforschung. (2015). *SOEP 2015 – Erhebungsinstrumente 2015 (Welle 32) des SOEP–Panels: SOEP Survey Papers 274: Series A*. DIW/SOEP.

Torrès, O., & Thurik, R. (2019). Small business owners and health. *Small Business Economics*, *53*(2), 311–321. https://doi.org/10.1007/s11187-018-0064-y

Unger, J. M., Rauch, A., Frese, M., & Rosenbusch, N. (2011). Human capital and entrepreneurial success: A meta-analytical review. *Journal of Business Venturing*, *26*(3), 341–358.https://doi.org/10.1016/j.jbusvent.2009.09.004

Van der Zwan, P., Hessels, J., & Rietveld, C. A. (2018). Self-employment and satisfaction with life, work, and leisure. *Journal of Economic Psychology*, *64*, 73–88. https://doi.org/10.1016/j.joep.2017.12.001

Van Praag, C., & Cramer, J. (2001). The Roots of entrepreneurship and labour demand: Individual ability and low risk aversion. *Economica*, *68*(269), 45–62. Retrieved March 27, 2021, from https://doi.org/10.1111/1468-0335.00232

Wagner, J. (2007). What a difference a Y makes—Female and male nascent entrepreneurs in Germany. *Small Business Economics*, *28*(1), 1–21. https://doi.org/10.1007/s11187-005-0259-x

Wagner, G. G., Frick, J., & Schupp, J. (2007). The German Socio-Economic Panel Study (SOEP): Scope, evolution and enhancements. *Schmollers Jahrbuch*, *127*(1), 139–169. https://www.diw.de/de/diw_01.c.450791.de/publikationen/soeppapers/2007_0001/the_german_socio-economic_panel_study__soep___scope__evolution_and_enhancements.html

Welter, F., May-Strobl, E., Wolter, H.-J., & Günterberg, B. (2015). *Mittelstand im Wandel. Institut für Mittelstandsforschung Bonn* [SMEs in transition. Institute for SME Research Bonn]. https://www.ifm-bonn.org/fileadmin/data/ redaktion/publikationen/ifm_materialien /dokumente/IfM-Materialien-232_2014.pdf

Welter, F., Baker, T., & Wirsching, K. (2019). Three waves and counting: The rising tide of contextualization in entrepreneurship research. *Small Business Economics*, *52*(2), 319–330. https://doi.org/10.1007/s11187-018-0094-5

CHAPTER 6

DISABILITY AND ADVERSE IMPACT

Creating Inclusive Selection Practices for Individuals With Disabilities

Nicole Strah
University of North Carolina at Charlotte

Deborah E. Rupp
George Mason University

Jessie A. Cannon
George Mason University

ABSTRACT

Individuals with disabilities face many barriers to selection and promotion in the workplace. One such barrier is that (ostensibly) neutral selection practices can adversely impact individuals and groups with disabilities. However, disability-related adverse impact has not been the subject of extensive human resource management (HRM) research, likely due to the challenges in conducting such research. To address this issue, we integrate adverse impact research and legal decisions/perspectives on adverse impact in the context of disability status. That is, we review how the courts and legal scholars have approached disability-related adverse impact in order to provide context that could influence theoretical and methodological perspectives within

Forgotten Minorities in Organizations, pp. 177–206
Copyright © 2023 by Information Age Publishing
www.infoagepub.com
All rights of reproduction in any form reserved.

psychological and HRM research on disability-related adverse impact, which in turn, would facilitate the advancement of this research. We begin by examining the history of the Americans with Disabilities Act [ADA] discrimination legislation and case law. Next, we focus on the potential for common selection tools to produce adverse impact against those with disabilities. Then, we discuss theoretical and practical issues in studying disability-related adverse impact and contrast two legal frameworks, the well-established accommodation framework and less-well-established (in terms of disability) disparate impact framework. We conclude by proposing an agenda for future research that includes potential steps for identifying disability-related adverse impact, ways to address adverse impact within selection contexts, and practical ways to build inclusive selection systems.

Workers with disabilities face numerous organizational entry and succession barriers (Colella & Bruyère, 2011). Indeed, the unemployment rate of individuals with disabilities is almost double that of individuals without disabilities (12.6% compared to 7.9%; Bureau of Labor Statistics [BLS], 2021).[1] The underemployment of this group is especially problematic as individuals with disabilities comprise a large percent of the total population (27%; Taylor, 2018), meaning a great deal of our society is at a higher risk for underemployment. One significant barrier to those with disabilities obtaining desirable employment is that (ostensibly)[2] neutral selection and promotion practices can disadvantage these individuals. Specifically, many selection tools and methods have the potential to produce lower scores for individuals with varying disabilities (e.g., Brannick et al., 1992; Kotov et al., 2017; Saxena & Morris, 2019), resulting in lower selection rates for these individuals compared to those without disabilities (i.e., adverse impact against those with disabilities; Dunleavy & Morris, 2017).

If these subgroup differences in selection scores do *not* reflect real differences in the knowledge, skills, abilities, and other characteristics (KSAOs) required to perform *essential job functions*, then the selection practices unnecessarily, and perhaps illegally, limit employment opportunities for applicants with disabilities. That is, disability-related adverse impact can result in organizations not hiring or advancing individuals with disabilities who, in actuality, could have performed the job well. This is ethically and practically problematic for organizations as these organizations may not only be unfairly (and potentially illegally) denying individuals with disabilities opportunities, but are also missing the chance to increase employee diversity and hire individuals who can make important contributions to the organization.

Despite the clear negative implications of selection tools creating adverse impact against individuals with disabilities, adverse impact research has largely focused on race/ethnicity differences and, to a lesser extent, sex differences (e.g., Bobko & Roth, 2013; Dean et al., 2008). In fact, Ployhart and Holtz (2008) noted that we know little about subgroup differences in scores on many selection tools beyond Black-White differences. However, disability-related selection research can be meaningfully extended to include the research thus far established on adverse impact as well as the unique considerations needed when studying adverse impact in the context of disability. The importance of adverse impact against those with disabilities has only recently received some limited attention in the context of personality assessments (Colella & Bruyère, 2011; Saxena & Morris, 2019). In this chapter, we build on this research and call for a deeper analysis of adverse impact as it pertains to disability. While we seek to begin an evidence-based dialog on disability-related adverse impact, our main goal is to highlight the importance of future work in this area and identify clear paths for such research to take.

Understanding the unique considerations associated with adverse impact in the context of disability matters for the development of both organizational theory and practice. Indeed, our field's current lack of focus on this topic diminishes organizations' ability to identify problematic practices and increase disability-related workforce diversity. Therefore, we argue that disability-related adverse impact is an important topic deserving attention within both the disability and selection literature. Because such little research has been conducted in this area and because adverse impact research is often interconnected with and driven by public policy, in this review, we discuss disability-related adverse impact from a legal perspective. We believe this legal perspective will encourage future disability-related research because: (1) a Since courts and legal scholars have devoted relatively more attention to disability-related adverse impact, this legal lens can guide the identification of important disability-related considerations in psychological research and HRM practice; and (2) the possibility that organizations may be accused of either disparate[3] treatment or disparate impact under the ADA can catalyze new research given its implications for improving organizations' legal compliance.

We first examine the history of discrimination legislation and case law (specifically that which is tied to the ADA). Next, we focus on the potential for common, facially-neutral selection tools to produce adverse impact against those with disabilities. We then discuss theoretical and practical issues in studying disability-related adverse impact. Next, we contrast two legal frameworks, the well-established (accommodation) and less-well-established (disparate impact) legal frameworks that potentially allow facially neutral selection tools to be challenged under federal law.

Our integration of adverse impact research and legal discussions on disability-related adverse impact has noteworthy implications for how we can advance both research and practice related to adverse impact. Our proposed agenda for future research includes not only potential steps for identifying disability-related adverse impact but also preliminary suggestions for addressing or preemptively mitigating this adverse impact within selection contexts, which would allow more inclusive selection systems to be built. Table 6.1 contains our propositions for future research, and Table 6.2 contains practical implications, which we discuss in the sections that follow.

Table 6.1

Propositions for Future Research on Disability-Related Adverse Impact

Proposition 1: Different selection practices will vary in the extent to which they create adverse impact across different disability subgroups in a manner that can be predicted by theory. (p. 9)

Proposition 2: Conducting a diversity-inclusive job analysis (one focused on essential job functions) will allow selection practices to be chosen that contain less adverse impact. (p. 26)

Proposition 3: Considering the independent components of selection practices (e.g., underlying construct, methods used to assess construct) will allow organizational researchers to identify the source of disability-relevant adverse impact and mitigate this adverse impact where appropriate. (p. 32)

Table 6.2

Implications for HRM Practice

1. Assessing disability-related adverse impact is important, and organizational researchers should develop theoretically and practically sound approaches to assess how individuals with disabilities are disadvantaged by facially neutral selection systems.
2. Conducting a diversity-inclusive job analysis (one focused on essential job functions) will allow selection practices to be chosen that contain less adverse impact against individuals with disabilities.
3. A modular approach to selection, wherein specific aspects of selection tools are assessed (e.g., constructs, formats), should be adopted to create a more nuanced approach to increasing inclusivity within selection.

THE AMERICANS WITH DISABILITY ACT (ADA) AND OSTENSIBLY NEUTRAL SELECTION PRACTICES

To provide context for our discussions on theoretically and practically advancing research on *adverse impact* (when practices disproportionately screen out members of a demographic subgroup) and how the legal literature on *disparate impact* (a legal framework where the presence and justifiability of adverse impact is investigated; Vodanovich & Rupp 2022) can inform the study of adverse impact, we briefly define the legal frameworks the ADA offers for applicants or employees disadvantaged by ostensibly neutral practices.

The ADA was originally passed in 1990 and amended in 2008 (as the Americans with Disabilities Amendments Act, or ADAA). It protects applicants and employees from discrimination due to their disability, and applies to both private and municipal organizations. To initiate a claim, plaintiffs must provide sufficient evidence that an ADA claim is appropriate by demonstrating that they (1) have an impairment that "substantially limits one or more major life activities," have a record of the impairment, or have been regarded as being impaired; and (2) can complete the *essential job functions, with or without accommodations*[4] (ADA, 1990; Gutman et al., 2011; Vodanovich & Rupp, 2022). The second standard is particularly important in this context. That is, the essential job functions requirement necessitates the performance of job duties be assessed in relation to the following criteria "(a) the position exists to perform the function, (b) there are a limited number of other employees available to perform the function, or among whom the function can be distributed, and (c) a function is highly specialized, and the person is hired for the special expertise or ability to perform it" (Mitchell et al., 1997; p. 7).[5]

The most common ADA case focuses on the failure to accommodate, where an employer is charged with not providing a reasonable accommodation that was requested by an individual with a disability (Gutman et al., 2011). Far less common are disparate impact claims, where facially neutral procedures are shown to disproportionately disadvantage job applicants with disabilities. That said, the basic motivation underlying both legal frameworks is fundamentally the same, in that both focus on removing ostensibly neutral barriers for applicants or employees with disabilities (Crossley, 2004). However, legal scholars have noted the largely untapped potential of the disparate impact framework to improve the treatment of those with disabilities in the workplace (Stein & Waterstone, 2006). Specifically, a disparate impact case considers whether neutral selection practices disadvantage individuals with disabilities (i.e., create adverse impact), and, therefore, whether the practice should exist at all (rather than focusing on how individuals can be fairly accommodated when engaging with that practice).

DISPARATE IMPACT, ADVERSE IMPACT, AND DISABILITY

As alluded to earlier, *adverse impact* occurs when an employment practice disproportionately harms members of a demographic subgroup, despite its neutral or seemingly neutral intent (Vodanovich & Rupp, 2022). We use *disparate impact* to refer to the legal framework under which it can be shown that an organization illegally disadvantaged a protected group through unjustifiable practices that created the adverse impact.

The first step in understanding and mitigating disability-related adverse impact is identifying common selection tools' *general* potential to create adverse impact, which has typically been done through statistics that compare the scores demographic subgroups have obtained on selection measures or compare selection rates across demographic subgroups. Exploring the potential adverse impact created by different practices/methods allows for academic inquiry into the presence, nature, and origins of these subgroup differences.

Disability, as it has been defined legally, can refer to a variety of impairments as long as these impairments influence one or more of an individual's important life functions (ADA, 1990). The Centers for Disease Control and Prevention (CDC, 2020b) lists several examples of functions that can be impaired in such a manner, including seeing, hearing, moving, thinking, remembering, learning, communicating, mental health, and social relationships. Therefore, there are many reasons a selection tool—due to either the construct assessed by the tool, or the method used to assess the construct—might disproportionately screen out individuals from at least one disability group (Wiernik et al., 2019). For example, researchers have noted that individuals with certain impairments (e.g., depression, anxiety, personality disorders) will typically score lower on specific personality traits (Kotov et al., 2017; Saulsman & Page, 2004; Stone-Romero, 2005; Melson-Silimon et al., 2019), which, when used for selection, is likely to lead to lower selection rates for these groups (Saxena & Morris, 2019). The effect sizes for some of these relationships are fairly large.[6] Similarly, the use of cognitive tests for selection presents obvious difficulties for individuals with disabilities related to learning, remembering, attention, and processing (Bertelli et al., 2018; Shields et al., 2020). Additionally, Brannick et al. (1992) reported that those with learning disabilities and pre-lingual hearing impairments scored lower on the SAT, on average, compared to those without disabilities. Finally, legal claims have been filed by applicants with autism who had trouble completing interviews due to communication barriers even though these applicants argued that they had actually already been performing the essential job functions (*Leskovisek v. Ill. Dep't of Transp.*, 2018).

The point of these examples is to demonstrate the viability of disability-related adverse impact. However, this research paints far from a complete picture. It is still unclear the extent to which common selection practices will create adverse impact for different disability groups and the reasons for its existence. Therefore, research is needed to understand how selection practices might systematically disadvantage individuals with various disabilities. Further, future research should establish theory that can explain the presence, strength, and origins of adverse impact that specific selection practices create across different disability subgroups. The identification of underlying explanations for subgroup differences within a given situation may range from being clear and parsimonious (e.g., cognitive ability tests creating adverse impact for individuals with learning disabilities) to being less obvious to HRM researchers (e.g., cognitive ability tests creating adverse impact for individuals with hearing impairments; Brannick et al., 1992), making adverse impact against applicants and employees with disabilities a rich area for future research. The development of such theory can drive future research and practical discussions on appropriate ways to explore, discuss, and address the issue of adverse impact.

Proposition 1: Different selection practices will vary in the extent to which they create adverse impact across different disability subgroups in a manner that can be predicted by theory.

BARRIERS TO RESEARCHING ADVERSE IMPACT

There are several ways in which the disability-related adverse impact context is unique (compared to, for example, race-related adverse impact). First, there is an issue regarding how disability-related adverse impact can be identified (e.g., using adverse impact statistics), leading some to question the feasibility or usefulness of adverse impact analysis in this context (Brannick et al., 1997). Second, the disability context illuminates additional issues not typically considered when researching whether adverse impact is illegitimate (i.e., not job-related). Specifically, the disability context presents additional considerations within performance measurement (i.e., whether only the essential components of a job should be measured), making the establishment of job-relatedness under ADA standards more complicated. Third, mitigating disability-related adverse impact requires a more nuanced approach to identifying precisely which part of a selection tool is disadvantageous to individuals with disabilities. Specifically, adverse impact can arise from the construct being assessed or the method being used to measure the construct.[7]

We use disability discrimination legislation and ADA case law as a lens to consider each of these issues. The following sections present two legal frameworks, the widely used *failure to accommodate* framework and the lesser used *disparate impact* framework.

Failure to Accommodate

The ADA specifically requires that organizations accommodate individuals with disabilities by modifying practices, tools, policies, or environments that appear neutral but disadvantage these individuals (e.g., an applicant who is blind may request an accommodation for a selection test to be administered orally; Gutman et al., 2011). To initiate an accommodation claim, once plaintiffs prove they have a disability and are reasonably qualified for the essential functions of the job, they can articulate that a reasonable accommodation exists that would have allowed them to perform well on the selection tool and/or the essential functions of the job (that the defendant failed to provide). If a plaintiff successfully asserts this argument, the organization can employ several defenses: the accommodation is unreasonable (e.g., requires changing essential job functions); the plaintiff did not work with the employer to find a reasonable accommodation; the accommodation would not sufficiently enable the plaintiff to perform all essential job functions; the accommodation causes undue hardship for the organization (i.e., it is too challenging or expensive to be reasonable); or the disability would pose a danger to the plaintiff or others in the work environment (Gutman et al., 2011).

On one hand, this accommodation framework does not require individuals to prove that a selection practice creates adverse impact against a disability group. However, this framework does place a rather large burden on individuals with disabilities to navigate through selection systems that are (perhaps unnecessarily) not inclusive. That is, this framework often places the burden on applicants with disabilities to anticipate the nature of the selection tools they will encounter and request appropriate accommodations, even if the tool itself is not related to the focal job. An alternative framework that seems to lessen this burden is the disparate impact framework.

Disparate Impact

The disparate impact legal scenario was originally established by the Supreme Court under Title VII of the Civil Rights Act of 1964 (*Griggs v. Duke Power Co.*, 1971; *Albemarle Paper Co. v. Moody*, 1975), and consists of three general phases. In the first (i.e., *prima facie*) phase, plaintiffs need to prove that the selection practice disproportionately disadvantages a protected group (i.e., adverse impact is present). This can manifest as plaintiffs providing statistical evidence that the selection tool results in a statistically lower proportion of the disadvantaged group passing through a selection hurdle or being selected by the organization compared to the favored group (Dunleavy & Morris, 2017). In the second phase, defendants (the organization) must prove that despite adversely impacting a demographic subgroup, the selection method measures job-related characteristics and is consistent with business necessity. Finally, in the third phase, plaintiffs can counter by showing alternative tools exist that are similarly job-related and demonstrate less adverse impact.

The ADA concretely addresses the principles of the disparate impact framework, listing under its definition of disability discrimination:

> using qualification standards, employment tests or other selection criteria that screen out or tend to screen out an individual with a disability or a class of individuals with disabilities unless the standard, test or other selection criteria, as used by the covered entity, is shown to be job-related for the position in question and is consistent with business necessity. (ADA, 1990)

The U.S. Supreme Court has also specifically affirmed the use of disparate impact theory under the ADA, stating that "both disparate treatment and disparate impact claims are cognizable under the ADA" (*Raytheon Co. v. Hernandez*, 2003).

However, disparate impact has three unique considerations under the ADA compared to its application under Title VII (under which race, religion, sex, color, and national origin discrimination claims may be made). First, identifying disability-related adverse impact faces unique challenges. The ADA typically considers the circumstances of an *individual* (e.g., determining whether an employee's impairment limits a major life activity, determining whether an individual is qualified to perform essential job functions; Gutman et al., 2011), a practice that conflicts with disparate impact theory's typical focus on the disproportionate screening out of *groups* of applicants (which relies on adverse impact statistics). Second, the requirement that organizations demonstrate the job-relevance and business necessity of selection methods may be complicated by the additional considerations of essential job functions and accommodations as required by the ADA. Third, the disability context highlights that specific aspects of a selection tool (e.g., the construct measured, the format of a selection test) can create adverse impact.

Due to these unique considerations, as well as the fairly limited number of disparate impact cases argued under the ADA, we are not able to confidently assert the precise manner in which adverse impact is or will be investigated within the disparate impact framework across different legal jurisdictions. However, the legal context has given far more attention to investigating disability-related adverse impact than has HRM research, and the manner in which the courts and legal scholars have discussed and approached these three considerations can aid HRM scholars' understanding of parallel challenges in (1) identifying disability-related adverse impact, (2) validating selection tools that may contain adverse impact, and (3) building inclusive selection systems by considering the effect of individual aspects of selection tools.

Challenges in Identifying Disability-Related Adverse Impact

As mentioned earlier, adverse impact is typically investigated within HRM research through the exploration of subgroup differences in scores on common selection tools (which would lead to differential selection rates between subgroups). However, identifying adverse impact within a disability context requires additional considerations related to data collection and appropriately grouping individuals. Legal research and court decisions related to the ADA have considered such issues and have taken different perspectives toward identifying adverse impact.

One challenge revolves around how many individuals may wish not to disclose their disability, making data hard to collect (Pregerson, 2011; Santuzzi & Waltz, 2016). Further, the Equal Employment Opportunity Commission (EEOC, 2002) states that employers are not allowed to ask applicants whether they have a disability. However, the EEOC also provides an exception to this rule. Specifically, EEOC guidance states that employers can ask applicants if they would voluntarily indicate their disability status, if these employers are using the information to proactively improve the work experiences or opportunities of individuals with disabilities (EEOC, 1995; EEOC, Employers Guide).[8] Indeed, the EEOC has suggested that asking applicants to voluntarily self-identify as having a disability is appropriate as long as applicants are not disadvantaged if they choose not to self-report such data, and as long as the organization uses the data only for affirmative action purposes (Vodanovich & Rupp, 2022). However, this language seems to refer to asking individuals simply if they have a disability (cf., OFCCP Voluntary Self Identification Form). It is unclear whether organizations would be allowed to ask employees if they would voluntarily disclose the *nature or severity* of their disability, two pieces of information that could be important for grouping individuals for the sake of adverse impact analyses —an issue we discuss next.

A broader challenge (one that goes beyond data collection restrictions) is identifying the correct individuals to include in comparative, adverse impact analyses. Although some legal commentators note that those with disabilities can be grouped together in a similar manner to race or sex (Stein & Waterstone, 2006), grouping based on disability status faces barriers race and sex groupings do not. Stein and Waterstone (2006) make the case that many individuals with disabilities can be similarly affected by policies and practices, making adverse impact investigations appropriate. However, innumerable impairments exist as well as important qualitative differences between the experiences of the individuals with the same general impairments, which makes grouping these impairments into manageable categories to calculate adverse impact challenging. For example, in *Prewitt v. United States Postal Serv.* (1981) the court states:

> one difference [referring to disparate impact as it is typically applied, as compared to the application of disparate impact under the ADA] ... is that, when assessing the disparate impact of a facially-neutral criterion, courts must be careful not to group all handicapped [*sic*] persons into one class, or even into broad subclasses. This is because "the fact that an employer employs fifteen epileptics [*sic*] is not necessarily probative of whether he or she has discriminated against a blind person [*sic*]."[9]

The many possible qualitative differences between any two individuals with (the same or different) impairments (and thus how they are affected by organizational practices) is likely at least part of the reason the definition of disability within the ADA is clearly focused on how an individual's life is impacted by an impairment, not their medical diagnosis (ADA, 2008). Adding additional complexity to this challenge, two individuals with the same disability may have differing abilities to carry out the essential functions of a job, with or without a reasonable accommodation. Evidence of this ability is one of the requirements for making a *prima facie* ADA case of discrimination (Gutman et al., 2011; Vodanovich & Rupp, 2022).

Courts and regulatory agencies have provided differing opinions on how individuals can provide evidence that they have faced adverse impact under the ADA, as well as the extent to which gathering data and comparing one's group to other groups in the organizations is necessary. The ADA specifically dictates that selection criteria cannot disproportionately screen out *individuals* with disabilities or a class of individuals with disabilities. This language suggests that, unlike Title VII, a single plaintiff with a disability can make a claim that an organization's neutral policy or practice disadvantages them, *individually* (*Williams v. ABM Parking Servs*, 2017). However, in practice, the courts have made contrary rulings on whether individuals can provide evidence that they were individually disadvantaged or whether they must provide subgroup statistical comparisons to evidence adverse impact. Below we review (1) court opinions that have focused on specific statistical evidence of a neutral practice's impact on subgroups with and without disabilities (i.e., typical adverse impact statistics); (2) court rulings that have allowed a broader use of subgroup statistical comparisons to indicate adverse impact; and (3) court rulings that have allowed an *individual* to argue they were disadvantaged by a neutral practice due to their disability (see Table 6.3).

Table 6.3

***Criteria Required for Plaintiffs to Meet Their Disparate Impact
Prima Facie Burden Under the ADA***

1. Plaintiff proves they qualify under the ADA's standard of "disability" by showing that
    they:
    - Have an impairment that "substantially limits one or more major life activities"
      (ADA, 1990) **OR**
    - Have a record of the impairment **OR**
    - Have been regarded as being impaired
2. Plaintiff shows they can perform the essential job functions with or without
    accommodations by showing the ability to perform:
    - the job tasks that the position exists to perform
    - the tasks for which there are a limited number of other employees available to
      perform
    - the (specialized) tasks that the plaintiff was/would be hired to perform
3. Plaintiff provides evidence of adverse impact (i.e., that a selection measure
    disproportionately screens out those with disabilities)

**Cases involving specific subgroup comparisons of selection rates
(e.g., flow statistics).** Several circuit courts have opined that group-based,
statistical evidence (seemingly, perhaps, from the same organization) is
necessary for an ADA disparate impact case. In *Lopez v. Pac. Mar. Ass'n*
(2011) the Ninth Circuit Court heard a disability case wherein the plaintiff, a recovering drug addict, was rejected from the applicant pool after
testing positive for marijuana during a pre-employment drug test. More
importantly, the company's "one-strike rule" prevented the plaintiff from
consideration for any future jobs with the organization. The applicant
alleged this "one-strike rule" created adverse impact for recovered drug
addicts. The Ninth Circuit rejected this argument as the plaintiff did not
provide statistical or anecdotal evidence that the rule resulted in a lower
number of qualified, recovering drug addicts being selected for the job
compared to the proportion in the (potential) applicant pool. However,
the court noted that it did not consider the aspects of the ADA statute
that specifically address selection practices screening out individuals with
disabilities (Sec. 12112 (b)(6)). Instead, this ruling was issued based on the
plaintiff's argument that disparate impact under the ADA should follow
the rules outlined under Title VII. The court stated:

> although Defendant will never hire those people and thus their selec-
> tion rate always will be zero, we still do not know how many recovered
> drug addicts Defendant hires versus how many recovered drug addicts it
> turns away, nor do we know how many of those turned away are not drug
> addicts, recovering or otherwise to create a genuine issue of fact. Under
> the theory that Plaintiff chose to pursue, Plaintiff must have produced

evidence from which a factfinder reasonably could conclude that the one-strike rule results in fewer recovered drug addicts in Defendant's employ, as compared to the number of qualified recovered drug addicts in the relevant labor market.

Interestingly, the dissenting opinion does acknowledge the burden placed on plaintiffs under this ruling (cf. Pregerson, 2011). Specifically, Judge Pregerson argued that statistical evidence for disparate impact cases should not be required under the ADA and that such a requirement would be unreasonable given the low likelihood that recovering addicts would be willing to identify themselves for data collection.

Corroborating the majority opinion of *Lopez* (2011), in *Roberts v. City of Chicago* (2016), the Seventh Circuit Court opined that plaintiffs must provide "factual content" demonstrating a significant disparity between those with and without disabilities to provide evidence that the defendant's medical screenings disproportionately disadvantaged those with disabilities. Similarly, in *Smith v. Miami-Dade County* (2015), the 11th Circuit Court ruled against a plaintiff who asserted that a refusal to rehire employees with a history of absences disparately impacts those with disabilities. The court stated that the plaintiff would have needed to provide comparative evidence (between employees with and without disabilities) convincing enough to infer causation as opposed to demonstrating that a small number of people were impacted by a neutral policy. This standard poses a challenge given that many organizations do not collect disability data, or even if they do, data that specifies the precise nature of employees' disabilities. This means applicants are very unlikely to have access to the data they would need to initiate a case. From an ethical perspective, organizations' careful consideration of how such data could be collected could improve their ability to identify and investigate potentially problematic practices that are suppressing their ability to maintain a diverse workforce.

In general, these jurisdictions have set standards for evidencing adverse impact similar to the approach taken within HRM (i.e., statistical evidence that one demographic subgroup is disadvantaged compared to another by a specific practice). Research studies have explored the race-based adverse impact potential of selection tools such as cognitive ability tests, personality inventories, and assessment centers (e.g., Ployhart & Holtz, 2008). This research (along with research on the impact of various selection strategies on adverse impact, e.g., Finch et al., 2009; Rupp et al., 2020) can give organizations an idea of the extent to which their own practices might disadvantage specific groups, and prompt targeted, local investigations of these practices. However, the extent to which we will ever be able to amass enough empirical data on subgroup differences across disability subgroups to be useful in this manner is questionable given the barriers to collecting and analyzing such data.

Cases involving broader sociological evidence (stock statistics). The broader history of disparate impact case law suggests that there is a certain amount of flexibility in how adverse impact can be evidenced (beyond demonstrating that a specific organization's policy disadvantaged a specific subgroup of applicants). In the case that set the standards for disparate impact, *Griggs v. Duke Power Co.* (1971), plaintiffs did not provide the specific statistics of how the practice of requiring the completion of high school resulted in a disproportionate number of White employees selected to transfer into higher paying jobs at Duke Power. For example, they did not provide statistics showing that fewer Black candidates were selected for these jobs compared to White candidates due to the criteria of requiring the completion of high school). Instead, the court considered census data showing that fewer Black individuals, relative to White individuals, obtained high school diplomas. Thus, the disadvantage for Black applicants of requiring a high school education could be inferred. Some cases have also allowed for statistics where the demographic composition of the organization was compared to that of the relevant labor market (Kuang & Ramos, 2017; Saxena & Morris, 2019; as is also implied in *Lopez v. Pac. Mar. Ass'n,* 2011). These approaches provide opportunities to demonstrate adverse impact even when data is challenging to obtain.

The Fifth Circuit Court has set a different standard for disparate impact evidence. This standard requires subgroup comparisons, but does not necessarily require statistical evidence. Specifically, in *Garcia v. Woman's Hospital of Texas* (1996), the court ruled that the plaintiff could meet her *prima facie* burden for a pregnancy-related disparate impact case (wherein a nurse was fired for the inability to lift 150 pounds) by providing evidence from a medical professional that "all or substantially all pregnant women would be advised by their obstetrician not to lift 150 pounds," shifting the burden to the employer to prove that lifting 150 pounds is job-relevant or a business necessity for nurses. This opinion was affirmed in *Stout v. Baxter Healthcare Corp.* (2002) where the court noted that it is possible for plaintiffs to meet their *prima facie* burden for a disparate impact case without providing statistical evidence. Importantly, court opinions have noted that in these instances, an "all or substantially all" requirement should be applied if probative statistics are not used. For example, in the Fifth Circuit case *Wallace v. Magnolia Family Services LLC.* (2015), the plaintiffs argued that statistics should not be needed to establish that Black individuals were disproportionately impacted by criminal background checks. However, the court did not agree with this argument, considering the plaintiff could not offer any kind of proof that substantially all Black individuals have criminal backgrounds.

The *Garcia* ruling may shed light on how adverse impact can be evidenced by individual plaintiffs in ADA cases. For example, when examining the adverse impact of an interview on applicants with Autism, evidence can be found within the definition of the disorder diagnosis itself, with lower social and communicative proficiency characterizing (perhaps substantially all) all individuals with this diagnosis (CDC, 2020a).[10] Therefore, if circuit courts are willing to accept evidence from medical experts that symptoms of certain disorders or conditions would prevent substantially all applicants with this disability from successfully engaging in the selection process, despite being qualified for the job, establishing a *prima facie* case of disparate treatment under the ADA becomes more achievable.

Ultimately, these approaches create some additional ideas for how disability-related adverse impact can be studied in HRM research. While still susceptible to many of the same barriers we describe above (availability and accuracy of disability data), approaching disability-related adverse impact research from a broader perspective and drawing inferences from the results might allow some additional opportunities for investigations. For example, researchers might be able to compare the practices of organizations with high as compared to low disability representation.

Cases involving individual situations. The circuit courts that have set precedent requiring statistical comparison evidence for demonstrating adverse impact under the ADA disparate impact framework have seemingly placed a high burden on plaintiffs. However, several courts and regulatory agencies have acknowledged adverse impact as a potentially individual-level concept, mostly in cases that have seemingly been approached within an accommodation framework. In these cases, courts have acknowledged that individuals with disabilities have been screened out by an organization's practices or criteria, entirely bypassing the process of demonstrating that a whole group of individuals is disadvantaged by a neutral practice. Instead, these cases focus on a single individual who was disadvantaged.

For example, in *Rohr v. Salt River Project Agric. Improvement & Power Dist* (2009), the Ninth Circuit assessed an accommodation case that spoke directly to adverse impact and disparate impact concepts. Specifically, the defendant argued that a plaintiff was not qualified for a welding job as the plaintiff was not able to complete a recurrent respirator certification test (due to his high blood pressure, a symptom of diabetes). However, using the section of the ADA that references adverse impact/disparate impact concepts (i.e., organizations are prohibited from using non-job-related tests that tend to screen out individuals with disabilities), the plaintiff argued the test itself was discriminatory. The court opined that after

[i]t was undisputed that the respirator certification test screened out the employee due to his high blood pressure, which was a complication of his diabetes.

This means that the court (in a decision that seemingly contradicts the Ninth Circuit's earlier ruling in *Lopez v. Pac. Mar. Ass'n*, 2011), accepted the premise that a test (disparately) screened out the individual employee due to the employee's disability (without requiring evidence that other employees with disabilities were similarly disadvantaged). Consequently, the organization was required to defend the test by providing proof that the test was related to the (essential) functions of the job and consistent with business necessity, which the organization failed to do.[11] A similar example appears in an EEOC final decision on federal appeals (Blue, 2015).[12] Specifically, no statistical evidence was used to determine that a woman with a shoulder injury was disadvantaged by a 70-pound lifting standard (*Complainant v. USPS*, 2013). Subsequently, the EEOC determined that the test did not comprise careful measurement of the employee's abilities to perform the essential job functions (i.e., USPS employees were not frequently required to lift 70 pounds).

Other courts have explicitly considered the appropriateness of the concept of adverse impact on an individual basis via a disparate impact framework (e.g., *Williams v. ABM Parking Servs.*, 2017. In *Leskovisek v. Ill. Dep't of Transp.* (2018), an Illinois district judge noted the inconsistency between *Roberts v. City of Chicago* (2016) and section 12112(b)(6) of the ADA. Although previous precedent in Illinois (*Roberts v. City of Chicago*, 2016) states that plaintiffs must show that the organization's qualification standard caused a significant disparity between groups with and without disabilities within a disparate impact case, in *Leskovisek v. Ill. Dep't of Transp.* (2018), the Illinois district judge still allowed the disparate impact claim at hand to proceed into discovery despite the lack of statistical proof of adverse impact (i.e., subgroup disadvantage). This decision was based on the language in section 12112(b)(6) of the ADA that prohibits selection procedures that screen out *individuals* with disabilities. This Illinois judge specified that the issue could be raised again after discovery and that the plaintiffs could also have an opportunity during discovery to obtain statistical evidence of adverse impact. The court later determined that statistical evidence was not needed to meet the *prima facie* burden (*Leskovisek v. Ill. Dep't of Transp.*, 2020), but the court also labeled this case (wherein an individual is screened out due to their disability) as being a "disparate treatment type claim" rather than a disparate impact claim (disparate treatment is a different legal framework under the ADA; Gutman et al., 2011). The inconsistency between the requirement of statistical evidence under the disparate impact framework and the language of the ADA is an issue requiring deeper analysis (Alvarez et al., 2011).

Ultimately, approaching adverse impact on an individual basis presents interesting opportunities for future adverse impact research. Thinking about adverse impact in this way would allow for a more inclusive study of adverse impact, theoretically (while presenting new challenges for studying adverse impact empirically). Although evidence of adverse impact has typically been defined within the HRM literature as either mean differences across groups or group differences in selection ratios, we suggest that the legal literature we review here demonstrates that HRM adverse impact research should reevaluate what would appropriately evidence that an ostensibly neutral system was disadvantaging an individual with a disability. Specifically, researchers must consider whether group statistics are necessary or whether alternative evidence (e.g., evidence that can rely on the experiences of individuals) is able to provide rigorous and sufficient support for the presence of adverse impact.

Using Legal Perspectives to Inform HRM Research on Identifying Adverse Impact. Courts have taken differing positions on how job applicants can demonstrate adverse impact in the context of disability. As evidenced above, some of these approaches are unique to the disability context (i.e., allowing single individuals to argue they have been victims of adverse impact without showing supporting statistics). For courts that have required statistical evidence, it is unclear how they would decide which employees can be appropriately grouped together as being in the same "disability group" (though *B.C. v. Mount Vernon Sch. Dist.*, 2016, may provide preliminary insight[13]). However, these different legal perspectives can still inform how the HRM field might approach adverse impact research. Specifically, researchers should decide what adverse impact means theoretically and what empirical evidence would be sufficient to support the presence of adverse impact. Once adverse impact in the disability context is defined theoretically and empirically, academic research focused on uncovering adverse impact relevant to specific impairments/severity of impairments and specific selection methods could be illustrative to organizations and courts attempting to understand the disability-related adverse impact potential of various selection tools.

Establishing ADA-Compliant Job-Relatedness for Selection Practices

The potentially wide-reaching implications of disability-related adverse impact (i.e., across many different forms of disability and selection practices) requires a systematic and comprehensive approach to researching how disability-related adverse impact can be mitigated while not sacrificing selection practices that demonstrate strong predictive validity. The heart of this process consists of ensuring that successful performance of a job is carefully and fairly defined, and the selection practices used are job-relevant and therefore predict which applicants become successful performers. The ADA has much to offer in terms of understanding how successful job performance can be reasonably established in a manner inclusive to those with disabilities.

ADA and Job-Relatedness. To defend a charge of disparate impact in selection procedures under the ADA, employers must show that the practice that adversely impacts a disabled group is job-related, consistent with business necessity, and cannot be reasonably accommodated (29 CFR § 1630.15). Unlike the typical accommodation case, this step places a burden on the organization to justify the appropriateness of job qualifications or selection processes. This relieves the plaintiff from specifying and justifying an unmet accommodation during the selection process involving tools that were not job-related in the first place.

A ruling by the Ninth Circuit Court and a final decision made by the EEOC on a federal appeal further suggest that employers may even need to successfully defend a selection tool as being job-relevant *for essential job functions* (*Bates v. United States Parcel Serv.*, 2007; *Complainant v. USPS*, 2013), meaning job performance should not be considered in its entirety if it typically includes *nonessential* tasks or KSAOs. The EEOC published criteria for determining the essentiality of job functions (EEOC, 1991): (1) whether the job was created to serve the function or perform the task; (2) whether the task needs to be performed by one or a few individuals or can be distributed amongst many employees; (3) whether the task necessitates a high degree of skill and expertise.

The sparse amount of case law on disparate impact under Title I of the ADA means that we cannot confidently predict how future litigation under the ADA will unfold across various courts. However, these tentative legal perspectives offer HRM researchers a fruitful path forward for considering how validation processes can be modified to be more inclusive to those with disabilities (even before individual selection practices are chosen).

Using Legal Perspectives to Inform HRM Research on Validation. Through job analysis, the most important elements of a job, as well as the KSAOs needed to carry out these behaviors can be systematically identified (Morgeson et al., 2019). Job analysis data then form the basis for developing valid and fair HR systems by allowing organizations to develop and test whether selection practices are related to the job. These data also provide evidence that organizations can use to defend themselves if their selection methods are legally challenged. That being said, research has suggested that even job analyses completed with the best intentions can fail to represent inclusive perspectives on a job (Strah & Rupp, 2022).

To prioritize disability-related inclusivity and maximize ADA compliance, job analyses can identify the *essential* functions of jobs and the KSAOs (and minimum proficiency levels) needed to carry out these functions. Although the concept of identifying job functions and tying predictor constructs (i.e., KSAOs) to these job functions through job analysis is not new (Gatewood et al., 2015), attending to which job functions are *essential* adds an extra complication to job analysis procedures as not all tasks (even those rated as important) are necessarily essential.

The EEOC specifies that evidence of the essentiality of such tasks can be provided by (1) work experiences articulated by employees; (2) the amount of time employees spend on the task; (3) the severity of the consequence to the organization of the employee not completing the function; and (4) collective bargaining agreement stipulations (EEOC, 1991). The EEOC also considers employers' perceptions of essential job functions and the functions listed in job descriptions. Each of these strategies for assessing essentiality of job functions are either frequently used components of a job analysis or can be incorporated into a job analysis (Brannick et al., 1992; Gatewood et al., 2015; Mitchell et al., 1997; Morgeson et al., 2019). For example, employees can be asked to rate the severity of consequences that would result from any single employee not completing each task and how many other employees are typically able to substitute for an individual employee to complete each job function/task.

Mitchell et al. (1997) also suggested that employers could improve disability inclusion by conducting a job analysis focused on the outcomes required for a job as opposed to the actual tasks themselves (i.e., an outcome versus process orientation). Indeed, these authors suggested the job analysis method that could be most easily modified for ADA purposes is a functional job analysis, which focuses on the reasons why certain functions are needed, allowing different employee processes to reach the desired outcomes. This allows flexibility in how employees complete work, so long as a suitable result is reached. Job analysts can also identify minimum KSAO requirements (e.g., sensory, motor, and cognitive) for the essential job functions that would later serve as an important baseline to inform which selection practices are most appropriate (i.e., which practices represent both underlying constructs and method formats that align with the KSAOs needed for the job). Thus, applicants, in the selection context, are not expected to meet standards not required by the job itself. Such data may also inform which types of impairments may need to be accommodated as applicants work through the selection process, and what sorts of accommodations might be appropriate for different types and levels of disabilities.

Proposition 2: Conducting a diversity-inclusive job analysis (one focused on essential job functions) will allow selection practices to be chosen that contain less adverse impact against individuals with disabilities.

Further, while conducting a job analysis, multiple other types of information (i.e., equipment or tools used, working conditions) can be evaluated to proactively identify components of the job (for either essential or nonessential functions[14]) that can likely be accommodated, and existing accommodations for the job can also be identified.[15]

Using job analysis to parse through the different components of jobs (e.g., essential vs. nonessential; tasks vs. outcomes) also provides new and interesting avenues for understanding job performance, which has historically faced measurement challenges (Cascio & Aguinis, 2011). For example, it would be of both theoretical and practical value to better understand what makes some job tasks important to an organization, yet not essential to the job.

Building Inclusive Systems Via Every Component of a Selection System

The context of disability highlights the importance of ensuring the job-relevance and inclusiveness of every component of a selection system.

ADA and Individual Aspects of Selection Tools. The ADA states that discrimination in selection also constitutes:

> failing to select and administer tests concerning employment in the most effective manner to ensure that, when such test is administered to a job applicant or employee who has a disability ... such test results accurately reflect the skills, aptitude or whatever other factor of such applicant or employee that such test purports to measure, rather than reflecting the [impairment] of such employee or applicant. (ADA, 2008)

This passage implies that organizations should either ensure all aspects of a selection tool are job-relevant (e.g., only administer paper and pencil cognitive ability tests if it can be proven that all abilities required to complete the test are necessary for essential job functions), or, more realistically, identify both the job-related and the non-job-related aspects of each selection tool, so that alternative approaches to measuring KSAOs can be proactively developed.

Understanding precisely what is legally required by ADA 42 U.S. Code § 1211 – Discrimination (b)(7) when a disparate impact claim is being pursued is complicated. In most legal cases to date, if an employee cannot manage

Adverse Impact and Disability Status   197

the testing format, they would be expected to ask for an accommodation. However, using a disparate impact perspective, it is conceivable that disadvantaged employees, after an organization demonstrates that a selection tool is job-related, could then defer to the typical third stage of a disparate impact claim, by arguing that there is an alternative selection tool that is similarly job-related but causes less adverse impact. We have no knowledge of such an argument being used or responded to positively by the courts. However, this hypothetical scenario is useful for moving research forward by demonstrating the need to introduce nuance into our understanding of adverse impact in individual aspects of selection tools. Doing so informs how we can build HRM systems that are as preemptively inclusive to those with disabilities as possible.

Applying a Modular Approach to Increase Precision. Identifying the non-job-related aspects of a selection tool gives organizations the opportunity to mitigate non-job-related adverse impact. However, identifying such non-job-related aspects of selection tools can pose a problem for employers, given that selection tools are often conceptualized and studied holistically (e.g., adverse impact is typically studied for interviews as a whole; e.g., Ployhart & Holtz, 2008). Indeed, Arthur and Villado (2008) pointed out that predictor constructs (underlying job-relevant KSAOs) and predictor methods are often confounded, meaning we are often unsure whether adverse impact resides in the underlying KSAO of interest or the method of measuring that underlying KSAO. Addressing this conundrum is complicated by the fact that some commonly-used selection practices (e.g., interviews) often do not even report the underlying constructs of interest.

To address this limitation, Lievens and Sackett (2017) suggested that researchers and practitioners should adopt a *modular approach* to selection by breaking down each selection tool into its individual aspects: (1) the features of the method used to measure the underlying construct; and (2) the features of the underlying construct (i.e., KSAO) itself. This allows the cause of adverse impact to be more carefully traced to its specific source.

Methods used. Lievens and Sackett (2017) provided a useful taxonomy for characterizing predictor methods, which includes: stimulus format (e.g., textual, auditory); contextualization (i.e., to what extent the procedural context corresponds to the actual job); stimulus presentation consistency (the extent to which content presented to applicants is standardized and consistent); response format (the way in which applicants must respond to stimuli); response evaluation consistency (the level of standardization in evaluation of applicant scores); information source (e.g., self-reports; behavioral decisions; other reports); and instructions (i.e., general versus specific). The implications of each of these method choices were then summarized in terms of validity, construct saturation, subgroup differences, and applicant perceptions. This framework provides an invaluable resource to examine trade-offs in selection. However, the subgroup differences summarized are almost exclusively focused on Black-White differences, mirroring the extant adverse impact research and demonstrating the need for work on the role of disability within this framework.

As we have indicated throughout this chapter, when considering the disability-related inclusivity inherent to a selection system, to the furthest extent possible, the features of the method used to assess underlying constructs (KSAOs) should reflect the essential functions of the job. For example, a written cognitive ability test should reflect not only the cognitive abilities essential for the job, but also the visual abilities required. However, this goal is often not achievable. Therefore, at a minimum, all features of a method need to be examined for whether they are tied to the job's essential functions. If a method feature is not tied to the job's essential functions, but also generally does not appear likely to lower the predictive validity of the predictor construct, it may make sense to retain this method for the overall applicant sample. However, the company should begin to proactively assess alternative forms of this selection procedure (with foundationally equivalent method features) so that these alternative methods can be provided as accommodations when requested. Thus, research on alternative method features for measuring various underlying constructs is imperative. Increasing the flexibility of selection systems through this approach will enable organizations to respond to some of the most common accommodation needs that may be requested.[16]

Assessing an underlying construct in alternative yet equivalent ways is a complex undertaking. For example, the American College Testing (ACT) organization conducts extensive studies to evaluate and compare paper-and-pencil and online versions of a test to ensure construct equivalence and score comparability and to examine issues such as the time given to take the test (ACT, 2020). Concerns of test equivalency across different formats are valid, as was revealed in Lievens and Sackett's (2006) conclusion that, despite maintaining equivalent construct content, a video-based format of a situational judgement test demonstrated stronger criterion validity compared to the paper version of the test. Lievens and Sackett's (2017) framework gives researchers and practitioners a starting point for evaluating which methods are likely to affect the validity of tests. However, this work reveals that extensive future work is needed both in the realm of academia and practice to determine both appropriate tool equivalency and subgroup differences across typically used method features, within specific contexts.

Underlying constructs (KSAOs) measured. Although applicants with disabilities are more likely to challenge or request an accommodation for a method as opposed to an underlying construct (especially if that construct is clearly job-related), the organization still holds the ethical and social responsibility to ensure that the choice of KSAOs assessed during selection does not cause unfair adverse impact. That being said, preventing unnecessary adverse impact of predictor constructs requires deeper theoretical thought and empirical testing beyond stopping at the conclusion that an entire test is, or is not related to essential job functions.

For example, even though cognitive tests are predictive of performance across numerous jobs, the level of cognitive ability needed for different positions varies based on different factors (e.g., job complexity; Schmidt & Hunter, 1998, 2004), suggesting that the use of minimum cut scores might be more appropriate than a top-down selection strategy in some situations (in that it forces the organization to not screen out candidates who indeed have a level of KSAO proficiency commensurate with carrying out the most critical—and in the context of the ADA, essential—job tasks).[17] Additionally, subdimensions of cognitive ability can differentially predict job performance across different types of jobs (Schneider & Newman, 2015). This is important, as prior evidence suggests that subdimensions of cognitive ability can have different sub-group differences (e.g., across race; Outtz & Newman, 2010). The same concerns pertain to disability-related adverse impact. Therefore, the specific facets of constructs measured in a selection context need to be considered based on their own associations to the essential job functions (in relation to both content and criterion validity, as well as adverse impact pertaining to multiple demographic factors)—and not generalized validity evidence about the higher-order construct—to ensure they are appropriate for local use. Including dimensions of a construct that are not theoretically justified not only artificially limits the opportunities of those scoring lower on this dimension (which may vary by disability status), but also weakens the predictive validity of the predictor.

> **Proposition 3:** Considering the independent components of selection practices (e.g., underlying construct, methods used to assess construct) will allow organizational researchers to identify the source of disability-relevant adverse impact and mitigate this adverse impact where appropriate.

Additional Considerations in Creating Inclusive Selection Systems

Even though organizational researchers can investigate ways to make selection tools valid, inclusive to individuals with disabilities, and easily accommodated, no one can anticipate every accommodation that might be required. From a legal perspective, organizations are asked to flexibly and independently consider each accommodation requested. Indeed, previous work suggests that most accommodations requested are reasonable cost-wise (typically less than $500; Lee, 1996). From a practical perspective, it is worthwhile to consider that appropriate selection processes should be developed to assess individual applicants with disabilities if there is any doubt as to whether that applicant could or could not perform the essential functions of the job. A careful review of an applicant's previous work experience or a work sample may provide such information (Roth et al., 2005). Although work samples may be expensive and therefore impractical to integrate into typical selection systems, in some cases, allowing an applicant with a disability to perform the job function allows the highest level of fidelity in making such determinations, especially if they are able to demonstrate how they would complete the task with an accommodation. As such, developing an option for (even infrequent) work samples may also be in an organization's best interest.

Finally, we urge organizational researchers to interact with law-makers, attorneys, judges, litigation consultants, relevant agencies (e.g., EEOC), and legal scholars within this domain. Such interactions would not only allow organizational researchers to better understand the standards for providing evidence of adverse impact (which could further inform adverse impact research and the practical application of this research), but also potentially give organizational science a voice in future legislation and court opinions. Indeed, the field of HRM is well-positioned to offer thoughtful contributions to such policy decisions, particularly as research in disability-related adverse impact grows.

CONCLUSION

Within our review, we sought to highlight the importance of future psychological and HRM research on disability-related adverse impact. To do this, we first discussed the likelihood that common selection tools will produce disability-related adverse impact. Second, we discussed barriers to studying disability-related adverse impact, and used the legal literature as a lens to understand each of these barriers more deeply, as well as some potential solutions to these issues. Within this chapter, we did not argued that one specific tool or a combination of tools will increase the inclusion of people with disabilities. Instead, we argue that: (1) assessing disability-related adverse impact is important, and organizational researchers should develop theoretically and practically sound approaches to assess how individuals with disabilities are disadvantaged by facially neutral selection systems; (2) the criterion used in validation studies (i.e., job performance) should be carefully considered in terms of what components of a job are necessary (and likely essential); and (3) a modular approach to selection, wherein specific aspects of selection tools are assessed (e.g., constructs, formats), should be adopted to create a more nuanced approach to increasing inclusivity within selection. Ultimately, we believe this review offers theoretical and practical insights into the study of disability-related adverse impact and proposes an important research agenda wherein HRM scholars can advance an area of disability research which has heretofore been largely ignored.

REFERENCES

ACT. (2020). *ACT Technical Manual.* https://www.act.org/content/dam/act/unsecured/documents/ACT_Technical_Manual.pdf

Albemarle Paper Company. v. Moody, 422 U.S. 405 (1975).

Americans with Disabilities Act. (1990). Federal Register 56: 35726-35756.

Americans With Disabilities Act Amendments. (2008), 42 U.S.C. § 12101 et seq.

Alvarez, F. P., Nieman, M. F., & Russo, K. J. (2011, March). *Ninth circuit divided on applicable proof for disparate impact ADA claim brought by former addict.* JacksonLewis. https://www.jacksonlewis.com/resources-publication/ninth-circuit-divided-applicable-proof-disparate-impact-ada-claim-brought-former-addict

Arthur, W., Jr., & Villado, A. J. (2008). The importance of distinguishing between constructs and methods when comparing predictors in personnel selection research and practice. *Journal of Applied Psychology, 93*(2), 435–442.

BC v. Mount Vernon School Dist., 837 F.3d 152 (2d Cir. 2016).

Bates v. United Parcel Serv., Inc., 511 F.3d 974, 990 (9th Cir., 2007).

Bertelli, M. O., Cooper, S. A., & Salvador-Carulla, L. (2018). Intelligence and specific cognitive functions in intellectual disability: Implications for assessment and classification. *Current Opinion in Psychiatry, 31*(2), 88–95.

Blue, E. P. (2015). Job functions, standards, and accommodations under the ADA: Recent EEOC decisions. *Louis University Journal of Heath Law and Policy, 9,* 19–34.

Bobko, P., & Roth, P. L. (2013). Reviewing, categorizing, and analyzing the literature on Black-White mean differences for predictors of job performance: Verifying some perceptions and updating/correcting others. *Personnel Psychology, 66*(1), 91–126.

Brannick, M. T., Brannick, J. P., & Levine, E. L. (1992). Job analysis, personnel selection, and the ADA. *Human Resource Management Review, 2*(3), 171–182.

Bureau of Labor Statistics. (2021). *Persons with a disability: Labor force characteristics summary.* Economic News Release: https://www.bls.gov/news.release/disabl.nr0.htm

Cascio, W. F., & Aguinis, H. (2011). *Applied psychology in human resource management.* Pearson Prentice Hall.

Centers for Disease Control and Prevention. (2020a). *Autism spectrum disorder (ASD): What is ASD?* https://www.cdc.gov/ncbddd/autism/facts.html

Centers for Disease Control and Prevention. (2020b). *Disability and health promotion: Impairments, activity limitations, and participations restrictions.* https://www.cdc.gov/ncbddd/disabilityandhealth/disability.html

Colella, A., & Bruyère, S. (2011). Disability and employment. In S. Zedeck (Ed.), *APA handbook of industrial and organizational psychology* (Vol. 1, pp. 473–504). American Psychological Association.

Complainant v. USPS, Appeal No. 0120080613, 2013 WL 8338375, at *4 (E.E.O.C. Dec. 23, 2013).

Crossley, M. (2004). Reasonable accommodation as part and parcel of the antidiscrimination project. *Rutgers Law Journal, 35(3),* 861–958.

Dean, M. A., Roth, P. L., & Bobko, P. (2008). Ethnic and gender subgroup differences in assessment center ratings: A meta-analysis. *Journal of Applied Psychology, 93*(3), 685–691.

Dunleavy, E. M., & Morris, S. B. (2017). An introduction to adverse impact measurement in the EEO context. In S. B. Morris & E. M. Dunleavy (Eds.), *Adverse impact analysis: Understanding data, statistics, and risk* (pp. 3–28). Psychology Press.

EEOC v. Wal-Mart Stores, Inc., 477 F.3d 561, 568 (8th Cir., 2007).

Equal Employment Opportunity Commission. (1991). *The ADA: Your responsibilities as an employer.* https://www.eeoc.gov/laws/guidance/ada-your-responsibilities-employer.

Equal Employment Opportunity Commission. (1995). *Enforcement guidance: Preemployment disability—related questions and medical examinations.* https://www.eeoc.gov/laws/guidance/enforcement-guidance-preemployment-disability-related-questions-and-medical

Equal Employment Opportunity Commission. (2002). *EEOC enforcement guidance: The ADA: questions and answers.* https://www.eeoc.gov/laws/guidance/ada-questions-and-answers

Finch, D. M., Edwards, B. D., & Wallace, J. C. (2009). Multistage selection strategies: Simulating the effects on adverse impact and expected performance for various predictor combinations. *Journal of Applied Psychology, 94*(2), 318.

Garcia v. Woman's Hospital of Texas, 97 f.3d 810 (1996).

Gatewood, R. D., Field, H. S., & Barrick, M. (2015). *Human resource selection* (9th ed.). Wessex Press Inc.

Griggs v. Duke Power Co., 401 U.S. 424 (1971).

Gutman, A., Koppes, L. L., & Vodanovich, S. J. (2011). *EEO law and personnel practices.* Psychology Press.

Hotchkiss, J. L. (2003). Compensation: Wages and Benefits. In *The Labor Market Experience of Workers with Disabilities: The ADA and Beyond* (pp. 49–72). W. E. Upjohn Institute for Employment Research.

Kotov, R., Krueger, R. F., Watson, D., Achenbach, T. M., Althoff, R. R., Bagby, R. M., Brown, T. A., Carpenter, W. T., Caspi, A., Clark, L. A., Eaton, N. R., Forbes, M. K., Forbush, K. T., Goldberg, D., Hasin, D., Hyman, S. E., Ivanova, M. Y., Lynam, D. R., Markon, K., … Zimmerman, M. (2017). The Hierarchical Taxonomy of Psychopathology (HiTOP): A dimensional alternative to traditional nosologies. *Journal of Abnormal Psychology, 126*(4), 454–477.

Kuang, D., & Ramos, M. (2017). Workforce composition and utilization analyses. In S. B. Morris & E. M. Dunleavy (Eds.), *Adverse impact analysis: Understanding data, statistics and risk* (pp. 126–146). Routledge.

Lee, B. (1996). Legal requirements and employer responses to accommodating employees with disabilities. *Human Resource Management Review, 6*, 231–251.

Leskovisek v. Ill. Dep't of Transp., 305 F. Supp. 3d 925,933 (C.D. Ill. 2018).

Leskovisek v. Ill. Dep't of Transp., 506 F. Supp. 3d 553 (C.D. Ill. 2020).

Lievens, F., & Sackett, P. R. (2006). Video-based versus written situational judgment tests: a comparison in terms of predictive validity. *Journal of Applied Psychology, 91*(5), 1181.

Lievens, F., & Sackett, P. R. (2017). The effects of predictor method factors on selection outcomes: A modular approach to personnel selection procedures. *Journal of Applied Psychology, 102*(1), 43–66.

Lopez v. Pac. Mar. Ass'n, 657 F.3d 762 (2011).

Melson-Silimon, A., Harris, A. M., Shoenfelt, E. L., Miller, J. D., & Carter, N. T. (2019). Personality testing and the Americans with Disabilities Act: Cause for concern as normal and abnormal personality models are integrated. *Industrial and Organizational Psychology, 12*(2), 119–132.

Mitchell, K. E., Alliger, G. M., & Morfopoulos, R. (1997). Toward an ADA-appropriate job analysis. *Human Resource Management Review, 7*(1), 5–26.

Morgeson, F. P., Brannick, M. T., & Levine, E. L. (2019). *Job and work analysis: Methods, research, and applications for human resource management.* SAGE.

Outtz, J. L., & Newman, D. A. (2010). *A theory of adverse impact.* Routledge/Taylor & Francis Group.

Pregerson. Dissenting opinion in Lopez v. Pac. Mar. Ass'n, 657 F.3d 762 (2011).

Ployhart, R. E., & Holtz, B. C. (2008). The diversity–validity dilemma: Strategies for reducing racioethnic and sex subgroup differences and adverse impact in selection. *Personnel Psychology, 61*(1), 153–172.

Prewitt v. United States Postal Serv., 662 F.2d 292 (5th Cir., 1981).

Raytheon Co. v. Hernandez, 540 U.S. 44 (2003).

Roberts v. City of Chicago, 817 F. 3d 561 (2016).

Rohr v. Salt River Project Agric. Improvement & Power Dist, 555 F. 3d 850 (9th Cir., 2009).

Roth, P. L., Bobko, P., & McFarland, L. A. (2005). A meta-analysis of work sample test validity: Updating and integrating some classic literature. *Personnel Psychology, 58*(4), 1009–1037.

Rupp, D. E., Song, Q. C., & Strah, N. (2020). Addressing the so-called validity–diversity trade-off: Exploring the practicalities and legal defensibility of Pareto-optimization for reducing adverse impact within personnel selection. *Industrial and Organizational Psychology, 13*(2), 246–271.

Santuzzi, A. M., & Waltz, P. R. (2016). Disability in the workplace: A unique and variable identity. *Journal of Management, 42*(5), 1111–1135.

Saulsman, L. M., & Page, A. C. (2003). Can trait measures diagnose personality disorders? *Current Opinion in Psychiatry, 16*(1), 83–88.

Saxena, M., & Morris, S. B. (2019). Adverse impact as disability discrimination: Illustrating the perils through self-control at work. *Industrial and Organizational Psychology, 12*(2), 138–142.

Schmidt, F. L., & Hunter, J. E. (1998). The validity and utility of selection methods in personnel psychology: Practical and theoretical implications of 85 years of research findings. *Psychological Bulletin, 124*(2), 262–274.

Schmidt, F. L., & Hunter, J. (2004). General mental ability in the world of work: Occupational attainment and job performance. *Journal of Personality and Social Psychology, 86*(1), 162–173.

Schneider, W. J., & Newman, D. A. (2015). Intelligence is multidimensional: Theoretical review and implications of specific cognitive abilities. *Human Resource Management Review, 25*(1), 12–27.

Shields, R. H., Kaat, A. J., McKenzie, F. J., Drayton, A., Sansone, S. M., Coleman, J., Michalak, C., Riley, K., Berry-Kravis, E., Gershon, R. C., Widaman, K. F., & Hessl, D. (2020). Validation of the NIH Toolbox Cognitive Battery in intellectual disability. *Neurology, 94*(12), e1229-e1240.

Smith v. Miami-Dade County, 621 Fed. Appx. 955 (2015).

Society for Industrial and Organizational Psychology. (2018). Principles for the validation and use of personnel selection procedures (5th ed.). *Industrial and Organizational Psychology, 11*(S1), 1–97.

Stein, M. A., & Waterstone, M. E. (2006). Disability, disparate impact and class actions. *Duke Law Journal, 56*, 861–922.

Stone-Romero, E. F. (2005). Personality-based stigmas and unfair discrimination in work organizations. In B. Dipboye & A. Colella (Eds.), *Discrimination at work: The psychological and organizational bases* (pp. 255–281). Erlbaum.

Strah, N., & Rupp, D. E. (2022). Are there cracks in our foundation? An integrative review of diversity issues in job analysis. *Journal of Applied Psychology, 107*(7), 1031–1051. https://doi.org/10.1037/apl0000989

Stout v. Baxter Healthcare Corp., 282 F.3d 856 (5th Cir. 2002).

Taylor, D. (2018). Americans with disabilities: 2014. *United States Census Bureau.* https://www.census.gov/content/dam/Census/ library/publications/2018/demo/p70-152.pdf

Vodanovich, S. J., & Rupp, D. E. (2022). *Employment Discrimination: A Concise Review of the Legal Landscape.* Oxford University Press.

Wallace v. Magnolia Family Servs., LLC, 2014 WL 7369673, *3 (E.D. La. Dec. 29, 2014).

Williams v. ABM Parking Servs., 296 F. Supp. 3d 779 (E.D. VA, Oct. 31, 2017).

Wiernik, B. M., Bornovalova, M., Stark, S. E., & Ones, D. S. (2019). Constructs versus measures in personality and other domains: What distinguishes normal and clinical? *Industrial and Organizational Psychology, 12*(2), 157–162.

NOTES

1. We also note that individuals with disabilities face a number of other barriers to success in the workforce (e.g., low compensation, Hotchkiss, 2003).
2. We use the term "ostensibly" here to draw attention to how selection tools and methods can seemingly be neutral in that they may not purposefully discriminate against individuals with disabilities, but nonetheless disadvantage these individuals.

3. Note we use both the terms adverse impact and disparate impact throughout this text. Even though these terms are often used interchangeably by many scholars, following Dunleavy and Morris (2017), we use the term disparate impact to refer to the specific legal theory of discrimination and adverse impact to refer to evidence that a neutral practice results in a disadvantage for a legally protected group (a disadvantage which, as we cover later, may be defensible within a disparate impact framework).

4. Although the employee has the burden of demonstrating that they can perform the essential functions of the job, several courts have ruled that the employer must communicate the essential functions of the job so that the employee can argue/demonstrate they can complete these functions (*Bates v. UPS*, 2007; *EEOC v. Wal-Mart Stores Inc.*, 2007).

5. Evidence of these criteria that are considered by the EEOC include (1) an employer's judgement, (2) a job description (written prior to job advertisement and selection), (3) the work experiences of previous or current employees, 4) amount of time that employees spend on the job function, (4) the consequences that result from the function not being performed by the employee in question, (5) standards set by collective bargaining agreements (EEOC, 1991).

6. For example, Kotov et al. (2010) found that those with obsessive compulsive disorder (OCD) had higher neuroticism ($d = 2.07$), lower extraversion ($d = -1.12$), and lower conscientiousness ($d = -.97$) than those without OCD. Those with generalized anxiety disorder scored higher on neuroticism ($d = 1.96$), lower on extraversion ($d = -1.02$), and lower on conscientiousness ($d = -1.13$) compared to those without generalized anxiety disorder. Those with persistent depressive disorder (dysthymia) scored higher on neuroticism ($d = 1.93$), lower on extraversion ($d = -1.47$), lower on conscientiousness ($d = -1.24$), and lower on openness ($d = -.57$) than those without. Those with PTSD scored higher on neuroticism ($d = 2.25$), lower on extraversion ($d = -.79$), and lower on conscientiousness ($d = -1.02$) than those without. Saulsman and Page (2004) reported large correlations between neuroticism and borderline personality disorder ($r = .49$), avoidant personality disorder ($r = .48$), and dependent personality disorder ($r = .41$); between extraversion and histrionic personality disorder ($r = .42$) and avoidant personality disorder ($r = -.44$); and between agreeableness and paranoid personality disorder ($r = -.34$) and antisocial personality disorder ($r = -.35$).

7. Though we note such an approach would likely also be useful for adverse impact research, more broadly.

8. Disability-related question(s) should be asked in such a way that clearly indicates (1) providing disability information is voluntary; (2) the information will be used only to benefit those with disabilities; and (3) steps will be taken to ensure this disability-related data is kept confidential and only used for appropriate purposes as specified under the ADA. Data related to these inquiries need to also be gathered on a separate form such that applicants' disability information is not connected with their application. For online applications, this information should not be maintained in the same database as job applications.

9. We endeavored to use person-first language throughout this text. However, we sometimes necessarily deviated from this goal when directly quoting other sources.

10. Though we note that how a disability is defined by sources such as the CDC would not always align with (and in fact may often differ greatly from) disability as it is defined under the ADA.

11. As an aside, because the court was still unclear about whether the plaintiff was able to perform all essential job tasks, which, as we discussed above, is a necessary condition for a plaintiff to initiate an ADA case, the court remanded the case back to lower courts for further scrutiny.

12. The EEOC has the right to adjudicate discrimination complaints made against federal employers. Although not the same as traditional legal precedent, these cases give an indication of the logic the EEOC endorses.

13. In this Title II ADA case, a disparate impact charge was brought against a school for having a policy that assigned students to classes in a manner that disadvantaged those with disabilities. The plaintiffs provided statistics comparing the class assignments of students with and without disabilities, with disability labeled in the data based on students who qualified as disabled under the Individuals with Disabilities Education Act (IDEA). The Second Circuit Court ruled that these statistics were not sufficient as the IDEA disability categorization did not comprise sufficient overlap with the definition of a disability under the ADA, meaning it was unclear how many of the students identified as disabled in the data would be determined disabled under the ADA.

14. Both essential and nonessential job functions can be accommodated. However, if accommodations are not available or reasonable, employees with disabilities need not perform functions at all if they are not essential (ADA, 1992).

15. Accommodations are important for employers to document because proof of previous accommodations made can both inform employers on the plausibility of future requested accommodations and protect employers from mistakenly asserting that accommodations are not reasonable in a legal case when similar accommodations were previously made.

16. The website askjan.org provides helpful information about common disabilities and suggestions for how to provide accommodations.

17. The *Principles for the Validation and Use of Personnel Selection Procedures* (SIOP, 2018) explicitly recommend such an approach when diversity is a goal.

CHAPTER 7

DOES CONSCIOUS, SOCIAL, AND UNCONSCIOUS BIAS INFLUENCE EMPLOYMENT DECISIONS ABOUT MILITARY VETERANS?

Cristina Rosario DiPietropolo
Leader Essentials Group

Robert C. Ford
University of Central Florida

Henrique Correa
Rollins College

ABSTRACT

Research has shown that there are often conflicting stereotypes about military veterans (Stone, C. et al., 2017; Stone, C., & Stone, D., 2015). For instance, veterans are stereotyped as having mental health problems, including depression, post-traumatic stress disorder, unpredictable behaviors, and difficulties transitioning from military to civilian organizations (Schreger & Kimble, 2017). However, recent surveys revealed that veterans are often stereotyped positively today, and the majority of people in the U.S. believe

Forgotten Minorities in Organizations, pp. 207–238
Copyright © 2023 by Information Age Publishing
www.infoagepub.com
All rights of reproduction in any form reserved.

that veterans are more honorable, patriotic, hard-working, and disciplined than their civilian counterparts (Pew Research Center, 2019). Given these findings, the present study examined the degree to which hiring managers were biased in favor of veterans. In particular, it assessed the extent to which hiring managers' conscious, social, and unconscious biases favored veterans and influenced employment decisions about them. The results revealed that conscious and social biases were positively related to employment decisions about veterans. Implications for future theory, research, and practice are considered.

Many psychologists believe that biases are an inherent part of human decision-making (Kahneman & Tversky, 1977). Bias is often defined as "a personal and sometimes unreasoned judgment" (Merriam-Webster, n.d.) that serves to prejudice decisions in favor of or against one thing, idea, person, or group in comparison with another. One major problem with biases in the hiring process is that they may prevent talented applicants from being hired by organizations which harms both the organization and the individual. Consequently, much research has been done to examine how a hiring manager's biases can influence their judgments about an applicant's fit for a job (Chamberlain, 2016). In light of these problems, the passage of Title VII of the Civil Rights Act in 1964 (Equal Employment Opportunity Commission [EEOC], 2019), and other employment laws, have been passed to prevent unfair discrimination against women, ethnic and racial minorities, older applicants, and other protected group members. Thus, organizations have introduced a number of practices to preclude biases from influencing selection decisions, including interviewer training, standardized interview questions, and the use of valid selection techniques (Ployhart et al., 2017).

Given the possible legal consequences associated with biases in the selection process, organizations spend considerable time and effort trying to eliminate unfounded and unreasoned judgments from influencing these decisions. Thus, considerable research has been done to investigate the impact of interviewer bias on employee selection (Ployhart et al., 2017). Results of this research have shown that many individuals (including military veterans) are stereotyped negatively, which biases selection decisions about them (Koch et al., 2015; Stone, C. et al., 2017). Stereotyping is defined as "over-generalized beliefs about members of a category that are typically negative" (Stone, C. & Stone, D., 2015, p. 70), and research has consistently shown that stereotypes have a negative impact on hiring decisions (Derous et al., 2016; Latu et al., 2015; Messner et al., 2011).

Although there is considerable research on the effects of stereotyping and biases on ratings of job applicants (Stone, E. et al., 1992), relatively little research has examined the extent to which these biases are against or in favor of military veterans (Stone, C. & Stone, D., 2015). It is estimated that 250,000 U.S. military members leave the military each year, and the vast majority of them seek to enter the civilian workforce (Dupree, 2018). Further, research has shown that some organizations are reluctant to hire veterans, but other organizations are very enthusiastic about hiring them (Lewis, 2013). The primary reasons for this are that stereotypes about military veterans are both negative and positive (Stone, C. & Stone, D., 2015). For example, some research has found that military veterans are thought to have mental health problems including depression, post-traumatic stress disorder (PTSD), unpredictable behaviors, and difficulties transitioning from the military into civilian organizations (Schreger & Kimble, 2017). One survey conducted by the Society for Human Resource Management (SHRM, 2017) reported that one in three employers list concern with possible PTSD as a reason that they do not hire military veterans (Lewis, 2013).

Despite these negative stereotypes, research has also shown that many veterans are perceived to have distinct abilities and valuable skills developed in the military that are important sources of talent in civilian organizations, such as computer programming and cybersecurity skills (Davis & Minnis, 2017). Further, a recent survey by Pew Research Center (2019) found that the majority of U.S. citizens believe that military veterans are more honorable, hard-working, patriotic, and disciplined than those who have not served in the military. Although these views are positive, they may be unfounded stereotypes, just like the negative perceptions noted above, and further research is needed to determine the extent to which (negative or positive) biases about military veterans affect employment decisions about them. As noted above, some major organizations actively seek out and hire military veterans and argue that they make excellent employees. These organizations include, but are not limited to, Amazon, General Electric, Wal-Mart, Charles Schwab, USAA, Dupont, Comcast, USAA, CSX, and Spectrum (Opengart, 2020; Stone, C. & Stone, D., 2015). Further, a SHRM (2017) survey found that veterans are often an untapped source of talent with wide-ranging experience and competencies learned in the military. This survey revealed that veterans often demonstrate greater subject matter expertise, possess on-the-job training, and have advanced information technology, logistics, transportation, supply chain management, and public relations skills. They also have unique talents in leadership, teamwork, problem-solving, attention to detail, and global perspectives (SHRM, 2017).

In spite of these positive perceptions of veterans, hiring managers often have inconsistent views about them, which suggests that more research is needed to understand hiring managers' perceptions of veterans in the employment process. Further, it is important to determine how these perceptions affect employment decisions about those with prior military service (Stone, C. & Stone, D., 2015). Given that many human resource professionals have not served in the military and do not have experience working with military veterans (Opengart, 2020), they may not understand how training and experience developed in the military transfers to civilian jobs or how military roles might be different than civilian roles. Thus, a greater understanding of how hiring managers view veterans is needed so that these individuals do not experience unfair discrimination and have equal opportunities to suitable jobs. Improving the selection process for military veterans is not only beneficial from an economic standpoint, but it can also have a direct impact on an organization's diversity, creativity, and performance (Stone, C. et al., 2017). In addition, it can enable veterans to gain access to meaningful jobs and have a fulfilling work life.

Given the conflicting stereotypes about military veterans, they still have difficulties gaining access to jobs, but surveys show that perceptions of veterans are much more positive today than they have been in many years (Pew Research Center, 2019; SHRM, 2017). As a result, the primary purpose of this chapter is to report the findings of a study that assessed the degree to which past military service might have a positive influence on hiring managers' selection decisions in organizations. In addition, this research examined the degree to which hiring managers' perceptions are affected by conscious, social, and unconscious biases. One reason to consider these issues is that previous research has shown that conscious, social, and unconscious biases influence selection decisions about veterans and other minorities (Dijksterhuis & Nordgren, 2006; Latham, 2019; Messner et al., 2011). These issues will be considered in more detail below.

THEORETICAL FRAMEWORK

Early research on bias focused on how it influences human rationality in the decision-making process (Heider, 1958; Jones & Davis, 1965; Tversky & Kahneman, 1974). Numerous studies have since provided empirical evidence on the relationship between interviewers' initial impressions and final decision-making outcomes (Dougherty et al., 1994; Macan & Dipboye, 1990).

Given that research has shown that biases affect selection decisions, the current study is based on the model of social cognition (Miller & Brewer, 1984). Social cognition has been widely used to understand and explain the effects of stereotypes on job-related decision-making (Stone & Colella, 1996). This model suggests that when we encounter an individual, we assign the person to a category (e.g., man, woman, older person, military veteran, civilian). This category assignment then elicits stereotypes about the person and, in turn, influences job-related expectancies (e.g., anticipatory beliefs about the veteran's ability to perform the job). In turn, job expectancies affect job ratings, hiring decisions, job assignments, and other actions taken by an organization.

An example of this process is as follows. When we encounter veterans, they may be categorized when they reveal their prior military experience on their resumes or during a job interview. Once a person is categorized as a veteran, then the model of social cognition predicts that they are subsequently stereotyped by raters, both positively and negatively. Research has indicated that veterans are often stereotyped as (a) mentally ill (e.g., having depression or PTSD), (b) rigid, (c) prone to alcohol and drug abuse, (d) having anger management issues, (e) likely to exhibit violent behaviors, (f) disposed to withdrawal behaviors, (g) having difficulty adapting to the civilian workforce, and (h) lacking the ability to transfer military skills to the civilian workforce (Stone, C. & Stone, D., 2015; Stone, C. et al., 2017). However, other studies have shown veterans are perceived to be (a) disciplined, (b) dependable, (c) resilient, (d) trustworthy, and they are believed to have (e) good teamwork skills, (f) excellent leadership skills, (g) a strong work ethic, and (h) high levels of maturity (U.S. Department of Veteran Affairs [USDVA], 2015; Stone, C. et al., 2017). Beyond these positive and negative stereotypes, other factors may influence stereotypes about military veterans, including their specific job-related skills, the unique knowledge gained in the military (e.g., information technology, logistics), and their amount of work experience (Stone, C. et al., 2017). Despite these arguments, it merits emphasis that little research has actually examined the degree to which stereotypes influence job-related expectancies and hiring decisions about veterans (Stone, C. et al., 2017).

Interestingly, stereotypes may also exist for civilians or those individuals who do not have prior military service. Some studies have shown that civilians may be stereotyped as (a) lacking patriotism, (b) having anti-war sentiments, (c) unwilling to sacrifice for their country, (d) unable to qualify for military service because of physical or behavioral limitations, and (e) having elitist attitudes (Dowling, 2018; Pew Research Center, 2011; Stilwell, 2015). Conversely, civilians may be perceived to be more (a) likely to take initiative, (b) creative, (c) emotionally stable, (d) adaptable, (e) having more business experience, (f) good social skill, and (g) more adaptability than military veterans (Stone, C. et al., 2017; Sundheim, 2013).

In spite of the stereotypes about veterans, very few empirical studies have examined the degree to which stereotypes influence hiring decisions about applicants who have prior military service (Steffens et al., 2019; Xu et al., 2021). However, results of two studies revealed that employers are less likely to hire veterans than those who do not have a military service background (Xu et al., 2021; Steffens et al., 2019). Other studies found that stereotypes and biases against veterans negatively affect employment decisions about them (Johnson et al., 2010; Joseph, 2004; Latu et al., 2015;

Muchnik et al., 2013; Messner et al., 2011; Schreger & Kimble, 2017; Vornholt et al., 2013).

Despite the widespread use of the model of social cognition, very few empirical studies have assessed the extent to which stereotypes about veterans influence job expectancies and employment decisions about them. However, there has been extensive research showing that unfavorable stereotypes often have a negative impact on job expectancies and selection decisions about other group members, including (a) women (Koch et al., 2015), (b) people with disabilities (Yosef et al., 2019; Stone, D. & Colella, 1996), (c) older applicants (Kaufmann et al., 2016), (d) racial and ethnic minorities (McCord et al., 2018), (e) religious minorities (Scheitle & Corcoran, 2018), (f) people with various national origins (Derous et al., 2016), (g) those with different sexual orientations (LGBTQ) (Caulley, 2017), and (h) people who are unattractive (Messner et al., 2011).

Most of the research on employment decisions about veterans has focused on negative stereotypes about them. However, Stone, C. and Stone, D. (2015) argued that individual differences in raters' attributes and backgrounds (e.g., values, previous contact with veterans) may affect the degree to which their views and employment decisions about veterans are favorable. One factor that may have a positive effect on raters' views of veterans is their own values. Raters vary in terms of their values regarding military service, patriotism, and the importance of protecting our country, and these values are likely to influence their reactions to applicants who are veterans. For example, raters with high patriotic values should be more likely to value military service than those with low patriotic values. As a result, they should be more likely to hire veterans than those who do not stress these values. Further, raters with patriotic values may also perceive that veterans' values are similar to their own, and these beliefs should positively influence their beliefs about veterans (Byrne, 1971). Another factor that may affect the rater's views of veterans is the reason why the veteran originally joined the military (Stone & Colella, 1996). For instance, veterans who joined the military because they were patriotic or wanted to protect their country should be rated more favorably than those who joined the military because they had few job opportunities or to avoid incarceration. The primary reason for this is that veterans who joined the military because they were patriotic should be viewed as having higher levels of integrity than those who joined for more pragmatic reasons (e.g., few job opportunities) (Stone & Colella, 1996). Further, veterans who joined the military for pragmatic reasons are likely to be held more responsible for the problems they experienced in the military (e.g., physical or mental illness) than those who joined for patriotic reasons. This argument is consistent with research that found that people with disabilities are viewed more negatively if they are perceived as responsible for their own fate (e.g., disabled due to a motorcycle accident) than if they are not (e.g., disabled because of a contagious illness) (Bordieri & Drehmer, 1984).

A third factor that may affect raters' views of veterans is the degree to which they have had previous positive contact with veterans (Stone & Colella, 1996). Suppose raters have had positive interactions with, or have family members or friends who are veterans. In that case, they should have gathered individuating information about them that can be used to dispel negative stereotypes. For example, if a rater has a friend who is a veteran and the person is intelligent, hard-working, adaptable, emotionally stable, and has no alcohol or drug problems, then they should be less likely to believe that negative stereotypes about veterans are accurate (Stone, C. & Stone, D., 2015). This individuating information should lead raters to perceive that many veterans have positive qualities, which should increase the extent to which they hire them. However, if raters have had little or no positive contact with veterans, they should be more likely to base their hiring decisions on negative stereotypes (Stone & Colella, 1996). Indirect support for this argument is provided by research on previous contact with persons with disabilities (Stone & Colella, 1996) or immigrants (Stone, D. et al., 2020). This and other research found that "positive intergroup contact decreases intergroup prejudice" (Pettigrew & Tropp, 2006, p. 766), and personal contact often enhances attitudes toward members of stigmatized groups. Other studies, however, showed that when raters have little positive contact with members of stigmatized groups, they make inferences about the person based on existing stereotypes (Corrigan et al., 2001; Taylor, 1981; Weinberg, 1976; Yuker, 1988).

Taken together, this research suggests that a number of raters' attributes (e.g., patriotic values, previous positive contact with veterans, and beliefs about why veterans joined the service) should have a positive influence on their views of veterans and employment decisions about them.

Although research has examined these raters' attributes in terms of reactions to stigmatized groups (e.g., people with disabilities or immigrants), we know of no empirical research that has examined the extent to which raters' attributes positively affect views about applicants who are military veterans. Thus, we examined the following three hypotheses:

Hypothesis 1: Hiring managers' will be more likely to hire military veterans than civilian applicants.

Hypothesis 2: Hiring managers' who perceive that veterans joined the military service because they had no other job opportunities will be less likely to employ them than if they feel they joined the military because they were patriotic.

Hypothesis 3: Hiring managers' who have had previous positive contact with military veterans because they have family or friends who served in the military will be more likely to hire them than those who have not had previous contact with them.

Biases That Affect Managers' Decisions About Military Veterans

Previous research has shown that there are three types of biases that affect hiring managers' decisions about stigmatized groups (Baumeister & Masicampo, 2011). The potential biases that may affect hiring managers' decisions regarding military veterans include conscious biases, social biases, and unconscious biases (Figure 7.1). Each of these biases is considered in more detail below.

Conscious Bias

One important type of bias that is likely to affect hiring managers' views of military veterans is conscious bias. Conscious biases are preconceived beliefs about individuals or groups, and the person with the bias is aware that they have these predetermined beliefs (Baumeister & Masicampo, 2011). Conscious biases are especially problematic in the employment process because these biases influence interviews, and interviews are often a primary source of information used in the hiring process (Derous et al., 2016). Indeed, research indicates that bias in the interview process plays a

Figure 7.1

Biases Potentially Influencing Employment Decisions Regarding Military Veterans

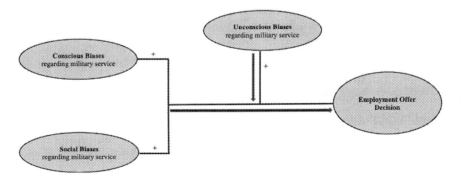

significant role in employee selection, where interview outcomes are prone to stereotypes and biases (Derous et al., 2016; Baumeister et al., 2010, Miller & Brewer, 1984).

An example of research done on conscious bias and its influence on the hiring process can be seen in the work of Vornholt et al. (2013). The authors investigated factors affecting the acceptance of individuals with disabilities in employment contexts. They conducted a comprehensive review of research on the topic and found that many raters have biased or preconceived views about employees with disabilities. Vornholt et al. (2013) found that when individuals have a biased view about the abilities of people with disabilities, that they are consciously aware of, they react negatively to working with coworkers with disabilities (Vornholt et al., 2013). Given these findings, we believe that when raters have a conscious bias for or against veterans, this is likely to affect their employment-related decisions. For example, during the Vietnam era, many U.S. citizens held a bias against members of the military who served in Vietnam because they were morally opposed to the war. As a result, they often stereotyped Vietnam-era veterans and mistreated them. However, recent research has shown that today people in the U.S. have extremely positive views about military veterans and perceive that they often make excellent employees (Pew Research Center, 2019; SHRM, 2017). Thus, we believe that, at the present time, hiring managers will be more likely to have a conscious bias in favor of military veterans than a conscious bias against them.

Although the arguments above appear reasonable, we know of no empirical research that has examined the degree to which a hiring manager's conscious bias influences employment decisions about military veterans. Thus, we offer the following hypotheses to guide research.

Hypothesis 4: Hiring managers' conscious biases in favor of military veterans will be positively related to hiring decisions about them.

Social Bias

A second type of bias that is likely to influence hiring managers' decisions about veterans is social bias. Social biases are those introduced by a person's social group (e.g., family, friends, coworkers and suggest that beliefs of social groups often influence judgments about others (Baumeister et al., 2010). For instance, if a person strongly identifies with a social group, their thoughts, beliefs, and actions may be influenced by the members of this group (Baumeister & Masicampo, 2011). Stated differently, if one's friends and family have positive views about military veterans, then their beliefs about military veterans are likely to be more positive than if their family and friends hold negative views about veterans.

Although considerable research has shown that one's social groups influence their beliefs (Ajzen & Fishbein, 1975), relatively little research has examined the relations between social and peer influences on employment decisions about military veterans. However, research has examined the effect of social interactions among coworkers on employees' beliefs about moral and ethical behavior (Joseph, 2004). The results of this study found that the biases of social group members influenced individuals' beliefs about moral behavior and ethical norms (Joseph, 2004). Thus, peer interactions and opinions of social group members may have an important influence on hiring managers' employment decisions. Other research has found that social groups can activate irrational and unreasonable judgments on the part of individuals, and these may, in turn, affect hiring decisions about military veterans (Ajzen & Fishbein, 1975).

Despite the arguments noted above, we know of no empirical research that has examined the effects of social group biases on hiring managers' employment decisions about veterans. Therefore, the following hypothesis is presented:

> **Hypothesis 5:** If hiring managers' social groups are positively biased toward military veterans, then the hiring manager will be more likely to hire veterans than if their social groups are negatively biased toward veterans.

Unconscious Bias

Another factor that is likely to affect employment decisions about military veterans is unconscious bias. Unconscious bias (or implicit bias) can be defined as biases or beliefs about individuals or groups that are outside of the person's awareness. In other words, the person is not consciously aware of their biases (Dovidio, 2001; Bargh & Morsella, 2008). The majority of research on unconscious bias is related to information processing that can occur unconsciously and outside of an individual's awareness (Bargh & Morsella, 2008; Messner et al., 2011; Dijksterhuis & Nordgren, 2006; Kawakami et al., 1999; Kawakami & Dovidio, 2001) but may be affected by the person's prior experiences. Research has shown that stereotypes are learned from prior experiences and are automatic, unintentional, and ingrained. Furthermore, stereotypes often influence raters' beliefs in ways that cause them to make decisions in favor of one person or group to the detriment of others (Knight, 2017). A review of studies on unconscious bias (Dovidio & Gaertner, 2004) found clear evidence that most individuals have deeply held negative beliefs about a number of minority group members (e.g., women, ethnic and racial minorities, veterans). These types of biases lead to subtle discrimination against minority groups without the rater's conscious awareness that they are biased. Thus, hiring managers may have unconscious biases against military veterans based on their antipathy toward war or the actions taken by some veterans during wars. Although they may not be consciously aware of these biases, these beliefs may still have a negative impact on employment decisions about veterans. Other research, such as Schreger and Kimble (2017), found that students enrolled in a psychology course held an implicit stereotype that military veterans were not mentally stable. The study assessed implicit bias with the Implicit Association Test (IAT) (Greenwald et al., 1998). The results revealed that participants held implicit biases towards veterans as being "somewhat more mentally unstable than civilians" (Schreger & Kimble, 2017, p. 6).

The Schreger and Kimble (2017) study is important for the present study in two ways. First, the researchers found unconscious biases towards military veterans' employment suitability which should negatively affect employment decisions about them. Second, the study suggested that hiring managers may have unconscious biases in favor of or against military veterans. Although Schreger and Kimble (2017) found that there are unconscious biases toward military veterans, the researchers did not provide an understanding of how these biases are formed or how they may affect employment decisions about veterans. Thus, a better understanding is needed of how unconscious biases about military veterans explain the challenges they experience during the employment process. Even though there has been some research on unconscious biases about racial and ethnic minorities (Dovidio, 2001), we know of no empirical research that has examined the influence of unconscious biases on employment decisions about military veterans. Therefore, we tested the following hypothesis:

Hypothesis 6: Hiring managers' unconscious positive biases toward military veterans will positively affect hiring decisions about them.

Taken together, we argue that three types of biases (conscious, social, and unconscious) may influence hiring managers' employment decisions about veterans, and we present several hypotheses to test these relations. Below, we present the methods used to test the hypotheses presented above.

METHODS

Overview: Experimental Design

In order to test the study's hypotheses, an experimental design was developed to examine the extent to which applicants who were military veterans were perceived more positively in the employment process than applicants who were civilians with no prior military service. It used a 1 x 2 experimental design and a fictitious employment scenario to examine whether an applicant's prior military service (civilian vs. military service background) affected employment decisions. The study also assessed the degree to which three types of biases (conscious, social, and unconscious) were related to employment decisions about veterans. It should be noted that the applicants' resumes in the study were identical except for the experimental manipulations of civilian versus military service. In addition, an online sampling process using Qualtrics was used to sample and collect data from a diverse sample of experienced hiring managers. This procedure increased the degree to which the sample was representative of hiring managers in the population as a whole.

Participants

The participants for this study were recruited utilizing Qualtrics, a survey technology solution, and the Experience Management (XM) platform (Molnar, 2019). Online data collection in behavioral research has become increasingly common and has gained popularity in research in psychology and cognitive science (Barnhoorn et al., 2015; Carpenter et al., 2018). As a result, modern survey software such as Qualtrics is "used to implement many of these studies and can administer a range of procedures, from questionnaires to randomized experiments" (Carpenter et al., 2018, p. 4). There are a number of advantages of online data collection, but one of the most important benefits is that the participants constitute a representative sample of the population of interest. Chang and Vowles (2013) offer numerous advantages to the online survey method. In particular, they note cost-effectiveness, targeted sample collection, unrestricted geographic coverage, and fewer processing errors as responses are recorded instantaneously online (Chang & Vowles, 2013). Ilieva et al. (2002) also indicate the advantages of online surveys regarding response times. Particularly, where online surveys are not only delivered instantly to participants, "the same applies to the speed of response" (Ilieva et al., 2002, p. 365). In addition, another significant advantage of the online survey method is the ability to increase the explanatory power of the findings. Specifically, larger online participant pools are more diverse, representative of the population (Molnar, 2019), and high-powered samples are accessible in short amounts of time (Paolacci & Chandler, 2014). As such, having the ability to reach a large and diverse online pool of participants with quicker response times increases reliability and generalizability (Kosinski et al., 2015).

There were 190 participants in this study, 101 women and 89 men, who were hiring managers located in the United States. Most of the participants identified as White or Caucasian ($n = 174$), with only six identifying as African American and 10 as Hispanic American. Thirty-two percent of the sample were between the ages of 35–44, and 37.4% had 12 years or more of hiring experience. Participants were fairly well educated, with 42.1% having a bachelor's degree and the largest group was from the Southeastern region of the U.S. (28.4%). The data reported here are part of a more extensive study that investigated both positive and negative biases towards military veterans. For the purpose of this chapter, an examination of positive stereotypes of veterans by hiring managers is discussed.

Pilot Study

To test the study's materials, a pilot study was conducted. This pilot test revealed the existence of a technical problem in how respondents accessed the questionnaire. This was corrected, and the correction was confirmed in a second pilot test. No other issues with the survey instrument were identified in the pilot study.

Measures

Conscious Bias

The "Susceptibility to Interpersonal Influence" scale (Bearden et al., 1989) was adapted to measure conscious bias. Participants were asked to respond to 10 items, including the following sample questions: (1) "I really admire those men and women who have served our country in our military"; and (2) "I think military veterans tend to maintain their aggressive behaviors as civilian employees" (see Appendix A for the full measurement tool). The original 10-item scale was used to collect data. All negative items were recoded. However, only six out of the 10 items were used in the final analyses as explained below. Participants used a 7-point Likert scale ("*1 = strongly disagree, and 7 = strongly agree*), and responses to the items were averaged to develop an overall score. Higher scores on the scale reflected more positive conscious bias for applicants who had military experience. The Cronbach's alpha reliability estimate for the six items was .728.

As a means of enhancing methodological transparency (Aguinis et al., 2018), the four items not included in the final analyses indicated above are items four, five, six, and seven (see Appendix A). The rationale for omitting these four items is that they could be considered ambiguous. For example, item six in Appendix A indicates, "I think those who wear military uniforms think differently than non-military." However, there is no referent to whom this question refers to (e.g., no different than business professionals, medical professionals, individuals from different cultures, etc.). Civilian (non-military) is not clear, and this is an example of why the item was omitted (Heggestad et al., 2019). Given that the measure included a variety of items that may or may not assess conscious biases, eliminating the ambiguous items increased the reliability of the scale (Heggestad et al., 2019). Methodological transparency regarding this measurement scale is intended to improve results reproducibility and improve the replicability of future research on this topic (Aguinis et al., 2018). The item reduction analysis of these four omitted items ensured only parsimonious, functional, and internally consistent items were included in the final analyses (Boateng et al., 2018).

Social Bias

Bearden et al.'s (1989) scale was likewise adapted to measure social bias. The scale included 10 items, including the following sample questions: (1) "Those people I ask for advice think that military veterans bring skills to work others do not have;" and (2) "Those people I ask for advice think that military veterans are hard to get along with in civilian jobs" (see Appendix A for the full measurement tool). Participants responded to items using a 7-point Likert scale (*1 = strongly disagree, and 7 = strongly agree*). The final measure of social bias was determined by averaging scores on these 10 items. All negative items were recoded. Higher scores on the measure reflected more positive social bias of military applicants. The Cronbach's alpha reliability estimate was .832.

Unconscious Bias

To measure unconscious bias, the Implicit Association Test (IAT), developed by Greenwald et al. (1998), was used and consisted of a total of seven blocks designed exclusively for this study, which compared a *target category* (i.e., picture of a military veteran and civilian model) and an *attribute dimension* with *target words across two category types* (i.e., *positive and negative words*). The speed of reaction time was used to assess unconscious bias and was calculated for each participant, measuring the associative strength between a given target category and an attribute dimension (Schreger & Kimble, 2017). This reaction time speed was used to determine whether or not the hiring manager felt an unconscious bias (for or against) military veterans. Although there are several ways to measure unconscious bias, the most prevalent sensory trigger is visual. Rather than measuring what individuals *believe*, the IAT measures what people *mentally associate* with the triggering object seen and its association with a memory (Carpenter et al., 2018). The Cronbach alpha reliability estimate for this scale was 0.861.

Employment Decision

The employment decision in the study was measured with a one-item scale that asked participants the following question: "Based on your review of the job description and resume, would you extend an offer of employment to the applicant?" Participants were asked to make a hiring decision using a 4-point Likert scale (*1 = definitely not, and 4 = definitely yes*). Higher scores on the measure reflected a greater intention to extend a job offer to the applicant.

Research Procedures

The following procedures were used for data collection. First, participants were given and asked to review and sign an informed consent form. Upon consent, they were randomly assigned to different treatment groups using a randomizer element in the Qualtrics survey flow. The materials were presented to the participants in the following order: (1) job posting, (2) resume, (3) employment offer decision question, (4) conscious bias questionnaire, (5) social bias questionnaire, and (6) the IAT used to measure unconscious bias. After completion of the tasks, participants were debriefed on the purpose and procedures used in the study.

Job Posting

The job posting selected for this study was taken from Indeed.com for a mid-level management position in supply chain and logistics in the domain of business management that would be a likely position for the candidate represented by the resume.

Resume

This research made use of a resume format developed by Stone, C. et al. (2017), modified to achieve this study's purpose. All fictitious applicants were male and either had no prior military service or prior military service in the U.S. Navy. The resumes were carefully constructed to represent common names and identical knowledge, skills, and abilities (KSAs). The only difference in resumes was the presence or absence of military service.

RESULTS

Multiple regression/correlational analyses were used to test the study's hypotheses. Table 7.1 presents the results of the multiple regression analyses, and tests for each hypothesis are presented below.

As can be seen in Table 7.1, the regression equation was statistically significant at the specified criterion ($R = .291$, $F(6,173) = 2.668$, $p = .01$). As a result, we were able to interpret the specific predictor variables.

Hypothesis 1

This hypothesis predicted that hiring managers would be more likely to offer employment to military veterans than civilian applicants. As can be seen in Table 7.1, the results of the regression analyses did not support this hypothesis ($\beta = .-02$, $t = -.27$, $p = .39$).

Table 7.1

Regression Analyses for Hiring Managers' Employment Offer[1]

Independent Variables	Dependent Variable Employment Offer	
	β	T
Military Veteran Status	-.02	-.27
Joined Military Because Had No Jobs Options	-.27	-2.54
Worked with Military Veteran	-.11	-1.30
Conscious Bias	.23	1.60
Social Bias	.22	1.79
Unconscious Bias	.07	1.06

Note: [1]$R = .291$, $F(6, 173) = 2.668$ $p = .01$.

Table 7.2

Correlations Table

	M	SD	1	2	3	4	5	6	7	8	9	10	11
Which category below includes your age?	3.55	1.04	-										
Gender Identification	1.53	0.50	0.002	-									
How many years of experience do you have making hiring decisions?	3.84	1.06	.512**	0.009	-								
Are you a military veteran?	1.07	0.26	0.044	-.220**	-0.015	-							
Civilian vs. Military Combined	0.66	0.47	0.069	0.112	0.093	0.031	-						
Had a family member who served in the military?	1.38	0.49	0.244**	0.081	.147*	0.236**	0.052	-					
Worked with someone who has served in the military?	1.73	0.44	0.197**	0.098	0.224**	0.171*	0.146*	0.302**	-				
Based on your review of the job description and resume, would you extend an offer of employment to the applicant?	3.22	0.63	-0.005	-0.098	0.012	0.096	0.014	0.043	0.019	-			
Conscious Bias	5.42	1.03	.256**	.244**	.267**	0.015	.253**	.187***	.432**	0.128	-		
Social Bias	5.16	0.96	.152*	.143*	.144*	0.026	.216**	.212**	.369**	.171*	.774**	-	
Unconscious Bias	1.34	0.48	-0.060	-0.076	-0.039	0.062	0.008	0.129	-0.002	0.065	-0.029	-0.009	-

Note: **. Correlation is significant at the 0.01 level (1-tailed).
*. Correlation is significant at the 0.05 level (1-tailed).

223

Hypothesis 2

Hypothesis 2 posited that hiring managers who perceived that veterans joined the military service because they had no other job opportunities would be less likely to employ them than those who felt people joined the military because they were patriotic. As shown in Table 7.1, the data from the present study showed statistically significant support for this hypothesis ($\beta = -.27$, $t = -2.54$, $p = .006$.). The more that hiring managers perceived that a veteran joined the military because they had no job offers, the lower the level of employment offers.

Hypothesis 3

This prediction predicted that hiring managers who have had previous positive contact with military veterans would be more likely to hire them than those who have not had previous contact with them. As can be seen in Table 7.1, the results of the study were in the hypothesized direction but did not reach statistical significance ($\beta = -.11$, $t = -1.30$, $p = .09$).

Hypothesis 4

Hypothesis 4 maintained that hiring managers' conscious biases in favor of military veterans would be positively related to hiring decisions about them. The data from the present study provided support for this hypothesis. Hiring managers' conscious biases in favor of veterans were positively related to employment offers ($\beta = .23$, $t = 1.60$, $p = .05$).

Hypothesis 5

This hypothesis predicted that hiring managers whose social biases were in favor of military veterans would be more likely to offer employment to them than those whose social biases were negative toward veterans. The results of the present study provided support for this hypothesis. The more that hiring managers had friends and family (social biases) in favor of military veterans, the more likely they would offer veterans employment ($\beta = .22$, $t = 1.79$, $p = .03$).

Hypothesis 6

Hypothesis 6 maintained that if hiring managers had positive unconscious biases toward military veterans, they would be more likely to offer employment to veterans. The data from the study did not provide support for this hypothesis ($\beta = .07$, $t = 1.06$, $p = .14$). However, the results were in the hypothesized direction.

Supplemental Analyses

Although no specific hypotheses were postulated, supplemental analyses were conducted to better understand the study's results. The findings of the supplemental analyses showed that managers' demographic variables were not related to employment offers. However, the results revealed that a number of managers' demographic variables were related to conscious and social biases. For example, managers' age was positively related to conscious ($r = .256$, $p < .01$), and social biases ($r = .152$, $p < .05$) in favor of veterans. Similarly, managers' years of making hiring decisions were positively related to conscious ($r = .267$, $p < .01$) and social ($r = .144$, $p < .05$) biases. Likewise, managers' previous contact with military veterans was positively related to conscious and social biases. In particular, if managers had family members who were military veterans, they were more likely to have conscious biases ($r = .187$, $p < .01$), and social biases ($r = .212$, $p < .01$) that were pro-military veterans. Finally, if managers had worked with military veterans they had more conscious biases ($r = .432$, $p < .01$) and social biases ($r = .369$, $p < .01$) favorable to veterans. These findings have important implications for future research on hiring veterans and should be included in that research.

DISCUSSION

Although most of the previous research on veterans has shown that they are often stereotyped negatively, which has an unfavorable impact on hiring decisions about them (Stone, C. & Stone, D., 2015), recent surveys have shown that the majority of U.S. citizens have much more positive views of veterans (e.g., they are disciplined and hard-working). Thus, we assessed biases (conscious, social, and unconscious) that may influence hiring managers and affect military veterans during the employment selection process. The results of the present study found that conscious and social biases in favor of veterans were positively related to hiring decisions about them. Further, the study found that attributions that veterans joined the service because they had no other job offers had a negative influence on employment decisions. These results have important implications for future theory, research, and practice on hiring veterans.

Implications for Theory

The present study's findings were inconsistent with previous research that found negative stereotypes of veterans had an unfavorable impact on hiring decisions about them (Stone, C. & Stone, D., 2019). Data from the present study revealed that hiring managers may have positive stereotypes about veterans and that these views are likely to have a favorable impact on employment decisions about them. Although these results are somewhat different than previous research, they still support the social cognitive model that argues that categorization and stereotyping influence job expectancies and hiring decisions. In this case, the stereotypes were positive, not negative, and had a positive impact on employment decisions. Thus, we believe that future research on veterans might base their predictions on social cognition and consider both positive and negative stereotypes.

However, it merits caution that both positive and negative stereotypes about individuals may not be accurate and may have a detrimental effect on employment decisions. For example, if hiring managers have inaccurate positive stereotypes of veterans, they may hire the person and expect that they will perform at an extremely high level. When the person does not perform at high levels, managers' expectations will be violated, and they may rate the person lower than they would have if they did not have such high expectations. Stated differently, inaccurate positive stereotypes about veterans may affect managers' job expectancies and lead them to believe that veterans will perform at inordinately high levels. These inaccurate job expectations are likely to harm veterans over time and lead them to receive low-performance ratings and fewer recommendations for promotion. Thus, both positive and negative stereotypes about veterans may lead to inaccurate decisions, which may have a negative effect on their performance ratings and pay raises. Therefore, hiring managers should strive to develop accurate projections about a veteran's potential rather than based on stereotyped performance expectancies. Accurate decision-making should benefit both veterans and employers.

The results of the present study also found that conscious and social biases influenced employment decisions about veterans, but unconscious biases were not related to these decisions. Baumeister and Masicampo (2011) argued that three types of biases (e.g., conscious, social, and unconscious) affect hiring managers' decisions about stigmatized groups. Conscious biases are preconceived beliefs about individuals or groups, and the person with the bias is aware of these predetermined beliefs (Baumeister & Masicampo, 2011). Social biases are those introduced by a person's social group (e.g., family, friends, coworkers and suggest that beliefs of social groups often influence an individual's judgments about others (Baumeister et al., 2010).

Unconscious bias (or implicit bias) can be defined as "biases or beliefs about individuals or groups that are outside of the person's awareness (e.g., the person is not consciously aware of their biases) (Dovidio, 2001; Bargh & Morsella, 2008). Research has shown that unconscious biases are related to information processing that can occur unconsciously and outside of an individual's awareness (Bargh & Morsella, 2008). The results of the present study revealed that hiring managers may be aware of their own biases about veterans or base their judgments or opinions on their social groups' views. If this is the case, then hiring managers should be trained to identify their personal biases and the biases of their friends and families and take steps to make sure that they do not influence hiring decisions. However, the present study did not find that hiring managers' biases were unconscious. Still, it is not clear if the lack of a statistically significant relationship resulted from the absence of unconscious biases or from measurement problems. For instance, the present study used the Implicit Association Test (IAT) that is typically used to measure biases against racial or ethnic minorities and may not accurately assess the degree to which there are unconscious biases for or against veterans. Thus, future research should use alternative measures for unconscious biases to examine the extent to which these types of biases affect employment decisions regarding veterans.

Implications for Research and Practice

Although the present study found that conscious and social biases affect employment decisions about veterans, future research is needed to identify the reasons for these biases (Stone & Colella, 1996). For example, specific factors associated with veterans may be related to these biases, including their perceived or actual disabilities, the type of military service (combat vs. non-combat), gender, the length of time served, the reason that the person joined the military, or the job skills developed in the military (Stone, C. & Stone, D., 2015). Similarly, research is needed to examine if factors associated with the rater are related to their biases for or against veterans, including their level of patriotism, personal experience in the military, prior contact with veterans, or views about war and combat (Stone, C. & Stone, D., 2015). Finally, research is needed to assess the degree to which the nature of the job affects biases about veterans, including the similarity of the job performed in the military, the skills and abilities requirements, and the extent to which the job requires skills learned in the military (e.g., teamwork, leadership). To date, there has been relatively little research on biases for or against veterans in the employment process, and much more research is needed to explain the factors affecting this process.

Apart from the implications for future theory and research, the results from this study have important implications for practice in organizations. As a result, organizations might use several mechanisms to decrease biases for or against veterans and develop more accurate decisions about them. Finding more effective means of utilizing the numerous talents of veterans is important, given the challenges that military veterans may face when entering the civilian workforce. The following sections will briefly consider several practical mechanisms to facilitate the inclusion of veterans in organizations to aid them in developing programs and procedures to eliminate biases and stereotypes in the hiring of military veterans.

Mechanism 1: Changing Affective and Behavioral Reactions Toward Military Veterans

In this study, we examined how hiring managers may perceive military veterans, which may be influenced by raters' cognitive, affective, and behavioral responses towards veterans. Direct changes in affective or emotional reactions to veterans may help reduce biases military veterans may experience in organizations (Stone & Colella, 1996). Thus, organizations might decrease negative biases by developing cross-cultural training to familiarize hiring managers with the cultural beliefs and practices of the military (Opengart, 2020). For instance, Hofstede's (1984) cultural dimensions could be used as a framework to differentiate between civilian and military cultures to better educate hiring managers about the cultural adjustment military veterans experience when transitioning into the civilian workforce (i.e., individualism vs. a collective team orientation, power distance/chain of command). Additionally, creating a more inclusive workforce should include designing programs and procedures focused on hiring and retaining military veterans, such as sponsorship and/or mentorship opportunities (Opengart, 2020; PsychArmor, 2021a; Stone, C. & Stone, D., 2015).

Mechanism 2: Directly Changing Negative Stereotypes about Military Veterans

There has been much discussion asserting that organizations may be able to directly influence the behaviors of their employees (Porter et al., 1975; Stone & Colella, 1996). Although Porter et al. (1975) suggest making rewards contingent on desired behaviors, there is a possibility that organizations can change the way military veterans are perceived and treated during the employment selection process. For instance, the development of diversity, equity, and inclusion (DEI) educational training specifically designed to dispel stereotypes regarding military veterans which are not always accurate or applicable to the vast majority of military veterans (e.g., rigid, mental instability, aggressive) is a first step in the right direction (Stone & Colella, 1996; Stone, C. & Stone, D., 2015). However, careful design of the type of training is crucial. Bezrukova et al.'s (2016) meta-analysis suggest that diversity training effectiveness is dependent on numerous factors, including content, length, audience, and accompanying diversity efforts. Thus, all DEI training should be for 3 to 12 months, depending on the size of the organization, and continued research is needed to investigate the effectiveness of these types of organizational strategies (Stone & Colella, 1996) to determine if they alter behavior (positively) towards veterans.

Additionally, results of this study found that veterans are often categorized and stereotyped positively in the employment process. Still, these beliefs may be inaccurate and lead to erroneous decisions. As a result, hiring managers may develop excessively positive job expectancies about veterans, and when these individuals do not perform at high levels, it will violate managers' expectancies. The violation of these expectancies may lead to low-performance ratings, fewer pay raises, or a lack of promotion recommendations. Thus, we believe that organizations should develop strategies to overcome unfounded stereotypes about veterans and ensure that decision-makers accurately perceive their job-related skills and abilities. Consistent with models of organizational change (Porter et al., 1975), we believe that organizations might use a variety of methods to modify inaccurate stereotypes about veterans and ensure that their skills and abilities are perceived accurately. For example, another approach that might be used to change stereotypes about veterans is to increase interpersonal contact with them. Veterans might be assigned to key work teams or become involved in informal group activities so that decision-makers can gather individuating information about them. Finally, another method for changing stereotypes about veterans is to publicize their key contributions and successes in organizations. Even though we expect these mechanisms to alter both positive and negative stereotypes about veterans, additional research is needed to assess their effectiveness.

Mechanism 3: Overcoming Social Biases Toward Veterans

This study revealed that social biases have a key impact on judgments about veterans. As a result, organizations might use training designed to show employees how to respond when members of their social groups espouse positive or negative stereotypes about veterans. They might also increase interpersonal contact (e.g., social events, work teams) between veterans and current employees so that employees can see veterans as individuals, not as members of a distant group. The increased contact with veterans should allow employees to see that individual veterans do not always fit the stereotypes of veterans as top performers, leaders, good team members, or resilient to stress. Despite these arguments, research is needed to examine the extent to which these methods increase accurate perceptions of veterans.

Mechanism 4: Overcoming Raters' Biases For or Against Veterans

The current study suggests that conscious and social biases may affect employment decisions about veterans. As a result, we believe that all raters should be trained in fair employment practices and held accountable for the types of decisions that they make about applicants and employees who are veterans (Cox, 1994). For example, managers could examine the types of decisions made about veterans and other group members to ensure they are not engaging in stereotyping rather than utilizing objective information to make employment decisions. These evaluations could then be used to evaluate raters' performance and determine specific outcomes. It is also recommended that organizations track the performance of veterans and determine if hiring decisions about veterans and other group members actually predict job performance. Although these mechanisms seem feasible, research is needed to assess their effectiveness.

Mechanism 5: Raters Acquiring Military Acumen

The current study has discussed how military veteran applicants may be viewed differently than civilian applicants in organizations. This may result from hiring managers having biased perceptions about the skills and abilities veterans acquire during their military service (Stone & Colella, 1996). Given that the typical civilian hiring manager has limited military experience, structured training programs can be developed to help hiring managers build their military acumen. This would include teaching the different rank structures across the different branches of the military so hiring managers, who do not have any experience with military veterans, are better able to identify transferable skills veterans can bring to the organization (SHRM, 2019).

Future Research

Further research on conscious, social, and unconscious biases is important in extending knowledge of bias and stereotyping in employee selection. Below, Several research opportunities are identified to expand understanding of the influence of bias in individual behaviors, including the employment selection process of the military veteran population.

First, future studies should include the different branches of service and different ranks within other branches of service to determine if different biases exist regarding the employment of military veterans. This would be especially important in comparing those with and without military service, military affiliations, or experience with military employees. Second, the military resumes in this study represented former active duty service members with civilian work experience after departing the military. Future research should investigate the degree to which active versus reserve military status influences hiring managers' decisions. Third, gender was held constant across all resume treatments in this study. Future research should also include female applicants to examine the effects of the IAT visual stimuli on unconscious bias and investigate higher levels of unemployment amongst female military veterans. Fourth, future research should consider replicating this study utilizing the theory of planned behavior (TPB) as a mediator with the possibility of unconscious bias (IAT) mediating the relationship between conscious and social bias in the employment offer decision. Implicit measures not only provide important information related to cognitive processing and initial reactions, but they are also well suited to measure socially sensitive issues such as stereotyping and preju-dice (Kawakami & Dovidio, 2001). Finally, future research should further investigate social desirability response and control for this potential bias when administering questionnaires (Crowne & Marlowe, 1960; van de Mortel, 2008). A greater understanding of perceived social biases shared among coworkers by hiring managers, and their impact on the employability of military veterans can potentially enhance military veterans' inclusivity within U.S. organizations.

CONCLUSION

This research study was designed to investigate and provide insight into biases that may affect the treatment of military veterans by hiring managers during the employment selection process. Specifically, the study examined the degree to which hiring managers were biased in favor of veterans and assessed the extent to which hiring managers' conscious, social, and unconscious biases favored veterans and influenced employment decisions about them. Results of this study revealed that conscious and social biases were positively related to employment decisions about military veterans. Thus, a more comprehensive understanding of the perceptions and treatment of military veterans by hiring managers requires that future research assess the cognitive, affective, and behavioral responses towards veterans.

We have argued, as do others (Davis & Minnis, 2017; Dickstein et al., 2010; Stone, C. et al., 2017), that veterans have distinct abilities and valuable skills developed in the military that are important sources of talent and which are typically undervalued and underutilized in organizations (Stone & Colella, 1996). Thus, a better understanding of the factors that influence the employment of military veterans by hiring managers may assist organizations in reducing biases that veterans experience as they seek civilian employment. However, negative stereotypes of veterans still exist.

Research has shown that veterans often have numerous problems gaining access to jobs and are often stereotyped negatively (e.g., mentally ill, suffering from depression or PTSD, being unpredictable, being prone to anger) (Schreger & Kimble, 2017; Stone, C. & Stone, D., 2015). However, the present study revealed that veterans could also be stereotyped positively, and these stereotypes will have a positive impact on ratings of their skills and abilities. However, as previously discussed, positive stereotypes may also have a negative impact on performance ratings, pay raises, and promotion recommendations over time. The results of the present study will enable hiring managers to develop more accurate job expectancies for military veterans and utilize the many skills and talents this segment of the population brings to the workforce. The goal of this study is to have a positive impact on military veterans' ability to gain access to satisfying job and career opportunities.

REFERENCES

Aguinis, H., Ramani, R. S., & Alabduljader, N. (2018). What you see is what you get? Enhancing methodological transparency in management research. *Academy of Management Annals*, *12*(1), 83–110.

Ajzen, I. (1991). The theory of planned behavior. *Organizational behavior and human decision processes*, *50*(2), 179–211.

Ajzen, I., & Fishbein, M. (1975). A Bayesian analysis of attribution processes. *Psychological Bulletin*, *82*(2), 261–277.

Bargh, J. A., & Morsella, E. (2008). The unconscious mind. *Perspectives on Psychological Science*, *3*(1), 73–79.

Barnhoorn, J. S., Haasnoot, E., Bocanegra, B. R., & van Steenbergen, H. (2015). QRTEngine: An easy solution for running online reaction time experiments using Qualtrics. *Behavior research methods*, *47*(4), 918–929.

Baumeister, R. F., & Masicampo, E. J. (2010). Conscious thought is for facilitating social and cultural interactions: How mental simulations serve the animal-culture interface. *Psychological Review*, *117*(3), 945.

Baumeister, R. F., Masicampo, E. J., & Vohs, K. D. (2011). Do conscious thoughts cause behavior? *Annual Review of Psychology*, *62*, 331–361.

Bearden, W. O., Netemeyer, R. G., & Teel, J. E. (1989). Measurement of consumer susceptibility to interpersonal influence. *Journal of Consumer Research*, *15*(4), 473–481.

Bezrukova, K., Spell, C. S., Perry, J. L., & Jehn, K. A. (2016). A meta-analytical integration of over 40 years of research on diversity training evaluation. *Psychological Bulletin*, *142*(11), 1227–1274. https://doi.apa.org/doi/10.1037/bul0000067

Boateng, G. O., Neilands, T. B., Frongillo, E. A., Melgar-Quiñonez, H. R., & Young, S. L. (2018). Best practices for developing and validating scales for health, social, and behavioral research: a primer. *Frontiers in public health*, *6*, 1–18. https://doi.org/10.3389/fpubh.2018.00149

Bordieri, J. E., & Drehmer, D. E. (1984). Vietnam veterans: Fighting the employment war. *Journal of Applied Social Psychology*, *14*(4), 341–347.

Byrne. D. (1971). The attraction paradigm. Academic Press.

Carpenter, T., Pogacar, R., Pullig, C., Kouril, M., Aguilar, S. J., LaBouff, J. P., Isenberg, N., & Chakroff, A. (2018). Survey-software implicit association tests: A methodological and empirical analysis. *Behavioral Research Methods*, *51*, 1–15.

Caulley, S. L. (2017). The next frontier to LGBT equality: Securing workplace-discrimination protections. *University of Illinois Law Review*, *2*(2), 909–964.

Chamberlain, R. P. (2016). Five steps toward recognizing and mitigating bias in the interview and hiring process. *Strategic HR Review*, *15*(5), 199–203. https://doi-org.ezproxy.rollins.edu:9443/10.1108/SHR-07-2016-0064

Chang, T. Z. D., & Vowles, N. (2013). Strategies for improving data reliability for online surveys: A case study. *International Journal of Electronic Commerce Studies*, *4*(1), 121–130.

Corrigan, P. W., Edwards, A. B., Green, A., Diwan, S. L., & Penn, D. L. (2001). Prejudice, social distance, and familiarity with mental illness. *Schizophrenia Bulletin*, *27*(2), 219–225.

Cox, T. (1994). *Cultural diversity in organizations: Theory, research and practice*. Berrett-Koehler Publishers.

Crowne, D. P., & Marlowe, D. (1960). A new scale of social desirability independent of psychopathology. *Journal of Consulting Psychology*, *24*, 349–354.

Davis, V. E., & Minnis, S. E. (2017). Military veterans' transferrable skills: An HRD practitioner dilemma. *Advances in Developing Human Resources*, *19*(1), 6–13.

Derous, E., Buijsrogge, A., Roulin, N., & Duyck, W. (2016). Why your stigma isn't hired: A dual-process framework of interview bias. *Human Resource Management Review*, *26*, 90–111.

Dickstein, B. D., Vogt, D. S., Handa, S., & Litz, B. T. (2010). Targeting self-stigma in returning military personnel and veterans: A review of intervention strategies. *Military Psychology*, *22*(2), 224–236.

Dijksterhuis, A., & Nordgren, L. F. (2006). A theory of unconscious thought. *Perspectives on Psychological Science*, *1*(2), 95–109.

Dougherty, T. W., Turban, D. B., & Callender, J. C. (1994). Confirming first impressions in the employment interview: A field study of interviewer behavior. *Journal of Applied Psychology*, *79*(5), 659–665.

Dovidio, J. F. (2001). On the nature of contemporary prejudice: The third wave. *Journal of Social Issues*, *57*, 829–849.

Dovidio, J. F., & Gaertner, S. L. (2004). The aversive form of racism. *The Psychology of Prejudice and Discrimination: Racism in America*, *1*, 1–52.

Dowling, M. (2018). *9 reasons candidates are disqualified from military service*. We Are The Mighty. https://www.wearethemighty.com/articles/9-top-reasons-you-will-be-disqualified-from-military-service/

Dupree, A. (2018). *The transition from a military to civilian career just got easier.* Retrieved January 7, 2019, from https://www.careerbuilder.com/advice/transition-from-military-to-civilian-career

Equal Employment Opportunity Commission. (2019). *Title VIII of the Civil Rights Act of 1964*. Retrieved January 6, 2019, from https://www.eeoc.gov/laws/statutes/titlevii.cfm

Greenwald, A. G., McGhee, D. E., & Schwartz, J. L. (1998). Measuring individual differences in implicit cognition: The implicit association test. *Journal of Personality and Social Psychology*, *74*(6), 1464–1480. https://doi.org/10.1037/0022-3514.74.6.1464

Heggestad, E. D., Scheaf, D. J., Banks, G. C., Monroe Hausfeld, M., Tonidandel, S., & Williams, E. B. (2019). Scale adaptation in organizational science research: A review and best-practice recommendations. *Journal of Management*, *45*(6), 2596–2627.

Heider, F. (1958). *The psychology of interpersonal relationships* (Vol. 37). John. https://doi.org/10.2307/2572978

Hofstede, G. (1984). Cultural dimensions in management and planning. *Asia Pacific Journal of Management*, 81–99.

Ilieva, J., Baron, S., & Healey, N. M. (2002). Online surveys in marketing research. *International Journal of Market Research*, *44*(3), 1–14.

Johnson, S. K., Podratz, K. E., Dipboye, R. L., & Gibbons, E. (2010). Physical attractiveness biases in ratings of employment suitability: Tracking down the "beauty is beastly" effect. *The Journal of Social Psychology*, *150*(3), 301–318.

Jones, E. E., & Davis, K. E. (1965). From acts to dispositions the attribution process in person perception. *Advances in Experimental Social Psychology*, *2*, 219–266.

Joseph, J. (2004). *How peers influence ethical decision-making in work organizations: Revisiting the social dimension*. American University.

Kaufmann, M. C., Krings, F., & Sczesny, S. (2016). Looking too old? How an older age appearance reduces chances of being hired. *British Journal of Management*, *27*(4), 727–739.

Kaufmann, M. C., Krings, F., & Sczesny, S. (2016). Looking too old? How an older age appearance reduces chances of being hired. *British Journal of Management*, *27*(4), 727–739.

Kawakami, K., Dion, K. L., & Dovidio, J. F. (1999). Implicit stereotyping and prejudice and the primed Stroop task. *Swiss Journal of Psychology/Schweizerische Zeitschrift für Psychologie/Revue Suisse de Psychologie*, *58*(4), 241–250.

Kawakami, K., & Dovidio, J. F. (2001). The reliability of implicit stereotyping. *Personality and Social Psychology Bulletin*, *27*(2), 212–225.

Knight, R. (2017). *7 Practical ways to reduce bias in your hiring process*. Harvard Business Review. https://hbr.org/2017/06/7-practical-ways-to-reduce-bias-in-your-hiring-process#

Koch, A. J., D'Mello, S. D., & Sackett, P. R. (2015). A meta-analysis of gender stereotypes and bias in experimental simulations of employment decision making. *Journal of Applied Psychology*, *100*(1), 128–161.

Kosinski, M., Matz, S. C., Gosling, S. D., Popov, V., & Stillwell, D. (2015). Facebook as a research tool for the social sciences: Opportunities, challenges, ethical considerations, and practical guidelines. *American Psychologist*, *70*(6), 543.

Latham, G. (2019). Unanswered questions and new directions for future research on priming goals in the subconscious. *Academy of Management Discoveries*, *5*(2), 111–113.

Latu, I. M., Mast, M. S., & Stewart, T. L. (2015). Gender biases in (inter) action: The role of interviewers' and applicants' implicit and explicit stereotypes in predicting women's job interview outcomes. *Psychology of Women Quarterly*, *39*(4), 539–552.

Lewis, K. R. (2013). *3 reasons why companies don't hire veterans*. http://fortune.com/2013/11/11/3-reasons-why-companies-dont-hire-veterans/

Macan, T. H., & Dipboye, R. L. (1990). The relationship of interviewers' preinterview impressions to selection and recruitment outcomes. *Personnel Psychology*, *43*(4), 745–768.

McCord, M. A., Joseph, D. L., Dhanani, L. Y., & Beus, J. M. (2018). A meta-analysis of sex and race differences in perceived workplace mistreatment. *Journal of Applied Psychology*, *103*(2), 137–163. https://doi.org/10.1037/apl0000250

Merriam-Webster. (n.d.). Bias. In *Merriam-Webster dictionary*. https://www.merriam-webster.com/dictionary/bias

Messner, C., Wänke, M., & Weibel, C. (2011). Unconscious personnel selection. *Social Cognition*, *29*(6), 699–710.

Miller, N., & Brewer, M.B. (1984). *Groups in contact*. Academic Press.

Molnar, A. (2019). SMARTRIQS: A simple method allowing real-time respondent interaction in Qualtrics surveys. *Journal of Behavioral and Experimental Finance*, *22*, 161–169.

Muchnik, L., Aral, S., & Taylor, S. J. (2013). Social influence bias: A randomized experiment. *Science*, *341*(6146), 647–651.

Opengart, R. (2020). Veterans in the civilian workplace: How human resources can facilitate the adjustment. *Organizational Dynamics*, 1–8. https://doi.org/10.1016/j.orgdyn.2020.100775

Paolacci, G., & Chandler, J. (2014). Inside the Turk: Understanding Mechanical Turk as a participant pool. *Current Directions in Psychological Science*, *23*(3), 184–188.

Pettigrew, T. F., & Tropp, L. R. (2006). A meta-analytic test of intergroup contact theory. *Journal of Personality and Social Psychology, 90*(5), 751–783. https://doi.org/10.1037/0022-3514.90.5.751

Pew Research Center. (2011). *The military-civilian gap: Fewer family connections* https://www.pewresearch.org/social-trends/2011/11/23/the-military-civilian-gap-fewer-family-connections/

Pew Research Center. (2019). *Key findings about America's military veterans.* https://www.pewresearch.org/fact-tank/2019/11/07/key-findings-about-americas-military-veterans/

Ployhart, R. E., Schmitt, N., & Tippins, N. T. (2017). Solving the supreme problem: 100 years of selection and recruitment at the Journal of Applied Psychology. *Journal of Applied Psychology, 102*(3), 291–304. https://doi.org/10.1037/apl0000081

Porter, L. W., Lawler, E. E., & Hackman, J. R. (1975). *Behavior in organizations.* McGraw-Hill.

PsychArmour Institute. (2021a). Creating a veteran mentoring program. Retrieved August 26, 2021, from https://psycharmor.org/courses/strategies-effective-veteran-hiring/

Scheitle, C. P., & Corcoran, K. E. (2018). Religious tradition and workplace religious discrimination: The moderating effects of regional context. *Social Currents, 5*(3), 283–300.

Schreger, C., & Kimble, M. (2017). Assessing civilian perceptions of combat veterans: An IAT study. *Psychological Trauma: Theory, Research, Practice, and Policy, 9*(S1), 12–18. https://doi.org/10.1037/tra0000191

Society for Human Resource Management Foundation (SHRM). (2019). Why hire a vet? The business case for hiring military veterans. Retrieved August 23, 2021, from https://www.shrm.org/foundation/ourwork/initiatives/engaging-and-integrating-military-veterans/Documents/13056-G-01_SHRMF_WhyHireVet.pdf

Society for Human Resource Management Foundation (SHRM). (2017). *Integrating and engaging veterans in the workforce.* Retrieved December 12, 2021, from https://www.shrm.org/foundation/ourwork/initiatives/engaging-and-integrating-military-veterans/documents/4-17%20vet%20summit%20report%20final.pdf

Steffens, M. C., Niedlich, C., Beschorner, R., & Köhler, M. C. (2019). Do positive and negative stereotypes of gay and heterosexual men affect job-related impressions? *Sex Roles, 80*(9), 548–564.

Stilwell, B. (2015). *Here's why most Americans can't join the military.* We Are The Mighty. https://www.wearethemighty.com/articles/americans-unfit-military-service/.

Stone, C. B., Lengnick-Hall, M. L., & Muldoon, J. (2017). The veteran myth: An experiment of HR managers' perceptions of US military veterans. In *Academy of Management Proceedings* (Vol. 2017, No. 1, p. 12963). Academy of Management.

Stone, C. B., & Stone, D. L. (2015). Factors affecting hiring decisions about veterans. *Human Resource Management Review, 25*(1), 68–79.

Stone, D. L., & Colella, A. (1996). A model of factors affecting the treatment of disabled individuals in organizations. *Academy of Management Review, 21*(2), 352–401.

Stone, D. L., Lukaszewski, K. M., Krueger, D. C., & Canedo, J. C. (2020). A model of factors thought to influence unfair discrimination against immigrants in organizations. *Diversity and Inclusion in Organizations, Special Series, Research in HRM,* 331–361.

Stone, E. F., Stone, D. L., & Dipboye, R. L. (1992). Stigmas in organizations: Race, handicaps, and physical unattractiveness. In *Advances in Psychology 82,* 385–457. North-Holland.

Sundheim, K. (2013). *15 Traits of the ideal employee.* Forbes. Retrieved September 2, 2021, from https://www.forbes.com/sites/kensundheim/2013/04/02/15-traits-of-the-ideal-employee/?sh=6ff47fb4161f

Taylor, S. E. (1981). A categorization approach to stereotyping. *Cognitive Processes in Stereotyping and Intergroup Behavior, 832114.*

Tversky, A., & Kahneman, D. (1974). Judgment under uncertainty: Heuristics and biases. *Science, 185*(4157), 1124–1131.

U.S. Department of Veteran Affairs (USDVA). (2015). *Positive outcomes of military service.* Retrieved September 14, 2021, from https://www.va.gov/vetsinworkplace/docs/em_positiveChanges.asp

van de Mortel, T. F. (2008). Faking it: Social desirability response bias in self-report research. *The Australian Journal of Advanced Nursing, 25*(4), 40–48.

Vornholt, K., Uitdewilligen, S., & Nijhuis, F. J. (2013). Factors affecting the acceptance of people with disabilities at work: A literature review. *Journal of Occupational Rehabilitation, 23*(4), 463–475.

Weinberg, N. (1976). Social stereotyping of the physically handicapped. *Rehabilitation Psychology, 23*(4), 115–124. https://doi.org/10.1037/h0090911

Xu, Q., Ye, C., Gu, S., Hu, Z., Lei, Y., Li, X., Huang, L., & Liu, Q. (2021). Negative and positive bias for emotional faces: Evidence from the attention and working memory paradigms. *Neural Plasticity, 2021.*

Yosef, L., Soffer, M., & Malul, M. (2019). From welfare to work and from work to welfare: A comparison of people with and without disabilities. *Journal of Disability Policy Studies, 29(4),* 226–234. https://doi.org/10.1177/1044207318782674

Yuker, H. E. (1988). *Attitudes toward persons with disabilities.* Springer.

APPENDIX A

Conscious and Social Bias Measurements

Conscious Bias (CB) Measurement Scale	Cronbach's Alpha (CB)	Social Bias (SB) Measurement Scale	Cronbach's Alpha (SB)
1. I really admire those men and women who have served our country in our military.	.728	1. Those people I ask for advice think that…Military veterans are great employees.	.832
2. I think military veterans tend to retain their aggressive behaviors as civilian employees.		2. Those people I ask for advice think that…Military veterans make great leaders.	
3. I am afraid that all veterans suffer from PTSD and are prone to violence.		3. Those people I ask for advice think that…Military veterans are more reliable employees.	
4. I think those who were in the armed services should be treated no differently than non-veterans.		4. Those people I ask for advice think that…Military veterans bring skills to the workforce others do not have.	
5. I think serving in the military is essentially no different than any other job.		5. Those people I ask for advice think that…Military veterans bring greater maturity to a workplace.	
6. I think those who wear military uniforms think differently than non-military.		6. Those people I ask for advice think that…Military veterans are more aggressive employees.	
7. I think those who served in the military did so because they had no better job options.		7. Those people I ask for advice think that…Military veterans can be dangerous to others because of PTSD.	
8. I think those who served in the military sacrificed a lot for our country.		8. Those people I ask for advice think that…Military veterans are hard to get along with in civilian jobs.	
9. I think veterans are true American heroes.		9. Those people I ask for advice think that…Military veterans do not make good employees.	
10. I think having a veteran working next to me would make me nervous.		10. Those people I ask for advice think that…Military veterans should not get hiring preferences just because of their service.	

238

CHAPTER 8

DEGREES OF INCARCERATION

Navigating Barriers to Employment

Catrina Palmer Johnson
Kent State University

Nicole C. Jones Young
Franklin & Marshall College

ABSTRACT

In the United States, 70 million adults possess a criminal history. The majority will return or remain in the community, allowing them—often mandating them—to seek employment. Yet because criminal history is among the most detrimental stigmas in the employment process, this population has limited options. Among the strategies that can assist individuals in lowering their perceived stigma during the employment process, the attainment of higher education is less understood. To gain further understanding, we conducted 21 interviews with men and women who were recently released from incarceration, seeking paid employment, and had completed or were pursuing a bachelor's, master's, or doctoral degree. With regard to managing the effects of stigma related to justice-involvement, we find that completion of a higher education degree provides formerly incarcerated individuals with (1) awareness of structural barriers that increase visibility of a criminal history, (2) confidence to disclose one's criminal history, (3) disposition to pursue a true-to-self provisional strategy, and (4) readiness to pursue a highly skilled occupation.

Forgotten Minorities in Organizations, pp. 239–273
Copyright © 2023 by Information Age Publishing
www.infoagepub.com
All rights of reproduction in any form reserved.
239

DEGREES OF INCARCERATION:
NAVIGATING BARRIERS TO EMPLOYMENT

Over 70 million adults in the United States possess a criminal history (The Sentencing Project, 2015), meaning they have been convicted of committing an offense and have served time within a correctional facility (i.e., prison or jail), completed or are under community supervision (i.e., probation or parole), or experienced a combination of the two.[1] Many of the approximately 700,000 individuals released from state and federal prisons each year (Strait & Eaton, 2017) are overwhelmed with the challenges of transitioning back to society, particularly securing employment. According to most recent research, on average, formerly incarcerated individuals are unemployed at a rate of approximately 27% (Couloute & Kopf, 2018), a status disproportionately concentrated among Black and Latinx individuals who are more likely to return to disadvantaged, low-income communities (Decker et al., 2015; Travis et al., 2014). While the size of those with a criminal history is large, the disproportionately negative employment outcomes and insufficient attention in addressing these issues, signal that these individuals may be representative of a forgotten minority.

Formerly incarcerated individuals face employment discrimination as a result of the stigma associated with criminal history. In comparison to other concealable stigmas, a criminal history can be requested and legally considered during the employment process (U.S. Equal Employment Opportunity Commission, 2012). Individuals with a criminal history often experience a variety of unique challenges as they attempt to gain entry into an organization, allowing criminal history to be considered one of the most detrimental stigmas (Pager, 2007). Yet, employment is paramount to secure basic necessities and resources, and it is often a condition of release to community supervision after incarceration. To decrease stigma and increase employability, individuals may look to acquire additional human capital, such as education credentials. According to the most recent study on educational attainment and the U.S. incarcerated population, 30% have less than a high school education—more than double the rate among Americans without a criminal history (U.S. Department of Education, 2014). At the collegiate level, less than 1% have a bachelor's degree (Couloute, 2018), as compared to 23.5% of the U.S. population who hold a bachelor's degree as their highest degree (U.S. Census, 2022). The association of carceral history and low education levels is salient and readily apparent on a job application. Thus, it is likely that employers are influenced not only by the stigma of an applicant's criminal history, but also to the stigma of low educational attainment in their hiring decisions.

Given that educational attainment can signal employment readiness within the labor market (Spence, 1973), individuals who obtain higher levels of education may positively affect their employment outcomes. This may be of particular relevance as we consider those with a criminal history, because many employers want to see some evidence of positive engagement prior to extending an offer of employment (Griffith & Young, 2017). Obtaining education, particularly higher levels of education, is one way that individuals with a criminal history can meet this informal requirement and attempt to lessen the common stereotype that ties justice-involvement to the assumption of low education levels.

While important to understand the employer's perspective, as Young and Ryan (2019) suggested, it is also important to understand more about this population from the perspective of the applicant. As such, to explore the effect of educational attainment on perceptions of securing employment, we engaged in 21 interviews with formerly incarcerated men and women who had completed or were in the process of completing a bachelor's degree. Our findings indicate that the completion of a higher education degree provides formerly incarcerated individuals with (1) awareness of structural barriers that increase visibility of a criminal history (2) confidence to disclose one's criminal history, (3) disposition to pursue a true-to-self provisional strategy, and 4) readiness to pursue a highly skilled occupation.

LITERATURE REVIEW

Stigma of a Criminal Record

Conceptualized as a social response to an attribute that others find discrediting (Goffman, 1963), stigma is often cited as the underlying factor in explaining the low employment rates among individuals with a criminal history. Research demonstrates an array of stigma-related consequences (Stone et al., 1992). For instance, based on the categorization of an applicant's stigma, stereotypes may influence perceptions, feelings, and behaviors toward that stigmatized individual or group (Stone & Colella, 1996). Generally, this results in discrimination (Baur et al., 2018; Link & Phelan, 2001). Moreover, when the stigma of criminal history coincides with another attribute, such as a racial or ethnic identity, the effect may be compounded, as the stigma of a criminal history is heightened for individuals who are also Black and/or Latinx.

While individuals with a criminal history will share some challenges with other stigmatized groups, such as racial minorities, women, or individuals with a disability, they are unique in that there are no federal civil rights laws to protect them from disclosing their criminal history or prevent its consideration in the hiring process (Young & Powell, 2015; Zeidner, 2014).

This lack of federal legal protection may justify prejudicial beliefs about and practices toward formerly incarcerated individuals. To address these distinct challenges, Young and Powell (2015), and subsequently Baur and colleagues (2018), developed theoretical models that detail how the stigma of a criminal history influences employers' hiring decisions, and how it varies in relation to factors including disclosure characteristics, characteristics of the offense, characteristics of the applicant, and characteristics of the observer.

Individuals do not have discretion over whether to conceal their criminal record. Thus, disclosure is typically unavoidable during the hiring process, where, even if it can be concealed on an initial application, it becomes a required disclosure at the interview stage or is revealed when a parole or probation officer contacts the employer to confirm an offer of employment (Young & Ryan, 2019). The decision to disclose or conceal is also nullified in many cases because criminal convictions are largely accessible to the public (Freeman, 2008), allowing anyone to search the criminal history of prospective or fellow employees (Anazodo et al., 2020).

The ever-present stigma, stereotypes, and discriminatory practices it can elicit in the labor market make it difficult for individuals with a criminal history to secure employment (Griffith et al., 2019). Fear of being victimized, issues of trustworthiness, cost, and concerns about the organization's reputation often hinder employers' willingness to hire this population (Anazodo et al., 2020; Griffith & Young, 2017; Holzer et al., 2004; Waldfogel, 1994), as do worries about increased workplace crime and negligent hiring claims (Leavitt, 2001; Zeidner, 2014). Moreover, recent research confirms the power of continuing discrimination, pointing to the persistence of racial profiling and stereotypes regarding criminality (Agan & Starr, 2018; Doleac & Hansen, 2016).

With limited opportunities, individuals with a criminal record are frequently relegated to low-wage and low-skilled occupations such as warehouse and construction work and positions in the restaurant and food service industry (Nally et al., 2014; Vuolo et al., 2017). These occupations are marked by high turnover, poor labor conditions, irregular schedules, and labor-intensive (Harding et al., 2019; Holzer et al., 2004; Purser, 2012; Western, 2002). Currently, at least 37 states have enacted "ban the box" laws and other legislation to help protect individuals with a criminal history from employment discrimination (Avery & Lu, 2021). Specifically, these policies frequently prohibit employers from asking about applicants' criminal history during the initial job application process. Findings from Griffith and Young (2017) indicated that hiring managers in ban the box states support hiring formerly incarcerated individuals, but also cited concerns related to safety, cost, and characteristics of the individual's offense; signaling that stigma may attenuate hiring decisions, regardless of legislation. In short, despite good-faith efforts to reform the legal context of hiring decisions, formerly incarcerated individuals cannot effectively conceal their criminal history and frequently find their employment options to be limited.

Education and Employment

Reentry studies have long documented the myriad challenges facing formerly incarcerated individuals, but scholars have recently begun to focus on the agency that these individuals demonstrate to overcome their adversities (Hwang & Phillips, 2020; Palmer & Christian, 2019). That is, rather than focus on the barriers they encounter, studies seek to uncover how these individuals actively strategize and intentionally engage in opportunities to create positive outcomes for themselves and their communities. For example, to improve their job prospects, formerly incarcerated individuals may participate in pre-release and reentry programs featuring vocational training or college-level courses. Research indicates that these programs significantly reduce the literacy and numeric skills gaps between formerly incarcerated individuals and similarly situated peers without carceral histories (Ositelu, 2019). Meta-analysis further reveals that participation in correctional education programs increases the odds of gaining post-release employment by 13% (Davis et al., 2013). Thus, potential employers may be treating such programs as a positive credential softening the impact of stigma (Bushway & Apel, 2012; Formon et al., 2018; Harding et al., 2019). To hiring managers willing to consider formerly incarcerated applicants, educational program completion appears to signal an applicant has a higher skill level, knowledge, and job readiness than comparable others (Pager, 2003).

Questions such as whether college-educated, formerly incarcerated individuals have exposure to better-paying jobs and working conditions remain unanswered. In an experimental study, using fictitious resumes and cover letters, Cerda-Jara et al. (2020) found that college-educated, formerly incarcerated men received half the number of hiring callbacks as college-educated men without a criminal record. Their results also revealed a familiar pattern with regards to race, as Black and Latino men received fewer callbacks than their white male counterparts. In the authors' supplementary qualitative interviews, participants described the difficulties of "oversharing," choosing to omit their criminal records, and avoiding job postings that indicated background checks. Thus, educational attainment cannot fully negate the stigma of criminal history, particularly when accounting for additional factors such as race and ethnicity.

However, it is unclear how individuals who are formerly incarcerated and college-educated may undertake the process of seeking employment, given their increased human and social capital. Understanding whether the personal and financial investment in a college degree (which, for the formerly incarcerated, can be considerably more difficult to attain) aids in ameliorating the stigma and stereotypes associated with a criminal history, lowers real and perceived barriers to employment, and benefits the individual in less tangible ways is a question of paramount importance. Thus, we center the job-seeker and ask the following research question:

> **RQ:** How does individuals' pursuit or completion of higher education after obtaining a criminal history affect their perceptions of (re)entry to the workforce?

METHODS

We used a phenomenological investigative approach to examine how the pursuit or completion of higher education affected formerly incarcerated individuals and their perceptions of (re)entry to the workforce. This method is most appropriate for the purposes of understanding the phenomenon of post-incarceration job-seeking from the perspective of those experiencing it (Merriam, 2002). Additionally, this approach moves beyond other qualitative techniques, such as observations and assessments (Moustakas, 1994), allowing us to directly capture the meaning of the phenomenon as a result of the relationship between the person and the context in which the experience is taking place (Merriam, 2002). Hence, a deliberative focus on formerly incarcerated individuals' employment experiences both during and after they obtained their degree is critical in exploring the labor market value of higher education for this subgroup of job-seekers.

Sample

We recruited a purposeful sample of formerly incarcerated individuals who had obtained (or were in the process of obtaining) a bachelor's degree from a statewide program administered by a public university located in a Mid-Atlantic, ban-the-box state. The program aims to reduce recidivism through higher education. Funded by private donors, it takes a comprehensive approach and partners with an array of institutions, including the state's Department of Corrections, Parole Board, and a variety of 2- and 4-year colleges. Its postsecondary courses are open to eligible individuals incarcerated in one of seven correctional facilities within the state. Traditionally, individuals in our study, completed coursework towards their associates degree while incarcerated and upon release, became eligible to transition into a bachelor's degree program at a 4-year institution, with the support of the program.

With the consent and support of the executive director, the primary author attended the program's orientation sessions at the start of the fall 2018, spring 2019, and spring 2020 semesters. This allowed the author to observe the communal environment cultivated by the program administrators and initiate relationships with potential participants. At the end of each orientation, the author was introduced and provided a chance to announce the study, including its motivations and purpose, to program participants. Afterward, the authors sent midsemester follow-up emails inviting students to participate in the present study. Additional participants were recruited through snowball sampling, encouraged to sign up for the study as other participants openly described their interview experiences as positive and therapeutic.

Our final sample ($n = 21$, see Table 8.1), was 76% men and 67% people of color (Black/African American and Latinx), with an average age of 37.6 years across a range from 26 to 60 years ($SD = 9.16$). Every participant had at least a high school diploma (otherwise, they could not have begun their college degree while incarcerated), 47% had a bachelor's or master's degree, and 53% were in the process of completing a four-year degree. At the time of the interviews, 76% were employed (with individuals most frequently citing their pre-incarceration occupation as carpentry, retail, kitchen work, and entry-level administration). Participants' criminal convictions varied,[2] although the most commonly reported were robbery, drug possession and distribution, and aggravated assault. Thirty-three percent of the sample had endured multiple periods of incarceration.

Table 8.1

Participants of Study

	Name	Age	Race	Gender	Highest Degree Obtained	Employed
1	Thomas	41	Black/African American	Male	Associate	No
2	Devon	29	Black/African American	Male	Some College Credit	Yes
3	Charles	46	Black/African American	Male	Associate	Yes
4	Lawrence	44	Other	Male	Associate	No
5	Ben	44	Black/African American	Male	Associate	Yes

(Table continued on next page)

Table 8.1 (Continued)

Participants of Study

	Name	Age	Race	Gender	Highest Degree Obtained	Employed
6	Isabella	26	Hispanic/Latino	Female	Associate	Yes
7	Joshua	60	White	Male	Bachelor	Yes
8	Juan	34	Hispanic/Latino & White	Male	Bachelor	Yes
9	Mike	34	Black/African American	Female	Associate	Yes
10	Darryl	42	Black/African American	Male	Associate	Yes
11	Carlos	28	Prefer not to respond	Male	Bachelor	Yes
12	Anthony	26	Black/African American	Male	Associate	Yes
13	Tiara	41	White	Female	Master	Yes
14	Sofia	40	Hispanic/Latino	Female	Master	Yes
15	Terrance	28	Hispanic/Latino	Male	Associate	Yes
16	Jordan	32	Black & Hispanic/Latino	Male	Master	Yes
17	Jason	49	Black & Native American	Male	Bachelor	No
18	Nicholas	26	White	Male	Bachelor	No
19	David	43	White	Male	Some college credit	No
20	Michelle	45	White	Female	Master	Yes
21	Eduardo	31	Hispanic / Latino	Male	Bachelor	Yes

Our sample was affected by structural conditions, as all those who participated in our study had been selected (generally by prison staff) for the educational program, and so they cannot represent the full U.S. prison population or even the entire population of their specific facilities. As Joshua shared, *"I was in there and then they accepted me [to the program]. I was glad that they did, because like 1,100 people applied and they only had a hundred [spots]... but they expanded it to 150 [spots for admission] because the request was so large."* Another participant, who was initially wait-listed recalled being told up-front, *"... Any of you who score high enough on this test, who have a high school diploma, who have five years to do as a total of your sentence, you are eligible for this college program. But there's a waiting list."* This indicates that even if individuals are aware of opportunities to help navigate the stigma of a criminal history, structural inequities prevent access to opportunities for all who may be interested. As such, those who wished to engage with higher education during their incarceration but were unable to do so were excluded from our sample.

Several participants of color raised another intriguing factor, telling us they had been hesitant to participate in the higher education program, because they were skeptical about its legitimacy. Given their perceptions of and history with the carceral system, as well as their current experiences in prison, respondents were doubtful whether a correctional institution was truly willing to invest in their growth, development, and long-term prospects. Ben expressed his initial reaction to the opportunity, *"Why would these people back there, they treat us like this, but then allow us to have access to this education? They dehumanize us on one hand but give us a tool that can make us effective when we get back if we utilize it properly. So I was skeptical for quite some time."* Others recalled wondering whether the credentials they earned were "real" and if their college credits would transfer if and when they were released from prison.

Procedure

Prior to their interviews, we restated the purpose and structure of our study for participants. Each was informed that they could opt-out of the study at any time during the interview process. As presented in the Appendix, we began with open-ended interview questions designed to elicit personal narratives about the participants' motivation to pursue higher education, experiences gained inside and outside of the classroom, and positive and negative employment experiences. Participants then had the opportunity to reflect on their personal and professional milestones. The interviews ended with a survey to capture demographic and socioeconomic information, as well as criminal offenses and employment history.

We conducted 14 face-to-face and 7 phone interviews lasting approximately 45 to 60 minutes from October 2018 to March 2020. It should be noted that phone was generally preferred to video conferencing tools (e.g., Zoom), as phone interviews generally do not require technical knowledge (including how to use the software) or present barriers in the form of computer and internet access. Face-to-face interviews were held in an open and public location at the university campus and were conducted by one or both authors. Upon completion, participants were compensated for their time with a $10 Dunkin' Donuts gift card. With participants' consent, each interview was audio recorded, then transcribed verbatim by a third-party, professional service and stored in a password-protected folder. We have assigned pseudonyms to all participants, and the interview excerpts provided in this chapter are only edited to remove verbal utterances such as "um" and "uh."

Data Analysis

We began data analysis by transcribing and coding the first five interviews independently. We identified similarities and differences across interviews, with each author conducting line by line, open coding of each interview transcript to identify salient themes, and then coming together to compare and discuss the coding in order to ensure inter-coder reliability. This process also revealed areas of our interview protocol where we might expand our inquiry in the subsequent interviews to better understand the nuances of pursuing higher education as an individual with a criminal history (Creswell et al., 2007; Yin, 2015). For example, our initial coding highlighted participants' classroom experiences as well as their process of selecting the jobs to which they applied. Subsequent category coding included themes about the credibility of a degree obtained while incarcerated, strategies for framing one's criminal history for employers, and the structural challenges to reentry that participants encountered in domains including education, employment, and housing. We continued data collection and analysis simultaneously until we ceased to find newly emergent patterns in the data (Creswell, 2013).

An important caveat is that many individuals within our sample had prior employment histories, which may have affected their perceptions that higher education is necessary for employment. Thus, decisions to obtain higher education were not necessarily predicated on individuals' sense that *they* needed it, but more so that they felt *society wanted them* to obtain a degree before allowing them access to opportunities. Thomas summarized, "*So this degree, I needed to be on my resume so that I can secure a job so I can do what I want to do…. The only thing that will probably give me a job, the way I look on paper, is for them to see the education. That I have the capacity to learn.*" In similar terms, Darryl shared, "*I started taking classes because I knew I was going to need a degree, personally, in order to get the job I wanted to be accepted back into society.*" It was using this analytical lens that we engaged in coding our data.

FINDINGS

Our findings draw attention to four mechanisms through which gaining higher education can impact the post-incarceration job search and transition into work: (1) awareness of structural barriers that increase visibility of a criminal history (2) confidence to disclose one's criminal history, (3) disposition to pursue a true-to-self provisional strategy, and (4) readiness to pursue a highly skilled occupation. Each mechanism figured into participants' beliefs about how higher education impacted employers' perceptions of their stigma. These findings along with sub-themes and implications for employment are highlighted in Table 8.2.

Awareness of Structural Barriers That Increase Visibility of a Criminal History

As previously articulated, a criminal record is an invisible, but frequently not a concealable stigma. Employment and higher education are littered with structural barriers to an individual's real ability to control the disclosure of their criminal history. Even when individuals were not required to disclose their record, our participants commonly assumed others could "see" it. As Carlos said of his classmates, *"In my mind, I'm paranoid. They know I can't talk on the weekends. I don't answer my phone at night or on the weekend. I can't meet them. How do they not know?"* Commonly, individuals like Carlos who live in designated facilities (e.g., halfway houses) after incarceration, are subject to highly regulated schedules; according to the United States Courts (2021), individuals on probation and supervised release are subject to court monitoring and determinations regarding where they can live, with whom they can associate, and during which hours they are required to be present at a particular location. These invisible restrictions become visible quickly when, as Carlos describes, an individual needs to provide a schedule of availability to a classmate or an employer. Isabella pointed out that recently released people and those subject to housing assignments and curfews became identifiable because, *"Well, you're not allowed to be on campus after 6:00 p.m...."* Individuals with more privileged identities may have been oblivious to the fact that a swath of classmates were gone by 6 p.m., but those with marginalized identities sometimes felt their stigma was readily apparent.

Technological know-how (or lack thereof) presented another possible avenue for unintended stigma disclosure. Individuals who are incarcerated have limited access to computers and other technology. Ben said when he was incarcerated, *"there was only MySpace. Facebook hadn't opened. People were on the waiting list for the iPhone."* Thus, by the time he was released, Ben *"hadn't even seen an iPhone yet."* Another participant, Eduardo, told us, *"I left [for prison] in '05, and I came home beginning of 2011. Like, when I left, it was like Nokias with a green screen. You know Nokias?"* Some individuals were able to quietly maneuver around these technology barriers, but others felt their criminal history stigma become visible as they engaged in team projects with other students on campus. Multiple participants shared stories related to their lack of comfort with the computer:

Table 8.2

Exemplar Quotes

Theme	Subtheme	Exemplar	Connection to Employment
	Appearance	Yeah kind of like, "Why are you here?" Maybe it wasn't race. Maybe it was cultural. Maybe they're looking at me as a street kid working in there, "Why is he here?" Back then, I didn't know how to tone it down dress-wise. Now I learned how to dress. I'm like crisp shirt, watch, ring, earring, hair cut with the parts all over the place. If I look in, "Who's this kid in the seat?" ~Jordan	Participants were cognizant of how their race and gender influenced others' perceptions about their skills and abilities. Professional attire, such as gray and black suits, translated to participants being approachable and considered for opportunities; whereas streetwear or what others may perceive as "unpolished" professional attire led participants to believe that they did not fit (or were unwelcomed) in certain environments.
		I had a black belt and bright-blue tie, and I thought I was killing it. I show up at the symposium, and I remember walking into the room. As soon as I walked in, I felt like I had a bright-red nose on. Everyone else had—their clothes were tailored. They were toned down. Their colors were charcoal gray and navy blue and black. Here I am bright, canary-yellow shirt on, blue tie. I looked crazy. ~Jordan	
		It's because I understand, as a Black man in America, perception is everything. Like I've sat on the train going to school, same bookbag, same books open in a sweat suit. People have literally stood up not to sit next to me. And I've been on that same train with them same people at the same time with my suit on, same book open and I've had a guy talk about he's a professor at [University]. "What are you studying? Oh, I'm an economics professor. Here's my card." Like, "You were here yesterday and you didn't care about me." ~Devon	
	Institutional Restrictions	In my mind, I'm paranoid. They know I can't talk on the weekends. I don't answer my phone at night or on the weekend. I can't meet them. How do they not know? ~Carlos	Institutional restrictions required participants to manage another level of adversity and often was a hinderance for gaining employment. Given parameters, such as curfews and required check-ins, participants
		Well, you're not allowed to be on campus after 6:00 p.m., so that's one thing that affects it. But other than that, I still am a full-time student with four classes. ~Isabella	

(Table continued on next page)

250

Table 8.2 (Continued)

Exemplar Quotes

Awareness of Structural Barriers that Increase Visibility of a Criminal History	I applied for other positions. They wanted to hire me but the stipulations, like the halfway house can come do a site check at any time and the calls and everything, so they weren't really comfortable with the whole idea of the halfway house, like a lot of places well, when you get out of the halfway house, come back. ~Mike	learned how to adapt their schedules to maximize their time in and out of the classroom, building relationships with their colleagues and potential employers.
	Yeah. It's a double transition. I'm on the campus at 40 years old. Of course. That's another, like, "Mm-hmm, you 40?" And then the part that was getting me was I'd be like, "Alright, I don't know how to use this computer. Can somebody show me?" They were like, "What do you mean?" I'm like, "Listen, I've been locked up for a certain amount of time. Eleven years, eleven months. I have not had technology. I don't know how to really do this." ~Darryl	Due to the time lost in prison along with the lack of access to technology while incarcerated, participants were not adequately trained to compete in the present workforce. The technological divide also impacted participants' abilities to adequately market their skills and abilities and submit electronic applications.
Digital Divide	For me, I was locked up for 2-1/2 years, so the impact wasn't that great, but for my work now, like especially the women that have done 30 years, when they come home, they're like, "You shouldn't even go to school this semester. You need to take a semester to learn how to email." Basic stuff. ~Sofia	
	Because it was like, we got here and we're like, "Okay, who knows that I was incarcerated? Is it written all over my face? Are they going to know that I don't know how to do this?" It had been ten years since I was in community college after high school. So even in those ten years, we were ten years before we were submitting papers at the end of class, and now we're submitting them online and I'm like, "I don't know how to do this. " ~Tiara	
Disclosure with University or University	Go talk to your professors on a human level. Fuck what grades you want. On a human level. "Hey, this is me. I'm in your class, this is my situation. I'm a non-traditional student in the sense that I'm older and how would you take being in my position? How would you go about it?" I've always done that. ~Devon	Participants' disposition to disclose their criminal history allowed them to share a more comprehensive story about themself that expanded beyond their period of incarceration. It
	I think being home and telling people, fortunately having people be accepting of it, gives you more confidence to be able to feel like you can tell	

(Table continued on next page)

251

Table 8.2 (Continued)

Exemplar Quotes

	related Employment	people. That's definitely a big factor. Which all of those little things happening previously now make me very confident when speaking with an employer or being able to tell them my background. Just that I've had that experience already of telling people. ~Nicholas	demonstrated their willingness to own their past behaviors but also move forward in a very intentional and productive manner by creating new opportunities.
Confidence to Disclose One's Criminal History		At first I was not comfortable at all but the more I have put my life on the line or my story out the more comfortable I get with it because it is my story. I have to own it, you know. ~Joshua	
		When I went to [University], and I met with the director that was supervising our lab, that was the first thing I said. She went "Oh, we don't have to—that's fine and this and that. You don't have to tell anybody." I said, "No, I do. Because I've got to get practice in explaining this situation, because I've never really done it in interviews or anything. I've always had little menial jobs that didn't require all of that or they didn't care about backgrounds. " –Lawrence	
	Disclosure with Non-University related Employment	Like, "No, [colleague] didn't tell me and we don't even run background checks." He just laughed. He's like, "We don't even run background checks, but I'm glad you were open and honest with me. But we don't even run background checks. So it wasn't even something that was on our radar." For me, it's like you never know, especially when you work in finance. My biggest thing is where I'm at, I don't want to be a liability. ~Devon	Participants felt the need to be honest to potential employers, as they did not want their lack of disclosure to lead to a loss of employment in the long run.
		She was like alright, "all we need to do is just go through the background check and do a drug screen and then we'll get you started." "Alright, before you do that, can we have a conversation first because I'm just letting you know if you're going to do the background check, there's going to be some things you're going to find and I'd rather let you know about it ahead of time." This way it's not a surprise and then kind of go from there. ~Juan	
	Confronting Disclosure	Depending on the person that I was engaging, depending on the vibe at the moment between the two, that would depend on how soon I bring it up, but I wanted to make it clear that I was going to bring it up regardless. I'm not ashamed of it ... because there's to many Americans that have that stigma to ignore. And I want people to know that their interactions with me, because	Participants were confident and transparent with sharing their past criminal history. This confidence also translated to their belief in being an

(Table continued on next page)

252

Table 8.2 (Continued)

Exemplar Quotes

Theme	Subtheme	Exemplar	Connection to Employment
		I'm going to be representative of the others that come behind me. ~Lawrence	exceptional and hard-working employee for a potential employer.
		I'm going to be straight when I'm asked a question. I'm going to be straight honest. And I know how to be, for lack of a better word, diplomatic with it. But I'm going to be straight because I'm not into lying, and I feel like I value myself a little more than I need to lie. ~Thomas	
		It's like being a salesman. When you going in you have to sell yourself. I suit myself up. I go in there with confidence and I put everything on the table. "Where do we go from here?" ~Mike	
	Establishing New Norms for Self	I was supposed to get off at 12 midnight. They walked into the job and said, "Listen, we need you to work three more hours, and if you don't want to work three hours extra, you will be terminated." So I worked the three hours, and at the end of the three hours, they came back to us and said, "Well, now you can leave without any repercussions." But it wasn't what they said, it was how they said it. You get what I'm saying? And so at that point I realized I was nothing but a slave. And I was a slave in prison. So I'm not going to be a slave out here. And I never went back. ~Charles	Participants no longer felt they had to subject themselves to unfair and discriminatory practices. They felt empowered to challenge workplace norms that were unjust and identified new opportunities that aligned with their vision and interests.
		... the night manager was just horrible. I was arguing with her all [the] time, just like you're not going to talk to me like you do the rest of them—like don't bring this person out of me, please. I'm not one of these kids who comes in here from high school or something. I'm a grown man. You're not going to disrespect me. ~Juan	
Disposition to Pursue a True-To-Self Provisional Strategy		I don't know if this is like a me thing or people who are in prison think you get into a job and it's just everybody realizing [is this] what I really want to do? Or, is this what I've been allowed to do? ~Juan	Participants were driven to identify career opportunities wherein they were valued for
		I couldn't be the young, aggressive Black guy. Yeah, I'm from the hood and I never stop being from the hood because it made me who I am, in my culture, my people, I love them, but you've got to learn how to navigate to an extent	

(Table continued on next page)

253

Table 8.2 (Continued)

Exemplar Quotes

Theme	Subtheme	Exemplar	Connection to Employment
		to where you don't lose your identity, but you can still be successful here. ~Devon	being their authentic selves, despite how it may be perceived by others. Being their authentic selves increased their confidence to make an impact in their work and communities.
		I would want to work for an employer who would respect my honesty and integrity, and actually appreciate that I'm willing to explain and not try to hide anything from them ... I wouldn't really want to work for an employer who wasn't comfortable with the fact that I'm a convicted felon. ~Nicholas	
	Authentic Self	I wrote a seven-part article in [news website]. At first I was not comfortable at all but the more I have put my life on the line or my story out, the more comfortable I get with it because it is my story. I have to own it, you know. ~Joshua	
		I just want to work with people just like me. People of Color, from the hood. I can relate to them. ~Sofia	Participants desired to directly identify the impact of their work by working with others who can benefit from their knowledge, skills, and abilities.
	Meaningful Work	Once I complete my degree. I want to go back and help other brothers and sisters who are involved. Not so much of the victim. I know everybody wants to help the victim, and they should. I want to help the perpetrator ... ~Charles	
		I'm not concerned about money. I'm not concerned about prestige. I just want to do what I can from the lowest microlevel to the largest macro level for real systemic reform. ~Lawrence	
Readiness to Pursue a Highly Skilled Occupation	Social & Community Based Work	What it is, our committee has a federal judge on it. He deals with a reentry program of his own. We have two county administrators. We had the Camden County Jail, population manager there. A person from motor vehicles is on our committee. We have a couple public defenders, several different nonprofit organizations. So what we do is they allowed me to be a part of this board because I guess I can give insight into what people need reintegrating, even though I don't have the powers that they have. ~Ben	Participants were able to leverage their prior criminal history into an asset rather than a detriment, in their chosen field. They were no longer working around their criminal history but using it as a tool to perform their job.
		But also it depends on what industry you're doing, you know? Because from what I've heard and from what I've witnessed, when it comes to, like, social	

(Table continued on next page)

Table 8.2 (Continued)

Exemplar Quotes

Theme	Subtheme	Exemplar	Connection to Employment
		work, they'd actually rather have somebody who has been in the system rather than somebody who has never been. ~Terrance	
		Not as a hindrance, but the job that I got in [City], I feel like that's why they hired me was because I had a criminal record. So the supervisor knew I had a story and I could really relate to these kids. ~Sofia	
	Entrepreneurship	I am, but I'm fortunate. I'm very, very fortunate that I actually support myself by speaking engagements, sharing the message of transformation toward education. So I get four or five speaking engagements a month. ~Jason	Entrepreneurship provided participants with an alternative career route to the traditional labor market, an environment in which they were likely to experience various degrees of employment discrimination as a result of their race and criminal history.
		Well, I'm going to be real with you. I'm not looking to work for anybody. Even as we're speaking, I'm working on building something for myself. ~Carlos	
		Like myself, I just came home in January and I'm attempting to start a small business but I'm barred from government loans because I'm still a citizen on parole supervision. ~David	
	Traditionally Excluded Spaces	Yeah, so I'm considering, in addition to that master's that I mentioned, I'm going to take the LSAT, not the GRE. So I'm going to try. I looked on the network I just told you about and there are 38 states included in this network, and several of the people have passed the bar and have been authorized to practice law in several different states. So that's kind of inspirational for me. ~Ben	In gaining educational credentials, participants became increasingly confident in pursuing careers that they have been traditionally excluded from. In entering new spaces, they sought to use the opportunity to give back and empower those with whom they had a shared experience.
		Then I just tried to weave women and gender studies and IT together. I've always wanted to be able to help women of color access—more than just writing a resume. Everybody just wants to teach you how to write a resume. There's so much more that you can do with technology. That's why I ended up with that. ~Sofia	
		I liked human resources because I wanted to go into business, but human resources had more of a—there was like more people. Human resources was a way for me to enjoy the aspect of business but make a difference. I went that route. ~Jordan	

255

"Alright, I don't know how to use this computer. Can somebody show me?" They were like, "What do you mean?" I'm like, "Listen, I've been locked up for a certain amount of time. Eleven years, eleven months. I have not had technology. I don't know how to really do this." (Darryl)

"Are they going to know that I don't know how to do this?" It had been ten years since I was in community college after high school … we were submitting papers at the end of class, and now we're submitting them online, and I'm like, "I don't know how to do this." (Tiara)

Throughout their educational pursuits, respondents spoke about the ways they felt their identity, behaviors, and appearances allowed others to "see" their stigma and stereotype them for their criminal backgrounds (Moran, 2012). In some instances, they described how working toward an advanced degree seemed to have altered stereotypical assumptions about individuals with a criminal history having low-level educations (Harlow, 2003). But, as articulated by Devon, participants frequently had to navigate assumptions related to their racial identity first:

… as a Black man in America, perception is everything. Like I've sat on the train going to school—same bookbag, same books open—in a sweatsuit. People have literally stood up not to sit next to me. And I've been on that same train with them same people at the same time with my suit on, same book open, and I've had a guy talk about he's a professor at [University]. "What are you studying? Oh, I'm an economics professor. Here's my card." Like, "You were here yesterday, and you didn't care about me."

Assumptions that tie race and criminality are so common in employment (Doleac & Hansen, 2020) and educational (Bennett et al., 2017) contexts that even when criminal history is not provided, Black and Latinx individuals are subject to a litany of racial microaggressions. Clothing can further reinforce stereotypes, as many use clothing as a proxy for assessing other factors such as a person's social class status (e.g., Gillath et al., 2012), education levels and capacities (e.g., Ball et al., 2002). Perceptions of social class status frequently affect day to day interactions (Gray & Kish-Gephart, 2013), a fact that had not escaped our participant who was treated differently depending on the clothes he wore as he commuted to campus.

Unsurprisingly, participants surmised that their criminal history might be visible in their appearance. Jordan recalled attending a research symposium and feeling exposed:

I had some tan khakis. I borrowed some brown shoes from somebody. I had a black belt and bright-blue tie, and I thought I was killing it. I show up at the symposium, and I remember walking into the room. As soon as I walked in, I felt like I had a bright-red nose on. Everyone else had—their clothes were tailored. They were toned down. Their colors were charcoal gray and navy blue and black. Here I am, bright, canary-yellow shirt on, blue tie. I looked crazy.

In this moment, Jordan realized that he was unaware when it came to the norms of professional dress—and he was sure that all of his colleagues saw it just as clearly, possibly even associating his clothing with his criminal history.

Despite the prevalence of negative perceptions about the formerly incarcerated and the sense that their own past was always on display, many participants also believed that the transferable skills they acquired on campus outweighed any potential downsides and stereotypes. Sofia pointed out that she belonged on campus and was proud to have gotten there: "*I used my street smarts to better myself and also take advantage. I deserve this, too. I don't feel bad because I was formerly incarcerated. I don't feel none of that. I'm in here studying just as hard or harder than some of these other kids.*" In part, the heightened sense of visibility with regard to their stigma appears to have contributed to the next finding: that pursuing higher education provided participants with a new confidence when it came to disclosing their criminal history.

Confidence to Disclose Their Own Criminal History

Two opposite effects occurred simultaneously for participants. First, participants believed their invisible stigma was actually visible, such that they were surprised when it was not known to others. Second, pursuing a degree on a college campus resulted in numerous opportunities, which demonstrated to participants that even if their criminal history was known, it did not necessarily *matter*. These factors in tandem may have resulted in the overall high level of confidence we observed with regard to stigma disclosure. Lawrence, who was employed in a research lab, told us he directly informed his supervisor of his criminal history in order to help build a credible relationship with her: "*… that was the first thing I said. She went 'Oh, we don't have to - that's fine,' and this and that. 'You don't have to tell anybody.' I said, 'No, I do. Because I've got to get practice in explaining this situation …'*" In the educational context of his job, Lawrence seemed to feel he could practice disclosures he would need to make with other employers in the future, and it helped him build confidence doing so.

When their transparency was met by others' receptiveness, it helped participants practice disclosing and framing their stories, thus substantiating and further supporting their confidence. As Lawrence implied above, some respondents seemed to regard the University as a safe space for these initial disclosures. Devon said:

> ... I tell people all the time, "[University] is your first opportunity to be open, because it's the university's obligation. Once you leave here, [they] don't got to do nothing. But while you're here, it's their obligation. You got to use that to your advantage no matter what your field is."

Similarly, Nicholas shared:

> I think being home and telling people, fortunately having people be accepting of it, gives you more confidence to be able to feel like you can tell people. That's definitely a big factor. Which all of those little things happening previously now make me very confident when speaking with an employer or being able to tell them my background.

As participants cultivated relationships with their professors, supervisors, and colleagues, they were able to humanize their criminal histories and seek advice about how to navigate future barriers, including the intersections of their records, race, age, and nontraditional collegiate career path, in the job market. When asked how he felt about his chances securing future opportunities, Mike declared, *"I'm one hundred percent confident. I'm the type of person, I feel like one door closes, ten more open. If one person tells me no, I know somebody out there somewhere is going to give me a chance. I'm not a bad person. I just made bad choices."* This positive, confident attitude seemed to exude from many participants, as they developed comfort in this higher education context.

However not everyone saw the University as a safe haven. Some specified that, colleges were still operating within an oppressive institutional context. Eduardo, a doctoral student, expressed his frustration with having to disclose his criminal record in his college application:

> I mean, even applying to here, like ... all the big-name schools, they still, for the graduate programs, I still had to check the box and explain myself, you know. It's frustrating for me because—I was surprised that I got accepted to [University] because I wrote a nasty one-paragraph statement about my prior conviction because I just feel like—I mean excuse my language—but I feel like it's so bullshit that I have to explain myself over and over and over for a crime that I never committed! You know? It irks me and part of going into academia is like trying to overcompensate that, and it's like this constant question of like, okay, at what point is my degree going to overshadow that?

Eduardo was the only person in our study to self-disclose that he was wrongfully convicted, yet his frustration highlighted his high level of self-confidence regarding having served time. He would not allow his stigma or required disclosure to stand in the way of his progress.

Disposition to Pursue a True-to-Self Provisional Strategy

"During transitions, people often develop multiple provisional constructions of possible new identities (i.e., provisional selves), which remain provisional until they have been rehearsed and refined with experience" (Koen et al., 2016, p. 660). As individuals search for strategies to bridge the gap between their current capabilities and their expectations about the capabilities they will need in future roles, provisional selves are a useful tool (Ibarra, 1999). As professionals try to move into more senior roles they may observe role models (e.g., role prototyping, identity matching), experiment with a set of provisional selves (e.g., through imitation, whether wholesale or via selective, true-to-self strategies), and seek to evaluate and select from those provisional selves (e.g., on the basis of self-reflection or even external evaluation).

While such strategies may prove successful for professionals seeking higher-level roles, they may also reinforce structural barriers to advancement by suggesting that only certain behaviors or types of people are suitable for certain spaces. As Juan reflected on one of his jobs, *"I don't know if this is like a me-thing or people who are in prison think you get into a job and it's just everybody realizing [is this] what I really want to do? Or, is this what I've been allowed to do?"* For Juan, questioning how he ended up in his position led him to conclude what he was "allowed" to do was not sufficient.

Formerly incarcerated individuals have generally been stigmatized and devalued in numerous instances throughout their lives. The participants in our study had access to mentors, but as they tried on provisional selves, many respondents indicated a strong concern about remaining their authentic selves. Adopting the true-to-self strategy often helped our participants gain insight into their own behaviors as they approached their job search and interacted with employers:

> I couldn't be the young, aggressive Black guy. Yeah, I'm from the hood and I never stop being from the hood because it made me who I am, in my culture, my people, I love them, but you've got to learn how to navigate to an extent to where you don't lose your identity, but you can still be successful here. (Devon)

> I would want to work for an employer who would respect my honesty and integrity, and actually appreciate that I'm willing to explain and not try to hide anything from them … I wouldn't really want to work for an employer who wasn't comfortable with the fact that I'm a convicted felon. (Nicholas)

Others' true-to-self provisional strategies explained why they chose to pursue or engage in certain work:

> I wrote a seven-part article in [news website]. At first, I was not comfortable at all, but the more I have put my life on the line or my story out, the more comfortable I get with it because it is my story. I have to own it, you know. (Joshua)

> Once I complete my degree, I want to go back and help other brothers and sisters who are [justice-]involved. Not so much of the victim. I know everybody wants to help the victim, and they should. I want to help the perpetrator ... (Charles)

This idea of staying true-to-self, manifested in various ways, including responses to negative, or even abusive, employer treatment. As Charles explained that he was uninterested in settling for disrespectful treatment at work:

> I was supposed to get off at 12 midnight. They walked into the job and said, "Listen, we need you to work three more hours, and if you don't want to work three hours extra, you will be terminated." So I worked the three hours, and at the end of the three hours, they came back to us and said, "Well, now you can leave without any repercussions." But it wasn't what they said, it was how they said it. You get what I'm saying? And so at that point I realized I was nothing but a slave. And I was a slave in prison. So I'm not going to be a slave out here. And I never went back.

Juan, too, declined to continue in a job when he felt disrespected:

> ... the night manager was just horrible. I was arguing with her all [the] time, just like, "You're not going to talk to me like you do the rest of them." Like, "Don't bring this person out of me, please. I'm not one of these kids who comes in here from high school or something. I'm a grown man. You're not going to disrespect me."

Many other provisional self-strategies, like imitation and external evaluation, seemed to resonate less with our study participants. Devon did not care whether he measured up on one external evaluation scale: *"Yo, to hell with the GPA...."* In fact, rather than listing their role models, participants told us they wanted employment opportunities where *they* could be the role models. As articulated by Sofia, *"I just want to work with people just like me. Of color, from the hood. I can relate to them."* Considering his future employment, David shared who he might serve:

... maybe as a small business advisor, financial advisor, whatever catastrophe, I'm willing to help those who had similar lived circumstances as myself to benefit from because we're a small demographic and the kind that's forgotten about or set aside or, you know, left to our own demise.

Those participants who did engage in other strategies, such as selective imitation, did so less to perform a particular job role than to advance in a broad sense, such as obtaining employment in a particular field or industry. For instance, Devon recalled a conversation with his mentor about completing internships when his mentor told him *"You're not doing any non-paid internships ever again."* It was clear as the interview continued that Devon had worked to adopt his mentor's assuredness, then applied that confidence in his future job search. In other cases, participants took on another's optimism, adding to their confidence in disclosing their previous incarceration.

In short, while a subset of employees who are new to their job roles may look to another individual to socialize them into an organization, some individuals may engage with provisional selves quite differently. In fact, for many individuals of marginalized identities, a part of their identity may actually be driven *not* to conform. They may prioritize true-to-self strategies that hinge on the idea that they may not be the type of person who has existed in a certain space before, and the importance of retaining their authenticity.

Readiness to Pursue a Highly Skilled Occupation

For our participants, attaining higher education seemed to encourage them to aim toward higher skill occupations. A number of participants shared an interest and readiness to secure employment in community-based occupations that would allow them to give back, contribute to reentry reform, and enact a higher purpose: *"It's like I could counsel them from first-hand experience. Then I can counsel them from my education, and then I can do the work based on my experience. It was like, 'this job is perfect.' I can do this, and it's meaningful,"* stated Jordan.

While industries such as financial services have been historically closed to individuals with a criminal history (Lichtenberger, 2006), social- and community-based organizations are generally considered open to and accepting of these individuals. Participants like Terrance mentioned this understanding, which may have helped him feel better aligned with the skills needed for a career in this field: *"... from what I've heard and from what I've witnessed, when it comes to, like, social work, they'd actually rather have*

somebody who has been in the system rather than somebody who has never been."
Lawrence added:

> Every situation is unique. I mean, you've got some organizations out here
> that are looking for that. They want people with that inside experience,
> that have really been through the criminal justice system. So, if I work for a
> nonprofit criminal justice reform, that's what they want.

Organizations at the local, state, and federal levels seek out formerly incarcerated individuals as they craft initiatives to reform the criminal justice system. When our participants were sought to provide in-depth insights about their layers of incarceration and reentry, they came to see themselves as highly skilled experts with valuable lived experiences. Several individuals were able to generate a stream of income through speaking engagements, as Jason described *"I'm very, very fortunate that I actually support myself by speaking engagements, sharing the message of transformation toward education. So, I get four or five speaking engagements a month."*

Other participants used their education to seek different paths, such as entrepreneurial ventures. Peter stated, *"I'm not looking to work for anybody. Even as we're speaking, I'm working on building something for myself."* Some participants already had prior entrepreneurial experience, like Thomas:

> I've never worked for anybody before. I had a paper route when I was 11
> years old. We started cutting hair in my house when I was about 14 years
> old. I was in the streets, then at 20 years old, I opened my own barber-
> shop, and then at 21 years old I started my own vitamin company. At 22
> years old, I opened a bar. Then I lost trial at 25. So I never worked for
> anybody before. I never wanted to ...

And he concluded that he never planned to. He aimed to own his own business. However, David shared that even those who plan to work for themselves can encounter barriers related to a criminal history: *"... because I'm a convicted felon who is a citizen on parole, I'm not able to get a small business administration loan ..."* It could have been discouraging, but David used this as an opportunity: *"... so essentially I have to figure out a creative way to find financing."*

Participants, specifically those majoring in professional fields such as business, technology, and law, were also confident in their ability to secure employment—even in industries that have not typically been open to hiring individuals with a criminal history. Sofia had always been intrigued with technology and hoped to use her expertise and education to benefit women of color with a criminal history:

Then I just tried to weave women and gender studies and IT together. I've always wanted to be able to help women of color access—more than just writing a resume. Everybody just wants to teach you how to write a resume. There's so much more that you can do with technology. That's why I ended up with that.

Sofia wanted to expand the scope of how individuals with a criminal history conceptualized technology so that others could share her view: technology is not only a tool, but a *field*—and one that needs more women of color to share their insights.

Devon may not have been ready to get hired as an accountant, but he described how he was able to secure an accounting internship. He then continued on to secure paid employment at another accounting firm: *"I was there [accounting firm] from 2016 to now. I just left them to go work for another accounting firm that he got me and now I'm currently working for his firm on a contractual basis ..."* Given the hiring restrictions common to many financial services companies, Devon might have had trouble following a traditional path from college degree to salaried accountant position. But he connected with a minority-owned firm where he could gain tangible experience, despite his criminal record, then advanced from his internship into a series of higher-level, higher-skilled positions. As he described his employment path, *"And you get a lot more with education. A lot more doors open up"* it became clear that higher education was a means to an end, for him and other participants.

DISCUSSION

Having a criminal history can severely limit individuals' employment opportunities, particularly if they also identify with other marginalized attributes. Our research shows how those who are provided access to educational opportunities and obtain degrees not only gain skills and capabilities, but they also find themselves able to use their degrees to reshape perceptions of the skills and capabilities of other formerly incarcerated people—and in the United States, that is a sizeable population. Broadly, participation in higher education provided our participants with an outlet to tell their stories and disclose their criminal histories to professors, colleagues, and supervisors. In these interactions, participants experimented with the most effective ways to bridge the gap between their current capabilities and their future plans. They gained clarity about the expectations of the workplace, practiced and built confidence in disclosing their criminal records, and considered how potential employers might regard their educational and incarceration experiences. The professional development programs and internships open to them through educational institutions made them more aware of professional norms, created alternate paths to advancement, and helped them gain perspective and begin to articulate their experiences with and critiques of institutional systems and norms (including institutions like prison).

The institutional restrictions common to prisons now extend well beyond the walls of a correctional facility and continue long after sentences are served. The limitations placed on the formerly incarcerated as they transition into half-way housing, parole, and probation often continue to limit their exposure to critical technological skills and employability. A criminal record can significantly restrict an individual's access to various occupations (e.g., nursing), resources (e.g., a driver's license), and rights (e.g., voting), as described in the National Inventory of Collateral Consequences of Conviction (2021).[3] And the compound negative effects when race and ethnicity intersect with criminal history stigma cannot be overstated.

As reiterated in our study, when the stigma of a criminal history does not prevent employment entirely, it still frequently determines the type of jobs formerly incarcerated individuals are exposed to and the fields they can access. Most individuals experiencing reentry are relegated to low-wage, low-skilled, high-turnover occupations. However, a college education increased our participants' perceptions of their employability. Higher education gave them the credentials to pursue careers from which they have traditionally been excluded. Directly and indirectly, formerly incarcerated individuals went on to educate their colleagues about the value of employing people like them and to find ways to give back to and empower others who shared their carceral status.

Participants referenced education as a means to an end, and they understood this option was not available to all of their peers. Multiple interviews included the various ways other incarcerated people were unable to access educational opportunities, such as housed in facilities with no available college courses, no open spots to enroll, or correctional staff that deny an individual's application to participate. After release, various restrictions often forced individuals to choose between urgently needed employment or attempting to pursue college in order to access better opportunities in the future. Employers interested in and open to hiring the millions of formerly incarcerated Americans seeking jobs would do well to remember that, however they privilege those who have attained college degrees, they cannot assume those who have not were unmotivated or uninterested in educational programs, vocational training, and other employment preparation. Very often, those individuals never had the chance.

Implications for Research

Despite the variation in individual circumstance, education is often referred to as the "great equalizer." Its documented positive effects on life outcomes include higher lifetime earnings and occupational advancement. Yet the idea of educational attainment as positively affecting employment outcomes becomes tricky in the context of a criminal history; many employers want to see some evidence of positive engagement prior to extending an offer of employment, and participation in educational programs can help moderate negative perceptions attached to incarceration history (Griffith & Young, 2017). Yet, the premise of education as the great equalizer does not adequately account for individual differences such as race, ethnicity, and social class, nor for systemic differences, such as resources allocated to specific educational institutions and to educational programs in specific carceral contexts (Bernardi & Ballarino, 2016; Growe & Montgomery, 2003). All of these substantially affect the access, receipt, and interpretation of educational attainment.

In revisiting assumptions about the value of education for employment, we encourage researchers to consider the actual effects of education for marginalized individuals' employment. For instance, there are known perceptual differences in the value hiring managers ascribe to certain types of higher education, such that an applicant who graduated from a Historically Black College or University (HBCU) may be less attractive than one who graduated from a predominantly White institution (PWI). Studies have repeatedly documented that having a college degree does not negate employers' perceptions of a criminal history or the combined effects of a criminal history and other stigmatized identities (Cerda-Jara et al., 2020). College does not "level the playing field" for job-seekers, least of all for those with a criminal record and other stigmatized identities. Therefore, we encourage scholars to undertake studies that might indicate the conditions under which a college degree makes a substantial difference for employment and other commensurate outcomes, with an eye to expanding opportunity for and better directing the investments made by marginalized individuals toward their future.

Moreover, as we continue to explore how different populations engage with the hiring process, we encourage researchers to consider how the employment selection process may highlight overlooked biases that functionally exclude those with a criminal history from hiring consideration. As many individuals must contend with a variety of additional restrictions after their period of incarceration has ended, employment opportunities that directly conflict with restrictions (e.g., curfew) could prevent the recently released from accepting those jobs.

Researchers may also reconsider the importance of context when hiring managers use certain types of information, such as education, as signals of characteristics valued in prospective employees (Spence, 1973). For instance, many applaud those who simultaneously work and attend school. However, this is often not an option for many formerly incarcerated people. Terrance was blunt, *"No, it was either/or. I was either, I could either work or go to school,"* as was Thomas, who said, *"You can't do both. So you have to work or go to school. I'm the only one from my halfway house out of the 250 that goes to [the University]."* Hiring managers must account for the various structural barriers that can impede individuals from accessing resources. In short, without fully understanding the larger context and structural restrictions, using educational attainment as a proxy is likely to further disadvantage already marginalized individuals in the labor market and beyond.

Implications for Practice

As managers grapple with the new organizational focus on diversity, equity, and inclusion, we encourage them to consider how applicants with a criminal history fit into this equation. Specifically, we encourage hiring managers and human resources (HR) practitioners to evaluate how their hiring process may disadvantage or prevent individuals with a criminal history from entering and thriving within their organizations. This conversation seems particularly relevant now as COVID-19 restrictions ease throughout the United States and we have a significant labor shortage (Segal, 2021).

While there is enormous disagreement regarding the reasons why individuals have not fully returned to the workforce, we know that the unemployment rate for those with a criminal history is generally considerably higher than the average unemployment rate, ranging from 18.4% to 43.6% (Couloute & Kopf, 2018). As stated in 2018 by the Society of Human Resource Management, "For many organizations, individuals with criminal records can be a good source of untapped talent." Thus, as employers consider their current hiring practices—and challenges—we encourage HR practitioners to utilize this moment as a way to expand and include individuals from various marginalized and forgotten identities. They may find an eager pool of applicants who can diversify their teams, add new perspectives, and compliment their workforces.

Limitations

As with any research, our study has limitations. The primary limitation relates to our sample, which is internally diverse in terms of gender, age, race and ethnicity, and levels of educational attainment and completion, though we interviewed only 21 individuals. Our sample likely overrepresents individuals who had positive outcomes compared to those who had a more negative or detrimental outcome (e.g., re-arrest, re-incarceration, relapse). Yet these perspectives are also a lived reality. Additionally, given that this study was conducted in a geographic region that has passed ban the box legislation, participants' employment experiences may be perceived as more favorable than formerly incarcerated individuals in non-ban the box states. As such, we encourage future research to build upon our findings and further engage with this population to gain greater insight into employment related issues for this population.

CONCLUSION

The analysis conducted in this article provides early insights into the ways higher education can affect formerly incarcerated individuals' perceptions of (re)entry to the labor market. As this population secures entry into traditionally excluded spaces, organizations may need to make a concerted effort to evaluate how to make this population feel more included and productive within this space. These concerted efforts become even more critical in our everchanging climate, evolving around the existing pandemic and racial injustice, which has exposed the many disparities that exist for various marginalized communities.

REFERENCES

Agan, A., & Starr, S. (2018). Ban the box, criminal records, and racial discrimination: A field experiment. *The Quarterly Journal of Economics, 133*(1), 191–235. https://doi.org/10.1093/qje/qjx028

Anazodo, K. S., Young, N. C. J., & Ricciardelli, R. (2020) Challenging the status quo: Organizational deviations towards socially responsible behaviours in the age of digitization. *The Annual Review of Interdisciplinary Justice Research, 9*, 206–236. https://www.cijs.ca/volume-9

Avery, B., & Lu, H. (2021). *Ban the box: US cities, counties, and states adopt fair-chance policies to advance employment opportunities for people with past convictions.* National Employment Law Project. https://www.nelp.org/publication/ban-the-box-fair-chance-hiring-state-and-local-guide/

Ball, S. J., Davies, J., David, M., & Reay, D. (2002). 'Classification' and 'Judgement': Social class and the 'cognitive structures' of choice of higher education. *British Journal of Sociology of Education, 23*(1), 51–72. https://doi.org/10.1080/01425690120102854

Baur, J. E., Hall, A. V., Daniels, S. R., Buckley, M. R., & Anderson, H. J. (2018). Beyond banning the box: A conceptual model of the stigmatization of ex-offenders in the workplace. *Human Resource Management Review, 28*(2), 204–219. https://doi.org/10.1016/j.hrmr.2017.08.002

Bennett, L. M., McIntosh, E., & Henson, F. O. (2017). African American college students and racial microaggressions: Assumptions of criminality. *Journal of Psychology and Behavioral Science, 5*(2), 14–20. https://doi.org/10.15640/jpbs.v5n2a2

Bernardi, F., & Ballarino, G. (Eds.). (2016). *Education as the great equalizer: A theoretical framework.* In *Education, Occupation and Social Origin.* Edward Elgar.

Bushway, S. D., & Apel, R. (2012). A signaling perspective on employment-based reentry programming: Training completion as a desistance signal. *Criminology & Public Policy, 11*(1), 21–50. https://doi.org/10.1111/j.1745-9133.2012.00786.x

Cerda-Jara, M., Eslter, A., & Harding, D. (2020). *Criminal record stigma in the college-educated labor market.* Institute for Research and Labor Employment. https://irle.berkeley.edu/files/2020/05/Harding_Jara-Cerda-Elster-brief.pdf

Couloute, L. (2018). *Getting back on course: Educational exclusion and attainment among formerly incarcerated people.* Prison Policy Initiave. https://www.prisonpolicy.org/reports/education.html

Couloute, L., & Kopf, D. (2018). *Out of prison and out of work: Unemployment among formerly incarcerated people.* Prison Policy Initiative. https://www.prisonpolicy.org/reports/outofwork.html.

Creswell, J. (2013). *Qualitative inquiry and research design* (1st ed.). SAGE.

Creswell, J. W., Hanson, W. E., Clark Plano, V. L., & Morales, A. (2007). Qualitative research designs: Selection and implementation. *The Counseling Psychologist, 35*(2), 236–264. https://doi.org/10.1177/0011000006287390

Davis, L. M., Bozick, R., Steele, J. L., Saunders, J., & Miles, J. N. V. (2013). *Evaluating the effectiveness of correctional education: A meta- analysis of programs that provide education to incarcerated adults.* RAND Corporation. https://www.rand.org/pubs/research_reports/RR266.html

Decker, S. H., Ortiz, N., Spohn, C., & Hedberg, E. (2015). Criminal stigma, race, and ethnicity: The consequences of imprisonment for employment. *Journal of Criminal Justice, 43*(2), 108–121. https://doi.org/10.1016/j.jcrimjus.2015.02.002

Doleac, J. L., & Hansen, B. (2016). *Does "ban the box" help or hurt low-skilled workers? Statistical discrimination and employment outcomes when criminal histories are hidden.* National Bureau of Economic Research. https://www.nber.org/system/files/working_papers/w22469/w22469.pdf

Doleac, J. L., & Hansen, B. (2020). The unintended consequences of "ban the box": Statistical discrimination and employment outcomes when criminal histories are hidden. *Journal of Labor Economics, 38*(2), 321–374. https://www.journals.uchicago.edu/doi/10.1086/705880

Formon, D. L., Schmidt, A. T., & Henderson, C. (2018). Examining employment outcomes of offender and nonoffender vocational program graduates. *International Journal of Offender Therapy and Comparative Criminology, 62*(9), 2781–2800. https://doi.org/10.1177/0306624X17735041

Freeman, R. (2008). Incarceration, criminal background checks, and employment in a low(er) crime society. *Criminology & Public Policy, 7*(3), 405–412. https://doi.org/10.1111/j.1745-9133.2008.00517.x

Gillath, O., Bahns, A. J., Ge, F., & Crandall, C. S. (2012). Shoes as a source of first impressions. *Journal of Research in Personality, 46*(4), 423–430. https://doi.org/10.1016/j.jrp.2012.04.003

Goffman, E. (1963). *Stigma: Notes on the management of spoiled identity.* Simon & Schuster.

Gray, B., & Kish-Gephart, J. J. (2013). Encountering social class differences at work: How "class work" perpetuates inequality. *Academy of Management Review, 38*(4), 670–699. http://dx.doi.org/10.5465/amr.2012.0143

Griffith, J. N., Rade, C. B., & Anazodo, K. S. (2019). Criminal history and employment: An interdisciplinary literature synthesis. *Equality, Diversity and Inclusion: An International Journal, 28*(5), 505–528. https://doi.org/10.1108/EDI-10-2018-0185

Griffith, J. N., & Young, N. C. J. (2017). Hiring ex-offenders? The case of ban the box. *Equality, Diversity and Inclusion: An International Journal, 36*(6), 501–518. https://doi.org/10.1108/EDI-04-2017-0066

Growe, R., & Montgomery, P. S. (2003). Educational equity in America: Is education the great equalizer? *Professional Educator, 25*(2), 23–29. https://files.eric.ed.gov/fulltext/EJ842412.pdf

Harding, D. J., Morenoff, J. D., & Wyse, J. J. (2019). *On the outside: Prisoner reentry and reintegration.* University of Chicago Press.

Harlow, C. W. (2003). *Education and correctional populations.* U.S. Department of Justice: Office of Justice Programs. https://www.bjs.gov/content/pub/pdf/ecp.pdf

Holzer, H. J., Raphael, S., & Stoll, M. A. (2004). How willing are employers to hire ex-offenders. *Focus, 23*(2), 40–43. https://www.irp.wisc.edu/publications/focus/pdfs/foc232h.pdf

Hwang, K. J., & Phillips, D. J. (2020). *Entrepreneurship as a response to labor market discrimination for formerly incarcerated people.* https://doi.org/10.13140/RG.2.2.22562.38080

Ibarra, H. (1999). Provisional selves: Experimenting with image and identity in professional adaptation. *Administrative Science Quarterly, 44*(4), 764–791. https://doi.org/10.2307/2667055

Koen, J., Van Vianen, A., Klehe, U. C., & Zikic, J. (2016). "A whole new future"— identity construction among disadvantaged young adults. *Career Development International, 21*(7), 658–681. https://doi.org/10.1108/CDI-02-2016-0019

Leavitt, J. (2001). Walking a tightrope: Balancing competing public interests in the employment of criminal offenders. *Connecticut Law Review, 34*(4), 1281–1301.

Lichtenberger, E. (2006). Where do ex-offenders find jobs? An industrial profile of the employers of ex-offenders in Virginia. *Journal of Correctional Education, 57*(4), 297–311. https://www.jstor.org/stable/23282804

Link, B. G., & Phelan, J. C. (2001). Conceptualizing stigma. *Annual Review of Sociology, 27*(1), 363–385. https://doi.org/10.1146/annurev.soc.27.1.363

Merriam, S. B. (2002). Introduction to qualitative research. *Qualitative Research in Practice: Examples for Discussion and Analysis, 1*(1), 1–17.

Moran, D. (2012). Prisoner reintegration and the stigma of prison time inscribed on the body. *Punishment & Society, 14*(5), 564–583. https://doi.org/10.1177/1462474512464008

Moustakas, C. (1994). *Phenomenological research methods.* SAGE.

Nally, J. M., Lockwood, S., Ho, T., & Knutson, K. (2014). Post-release recidivism and employment among different types of released offenders: A 5-year follow-up study in the United States. *International Journal of Criminal Justice Sciences, 9*(1), 16–34.

National Inventory of Collateral Consequences of Conviction. (2021). *What are collateral consequences?* https://niccc.nationalreentryresourcecenter.org.

Ositelu, M. O. (2019). *Equipping individuals for life beyond bars.* New America. https://www.newamerica.org/education-policy/reports/equipping-individuals-life-beyond-bars/executive-summary

Pager, D. (2003). The mark of a criminal record. *American Journal of Sociology, 108*(5), 937–975. https://doi.org/10.1086/374403

Pager, D. (2007). *Marked: Race, crime, and finding work in an era of mass incarceration.* The University of Chicago Press.

Palmer, C., & Christian, J. (2019). Work matters: Formerly incarcerated men's resiliency in reentry. *Equality, Diversity and Inclusion: An International Journal, 38*(5), 583–598. https://doi.org/10.1108/EDI-10-2018-0177

Purser, G. (2012). "Still doin' time:" Clamoring for work in the day labor industry. *Journal of Labor and Society, 15*(3), 397–415. https://doi.org/10.1111/j.1743-4580.2012.00400.x

Segal, E. (2021). *Worker shortage crisis is focus of new campaign by U.S. Chamber.* Retrieved June 2, 2021, from https://www.forbes.com/sites/edwardsegal/2021/06/01/us-chamber-launches-campaign-to-address-worker-shortage-crisis/?sh=3c45fd0676b1

Spence, M. (1973). Job market signaling. *Quarterly Journal of Economics, 87,* 355–374. https://doi.org/10.2307/1882010

Stone, D. L., & Colella, A. (1996). A model of factors affecting the treatment of disabled individuals in organizations. *Academy of Management Review, 21*(2), 352–401. https://doi.org/10.2307/258666

Stone, E. F., Stone, D. L., & Dipboye, R. L. (1992). Stigmas in organizations: Race, handicaps, and physical unattractiveness. In *Advances in Psychology* (Vol. 82, pp. 385–457).

Strait, A., & Eaton, S. (2017). Post-secondary education for people in prison. *Social Justice Funders Opportunity Brief,* No. 1. https://heller.brandeis.edu/sillerman/pdfs/opportunity-briefs/post-secondary-education-people-in-prison.pdf

The Sentencing Project. (2015). *Americans with criminal records.* https://www.sentencingproject.org/wp-content/uploads/2015/11/Americans-with-Criminal-Records-Poverty-and-Opportunity-Profile.pdf

Travis, J., Western, B., & Redburn, F. S. (2014). *The growth of incarceration in the United States: Exploring causes and consequences.* National Research Council of the National Academies.

U.S. Census. (2022). *Census Bureau releases new educational attainment data.* https://www.census.gov/newsroom/press-releases/2022/educational-attainment.html

U.S. Courts. (2021). *Chapter 3: Location monitoring (probation and supervised release conditions)*. Retrieved on May 31, 2021, from https://www.uscourts.gov/services-forms/location-monitoring-probation-supervised-release-conditions

U.S. Department of Education. (2014). *U.S. Program for the International Assessment of Adult Competencies (PIAAC) 2012/2014: Main study and national supplement technical report*. https://nces.ed.gov/pubs2016/2016036_rev.pdf

U.S. Equal Employment Opportunity Commission. (2012). *EEOC Enforcement Guidance*. Retrieved on November 25, 2019, from https://www.eeoc.gov/laws/guidance/arrest_conviction.cfm

Vuolo, M., Lageson, S., & Uggen, C. (2017). Criminal record questions in the era of "ban the box". *Criminology & Public Policy, 16*(1), 139–165. https://doi.org/10.1111/1745-9133.12250

Waldfogel, J. (1994). The effect of criminal conviction on income and the trust "reposed in the workmen". *Journal of Human Resources, 29*(1), 62–81. https://doi.org/10.2307/146056

Western, B. (2002). The impact of incarceration on wage mobility and inequality. *American Sociological Review, 67*(4), 526–546. https://doi.org/10.2307/3088944

Yin, R. K. (2015). *Qualitative research from start to finish*. Guilford.

Young, N. C. J., & Powell, G. N. (2015). Hiring ex-offenders: A theoretical model. *Human Resource Management Review, 25*(3), 298–312. https://doi.org/10.1016/j.hrmr.2014.11.001

Young, N. C. J., & Ryan, A. M. (2019). Criminal history and the workplace: A pathway forward. *Equality, Diversity and Inclusion: An International Journal, 38*(5), 494–503. https://doi.org/10.1108/EDI-04-2019-0140

Zeidner, R. (2014). Choices and chances: The dilemma of criminal background screening. *Human Resources Magazine*, 50–56. https://www.shrm.org/hr-today/news/hr-magazine/pages/0614-criminal-background-screens.aspx

APPENDIX

Interview Protocol

Education

1. Why did you begin taking classes while incarcerated?
2. Upon your release, what motivated you to continue to pursue your degree?
3. How did your incarceration history affect the degree you decided to pursue?
4. What are (or were) your expectations once you complete your bachelor's degree?

Connecting education to employment

5. Do you feel that your educational pursuit has been worthwhile (i.e.,—job attainment, role modeling, etc.)?
   a. PROBE—Why/How?
6. What types of professional development programs or networking activities were instrumental in preparing you for your current employment?
   a. PROBE—If none, "what types of professional development or networking activities would have been useful?
7. If employed—What types of transferable skills (e.g., communication, organization, negotiation) do you feel led to your current employment?
   a. If not currently employed—What types of transferable skills (e.g., communication, organization, negotiation) do you feel will assist you find employment?
8. How do you think employers perceive you now that you have your degree?

Employment

9. What are some of the challenges that you have encountered while trying to gain employment?
   a. How did you navigate these challenges?
10. How did you become aware of your current employer and position?
11. How did you feel explaining your criminal history to your current employer?
    a. If not employed—how do you feel explaining your criminal history to your future employer?

12. What are some of your short-term goals related to employment?
13. What are some of your long-term goals related to employment?
14. Anything additional you would like to share that may help in understanding your experiences in gaining employment?

NOTES

1. We use the broad term "individuals with a criminal history" throughout the article to capture all individuals who may have been systematically impacted by the carceral system. Not all individuals with a criminal history have served time in a correctional facility, but all individuals who have been incarcerated have a criminal history.
2. Convictions do not indicate the charged crimes were actually committed by the participant.
3. The National Inventory of Collateral Consequences of Conviction provides an accessible database of over 10,000 specific restrictions that differ by state, and even jurisdiction.

CHAPTER 9

THE IMPACT OF MENTOR RELATIONSHIP AND SUPERVISOR SUPPORTIVE FEEDBACK ON THE WORKING POOR

The Moderating Role of Self-Efficacy

Erika N. Williams
University of Southern Indiana

Michele L. Heath
Cleveland State University

ABSTRACT

The working poor are unique among employee groups due to proximity to poverty, both past and present. This proximity creates distinct perspectives, in addition to the noted barriers faced in their personal lives, which impact their behavior and success at work. Here we examine the impact of mentor relationship and supervisor supportive feedback on the working poor's job performance. This chapter argues that mentoring and supervisor supportive feedback will positively impact their self-efficacy and job performance. In addition, the presence of self-efficacy among the working poor positively

Forgotten Minorities in Organizations, pp. 275–298
Copyright © 2023 by Information Age Publishing
www.infoagepub.com
All rights of reproduction in any form reserved.

moderates the relationship between mentoring, supervisor supportive feed-back, and job performance. Despite the ongoing conversation surrounding this demographic, there is a lack of research on the challenges of the working poor within organizations. We hope this research will encourage further study in the area of working poor and organizations.

To date, there has been a lack of research on the working poor and the myriad challenges they face that potentially have a negative influence on their performance in the workplace (Leana et al., 2012). Although the U.S. is one of the world's wealthiest nations, over 38 million citizens live at or below the poverty level, and 7 million of those people are a part of the working poor (Bureau of Labor and Statistics [BLS], 2020). BLS defines the working poor as individuals who work at least 27 weeks in a year, but their income falls below the national poverty level (BLS, 2020). The working poor demographic has been a topic of many discussions, from education to the recent debates on minimum wage. For example, a study from the National Low Income Housing Coalition (Bravve et al., 2012) found that in the United States, there are no congressional districts where a resident who is a full-time, low-income worker could afford a two-bedroom apartment.

Furthermore, there has been an increase in unstable, low-wage jobs that do not pay enough to support a family due to stagnant wages (Policy Link, n.d.). Persistent poverty is the lived experience of the working poor in the United States. This experience has a pervasive influence that shapes their perspectives and behaviors, both personally and professionally. Scholars have indicated that poverty has an adverse effect on self-efficacy devel-opment, leading to a greater incidence of challenging outcomes for the working poor (Leana et al., 2012). Drawing from social cognitive theory (Bandura, 1989a), we offer the following research questions to guide this work:

1. How might mentor relationships and supervisor supportive feed-back impact the job performance of the working poor?
2. How might the working poor's self-efficacy moderate the rela-tionship between a working poor employee's job performance and mentor relationships and supervisor supportive feedback?

Because of their continued exposure to poverty and other related fac-tors, it is not surprising that the working poor face many challenges that impact their employment status. The working poor often face barriers that affect their ability to perform their jobs, travel to their jobs, and create circumstances leading to higher levels of absenteeism, tardiness, and other work-related issues that cause friction and negatively affect the organiza-tion (Leana et al., 2012). Some of the barriers include reliance on public transportation, lack of consistent childcare, juggling multiple jobs, and high-stress levels (Leana et al., 2012; Payne & Murty, 2019). Although many social and political proponents of increased minimum wage argue that a living income will address the concerns among this demographic (Thiede et al., 2015), there are other issues that arise from proximity to poverty that are more challenging to alleviate.

This chapter focuses on the perceived self-efficacy of the working poor and its impact on their work-related performance. Self-efficacy is described as a person's belief in their ability to execute actions that lead to a desired outcome (Bandura, 1977, 1986). Just as higher levels of self-efficacy can serve as a motivator, low self-efficacy can be demoralizing (Wuepper & Lybbert, 2017), leading to lower performance levels due to the perception that they lack the ability to perform at the required level. In addition, the individual may lack the requisite coping mechanisms that allow them to manage stress or make informed decisions (Bandura, 1977). This impacts overall job performance and can also lead to higher levels of turnover, which is a cost to the organization. Despite these factors, there is a paucity of research in organizational behavior and human resource management on these issues. As a result, the working poor can be considered members of "Forgotten Minorities" at work, and we believe research is needed to better understand their concerns and how to help them with their challenges. This research is beneficial to individuals, organizations, and the larger society. For example, as we recognize factors that can enhance the self-efficacy of the working poor, they can also increase their performance leading to greater job stability which is advantageous to organizations as well. Beyond the organizational benefits, improving workplace performance and outcomes are of value to society as it benefits families, health outcomes and potentially alleviates the self-perpetuating problems associated with poverty.

SOCIAL COGNITIVE THEORY

We base our study on social cognitive theory (Bandura, 1986). This theory argues that one of the major factors that affect motivation and performance is self-efficacy. Self-efficacy can be defined as the extent to which the individual believes they can master a particular skill or task (Bandura, 1977). Research has shown that self-efficacy beliefs affect motivation, attitudes, and behaviors. Bandura has noted that an individual's self-efficacy plays a major role in how goals, tasks, and challenges are approached (Bandura, 1994). Individuals who have high levels of self-efficacy are more likely to believe they can master challenging tasks and problems, and they typically recover more quickly from setbacks than those with low self-efficacy

(Bandura, 1989b). In contrast, those with low self-efficacy are less confident in their ability to perform a task, leading them to avoid challenging tasks or situations (Bandura, 1994). As a result, self-efficacy is an important determinant of behavior and performance in organizations, and we believe that it has a major impact on the work behavior of the working poor.

As noted previously, we maintain that low self-efficacy may be responsible for many problems affecting the working poor. For instance, if they have low self-efficacy, they may not perceive that they can successfully perform jobs in organizations. In addition, they may be more likely to give up when they face unforeseen problems (e.g., no childcare, transportation problems) or constructive criticism from supervisors. Given these arguments, one way to help the working poor gain access to and maintain jobs is to enhance their self-efficacy and train them to recover from setbacks experienced in life and work contexts.

In order to understand how self-efficacy influences behavior, Bandura's (1994) social cognitive theory argues that self-efficacy can be developed or increased by:

- **Mastery experience:** defined as personal success associated with performing tasks (e.g., people's self-efficacy is increased when they are able to perform a task successfully) (Bandura, 1994).
- **Social modeling:** defined as an identifiable role model that shows the processes used to perform a behavior or accomplish a task. (e.g., people's self-efficacy is increased when they observe a successful role model display the processes needed to accomplish a task) (Bandura, 1994).
- **Improving physical and emotional states:** this refers to the extent to which a person is rested and relaxed enough to attempt a new behavior. If a person with low self-efficacy is anxious or impatient, they will not be able to perform the task at hand. Furthermore, individuals' self-efficacy will be increased when their anxiety levels are decreased, and they can successfully perform tasks (Bandura, 1994).
- **Verbal persuasion:** the process of providing encouragement for a person to complete a task or achieve a certain behavior. For instance, if supervisors or coworkers provide supportive feedback that encourages a person to perform a task, their self-efficacy will increase (Bandura, 1994).

Taken together, the arguments noted above suggest that the self-efficacy of the working poor may be increased, and they will be motivated when they (a) can master a task, (b) observe a successful role model perform or explain how to perform a task, (c) decrease their anxiety levels, and (d) receive supportive feedback from supervisors or coworkers that encourages them to perform a task.

Given these arguments, we believe that two organizational factors that may help the working poor enhance their work-related self-efficacy and task performance are (a) mentoring and (b) supportive feedback from supervisors. First, mentoring should increase the self-efficacy of the working poor because it shows these individuals they can master or successfully perform a task. It also provides information on the processes needed to perform a task and offers insights on how to overcome setbacks or challenges that impede their performance. Second, we believe that supportive feedback from supervisors may also enhance the self-efficacy of the working poor. The primary reason for this is supportive feedback provides the individuals with encouragement that increases their motivation to learn, perform and persist in tasks. Thus, in the following sections, we provide predictions on how mentoring and supportive feedback are likely to affect the motivation and performance of the working poor. We also review the research on these relationships and offer hypotheses to guide future research on the issues.

LITERATURE REVIEW

Extant literature argues that there is a strong negative relationship between poverty and behavior (Leana et al., 2012). For example, Leana and colleagues (2012) note that low-income individuals have a keen desire to fit in the workplace, but they may not always have the skills and motivational levels to succeed in jobs. Due to their unique background, the working poor is a sociologically distinct group (Thiede et al., 2015) who work but consistently live at, or below, the poverty line. Even though leaders in our society consistently argue that hard work is a means for achieving upward mobility (Thiede et al., 2015), people who are confined to low-wage jobs due to lack of education, skills, and access cannot always work the number of hours needed to leave poverty behind (Alabdulkareem et al., 2018; Gorski, 2017). This suggests that individuals in low-wage jobs often struggle to break cycles that would assist them in moving out of poverty. These results imply that individuals from a working poor background work to survive and might have different ways of thinking about the world and work (Kraus et al., 2012). Research has demonstrated a negative relationship between social class and individuals' motivations and behaviors (Kraus et al., 2012).

The Working Poor

The literature offers multiple definitions of the working poor. For the purpose of this research, we define the working poor as individuals who work a minimum of 27 weeks in the year, yet their income falls below the official poverty level as stated by the U.S. government (BLS.gov, 2020; Leana et al., 2012). It is worth noting that in the United States, according to the BLS (2014), the working poor consisted of 11.7% Black, 11.7% Hispanic/Latino, 5.5% White, and 4.3% Asian. Women were 7.2% of the working poor, and 18.3% had less than a high school diploma (BLS, 2016).

Scholars have argued that members of the working poor face barriers that impact their employability. For example, personal barriers such as lack of access to childcare, limited skillsets, little to no work experience, providing care for elderly family members, and other family challenges can create additional difficulties for the working poor and make it hard for them to participate in training and educational programs (Payne & Murty, 2019). In his book that shared the personal narratives of the working poor, Shipler (2005) detailed the struggle of the working poor across the United States, citing drug and alcohol addictions, health problems (both mental and physical), as well as lack of access to reliable transportation, and frequent setbacks as constant problems facing the working poor.

Similarly, the Coalition on Human Needs notes that even though poverty has declined in recent years, members of the working poor face an uphill battle due to the high cost of living in the U.S. and the low minimum wage rate ("The High Cost," 2016). Indeed, individuals who live in poverty in the United States often pay a premium for goods and services such as food and higher rents in urban areas in order to have access to public transportation ("The High Cost," 2016). The need to stretch every dollar leaves this population more vulnerable to late fees and predatory loans ("The High Cost" 2016). When researching the use of food pantry services among the working poor, Berner and colleagues (2008) found that working individuals are more likely to revisit the food pantry because they often sacrifice their food budget to pay for other necessities (e.g., electricity, heating, transportation).

Members of the working poor often work in low-wage jobs with unpredictable work schedules that do not offer sick pay or paid leave, leaving them one illness away from either losing jobs or wages. Scholars have noted that our modern job market is highly insecure (Kalleberg, 2011), leaving the working poor doubly vulnerable to both employment and housing insecurity (Desmond & Gershenson, 2016).

Although there are government programs to support this group (e.g., SNAP, subsidized housing), research has demonstrated that these programs may not help the working poor overcome the barriers associated with low wage rates and job insecurity. The struggle to make ends meet makes it difficult, if not impossible, to amass savings or invest in assets that would push them toward financial security ("The High Cost," 2004). While much of the existing research on the working poor often focuses on urban environments, many rural areas fare no better than cities as they lack available work, or the wages are so low that it is nearly impossible to take care of one's family ("The High Cost," 2004).

Despite the widespread work-related problems faced by the working poor, little research has focused on their experiences in work organizations or the factors that affect their ability to overcome their challenges and become strong, successful members of the workforce. Thus, this study considers multiple factors that may enhance the working poor's self-efficacy, motivation, and work performance.

Job Performance

Performance is a multidimensional and dynamic construct central in the human resource management and industrial-organizational psychology literatures (Viswesvaran & Ones, 2000). Even though there are a number of definitions of performance, we use Viswesvaran and Ones's (2000) definition as "scalable actions, behavior, and outcomes that employees engage in or bring about that are linked with and contribute to organizational goals." (p. 216). For the purpose of this research, we will consider performance through the lens of behavior because the results that either support (or hinder) organizational goals are based on the behavior of individuals within that organization (Motowidlo & Kell, 2012). We agree with Motowidlo and Kell (2012) stance that focusing on individual behavior rather than results gives us the opportunity to understand motivation and other psychological processes affecting behavior.

There are several models of job performance, but one of the most prominent is by Campbell (1990). Campbell suggests that performance is a function of three primary determinants: declarative knowledge about the job, procedural knowledge on how to perform the job, and motivation. Declarative knowledge represents the knowledge of a given task's requirements. For instance, declarative knowledge includes knowledge of principles, facts, and ideas about a task (Campbell, 1990). Procedural knowledge is the knowledge about how to perform a task, and it includes cognitive skills, perceptual skills, mechanical skills, and interpersonal skills. Motivation is the third factor, and it refers to the choice to expend effort, decisions regarding the level of effort, and the choice to persist on a task (Campbell, 1990). It is critical because it reflects the direction, intensity, and persistence of behaviors (Campbell, 1990). Similarly, researchers have also argued that job performance is influenced by the accuracy of role perceptions or role clarity (Katz & Kahn, 1978). Other scholars have noted that successful job performance is likely to affect job satisfaction, organizational commitment, and the achievement of organizational goals (Bandura, 1997; Lawler & Porter, 1967; Sonnentag et al., 2008).

In view of the dimensions of job performance (Campbell, 1990) noted above, we believe that the job performance of the working poor may be increased by training programs that teach declarative knowledge. However, other methods may be needed to enhance procedural knowledge and motivation. For instance, one mechanism that is likely to increase procedural knowledge is mentoring. Mentors help individuals learn organizational roles and gain insights into the processes needed to perform a job. Another mechanism that may increase the motivation of the working poor is supportive feedback from supervisors. As a result, we consider these two important factors in the sections below.

Mentoring

As noted above, we believe that one mechanism that can enhance the self-efficacy and the motivation of the working poor is mentoring. A mentoring relationship refers to an arranged relationship through which the protégé benefits by receiving advice and direction from an experienced professional (Al Hilali et al., 2020). Scholars have studied this area of research by examining the role of mentors as well as the outcomes of protégés (Kram, 1985). Seminal work by Kram (1985) suggests that mentoring develops over four phases: initiation, cultivation, separation, and redefinition. In Kram's (1985) model, the time for development and transition of each stage varies from six months to five years, and she argues that mentors offer two types of functions, career functions and psychosocial functions (Ragins & Kram, 2007a, 2007b).

Furthermore, research by Ragins (2016) indicates that mentoring can enhance a protégé's self-efficacy, self-identity, and psychological safety in addition to improving their performance, socialization and reduce their turnover intentions. Mentoring has been found to support employees in times of stress due to the social support the relationship provides (Kram & Hall, 1989) as well as a means to overcome gender challenges in the workplace (Parker & Kram, 1993).

Scholars have found evidence that informal mentoring is more advantageous for protégés than formal mentoring (Ragins & Cotton, 1999). One reason for this may be that informal mentors provide higher levels of both career and psychosocial functions which may be credited to the fact that these informal relationships develop between individuals who easily identify with one another (Inzer & Crawford, 2005). On the other hand, formal mentoring is structured by the organization, and while the dynamics may be different, these relationships are still beneficial to all parties. For example, people who have the support of mentors tend to have higher wages and access to career-advancing opportunities (Inzer & Crawford, 2005; Nemanick, 2000). In ideal circumstances, the formal mentoring relationship offers a safe space to learn and develop, leading to improved performance and organizational commitment (Inzer & Crawford, 2005).

Taken together, the research reviewed suggests that mentoring provides important developmental opportunities for individuals, and we believe that it should enhance the self-efficacy of the working poor. If mentoring increases self-efficacy, it should also be an important means of increasing their motivation, role clarity, and work performance in organizations.

There are a number of ways that mentoring can assist the working poor. For example, mentoring can provide support to assist the working poor employee with the ability to deal with problems that might occur on the job and in their personal lives. Furthermore, an employee who is considered a part of the working poor can learn coping skills from the mentoring relationship to help them deal with setbacks they face on their jobs (e.g., layoffs) and personal lives. A mentor could also propose alternative ways of dealing with potential barriers to working (such as problems of child-care, transportation, and stress levels). Similarly, most organizations and communities provide resources that employees can take advantage of, but sometimes the resources are not advertised. A mentor can utilize social networks to ensure the working poor employee can access the appropriate resources in the organization and within the community. Ultimately, a mentor can provide guidance, motivation, emotional support, and role modeling (Brown & Trevino, 2014), as well as identifying the right resources to overcome adversities to support working poor employees.

An effective mentor can also be an invaluable guide for the working poor employee and help them consider job options, get new information, and identify the support they need (De Janasz et al., 2003). A working poor employee might have low job performance due to life's circumstances unrelated to the job. Still, mentors can act as a sounding board to help them overcome life's challenges and enjoy a satisfying work life.

Although the working poor employee might have different challenges than other employees, positive results from mentoring can help alleviate the difficulties faced by employees who are part of the working poor. For instance, Awaya and colleagues (2003) found that the mentoring journey involves the assembling of an equal relationship characterized by trust, the sharing of expertise, moral support, and knowing when to help and when to sit back. Research has shown that effective mentors balance support with challenge by providing opportunities and setting positive expectations (Walkington et al., 2020). Working poor employees could benefit from these challenges and opportunities to deal with both difficulties on the job and in life (Sanfey et al., 2013).

Although we believe that mentoring programs should enhance the working poor's self-efficacy, motivation, and performance, we know of no direct empirical research on these relations. Thus, we offer the following hypotheses to guide research.

Hypothesis 1: When the working poor have a mentoring relationship, they will have higher levels of (a) self-efficacy, (b) motivation, and (c) performance than when they do not have a mentoring relationship.

Supervisor Supportive Feedback

Another factor that may increase the self-efficacy of the working poor is supportive feedback from supervisors or coworkers. Supportive feedback refers to the encouragement and positive support provided by supervisors and others in the workplace (Dahling & O'Malley, 2011). Research has shown that supportive feedback positively impacts trust, employee attitudes, and psychological states (Dahling & O'Malley, 2011). It is also related to employees' work performance and organizational outcomes (Dahling & O'Malley, 2011). The characteristics of supportive feedback include informal feedback between supervisors and their charges such that the employee believes the feedback to be credible and thoughtful, whether the feedback is positive or negative (Dahling & O'Malley, 2011). Specifically, supervisor supportive feedback can be described as an environment of ongoing, thoughtful, constructive feedback that can be positive or negative (Alam & Singh, 2019; Dahling & O'Malley, 2011).

Research has demonstrated that supervision is one of the most valuable procedures that an organization can introduce, and it has wide-ranging benefits for both the employer and employee (Walsh & Arnold, 2020). Supervisor feedback reduces role and performance uncertainty among employees, allows them to correct problems, and modify their performance to meet the organization's expectations (Agho et al., 1993; Hutchison & Garstka, 1996; Komaki, 1986). When employees understand their roles, they tend to experience higher levels of satisfaction with their supervisor and their organization (Aziri, 2011).

Research has also shown that "supportive feedback environments fostered by supervisors leads to improvements in employee well-being and performance" (Gabriel et al., 2014, p. 487). Most supervisors are looking for ways to provide constructive feedback without tarnishing the supervisor-employee relationship. As a result, we believe that supportive supervisor feedback should be very beneficial to the working poor and increase their job satisfaction, pride, work performance, and lower turnover rates. We also believe that employees who are members of the working poor can use supportive feedback to increase their self-efficacy, motivation, and persistence on a task. The use of supportive feedback might also shift their mindset and help them believe that they can perform tasks and be successful on jobs (Gabriel et al., 2014).

Receiving feedback of any kind can be a challenge as individuals are prone to an emotional response as a part of the process. Although it may be difficult for many to receive feedback, this form of communication can benefit one's sense of self-efficacy (Bandura, 2000). Existing research has demonstrated that efficacy beliefs are multidimensional (Zimmerman, 1995). When supervisors cultivate an environment of supportive feedback, it can have a positive effect on employees' psychological states, including a greater sense of control and reduced feelings of helplessness at work (Dahling & O'Malley, 2011; Sparr & Sonnentag, 2008).

Feedback provides information about individual capability (Dimotakis et al., 2017) and guidance toward improvement (Bandura, 2000), which should affect personal and organizational outcomes. A well-trained and empathetic supervisor with strong communication skills can use social persuasion to guide employees with their feedback. Bandura (2000) states that social persuasion is influential for efficacy beliefs as it is a source of information, in this case, regarding one's performance at work. A good supervisor places employees in a position to succeed and can build their confidence with effective feedback and directions on how to apply the feedback. As a result, the employee will feel more empowered because they believe that they can succeed on the job.

Even though we believe that supervisory supportive feedback should enhance the self-efficacy, motivation, and performance of the working poor, we know of no empirical studies on these issues. Thus, we propose the following hypothesis:

Hypothesis 2: Supportive supervisory feedback will enhance the (a) self-efficacy, (b) motivation, and (b) job performance of the working poor (see Figure 9.1).

Outgroup Status Has a Negative Impact on Self-Efficacy

Another factor that is likely to affect the motivation and behavior of the working poor in organizations is that they are typically viewed as outgroup members, which has a negative impact on their social identity or self-concept. Tajfel and Turner (1979) introduced social identity theory and argued that one's social identity refers to "That part of an individual's self-concept which derives from his knowledge of his membership in a social group (or groups) together with the value or emotional significance

Figure 9.1

Conceptual Model

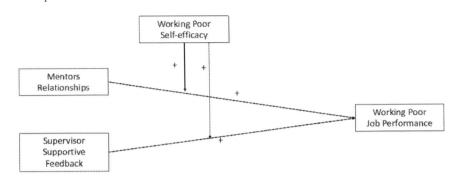

attached to that membership" (Tajfel, 1979, p. 63). The theory suggests that the groups (i.e., social class) to which individuals belong are critical to their source of pride and self-esteem (Jetten et al., 2015). The working poor consist of individuals who are grouped by their status in a hierarchy of social class based on their assets, educational attainment, occupation, income, and membership in a community (Loignon, & Woehr, 2018). Most working poor employees are on the lower levels of the hierarchies in society and often face challenges and adversities that members of higher social classes do not face (such as childcare, poverty, and transportation problems).

Research has shown that group memberships give us a sense of social identity and belonging (Jetten et al., 2017). Social identity theory argues that in-groups are dominant groups that typically have assets and social status, whereas outgroups are those that have few assets and social status (Scheepers & Ellemers, 2019). As a result, the working poor may identify themselves as outgroup members, which may negatively impact their self-perceptions, motivation, performance, and retention in organizations (Benson et al., 2017).

Social identity theory has also linked outgroup membership to self-efficacy in several studies (Brookes, 2015). Research has shown that groups tend to identify themselves with members who are similar to their own sense of self (Randel et al., 2018). Furthermore, individuals have greater connections with an ingroup than an outgroup (Tajfel & Turner, 1979), and people have a stronger connection with groups that have similar capabilities than dissimilar ones. Further, the association between SIT and self-efficacy has shown people believe that they have the same capabilities as their social groups (Tajfel & Turner, 1979). As a result, the working poor may perceive that they have low ability levels if other members of their group have limited capabilities. (Randel et al., 2018). Thus, members of the working poor may feel that they are part of an outgroup in organizations, which is likely to damage their morale and productivity. For instance, they may feel that compensation and reward systems are unfairly biased in favor of the ingroup and believe their opinions are not valued in group discussions. As a result, they may totally isolate themselves from others because they feel excluded in organizations. Research has also shown that outgroup members are more likely to leave the organization because they feel disrespected in organizations and perceive that members of the ingroup are more likely to receive promotions or positive outcomes (Northouse, 2013).

Given the arguments above, we believe that outgroup membership has a negative impact on a person's self-identity and self-efficacy. In support of these arguments, research has shown that individuals tend to self-select themselves into groups based on their own sense of self (Shore et al., 2011). Thus, we argue that if the working poor perceive that they are part of the outgroup they will have lower levels of self-efficacy which should negatively affect their motivation, performance, and intentions to remain with the organizations.

Although the arguments above seem reasonable, we are not aware of any research that has assessed the effects of outgroup status on the self-efficacy or motivation of the working poor. Thus, we propose the following hypotheses to guide research:

Hypothesis 3: When the working poor believe that they are part of an outgroup in organizations, they are more likely to have low (a) self-efficacy, (b) motivation, and (c) performance than when they perceive that they are part of an ingroup.

Self-Efficacy Moderates the Relationship Between Mentoring and Supportive Feedback and Job Performance

Based on Bandura's (1989a) social cognitive model, we also believe that self-efficacy will moderate the relationship between mentoring and job performance, and supportive feedback and job performance. In organizations, mentors influence their protégés by sharing and demonstrating behaviors that support them in the workplace, whereas supervisors are responsible for observing behavior and enforcing the organization's expectations. According to Bandura (1977), efficacy expectations are multidimensional drivers of behavior and motivation. They are also likely to have an important impact on performance (Heslin & Klehe, 2006). Extant research states that one's perception of self-efficacy impacts decisions, such as the goals one chooses to pursue, response to setbacks, and outcome expectations (Bandura, 1994). Furthermore, individuals with high levels of self-efficacy tend to work toward improvement of their ability to perform and seek information more than those with low self-efficacy, and these factors influence work engagement and performance outcomes (Heslin & Klehe, 2006).

In the sections above, we proposed that members of the working poor who have a mentor and supportive feedback from their immediate supervisor will have higher levels of job performance than those without a mentor or supportive feedback. However, it is clear that the person must also have high levels of self-efficacy in order to perform jobs. Thus, we argue that the self-efficacy of the working poor will moderate the relationship between (a) mentoring, and (b) supportive feedback and job performance. Given that self-efficacy perceptions drive motivation and behavior, if an employee expects that they will be successful and has a mentor who clarifies roles and provides supportive feedback, then their performance is likely to be higher than when the person does not expect to be successful.

We know of no research on the degree to which self-efficacy of the working poor moderates the relationship between (a) mentoring and (b) supportive feedback and job performance. We offer the following hypothesis to guide research:

Hypothesis 4: Self-efficacy of the working poor will moderate the relationship between mentoring relationships and job performance such that higher self-efficacy will increase job performance more than low self-efficacy.

Hypothesis 5: Self-efficacy of the working poor will moderate the relation between supervisory supportive feedback and job performance such that higher self-efficacy will increase job performance more than low self-efficacy.

In summary, based on Bandura's model of social cognition, we argued that the use of (a) mentoring and (b) supervisory supportive feedback should enhance the self-efficacy, motivation, and performance of the working poor. We also suggested that self-efficacy would moderate the relations between (a) mentoring and (b) supportive feedback and the job performance of the working poor. In addition, we proposed that if the working poor feel that they are members of an outgroup in organizations, these perceptions will have a negative impact on their perceptions of self-efficacy, motivation, feelings of inclusion, and retention in organizational settings.

DIRECTIONS FOR FUTURE RESEARCH

Despite the arguments in our chapter, we believe that research is needed to examine the degree to which (a) mentoring, and (b) supportive feedback enhances the self-efficacy and performance of the working poor. Even though we emphasized these two variables, we also believe that there are other factors that may enhance the self-efficacy of the working poor (e.g., successful role models, goal setting, mastery experiences).

For example, the use of successful role models from similar background may also improve their self-efficacy. One reason for this is that successful role models from working poor backgrounds should increase the extent to which individuals perceive that people like them are able to succeed on jobs. Furthermore, researchers have argued that goal setting should also help people enhance their self-efficacy (Bandura, 1989b). One reason for this is that when individuals work on tasks, they observe their own performance and evaluate their own progress toward their goals (Schunk, 1990). As a result, their self-efficacy is affected by their self-observation, self-judgment, and their achievement of goals (Schunk, 1990). In addition, when they feel that they are making progress toward their goals they are more likely to feel capable of improving their skills which leads them to set even more challenging goals. Thus, showing employees from working poor backgrounds how to set realistic goals and evaluate their progress toward meeting those goals is likely to increase their self-efficacy (Schunk, 1990). However, future research is needed to determine if successful goal attainment transfers to self-efficacy for those who are considered the working poor. These and other strategies might be used to increase the self-efficacy of these individuals, and help them move out of the category of the working poor.

IMPLICATIONS FOR PRACTICE

Although most of our chapter has focused on academic predictions about factors that affect the motivation and performance of the working poor, we believe that these predictions have important implications for practice in organizations. As a result, we highlight some of the practical mechanisms that might be used to enhance the self-efficacy, motivation, and performance of the working poor.

Mechanisms for Enhancing the Self-Efficacy, Motivation, and Performance of the Working Poor

We considered two strategies that might be used to enhance the self-efficacy of the working poor in the sections above, but we believe that other mechanisms might improve their self-efficacy as well.

Mechanism 1: Mastery Training

Mastery training creates real-world training experiences that prepare individuals for adverse circumstances or struggles by teaching methods to deal with organizational challenges (apa.org, n.d). As a result, we believe that training the working poor to successfully master tasks or their job will increase their self-efficacy, motivation, and performance. Thus, we recommend the following approaches to training: behavioral modeling training and creativity training.

One recommendation is to utilize behavioral modeling training, which means that individuals tend to inescapably learn things they see in a hands-on way (Srividya et al., 2018). Behavior modeling training (BMT), based on Bandura's social learning theory, refers to the process of showing employees how to do something by showing them the standard modeled behavior (Armanu et al., 2016). Behavior modeling usually consists of five steps: modeling, retention, rehearsal, feedback, and transfer of training. Research has demonstrated that trainees who received BMT with a combination of retention enhancement and practice led to significantly better cognitive learning than practice alone (Yi & Davis, 2007).

A second recommendation is to conduct creativity training. Creativity refers to the ability to generate ideas, solutions, or insights that are different yet viable (Stevenson et al., 2014). Research has demonstrated that creativity is best conceptualized not as a personality trait or general ability but as a behavior resulting from a particular pattern of personal characteristics, cognitive skills, and social environment (Zahra et al., 2013, p. 644). Creativity training focuses on cognitive skills and heuristics involved in skill application with practical exercises (Barak, 2010). Research has shown that creative activity can provide instructions to assist individuals in generating practical solutions and novel ideas to solve problems, and we believe that it should also enhance one's self-efficacy (De Jong & Den Hartog, 2007).

Mechanism 2: Successful Role Models Who Come From Working Poor Backgrounds.

We also believe that access to successful role models from similar backgrounds may increase the self-efficacy and motivation of the working poor. The literature defines a role model as a person who provides an example of behaviors that lead to the desired level of success (Lockwood, 2006). A number of researchers have suggested that individuals are drawn toward others with whom they perceive some similarity leading to a desire to emulate their behaviors (Gibson, 2004; Weaver et al., 2011). In addition, modeling or learning theories propose that models can be helpful when one needs to learn a new skill or task (Gibson, 2004).

When someone chooses a role model similar to themselves, it may be partly because they believe the other party has faced similar barriers and still found success (Lockwood, 2006). In the case of the working poor, finding a person who knows and understands their unique challenges may serve to positively affect motivation and confidence levels. Knowing someone has reached a level of achievement despite certain obstacles offers a path forward. Indeed, research by Brewer and Weber (1994) found that individuals who are a part of a minority group assess themselves more positively after contact with a successful member of their group. Finding a successful role model from the working poor community may well serve as a positive mechanism to improve the self-efficacy and workplace outcomes for similar members of that demographic.

Mechanism 3: Eliminating Ingroups and Outgroups in Organizations

We argued above that the working poor are likely to have lower self-efficacy when they perceive that they are part of outgroups rather than ingroups. Thus, we believe that eliminating the distinction between ingroups and outgroups may enhance the self-efficacy of the working poor. Research has shown that in-groups are typically individuals who are included and have power or influence in organizations whereas those in outgroups are typically excluded and have low power levels (Trepte & Loy, 2017). In an organizational context, some individuals might have more influence with decision-makers than are others. The working poor are often considered outgroup members, which means that they have little influence on decision makers, and this has a negative impact on their self-efficacy, morale, and performance (Ramsay et al., 2011).

There are several ways we could try to alleviate in-groups and outgroups in organizations. For example, we could create an inclusive culture by increasing positive group interactions on tasks or social events and hold supervisors accountable if a large number of individuals feel excluded in a unit or department. We could also make a concerted effort to provide all group members with positive recognition rather than recognizing just a few members of the ingroup. Research has shown that an inclusive culture also respects, values, and embraces cultural differences (Stoermer et al., 2016) so we would want to ensure that all members, not just members of the dominant culture, are given opportunities for promotion or rewards (Mor Barak, 2019).

Another strategy organizations might use to create an inclusive culture is to create opportunities for positive intergroup contact through formal team-building initiatives, assignment to tasks, or social activities that encourage diverse individuals to share their unique backgrounds and experiences. Although these strategies appear reasonable, research is needed to determine their effectiveness before they are implemented in organizations.

DISCUSSION

This chapter examined how mentor relationships and supervisor supportive feedback can increase a working poor employee's self-efficacy, motivation, and job performance. We believe that increasing their self-efficacy should give them opportunities to move to higher paying jobs in organizations. In particular, we argued, based on social cognition theory, that mentors should play an essential role in helping the working poor employee gain accurate role perceptions and obtain the feedback needed to increase their job performance and improve their skills and abilities (Schunk & DiBenedetto, 2000). In addition, we maintained that supportive feedback by supervisors and coworkers should provide encouragement to the working poor and enhance their motivation to move up the ladder to higher paying jobs. However, we also believe that organizations should offer support for these individuals by providing the necessary feedback, resources, and training. Understanding the factors that can contribute to the working poor's self-efficacy and motivation may also be used to create a more diverse workforce in organizations because many members of the working poor are often women and ethnic and racial minorities

The literature offers numerous examples surrounding the benefits of mentor relationships and supervisor supportive feedback. However, to date, we know of no research has examined the effects of these factors on the self-efficacy of the working poor. With the middle class fading away, the working poor is the next group of individuals that should be trained to seek better opportunities. Research has shown that organizations are more successful when they identify a diverse team for projects, and we believe that this team should include the working poor (Sanchez & Terlizzi, 2017). Most working poor employees tend to view work as a means to an end or as a functional activity necessary to support one's family. However, we believe that there are a number of strategies or interventions that organizations and communities might use to encourage members of the working poor to view work as a means of increasing their self-esteem, pride, and self-respect. There are also resources in communities to help employees seek new job opportunities, but members of the working poor may not be able to achieve higher paying jobs on their own. We believe that they need mentoring or other forms of help to gain the training needed or access to better jobs.

This chapter's central focus was to examine the potential moderating impact of self-efficacy on the motivation and performance of the working poor. Although resources are sometimes available to employees, they will need to organize and execute the next steps required to access these resources. Working poor employees should also be encouraged to believe in their ability to succeed. Self-efficacy is an inherent characteristic that is needed to enhance participation in mentoring programs and accept constructive feedback. The moderating role of self-efficacy may be important in encouraging the work poor employees to seek mentoring opportunities and supervisory feedback. The predictions in this chapter demonstrate the importance of first understanding the factors needed to increase self-efficacy and ultimately assist in moving an employee to a higher-wage position. This is particularly important for the working poor, and resources are required to help the working poor develop a plan for upward mobility. These predictions also demonstrate the importance of not simply relying on the employee alone, rather providing the tools and resources to motivate and encourage the employee. Organizations that invest time and effort into creating programs to build employee self-efficacy should develop a plan for the target audience.

CONTRIBUTIONS

This research contributes to the literature in several ways. The current theory on self-efficacy has not adequately considered individuals who are a part of the forgotten minorities at work, such as the working poor. The unique background these individuals bring to the workplace strongly influences their motivation, behaviors, and perspectives that influence their success at work. Indeed, scholars must consider that well-established thoughts on confidence and self-belief in the workplace may be challenged when we consider understudied groups. The research presented here contributes new ideas to the factors that potentially influence self-efficacy among the working poor. This chapter also examines interventions organizations can use to support the working poor to assist them with overcoming potential challenges that impact their performance at work.

CONCLUSION

Overall, this conceptual chapter provides insights regarding the challenges members of the working poor face and how these challenges impact their employment. We also offer suggestions that may help organizations assist the working poor in navigating personal barriers they may face on the job and in their personal lives.

Members of the working poor bring a unique presence to the workplace; however, the group is understudied by organizational scholars. Members of the working poor face obstacles that average working and middle-class employees do not; thus, it is important that we understand how organizations can support these individuals, particularly when they desire to improve their current socioeconomic status through work. While this chapter introduces concepts that may influence the working poor employee's success, empirical research is needed to clarify and improve our understanding of these relationships. We urge organization scholars to study the psychology of the working poor and understand how to transition these individuals toward a more satisfying work life.

REFERENCES

Agho, A. O., Mueller, C. W., & Price, J. L. (1993). Determinants of employee job satisfaction: An empirical test of a causal model. *Human Relations*, *46*(8), 1007–1027.

Alabdulkareem, A., Frank, M. R., Sun, L., AlShebli, B., Hidalgo, C., & Rahwan, I. (2018). Unpacking the polarization of workplace skills. *Science Advances*, *4*(7).

Alam, M., & Singh, P. (2019). Performance feedback interviews as affective events: An exploration of the impact of emotion regulation of negative performance feedback on supervisor-employee dyads. *Human Resource Management Review*, 100740.

Al Hilali, K. S., Al Mughairi, B. M., Kian, M. W., & Karim, A. M. (2020). Coaching and mentoring. concepts and practices in development of competencies: A theoretical perspective. *International Journal of Academic Research in Accounting, Finance and Management Sciences*, *10*(1), 41–54.

American Psychological Association. (n.d.). *APA Dictionary of Psychology*. Retrieved October 15, 2021, from https://dictionary.apa.org/mastery-training

Armanu, A., Djumilah, H., & Khusniyah, I. N. (2016). Extra-role behavior modelling: personality concept and the role of servant leadership. *Russian Journal of Agricultural and Socio-Economic Sciences*, *60*(12).

Awaya, A., McEwan, H., Heyler, D., Linsky, S., Lum, D., & Wakukawa, P. (2003). Mentoring as a journey. *Teaching and Teacher Education*, *19*(1), 45–56.

Aziri, B. (2011). Job satisfaction: a literature review. *Management Research & Practice*, *3*(4).

Bandura, A. (1977). Self-efficacy: toward a unifying theory of behavioral change. *Psychological Review*, *84*(2), 191.

Bandura, A. (1986). *Social foundations of thought and action*. Prentice Hall.

Bandura, A. (1989). Human agency in social cognitive theory. *American Psychologist*, *44*(9), 1175.

Bandura, A. (1989). Regulation of cognitive processes through perceived self-efficacy. *Developmental Psychology*, *25*(5), 729.

Bandura, A. (1994). Self-efficacy. In V. S. Ramachaudran (Ed.), *Encyclopedia of human behavior* (Vol. 4, pp. 71–81). Academic Press. (Reprinted in H. Friedman [Ed.], *Encyclopedia of Mental Health*. San Diego: Academic Press, 1998).

Bandura, A. (1997). *Self-efficacy: The exercise of control*. Macmillan.

Bandura, A. (2000). Cultivate self-efficacy for personal and organizational effectiveness. *Handbook of Principles of Organization Behavior, 2*, 11–21.

Barak, M. (2010). How the teaching of heuristic methods affects inventive problem-solving by middle school students. *Technology, Instruction, Cognition & Learning, 8*(3–4), 273–296.

Benson, A. J., Bruner, M. W., & Eys, M. (2017). A social identity approach to understanding the conditions associated with antisocial behaviors among teammates in female teams. *Sport, Exercise, and Performance Psychology, 6*(2), 129.

Berner, M., Ozer, T., & Paynter, S. (2008). A portrait of hunger, the social safety net, and the working poor. *Policy Studies Journal, 36*(3), 403–420.

Bravve, E., Bolton, M., Couch, L., & Crowley, S. (2012). *Out of reach*. http://nlihc. org/sites/default/files/oor/2012-OOR.pdf.

Brewer, M. B., & Weber, J. G. (1994). Self-evaluation effects of interpersonal versus intergroup social comparison. *Journal of Personality and Social Psychology, 66*(2), 268.

Brookes, J. (2015). The effect of overt and covert narcissism on self-esteem and self-efficacy beyond self-esteem. *Personality and Individual Differences, 85*, 172–175.

Brown, M. E., & Treviño, L. K. (2014). Do role models matter? An investigation of role modeling as an antecedent of perceived ethical leadership. *Journal of Business Ethics, 122*(4), 587–598.

Bureau of Labor Statistics. (2014). https://www.bls.gov/opub/reports/working-poor/2014/home.htm

Bureau of Labor Statistics. (2016). https://www.bls.gov/opub/reports/working-poor/2016/home.htm

Bureau of Labor Statistic. (2020). https://www.bls.gov/opub/reports/workingpoor/2018/pdf/home.pdf

Campbell, J. P. (1990). Modeling the performance prediction problem in industrial and organizational psychology. In M. Dunnette & L. M. Hough (Eds.), *Handbook of industrial and organizational psychology* (Vol. 1, 2nd ed., pp. 687–731). Consulting Psychologists Press.

Dahling, J. J., & O'Malley, A. L. (2011). Supportive feedback environments can mend broken performance management systems. *Industrial and Organizational Psychology, 4*(2), 201–203.

De Janasz, S. C., Sullivan, S. E., & Whiting, V. (2003). Mentor networks and career success: Lessons for turbulent times. *Academy of Management Perspectives, 17*(4), 78–91.

De Jong, J. P., & Den Hartog, D. N. (2007). How leaders influence employees' innovative behaviour. *European Journal of Innovation Management*.

Desmond, M., & Gershenson, C. (2016). Housing and employment insecurity among the working poor. *Social Problems, 63*(1), 46–67.

Dimotakis, N., Mitchell, D., & Maurer, T. (2017). Positive and negative assessment center feedback in relation to development self-efficacy, feedback-seeking, and promotion. *Journal of Applied Psychology*, *102*(11), 1514.

Gabriel, A. S., Frantz, N. B., Levy, P. E., & Hilliard, A. W. (2014). The supervisor feedback environment is empowering, but not all the time: Feedback orientation as a critical moderator. *Journal of Occupational and Organizational psychology*, *87*(3), 487–506.

Gibson, D. E. (2004). Role models in career development: New directions for theory and research. *Journal of Vocational Behavior*, *65*(1), 134–156.

Gorski, P. C. (2017). *Reaching and teaching students in poverty: Strategies for erasing the opportunity gap*. Teachers College Press.

Heslin, P. A., & Klehe, U. C. (2006). Self-efficacy. In S. G. Rogelberg (Ed.), *Encyclopedia of Industrial/Organizational Psychology*, *2*, 705–708.

Hutchison, S., & Garstka, M. L. (1996). Sources of perceived organizational support: goal setting and feedback 1. *Journal of Applied Social Psychology*, *26*(15), 1351–1366.

Inzer, L. D., & Crawford, C. B. (2005). A review of formal and informal mentoring: Processes, problems, and design. *Journal of Leadership Education*, *4*(1), 31–50.

Jetten, J., Branscombe, N. R., Haslam, S. A., Haslam, C., Cruwys, T., Jones, J. M., 3 Cui, L., Dingle, G., Liu, J., Murphy, S., Thai, A., Walter, Z., & Zhang, A. (2015). Having a lot of a good thing: Multiple important group memberships as a source of self-esteem. *PloS one*, *10*(5), e0124609.

Jetten, J., Haslam, S. A., Cruwys, T., Greenaway, K. H., Haslam, C., & Steffens, N. K. (2017). Advancing the social identity approach to health and well-being: Progressing the social cure research agenda. *European Journal of Social Psychology*, *47*(7), 789–802.

Kalleberg, A. L. (2011). *Good jobs, bad jobs*. Russell Sage Foundation.

Katz, D., & Kahn, R. L. (1978). Organizations and the system concept. *Classics of Organization Theory*, *80*, 480.

Komaki, J. L. (1986). Toward effective supervision: An operant analysis and comparison of managers at work. *Journal of Applied Psychology*, *71*(2), 270.

Kram, K. E. (1985). *Mentoring at work: Developmental relationships in organizational life*. Scott Foresman.

Kram, K. E., & Hall, D. T. (1989). Mentoring as an antidote to stress during corporate trauma. *Human Resource Management*, *28*(4), 493–510.

Kraus, M. W., Piff, P. K., Mendoza-Denton, R., Rheinschmidt, M. L., & Keltner, D. (2012). Social class, solipsism, and contextualism: How the rich are different from the poor. *Psychological Review*, *119*(3), 546.

Lawler, E. E., III, & Porter, L. W. (1967). The effect of performance on job satisfaction. *Industrial Relations: A Journal of Economy and Society*, *7*(1), 20–28.

Leana, C. R., Mittal, V., & Stiehl, E. (2012). PERSPECTIVE—Organizational behavior and the working poor. *Organization Science*, *23*(3), 888–906.

Lockwood, P. (2006). "Someone like me can be successful": Do college students need same-gender role models? *Psychology of Women Quarterly*, *30*(1), 36–46.

Loignon, A. C., & Woehr, D. J. (2018). Social class in the organizational sciences: a conceptual integration and meta-analytic review. *Journal of Management*, *44*(1), 61–88.

Mor Barak, M. E. (2019). Erecting walls versus tearing them down: Inclusion and the (false) paradox of diversity in times of economic upheaval. *European Management Review*, *16*(4), 937–955.

Motowidlo, S. J., & Kell, H. J. (2012). Job performance. *Handbook of Psychology, Second Edition*, *12*.

Nemanick, R. C., Jr. (2000). Comparing formal and informal mentors: Does type make difference?. *Academy of Management Perspectives*, *14*(3), 136–138.

Northouse, P. G. (2013). *Leadership: Theory and practice* (6th ed.). SAGE.

Parker, V. A., & Kram, K. E. (1993). Women mentoring women: Creating conditions for connection. *Business Horizons*, *36*(2), 42–52.

Payne, T. B., & Murty, K.S. (2019). *Balancing the odds: Women's perceptions of personal barriers and life satisfaction on transitioning to work*. Green Legacy.

Policy Link. (n.d). https://www.policylink.org/data-in-action/overview-americaworking-poor

Ragins, B. R. (2016). From the ordinary to the extraordinary. *Organizational Dynamics*, *45*(3), 228–244.

Ragins, B. R., & Cotton, J. L. (1999). Mentor functions and outcomes: a comparison of men and women in formal and informal mentoring relationships. *Journal of Applied Psychology*, *84*(4), 529.

Ragins, B. R., & Kram, K. E. (Eds.). (2007). The roots and meaning of mentoring. In *The handbook of mentoring at work: Theory, research, and practice* (pp. 3–15). SAGE.

Randel, A. E., Galvin, B. M., Shore, L. M., Ehrhart, K. H., Chung, B. G., Dean, M. A., & Kedharnath, U. (2018). Inclusive leadership: Realizing positive outcomes through belongingness and being valued for uniqueness. *Human Resource Management Review*, *28*(2), 190–203.

Ramsay, S., Troth, A., & Branch, S. (2011). Workplace bullying: A group processes framework. *Journal of Occupational and Organizational Psychology*, *84*(4), 799–816

Sanchez, O. P., & Terlizzi, M. A. (2017). Cost and time project management success factors for information systems development projects. *International Journal of Project Management*, *35*(8), 1608–1626.

Sanfey, H., Hollands, C., & Gantt, N. L. (2013). Strategies for building an effective mentoring relationship. *The American Journal of Surgery*, *206*(5), 714–718.

Scheepers, D., & Ellemers, N. (2019). Social identity theory. In K. Sassenberg & M. L. W. Vliek (Eds.), *Social psychology in action* (pp. 129–143). Springer.

Schunk, D. H. (1990). Goal setting and self-efficacy during self-regulated learning. *Educational Psychologist*, *25*(1), 71–86.

Schunk, D. H., & DiBenedetto, M. K. (2020). Motivation and social cognitive theory. *Contemporary Educational Psychology*, *60*, 101832.

Shipler, D. K. (2005). *The working poor: Invisible in America*. Vintage.

Shore, L. M., Randel, A. E., Chung, B. G., Dean, M. A., Holcombe Ehrhart, K., & Singh, G. (2011). Inclusion and diversity in work groups: A review and model for future research. *Journal of Management*, *37*(4), 1262–1289.

Sonnentag, S., Volmer, J., & Spychala, A. (2008). Job performance. *The SAGE Handbook of Organizational Behavior*, *1*, 427–447.

Sparr, J. L., & Sonnentag, S. (2008). Fairness perceptions of supervisor feedback, LMX, and employee well-being at work. *European Journal of Work and Organizational Psychology*, *17*(2), 198–225.

Srividya, M., Mohanavalli, S., & Bhalaji, N. (2018). Behavioral modeling for mental health using machine learning algorithms. *Journal of Medical Systems*, *42*(5), 1–12.

Stevenson, C. E., Kleibeuker, S. W., de Dreu, C. K., & Crone, E. A. (2014). Training creative cognition: adolescence as a flexible period for improving creativity. *Frontiers in Human Neuroscience*, *8*, 827.

Stoermer, S., Hildisch, A. K., & Froese, F. J. (2016). Culture matters: The influence of national culture on inclusion climate. *Cross Cultural & Strategic Management*.

Tajfel, H., & Turner, J. (1979). *Social identity theory*. https://learning-theories.com/social-identity-theory-tajfel-turner.html

The high cost of being poor. (2004). https://files.eric.ed.gov/fulltext/ED485918.pdf

The high cost of being poor in the U.S. (2016, September 20). https://www.chn.org/wp-content/uploads/2019/02/Final-CHN-Natl-Census-Poverty-Report-9.20.16.pdf

Thiede, B. C., Lichter, D. T., & Sanders, S. R. (2015). America's working poor: Conceptualization, measurement, and new estimates. *Work and Occupations*, *42*(3), 267–312.

Trepte, S., & Loy, L. S. (2017). Social identity theory and self-categorization theory. *The International Encyclopedia of Media Effects*, 1–13.

Viswesvaran, C., & Ones, D. S. (2000). Perspectives on models of job performance. *International Journal of Selection and Assessment*, *8*(4), 216–226.

Walkington, H., Stewart, K. A., Hall, E. E., Ackley, E., & Shanahan, J. O. (2020). Salient practices of award-winning undergraduate research mentors–balancing freedom and control to achieve excellence. *Studies in Higher Education*, *45*(7), 1519–1532.

Walsh, M. M., & Arnold, K. A. (2020). The bright and dark sides of employee mindfulness: Leadership style and employee well-being. *Stress and Health*, *36*(3), 287–298.

Weaver, R., Peters, K., Koch, J., & Wilson, I. (2011). 'Part of the team': professional identity and social exclusivity in medical students. *Medical Education*, *45*(12), 1220–1229.

Wuepper, D., & Lybbert, T. J. (2017). Perceived self-efficacy, poverty, and economic development. *Annual Review of Resource Economics*, *9*, 383–404.

Yi, M. Y., & Davis, F. D. (2001). Improving computer training effectiveness for decision technologies: Behavior modeling and retention enhancement. *Decision Sciences*, *32*(3), 521–544.

Zahra, P., Yusooff, F., & Hasim, M. S. (2013). Effectiveness of training creativity on preschool students. *Procedia-Social and Behavioral Sciences*, *102*, 643–647.

Zimmerman, B. J. (1995). Self-efficacy and educational development. *Self-Efficacy in Changing Societies*, *1*(1), 202–231.

CHAPTER 10

CALLING FOR MORE ORGANIZATIONAL RESEARCH ON SOCIOECONOMIC STATUS

Elisabeth R. Silver, Cassandra N. Phetmisy, Naomi Fa-Kaji
Rice University

Abby Corrington
Providence College

Linnea C. Ng
Lawrence University

Mikki Hebl
Rice University

ABSTRACT

Socioeconomic status (SES) refers to the social standing of an individual or group of people, and reflects a combination of income, education, and occupation (American Psychological Association, 2020). In this chapter, we argue that both theoretical and empirical research on SES is lacking in organizational science. We present a model in the current research (ASA; Schneider, 1987) that breaks down the impact of SES in three separate stages of the employment cycle: attraction, selection, and attrition. For each stage, we consider both the perspective of the individual who may be low in SES (self)

Forgotten Minorities in Organizations, pp. 299–328
Copyright © 2023 by Information Age Publishing
www.infoagepub.com
All rights of reproduction in any form reserved.
299

and how other organizational members (others) perceive those who may be low in SES. We conclude that scholars and organizations can better understand the impact of SES by studying a wider range of both employees within organizations and industries themselves to ensure that research reflects the experiences of those across the SES spectrum. We emphasize the importance of focusing on those outside the highest organizational echelons, as those in management and leadership are overrepresented in organizational research. We also suggest a number of important avenues for future research on SES in organizations, such as considering unique stressors, the meaning of work, and subjective perceptions of status at work.

Income inequality in the U.S. has steadily increased over the past 50 years, with the proportion of income earned by upper-class families growing and the proportion earned by lower- and middle-class families decreasing (Schaeffer, 2020). In 2018, 11.8% of people living in the U.S. lived at or below the poverty level of $25,465 in yearly income for a family of four (U.S. Census Bureau, 2019). According to estimates adjusted for cost of living and other demographic factors, 44% of workers between the ages of 18 and 64 years are low-wage workers, defined as those earning less than 66% of the median income for a given community (Ross & Bateman, 2019). Moreover, all of the 10 most common occupations in the United States, together constituting one-fifth of the U.S. labor force, are entry-level and non-managerial (Bergman & Jean, 2016). Because those with low socioeconomic status (SES) comprise a large and increasing portion of the workforce, understanding the influence of SES on organizational outcomes is paramount. Despite this urgent need for research, the experiences of low-SES individuals in the workplace are poorly represented in the industrial-organizational (I-O) psychology literature: from 2012 to 2014, only 9% of articles published in top I-O psychology journals specifically investigated samples of low-SES workers (Bergman & Jean, 2016). Research on social class is also underrepresented in related fields, such as organizational behavior (OB) and human resources (HR; Loignon & Woehr, 2018). Because such a small proportion of organizational research pertains to workers from low-SES backgrounds, it is difficult to determine whether existing organizational theories and findings generalize to this sizable population. Including workers from low-SES backgrounds in organizational research is the first step to addressing this too-often forgotten minority.

We use the term "SES" to broadly describe the social standing of an individual or group of people, reflecting one's economic resources and associated sociocultural experiences (American Psychological Association [APA], 2020; Gray & Kish-Gephart, 2013). SES is used to make comparisons in society and is often divided into three levels (i.e., low, middle, and high). In the present review, we use the terms *social status*, *SES*, and *social class* interchangeably. Reflecting the multidimensional nature of SES as a social, economic, and cultural construct, operationalizations of SES in psychological research include both objective measures (e.g., educational attainment, occupational level, income) and subjective SES measures assessing participants' perceptions of their own socioeconomic rank relative to others in a comparison group (Ostrove et al., 2000).

Research in some disciplines, such as sociology, education, and medicine, has made strides in uncovering the importance of SES as a predictor of life outcomes and wellbeing. Lower SES is linked to poorer physical and psychological outcomes (Signorello et al., 2014), and experiencing financial scarcity influences cognition by leading to a high level of focus on life sufficiency goals, leaving fewer cognitive resources for non-critical but nonetheless highly important ones (Mullainathan & Shafir, 2013). Social class often corresponds with cultural differences that impact one's sense of self, permeating many aspects of social interactions (Stephens et al., 2019). What is surprising, then, is the scarcity of organizational research on the subject. SES is rarely studied as a focal topic in organizational diversity research, despite research suggesting that it has comparable effects on occupational achievement relative to those of personality traits and IQ (Roberts et al., 2007).

We propose three primary factors that have led to the glaring absence of SES in analyses and discussions in organizational research. First, organizational theories surrounding SES are lacking. Theory is generated as both a response to empirical data and a guide for future investigation. Compared to the empirical attention that other social identities (e.g., race, gender, age, sexual orientation) have received in organizational research, work focused primarily on SES is modest. Thus, there is a ripe opportunity for organizational research to focus on this often-forgotten group and develop theories on its members' experiences in organizations. Second, the study of SES is complicated in that it often overlaps with other systems of oppression, and, as a result, can covary with other demographic characteristics. Many individuals are targeted by intersecting biases and systemic disadvantage (Cole, 2009), and SES is correlated with race, ethnicity, health, and education (APA, 2021; Williams et al., 2019). Disentangling these relationships often requires many participants, intricate designs, and theoretical consideration. Third, SES can be difficult to identify and define. In the U.S., it is taboo to discuss income, particularly in White middle- and upper-class environments, based on social norms and a desire to avoid feelings of economic guilt (Pinsker, 2020). Instead of discussing income directly, people signal their SES by referencing classed personal and professional experiences (e.g., education, occupational history; Pinsker, 2020). Defining SES is also difficult because it is more malleable across time and space than other demographic identities (Phillips et al., 2020).

In the context of the meritocratic values espoused in the U.S. (i.e., the notion that people can "pull themselves up by their bootstraps"), many believe that they can change their SES and actively try to do so (Phillips et al., 2020). Consequently, measuring and understanding SES at any given time can be challenging.

To address these challenges, we review research published in management, HR, and I-O psychology journals, including *The Academy of Management Review, The Academy of Management Journal, Journal of Organizational Behavior, Personnel Psychology,* and *Journal of Applied Psychology.* We also extend our perspective to include social psychology outlets (e.g., *Journal of Personality and Social Psychology, Journal of Applied Social Psychology,* and *Personality and Social Psychology Bulletin*), and sociology outlets (e.g., *American Sociological Review, American Journal of Sociology,* and *Journal of Social Issues*). We supplement our interdisciplinary perspective with additional literature searches for studies of socioeconomic status and social class as it intersects with various stages of the employment cycle.

ASA FRAMEWORK AND LITERATURE REVIEW

We begin by reviewing relevant research on SES in organizations, using the attraction-selection-attrition model (ASA; Schneider, 1987) as an organizing framework. According to the ASA model, employees' characteristics and their interactions with colleagues drive organizational behavior and change, emphasizing that people self-select into and out of organizations based on the perceived fit between themselves and the culture created by incumbents (Schneider, 1987). People are drawn to or repelled by certain organizations, a process that shapes three important organizational processes: attraction, selection, and attrition (Schneider, 1987). Through these processes, members of organizations often become increasingly homogenous over time (Dickson et al., 2008).

Because SES is inherently social in nature, based on its foundation in relative rankings (i.e., low, middle, high), we integrate the ASA framework with a dyadic interaction model that has been used to understand prejudice (Hebl & Dovidio, 2005). Through this dyadic lens, we consider the organizational implications of intraindividual and interpersonal experiences tied to SES, or "classed" experiences. Thus, we augment the ASA model by considering not only how SES influences one's *own* affect, behavior, and cognitions, but also how *others'* perceptions of an individual's SES influence organizational processes. We organize our review by examining these two interrelated axes, depicted in Table 10.1. This first axis draws from Schneider's (1987) ASA framework to explore how each step in the model impacts socioeconomic diversity in organizations. The second axis, which we refer to as "self versus other," explores the workplace implications of SES for workers from low-SES backgrounds themselves (self), and for perceivers of low-SES individuals in the organization (other). By combining these frameworks, we move toward understanding the multifaceted ways that SES impacts individuals in organizations and we provide recommendations for future research and practice.

Table 10.1

Theoretical Integration of Socioeconomic Influences in the Employment Life-Cycle

	Attraction	Selection	Attrition
Self	Do I want to work here?	Should I apply for this position?	Do I want to keep working here?
Other	Do I want this person to work here?	Should this applicant be hired?	Do I want this person to advance here?

ATTRACTION

The first stage in the ASA model is attraction (Schneider, 1987), which describes the process by which people perceive an organization as appealing and desire to join it. People are differentially attracted to organizations as a function of their values, interests, personality, and perceived fit between these characteristics and those of the organization (Cable & Judge, 1996). In this section, we discuss how SES influences individuals' attraction to organizations and the extent to which others perceive applicants who vary in SES as worthy of attraction efforts.

Self: Do I Want to Work Here?

At the attraction stage, culture, and access impact applicants' engagement with organizations. Many people learn about job opportunities through informal networks (Amis et al., 2020). Consequently, information about job opportunities at organizations with a predominantly middle- and upper-class workforce is more likely to reach those from similar backgrounds. Indeed, work on disparities in hiring based on race, often intersecting with SES due to systemic racism, has found that organizations' reliance on referrals when searching for potential new hires, as well as the segregation of social networks, can contribute to the exclusion of members of marginalized racial groups from desirable jobs (see Pedulla & Pager, 2019). Similar forces may influence socioeconomic disparities in knowledge about job opportunities.

A recent review highlighted how social ties of varying strengths intersect with social class inequalities, such that the smaller, stronger networks of low-SES individuals help people reach interdependent goals and survive resource scarcity (Carey & Markus, 2017). By contrast, the bigger, weaker social networks of high-SES individuals help people thrive and reach personal goals. Bigger and weaker social networks are more advantageous for learning about desirable jobs and advancing in organizations once employed (Granovetter, 1973). The breadth and depth of social ties to which individuals turn in times of employment uncertainty also differ as a function of social class: when employment status is threatened, those from lower social classes seek support from a smaller number, but stronger set, of social ties than those from higher social classes do (Smith et al., 2011). Likewise, during the transition from youth to adulthood, low-SES individuals more often form mentoring relationships with family members than they do with non-familial others, and the content of mentorship tends to focus less on career advice relative to that given to high-SES youth (Raposa et al., 2018). Thus, low-SES people seeking employment may be at a disadvantage, as the number of others inside organizations who are able to provide recommendations or advice is smaller. Applied to organizational attraction, the positive relationship between wealth and social network size indicates that if it is indeed "all about who one knows," organizations are more likely to attract an applicant pool that is socioeconomically homogenous and advantaged than one that is socioeconomically diverse.

In addition to equity issues related to word-of-mouth recruitment, recruitment for jobs and internships often occurs in higher-SES spaces such as elite college campuses, making it difficult for low-SES individuals to learn about and access these opportunities (Rivera, 2015). Unpaid internships, which often serve as a path to future employment, are yet another mechanism of social inequality maintenance, as only those with other means of financial support can take advantage of these opportunities. A lack of material resources may present further barriers to job entry—less flexible work schedules and a lack of paid leave within working-class jobs (Kossek & Lautsch, 2018) can leave little time to conduct a job search or interviews. Even when low-SES applicants *are* able to devote the same amount of effort to a job search as high-SES applicants, they tend to conduct less effective job searches (i.e., leading to fewer job interviews and offers) than upper-class individuals (Fang & Saks, 2020). Furthermore, a limited financial safety net may make it difficult for job seekers from low-

SES backgrounds to take advantage of opportunities that are high-risk, but offer a higher reward, such as jobs in start-up companies and emerging industries.

Finally, job seekers from low-SES backgrounds may perceive a lack of fit at organizations with predominantly middle- and upper-class cultural practices, values, and norms. Applicants may interpret cultural differences as a sign that they lack the job skills necessary for a position and therefore need not apply. For instance, research finds that women are more likely than men to discount themselves for certain jobs if they do not meet all of the requirements for a position (Mohr, 2014). The tendency to apply for jobs only when all qualifications are met may extend to low-SES jobseekers as well and is particularly troubling given that low-SES individuals have less access to voluntary learning experiences that could allow them to meet position requirements (Pitesa & Pillutla, 2019).

Other: Do I Want This Person to Work Here?

As mentioned previously, recruitment efforts concentrated in elite universities selectively sample applicants from a limited (i.e., upper) social class (Rivera, 2015). Further restricting the applicant pool, the discourse on top companies' recruitment websites for recent college graduates is centered on ambiguous ideals like ambition, innovativeness, and curiosity, rather than on the concrete knowledge, skills, and abilities that applicants need within desired roles (Handley, 2018). It is also common for companies to encourage prospective applicants to align their identity to that of the company's brand while also being authentic to themselves (Handley, 2018). Rather than providing constructive, actionable steps for applicants, these websites promote a cultural ideal (i.e., an employable college graduate) that is made for and by those with the highest social status. Including these messages in recruitment materials may deter low-SES applicants from pursuing a job based solely on their perceived lack of fit with the elite values that its current members espouse, regardless of the prospective applicant's objective qualifications.

In addition to organizational barriers, psychological research on identities other than social class suggests that prejudice in interpersonal interactions potentially directs recruitment efforts away from those who are or who are perceived as being low-SES. Research on aversive racism— that is, the phenomenon in which White individuals harbor high levels of implicit racial bias despite explicitly espousing egalitarian attitudes (Gaertner & Dovidio, 1986)—is particularly informative. A precondition for aversive prejudice to manifest is the ability to point to characteristics that are not clearly related to a stigmatized identity. For instance, although comparable White and Black applicants receive similar judg-ments on deserved pay and hire ability, Black applicants are rated lower on "soft skills," emotional stability, and seriousness about work (Gilbert & Lownses-Jackson, 2005). Moreover, White applicants with ambiguous qualifications for a job are evaluated more positively than Black applicants with ambiguous qualifications (Dovidio & Gaertner, 2000). Certainly, social class and race are different social identities. Nevertheless, research on aversive prejudice suggests that HR professionals may be especially likely to justify overlooking applicants from lower-class backgrounds based on, for example, attending a less prestigious college, speaking, or dressing in ways that indicate their social class (and are deemed "unprofessional"), or not sharing the same expensive, restrictive hobbies and social circles as existing employees. Indeed, the previously mentioned research examining organizations' recruitment websites demonstrates that recruitment mate-rials may overemphasize ambiguous characteristics, which are especially likely to allow biases to flourish.

SELECTION

The second employment stage in the ASA model is selection, which involves evaluating candidates and choosing whom to hire according to how well the candidate matches a role's qualifications (Schneider, 1987). Employees are not randomly assigned to workplaces; rather, formal (e.g., structured inter-views) and informal processes (e.g., perceptions of fit) lead some people to be chosen to enter or advance in an organization. In this section, we discuss how SES influences individuals' decisions to seek and accept employment opportunities. We then examine how classed norms influence hiring and promotion decisions for applicants across the SES spectrum.

Self: Should I Apply for This Position?

The belief that one's social class is mutable and a reflection of one's willingness and ability to work can obscure the important role that SES plays in determining who is included in applicant pools, which quali-ties are valued, and how applicants are evaluated. Such processes can be particularly problematic when there is a disconnect between the qualities that hiring managers use in selection decisions and the qualities that are actually needed for a given role. Research on self-fulfilling prophecies has found that evaluator expectations can influence performance in job interviews, by both changing applicants' behavior and biasing evaluators' perceptions of that behavior (Word et al., 1974). Evaluation procedures that indicate a preference for traits associated with high SES (e.g., previous unpaid internship experience, personal connections to current employees) can signal to low-SES applicants that they are not a good fit for the organization. Navigating these signals of fit can drain the applicants' cognitive resources by invoking identity management concerns (Madera et al., 2012) and stereotype threat (Major & O'Brien, 2005). Indeed, when individuals are aware of negative stereotypes regarding a group they belong to, the fear of confirming these negative stereotypes is cognitively taxing and can harm performance (Steele, 1997). Class biases and disparities can therefore influence selection in many ways—by influencing who is considered, defining the skills and traits that are valued by hiring managers, and hampering applicant performance through mechanisms such as stereotype threat.

Just as social identity processes may influence the anticipated outcome of selection processes for low- versus high-SES applicants, systemic logistical barriers play a role in determining the costs and benefits of entering the application cycle. A recent longitudinal study from DeOrtentiis and colleagues (2021) found associations between social class and a number of antecedents of job search behaviors. They found that applicants from lower social classes reported lower job search intensity than their higher-class counterparts, an effect that was mediated by lower job search self-efficacy. Consequently, low-SES applicants may be at a disadvantage when navigating selection processes by virtue of restricted access to job search tools (e.g., time for selection procedures, internet access, coaching) and support outside of work (e.g., childcare, transportation). Moreover, those who reported lower subjective social class status tended to accept job offers more frequently than higher-class applicants, suggesting that the ability to wait for more attractive job offers during selection is concentrated among high-SES applicants, making it more difficult for low-SES applicants to accumulate a variety of options.

Norms regarding self-presentation in interview settings may also deter qualified low-SES applicants from pursuing employment opportunities when they do not have the business casual or business formal clothing often required to be evaluated positively in interview settings (Bardack & McAndrew, 1985). The disproportionate financial burden of this demand on low-SES applicants is so pervasive that some university career centers offer students a lending library of free business casual or business formal clothing (e.g., University of Michigan, 2021). Revising standards for interview attire to reflect an organization's typical dress code or by asking interviewers to evaluate applicants regardless of their clothing may signal to applicants that they will receive fair consideration. Decision makers in organizations should think carefully about the assumptions embedded in their selection practices to benefit from skills and knowledge of those who may not fit an organization's prototype but can offer valuable insights.

Other: Should This Applicant Be Hired?

As with other social identities, social class is a demographic characteristic relevant to selection, particularly as it relates to interpersonal interactions, stigmatization, and stereotyping. The stereotype content model (SCM; Fiske et al., 2002) offers a useful framework for understanding how group-based stereotypes along dimensions of competence and warmth impact social class disparities in selection. Research using the SCM finds that high-SES individuals are perceived as highly competent but unkind (or cold), and low-SES individuals are perceived as relatively less competent but warm (Durante et al., 2017). These so-called ambivalent judgments, in which groups are stereotyped as possessing both positive and negative qualities simultaneously, may seem less pernicious than negative judgments alone. Nonetheless, social class stereotypes maintain SES inequalities by justifying high-SES individuals' status by virtue of their perceived competence (Durante & Fiske, 2017). Further, recent research suggests that when a group of people appears to have greater economic inequality, SES stereotyping is more pronounced than when groups appear to be more socioeconomically homogenous (Connor et al., 2021). During selection, when applicant pools may contain individuals from varying SES backgrounds, this finding implies that negative stereotypes of low-SES groups are more salient. Applicants perceived to be low-SES may be judged by recruiters as kind but incompetent, advantaging those perceived as high-SES in competitions for well-paying jobs.

Relatedly, system justification theory posits that stereotypes position social inequalities as permissible and fair (Jost & Banaji, 1994). Applied to SES, economic system justification describes "the belief that the capitalist system provides individuals with equal opportunity to succeed, and that outcomes are based upon personal deservingness and merit" (Goudarzi et al., 2020, p. 2). Under this view, economic inequality is a righteous outcome of a meritocratic system. To this point, Goudarzi and colleagues (2020) found that participants who perceived the economic system as just demonstrated blunted negative affect in response to videos depicting homelessness relative to those who did not perceive the economic system as just. Economic system-justifiers also exhibited blunted physiological responses to homeless people (Goudarzi et al., 2020). Thus, perceiving economic inequality as the product of individual failure in a fair system, rather than of systemic failures in an unjust system, decreases empathetic responses to low-SES individuals.

In practice, processes used in hiring practices can introduce additional pitfalls. Unstructured interviews are especially prone to bias, as interviewers tend to evaluate applicants from backgrounds similar to their own more positively than those from dissimilar backgrounds (Buckley et al., 2007;

McDaniel et al., 1994). Given the large representation of middle- and high-SES individuals in white-collar occupations, this bias disadvantages lower-SES job applicants. Rivera (2015) found that hiring managers in elite professional service firms often relied on feelings of excitement when evaluating mock applicants. Their excitement stemmed from learning information about an applicant that signaled a high-class background similar to that of the interviewer. Leisure activities associated with wealth (e.g., travel, lacrosse, and other costly sports) were points of connection between evaluators and applicants. Many of these activities require a substantial investment of time and money over a long time period, indicating not just the applicant's current high SES, but also the SES of the family in which they were raised (Rivera, 2015). The weight given to these class markers is even more remarkable given that the mock applicants evaluated by hiring professionals were almost exclusively students from elite colleges and universities. This finding suggests that those from low-SES backgrounds continue to face class discrimination even when they have gained entry into high-SES spaces (Rivera, 2015).

The class-based consequences of flawed selection processes are exacerbated by pervasive negative stereotypes (e.g., Durante et al., 2017). Vázquez and Lois (2020) found that highly materialistic participants were less likely to select or recommend an applicant perceived as low-SES than they were an applicant perceived as high-SES. They also found that, relative to a low-performing, high-SES peer, participants reported less desire to work on a team and interact with a low-performing, low-SES peer. However, when a low-SES peer was described as performing highly in the past, participants were equally likely to want to work with her as they were a high-performing, high-SES peer. These results suggests that low-SES applicants may be judged more harshly than high-SES applicants with the same (poor) performance record, and that bias disadvantages low-SES applicants most when there is ambiguity around applicants' future ability to perform.

ATTRITION

The third stage in the ASA model is attrition. Attrition occurs when employees recognize a mismatch between their values and the organization's goals, motivating their departure from an organization. When people do not feel that they belong or perceive poor person-organization fit, they are likely to leave their jobs (Cable & Judge, 1996). In this section, we explore how social class stereotypes, cultural differences (both real and perceived), and impression management can wear on employees and contribute to attrition. Specifically, we discuss how individuals' SES influences their decision to remain with or turnover in organizations. Additionally, we examine the extent to which other employees help promote a sense of belonging among their low-SES coworkers and work to prevent their departures.

Self: Do I Want to Keep Working Here?

The decision to leave an organization can mark the culmination of challenges faced by workers from low-SES backgrounds. Stereotypes can inform which roles and tasks seem most "appropriate" for individuals with certain social identities, further perpetuating disparities based on notions of "fit." Social class may influence the tasks and roles that workers are assigned to, with implications for compensation and career advancement. Much of the work on disparities in role and task allocation focuses on how such practices contribute to race- and gender-based inequality (e.g., Miller & Roksa, 2020). These findings likely extend to SES, given that social class groups are stereotyped as differing on traits relevant to organizational functions (see previous discussion). The best jobs are sometimes reserved for those perceived to fit the "ideal worker" prototype: a person who is fully committed to his (the prototype is almost always male) job and prioritizes work over other obligations (Acker, 1990). The "ideal worker" is therefore only achievable for those who have few obligations outside of work, close others who can tend to outside obligations, or the financial resources to pay others to perform extra-work roles.

Workers from low-SES backgrounds may have less mobility within organizations, making it difficult to gain experience in a broad range of organizational functions and providing fewer opportunities to demonstrate skills. Furthermore, the tendency toward homophily means that even when individuals from historically marginalized groups can cultivate extensive professional networks, they are unlikely to benefit from their networks to the same degree as their more privileged peers, who typically have greater access to those with decision-making power (James, 2000). To this point, employees from upper- and upper-middle-class backgrounds reap greater career advancement benefits from mentoring than comparable low-SES peers (Whitely et al., 1991). Additionally, although rising in formal organizational rank is typically associated with a rise in pay, the monetary benefits tend to be greater for those from high-SES backgrounds (Laurison & Friedman, 2016), suggesting that incentives for gaining organizational power are more limited for low-SES employees.

Because of the negative stereotypes associated with low SES (e.g., Durante et al., 2017), SES-related social identity threat can incur psychological costs, especially when individuals are part of a prestigious organization in which cross-class interactions are likely to occur (Gray & Kish-Gephart, 2013). For instance, low-SES students at an elite university reported poorer academic fit with the institution than their high-SES peers, and, unlike their high-SES peers, low-SES students experienced cognitive depletion after discussing academic achievement (Johnson et al., 2011). Gray and Kish-Gephart (2013) conceptualized such costs as a form of intraindividual *class work* undertaken by low-SES employees in cross-class interactions. They described four major types of within-person class work among low-SES employees: accepting meritocratic beliefs, centralizing an identity unrelated to SES, expressing pride in their unique classed experiences, and/or denigrating upper-class members. This class work demonstrates how stigma associated with low SES can create identity management concerns (i.e., how employees manage concealable identities at work), introducing another potential cognitive burden. Although social class often can be deduced from observable characteristics, how members of different social classes negotiate these identities interpersonally is another matter. Suppressing a stigmatized identity is associated with poorer organizational outcomes, including greater perceived discrimination, higher turnover intentions, and lower job satisfaction (Madera et al., 2012). Clair and colleagues (2005) note that "passing" as a member of a nonstigmatized group may afford benefits but is also associated with potential costs to felt authenticity, connection to coworkers, and fear of discrimination.

Classed cultural differences can make it difficult for low-SES employees to build relationships within organizations—relationships that can impact their sense of belonging and potential for career growth. SES encompasses not only material resources but also cultural capital, "a set of socially rare and distinctive tastes, skills, knowledge, and practices" (Loignon & Woehr, 2018, p. 64; see also Bourdieu, 1984). In the workplace, work scripts (i.e., appropriate behaviors for a given work role and setting) constitute one such distinctive practice (Stone-Romero et al., 2003). According to Stone-Romero and colleagues (2003), work scripts are culturally defined, both in terms of organizational culture and individual employees' cultural background. Employees of different class backgrounds may therefore bring different expectations to the same work role, creating friction that wears on interpersonal work relationships.

Interpersonal relationships at work can provide employees with the information and mentorship required to learn the scripts that define a certain role (Stone-Romero et al., 2003), but low-SES employees may be disproportionately excluded from such mentorship and socialization experiences (Whitely et al., 1991). Research suggests that individuals from lower status social groups (i.e., women, people of color) tend to reap greater material benefits from privileged mentors (i.e., White men) than they do from mentors similar to themselves or in the absence of mentorship (Dreher & Cox, 1996). However, more recent work in educational settings has found that members of lower status social groups benefit more from mentors who share their marginalized identity than those who do not in terms of academic performance, retention, and belongingness (Blake-Beard et al., 2011; Dennehy & Dasgupta, 2017). Although it remains unclear how these relationships might apply to social class, mentors from lower-SES backgrounds themselves may provide better insight into an organization's classed culture and norms to low-SES mentees than mentors who have not needed to engage in similar types of class work. Because of their relatively senior status, mentors may be situated to push back on classed norms in organizations to create a more inclusive climate for mentees at not only the interpersonal level, but also the organizational level.

Finally, qualitative studies of upwardly mobile employees support the notion that mismatches in cultural capital exclude currently or formerly low-SES employees. In one study, previously economically disadvantaged White men in a professional service firm described feelings of isolation from their upper-class colleagues and alienation from their work environment, despite being highly skilled in the work in itself (Giazitzoglu & Muzio, 2020). Participants described how class distinctions were reinforced by differences on dimensions such as speech, mannerisms, clothing, food preferences, and educational background, preventing participants from being perceived by others as organizational insiders. Adopting the cultural milieu of their organization strained ties with their community outside of work, highlighting how classed norms can create conflict between one's work identity and personal identity. However, differences in class background are not always experienced as negative: indeed, participants cited the diligence and unique perspectives they had on account of their class background as assets they brought to their jobs.

Other: Do I Want This Person to Advance Here?

Research suggests that individuals' lay beliefs about the characteristics of effective leaders are incongruent with stereotypes of low-SES groups (Martin et al., 2017; Offermann et al., 1994). The traits believed to characterize effective leaders include dedication, charisma, intelligence, and sensitivity (Offermann et al., 1994). Perceptions of intelligence and dedication, in particular, may conflict with the belief that low-SES groups are lower in competence (Durante et al., 2017) and that hard work will necessarily lead to economic gains (Goudarzi et al., 2020), creating a perceived mismatch between the traits of leaders and those of low-SES groups. Supporting this perspective, research estimates that low-SES individuals are less likely than higher-class employees to become managers. This class disparity is comparable in magnitude to that experienced by women (versus men) and that of Black employees (versus White employees; Ingram, 2021; Oh & Ingram, 2019).

Further complicating the role SES plays in judgments of an employee's advancement potential, research on decisions in mock trials suggests that low-SES defendants are more harshly punished than high-SES defendants (Mazzella & Feingold, 1994). Similarly, Rosette and Livingston (2012) found that Black women leaders were punished more harshly for missteps than White men, Black men, and White women, all of whom were perceived as more prototypical of leaders than Black women. These findings suggest that when low-SES employees make mistakes at work, they may face harsher repercussions than high-SES employees would, and that these outsized penalties may be even greater for those in leadership due to the incongruence between low-SES and leadership stereotypes. Consequently, low-SES employees may find themselves contending with job stagnation and job dissatisfaction. If low-SES workers indeed face stereotype-imposed barriers to upward organizational mobility, subsequent job dissatisfaction could lead to turnover intentions (Rubenstein et al., 2015).

Just as culturally bound work scripts can negatively impact an employee's desire to remain in a job, they can also negatively impact others' evaluations of an employee, leading to exclusion (Stone-Romero et al., 2003). For instance, in interpersonal interactions, low-SES people tend to be more engaged listeners than their high-SES counterparts—a subtle cue that signals social status to otherwise unaware observers (Kraus & Keltner, 2009). Although low-SES employees may see such affiliative behavior as expected and normative work conduct, high-SES interaction partners may perceive it as inappropriate, thereby disrupting cohesion. These disconnects in social norms can hinder the retention of lower-SES employees when coworkers and supervisors do not perceive their interpersonal styles as being an adequate fit within an organization.

The blurring of work and social boundaries can also perpetuate inequality in organizations by constructing barriers to entry for low-SES employees. Informal knowledge sharing often occurs during extra-work social activities with coworkers. Such activities can be less accessible to employees from low-SES backgrounds due to the monetary resources and time investment they require. In one interview study, academics from working-class backgrounds described feelings of isolation because they could not afford to participate in informal social activities (Waterfield et al., 2019). Echoing the findings of Giazitzoglu and Muzio (2020), participants noted that even when they did have the economic capital to participate in social events, class differences were apparent from differences in cultural capital. One participant remarked, "you always remain slightly an outsider. And that's not a bad thing. To me, that's a good thing" (p. 378). In this sense, classed experiences provided some participants with uniqueness and insight. Although feelings of distance and judgment from coworkers due to social class differences may wear on employees from low-SES backgrounds, these differences are not always a point of pain, but also can be a point of pride in their identity. Embracing these different perspectives and backgrounds rather than advocating assimilation to existing high-class norms may enable organizations to benefit from the insights and skills that employees from low-SES backgrounds bring.

Finally, systematic differences in work-life flexibility across SES strata (i.e., work-life inequality) can create classed differences in the constraints imposed by extra-work relationships. Relative to employees in upper- and middle-class jobs, employees in lower-class jobs have less advance notice in scheduling and lower access to schedule flexibility, paid leave, control over workload, and arrangements such as telecommuting (Kossek & Lautsch, 2018). Employees in lower-SES occupations often do not benefit from federally mandated unpaid leave policies like Family and Medical Leave of Absence, given that time off is unpaid. Although control over workload can be beneficial to employees in upper- and middle-class jobs, this type of flexibility for those in lower-class occupations often entails flexibility from the perspective of employers (e.g., forcing workers into part-time status to avoid benefits obligations) rather than employees (Kossek & Lautsch, 2018). Thus, work-life inequality can impose demands that uniquely contribute to the attrition of low-SES employees.

IMPLICATIONS FOR HR MANAGEMENT AND DIRECTIONS FOR FUTURE RESEARCH

We now highlight fruitful avenues of research aimed at learning more about the impact of SES on organizational experiences and outcomes. We categorize these areas by three main topics, describing their significance within the ASA framework. First, researchers should explore the insidious ways that organizational hierarchies reproduce the SES inequality in broader society. Second, because low-SES workers are a forgotten minority in research, the field does not yet have a robust understanding of the unique organizational stressors and experiences associated with socioeconomic diversity. Third, individuals hold many social identities and adopting an intersectional lens can aid in our understanding of class-based experiences as well as the experiences of employees more broadly.

Organizational Hierarchy Reproducing Societal SES Inequality

The context of organizations is particularly ripe for research on SES due to the formal hierarchies that often regulate who *should be* attracted to, selected into, or left out of organizational spaces. To investigate how these hierarchies are created and reinforced, increased attention is being devoted to expanding SES operationalizations to include both objective measures (e.g., education, income) and subjective measures (e.g., perceived status compared to most Americans, compared to most employees in one's organization; Ostrove et al., 2000). Future research should explore the consequences of perceived (i.e., subjective) SES inequality within organizations and how organizational culture exacerbates or mitigates the strains arising from this inequality to influence attraction and attrition. Including subjective SES can allow researchers to better investigate the assessments people make about their relative status, which may affect their perceptions, decisions, and behaviors at work. Ideally, these findings could be leveraged to improve conditions for low-SES workers, who are often ignored in organizational decisions and hold less power. For instance, do low-SES workers feel that their contributions are valued compared to workers in higher-paid positions? How can organizations prioritize issues that primarily affect low-SES workers? To what extent do low-SES workers have the power to voice concerns to decision-makers?

Hypothesis 1: When an organization's structure, policies, and culture replicate and/or exacerbate broader societal inequalities, workers from low-SES backgrounds are less likely to be (1) attracted to the company, (2) selected into the company, and (3) remain at the company than high-SES peers.

Although low-SES workers may be deemed expendable by organizations, their preferences and needs can significantly influence the labor market. Recently, much attention has been given to the "labor shortage" in the U.S., in which traditionally lower-paid positions (e.g., retail and restaurant industries) are short-staffed (Kosik, 2021). Discourse on the topic has highlighted that these industries do not provide livable wages, good working conditions, or health benefits (Long, 2021), resulting in workers leaving such positions. Researchers should investigate the career decisions that these workers are making and their implications for negotiating class stigma in organizations. Future research may also investigate the motivations involved in voluntary turnover among low-SES workers under varying levels of financial flexibility.

Hypothesis 2: Low-SES workers' decisions and motivations to enter or leave an organization can be significantly influenced by markers of inequality, such as extremely poor working conditions, absence of fair compensation, and/or unequal access to resources, benefits, and opportunities.

There is also an understudied portion of low-SES workers participating in gig and on-demand work (e.g., freelancers, contractors, rideshare drivers, delivery services). The effects of these precarious employment situations are poorly understood, and research should examine organizational phenomena within this sector, such as the factors that uniquely attract people into gig and on-demand work. For instance, although gig and on-demand work may be less predictable compared to traditional forms of work, how might enhanced feelings of autonomy attract low-SES workers? Research demonstrates that workers who engage in on-demand work may experience more intrinsic motivation and subsequent organizational identification (Rockmann & Ballinger, 2017). However, the recent passage of legislation in California aimed at classifying gig workers as "independent contractors" who are not entitled to the same benefits as "employees" could make gig workers more vulnerable to exploitation (Conger, 2020). As the organizational structure of gig work shifts, it may be worthwhile for researchers to study the factors that workers consider when choosing, entering, and leaving these positions.

> **Hypothesis 3:** Compared to high-SES and middle-SES workers, low-SES workers are more attracted to gig and on-demand work, to the extent that they offer psychological benefits, such as autonomy and motivation, that are often restricted in traditional forms of work.

Classed Workplace Stressors and Experiences

The workplace stressors faced by low-SES employees have yet to be fully recognized in the literature. Despite the inclusion of blue-collar workers in, for example, work on occupational safety in manufacturing (Clarke, 2006), research with low-SES employees more often focuses on accident prevention than on topics such as succession, motivation, and organizational commitment. Future research should consider the working environments of low-SES employees, especially because poor working conditions may lead to worse health outcomes, lower well-being, and attrition (Arnoux-Nicolas et al., 2016; Robone et al., 2011). Once low-SES workers are selected into an organization, they may face unique challenges that their higher-SES counterparts in the same organization do not. For instance, low-SES workers are more likely to have jobs that require closer supervision and less autonomy (Hout, 1984). Many low-SES workers are in positions of economic vulnerability, and thus face greater job stress from threats to job security (Shoss, 2017). This vulnerability highlights the need for a greater understanding of how workers in blue-collar professions experience organizational outcomes typically studied in higher-income occupations. It also demonstrates that the factors contributing to attrition among employees in lower-paid occupations may be different in both quality (i.e., job stress from economic vulnerability versus job stress from nature of work) and quantity (i.e., desired versus actual level of job autonomy).

> **Hypothesis 4:** SES moderates the type of stressors experienced at work, such that low-SES workers more often experience stressors related to finances and working conditions than middle- and high-SES employees, and the extent to which stressors impact attrition, such that low-SES employees require higher levels of stress to decide to attrit.

It is important to also investigate how low-SES workers construct their relationships with work. Understanding how workers create meaning and derive value from their work can inform us of the unique experiences of low-SES workers, as well as reveal the most salient reasons workers are attracted to their work. Research has focused on employees' desire to generate meaning through their work (Allan et al., 2016); however, this meaning may differ based on the needs of workers. For example, some research indicates that perceptions of work-life balance differ between white- and blue-collar workers, such that white-collar workers prioritize time flexibility whereas blue-collar workers prioritize wage earning (Warren, 2015). Other research suggests that high-SES individuals value finding independence and exploring curiosities in one's career, and low-SES individuals focus on getting their job tasks done without bringing attention to themselves (Weininger & Lareau, 2009). SES also influences ways of relating to others (Kraus & Stephens, 2012), with implications for workplace relationships. For instance, because people from low-SES backgrounds tend to show higher levels of interdependency and desire for community compared to their high-SES counterparts (Stephens et al., 2012), relationships with coworkers and supervisors may be more impactful for attracting and retaining lower-SES workers compared to higher-SES workers.

> **Hypothesis 5:** SES influences the factors that attract employees to organizations, with lower-SES workers prioritizing pay, coworker relationships, and working conditions and higher-SES workers prioritizing independence and flexibility.

Intersection of SES With Other Social Identities

Intersectionality theory posits that people's social identities are multifaceted, forming combinations that delineate one's privileges and disadvantages depending on their identification with multiple social groups, such as one's race, ethnicity, gender, religion, and more (Cole, 2009; Crenshaw, 2019). Social identities such as SES play a role in shaping behaviors and perceptions (Weininger & Lareau, 2009). Consequently, those who share one identity do not necessarily share the same experiences due to the multiple identities that the individuals within one group may hold. Because systems of oppression often intersect and overlap to influence access to economic resources, considering these overlaps and their implications for the workplace is especially crucial when it comes to SES. For instance, Black and Hispanic women disproportionately hold more low-wage jobs in the U.S., and the most vulnerable low-wage workers are "older, female, Black, Latino or Hispanic," or have a disability (Ross & Bateman, 2019, p. 12). Given that low-wage workers are already an under-researched population, the unique experiences of these populations may continue to be overlooked.

Just as SES impacts employees' experiences, other identities simultaneously influence important social, physical, and mental health outcomes (e.g., Assari, 2017). Systemic racism results in fewer economic opportunities for some people of color: Black and Hispanic men and women tend to earn less than their White counterparts at equal educational attainment levels, with Black and Hispanic employees sometimes earning less than White employees with *less* education (Williams et al., 2010). Research also finds that within low-income working populations, women of color are more likely to experience general and sexual harassment at work compared to White women (Krieger et al., 2006; McLaughlin et al., 2012), increasing the risk of poor mental health, attrition, and financial stress (McLaughlin et al., 2017). Due to intersecting identities with one's SES, as well as racialized conceptions of social class (Lei & Bodenhausen, 2017), employees are often subject to differential opportunities and experiences once they are hired. Thus, it is important to use an intersectional lens for investigating organizations' roles in shaping and preventing differential outcomes tied to employee treatment, earnings, and wellbeing.

HR management scholars can explore the mechanisms in the occupational realm that specifically aid in (a) sustaining SES disparities and (b) understanding the heterogeneity of classed experiences due to intersections of multiple identities. Using the ASA framework, researchers can investigate the antecedents and consequences of SES disparities as they relate to intersecting identities. For instance, are there systematic class, race, and gender differences for initial starting salary within the same occupational roles? If so, how can organizations change their selection procedures to eliminate inequalities? How might job insecurity and discrimination differently affect workplace experiences depending on low-SES employees' other demographic identities?

Hypothesis 6: Although likely to affect employees at all SES levels, low-SES workers with (versus without) intersecting marginalized identities are at a significantly increased risk of experiencing unfair treatment during selection processes and while working in their position, which may ultimately result in poorer personnel outcomes and attrition.

IMPLICATIONS FOR HR MANAGEMENT AND PRACTICE IN ORGANIZATIONS

Our review offers three key implications for efforts to decrease attrition among low-SES employees working in organizations that may offer upward mobility. First, establishing clear and uniform evaluation criteria and accessible (i.e., paid) development opportunities would likely benefit employees of all SES backgrounds, but may disproportionately benefit those from low-SES backgrounds. Second, providing funding dedicated to social activities or organization-sponsored social activities could help create opportunities for building informal networks and camaraderie to foster inclusion of low-SES employees. Finally, just as organizations are becoming increasingly interested in fostering inclusive climates for diversity with respect to employee gender, sexual, and racioethnic identity, similarly recognizing the benefits of diverse perspectives based on social class could help organizations retain talented employees from low-SES backgrounds.

Despite the widely held and erroneous belief in merit-based economic mobility, national economic and social inequality is on the rise (Reeves, 2018). It is therefore more important than ever for organizational leaders to ensure that they do not perpetuate class-based inequity. Currently, however, many common organizational practices and policies do just that. Organizations are affected by their potential and existing employees' SES in many ways, whether leaders and HR personnel recognize it or not. To create equitable opportunities and working conditions for all people, organizational leadership and HR personnel must consider the ways in which SES shapes organizational practices and outcomes—such as hiring practices and low-SES employees' feelings of belonging. Guided by the ASA model, we present several recommendations for organizational leadership and HR personnel to consider as part of efforts to reduce class-based inequality within organizations.

Even when not explicitly or immediately evident, class bias perniciously seeps into perceptions of others. Much of the bias against low-SES individuals is prominent in the hiring phase, and—similar to other types of discrimination (e.g., racism, sexism)—class discrimination is often subtle.

That is, selection decisions are influenced by applicant characteristics that are closely (but not explicitly) associated with SES, such as appearance, educational background, and speech style (Kraus et al., 2019; Peterman, 2018). For example, a common physical trait that employers may associate with low SES is dental health (e.g., broken, stained, or missing teeth; Peterman, 2018). Research also indicates that evaluators attend to speech-related cues that are related to SES (e.g., pronunciation, tone, rhythm) and that judgments of fit, competence, starting salary, and bonuses are made in accordance with these cues (Kraus et al., 2019). Similarly, employers may discriminate against low-SES applicants by screening out applicants living in low-SES geographic areas, citing distance from the office as justification for not hiring them. Additionally, many employers have begun to require college degrees for entry-level jobs that have historically required only a high school or associate degree (Peterman, 2018).

There are several actions that HR personnel can take to remediate the class-based biases entrenched in selection systems. First, they can ensure that they recruit (i.e., attract) job candidates from a diverse array of populations, including community and state colleges, rather than relying primarily on elite universities and employee referrals (Rivera, 2015). Second, they can standardize hiring and promotion procedures, such as eliminating unstructured interviews, which are fraught with bias and job-irrelevant information, and instead using structured interviews with predetermined evaluation criteria (Bohnet, 2016). Third, organizations can ensure that hiring committees themselves are diverse—composed of people from a variety of social and economic backgrounds. Fourth, organizations should evaluate their selection tools. Many preemployment cognitive ability tests, for example, result in adverse impact when used alone (Schmitt et al., 1997). To overcome this potential source of bias, HR personnel should use information from multiple sources when making employment decisions.

There are also post-hiring changes that HR personnel can implement to ensure that employees from all economic backgrounds thrive in the workplace (i.e., do not attrit). First, they can ensure that access to resources, such as developmental opportunities, are not predicated on possessing a certain threshold of economic capital. For instance, HR can cover expenses related to developmental opportunities (such as conferences and boot-camps) intended to increase employees' job-relevant knowledge, skills, and abilities. Moreover, organizational leaders should take care when planning social events to ensure that low-SES employees are not inadvertently put at a disadvantage. Such events could be held during work hours to avoid incurring additional childcare or eldercare costs. Employee events should also be hosted in locations that are not cost-prohibitive and where people of all socioeconomic strata feel that they belong, rather than at exclusive venues such as country clubs. Finally, organizations can implement mentorship programs that focus on increasing confidence, building a professional identity, and role modeling (Allen et al., 2017). These programs may be most helpful if mentors have come from similar SES backgrounds as mentees (Blake-Beard et al., 2011, Dennehy & Dasgupta, 2017), given that they may be better able to relate to their mentee and prepare them for new, class-based experiences at work.

CONCLUSION

In a 2009 paper, Christie and Barling stated that, in organizational research, SES has been "treated as [a] nuisance variabl[e] whose influence must be excluded" (p. 1474). We agree with this perspective, arguing that too little attention has been paid to the impact of SES on psychological and organizational outcomes. Low-SES individuals comprise a substantial portion of the U.S. workforce, yet upper- and middle-class samples dominate the organizational literature. Disproportionate focus on upper- and middle-class samples can lead to overgeneralizations from empirical research. To this end, we encourage researchers to study the experiences of individuals who are lower in SES, a population that is growing in number as income inequality increases. Based on our review of the individual and interpersonal role of SES in organizational attraction, selection, and attrition, we conclude that researchers and practitioners can better understand the impact of SES in the workplace by sampling from a more diverse pool of employees and organizations. We also suggest that research on SES in organizations consider unique stressors, the meaning of work, and subjective perceptions of status at work. It is our hope that such research will ultimately pave the way for individuals of all SES backgrounds to thrive in their workforce contexts.

REFERENCES

Acker, J. (1990). Hierarchies, jobs, bodies: A theory of gendered organizations. *Gender & Society, 4*(2), 139–158. https://doi.org/10.1177/089124390004002002

Allan, B. A., Autin, K. L., & Duffy, R. D. (2016). Self-determination and meaningful work: Exploring socioeconomic constraints. *Frontiers in Psychology, 7.* https://doi.org/10.3389/fpsyg.2016.00071

Allen, T. D., Eby, L. T., Chao, G. T., & Bauer, T. N. (2017). Taking stock of two relational aspects of organizational life: Tracing the history and shaping the future of socialization and mentoring research. *Journal of Applied Psychology, 102*(3), 324–337. https://doi.org/10.1037/apl0000086

American Psychological Association. (2020). *Socioeconomic status.* https://www.apa.org/topics/socioeconomic-status/

American Psychological Association. (2021). *Education and socioeconomic status.* https://www.apa.org/pi/ses/resources/publications/education

Amis, J.M., Mair, J., & Munir, K. (2020). The organizational reproduction of inequality. *Academy of Management Annals, 14*, 195–230. https://doi. org/10.5465/annals.2017.0033

Arnoux-Nicolas, C., Sovet, L., Lhotellier, L., Di Fabio, A., & Bernaud, J.-L. (2016). Perceived work conditions and turnover intentions: The mediating role of meaning of work. *Frontiers in Psychology, 7.* https://doi.org/10.3389/fpsyg.2016.00704

Assari, S. (2017). Social determinants of depression: The intersections of race, gender, and socioeconomic status. *Brain Sciences, 7*(12), 1–12. https://doi. org/10.3390/brainsci7120156

Bardack, N. R., & McAndrew, F. T. (1985). The influence of physical attractiveness and manner of dress on success in a simulated personnel decision. *The Journal of Social Psychology, 125*(6), 777–778. https://doi.org/10.1080/00224545.1985 .9713553

Bergman, M. E., & Jean, V. A. (2016). Where have all the "workers" gone? A critical analysis of the unrepresentativeness of our samples relative to the labor market in the industrial–organizational psychology literature. *Industrial and Organizational Psychology, 9*(1), 84–113. https://doi.org/10.1017/iop.2015.70

Blake-Beard, S., Bayne, M. L., Crosby, F. J., & Muller, C. B. (2011). Matching by race and gender in mentoring relationships: Keeping our eyes on the prize. *Journal of Social Issues, 67*(3), 622–643. https://doi.org/10.1111/j.1540-4560.2011.01717.x

Bohnet, I., (2016). *How to take the bias out of interviews.* Harvard Business Review. https://hbr.org/2016/04/how-to-take-the-bias-out-of-interviews

Bourdieu, P. (1984). *Distinction: A social critique of the judgement of taste.* Routledge.

Buckley, M. R., Jackson, K. A., Bolino, M. C., Veres, J. G., & Feild, H. S. (2007). The influence of relational demography on panel interview ratings: A field experiment. *Personnel Psychology, 60*(3), 627–646. https://doi.org/10.1111/j.1744-6570.2007.00086.x

Cable, D. M., & Judge, T. A. (1996). Person-organization fit, job choice decisions, and organizational entry. *Organizational Behavior and Human Decision Processes, 67*(3), 294–311. https://doi.org/10.1006/obhd.1996.0081

Carey, R. M., & Markus, H. R. (2017). Social class shapes the form and function of relationships and selves. *Current Opinion in Psychology, 18*, 123–130. https://doi.org/10.1016/j.copsyc.2017.08.031

Clair, J. A., Beatty, J. E., & Maclean, T. L. (2005). Out of sight but not out of mind: Managing invisible social identities in the workplace. *Academy of Management Review, 30*(1), 78–95. https://doi.org/10.5465/amr.2005.15281431

Clarke, S. (2006). The relationship between safety climate and safety performance: a meta-analytic review. *Journal of Occupational Health Psychology, 11*(4), 315–327. https://doi.org/10.1037/1076-8998.11.4.315

Christie, A. M., & Barling, J. (2009). Disentangling the indirect links between socioeconomic status and health: The dynamic roles of work stressors and personal control. *Journal of Applied Psychology, 94*(6), 1466–1478. https://doi. org/10.1037/a0016847

Cole, E. R. (2009). Intersectionality and research in psychology. *American Psychologist,* *64*(3), 170. https://doi.org/10.1037/a0014564

Conger, K. (2020, November 4). *Uber and Lyft drivers in California will remain contractors.* The New York Times. https://www.nytimes.com/2020/11/04/technology/california-uber-lyft-prop-22.html

Connor, P., Varney, J., Keltner, D., & Chen, S. (2021). Social class competence stereotypes are amplified by socially signaled economic inequality. *Personality and Social Psychology Bulletin, 47*(1), 89–105. https://doi.org/10.1177/0146167220916640

Crenshaw, K. (2019). *On intersectionality: Essential writings.* New Press.

DeOrtentiis, P. S., Van Iddekinge, C. H., & Wanberg, C. R. (2021). Different starting lines, different finish times: The role of social class in the job search process. *Journal of Applied Psychology.* Advance online publication. https://doi.org/10.1037/apl0000915

Dickson, M. W., Resick, C. J., & Goldstein, H. W. (2008). Seeking explanations in people, not in the results of their behavior: Twenty-plus years of the attraction-selection-attrition model. In D. B. Smith (Ed.), *The people make the place: Dynamic linkages between individuals and organizations* (pp. 5–36). Taylor & Francis Group/Lawrence Erlbaum Associates.

Dennehy, T. C., & Dasgupta, N. (2017). Female peer mentors early in college increase women's positive academic experiences and retention in engineering. *Proceedings of the National Academy of Sciences, 114*(23), 5964–5969. https://doi.org/10.1073/pnas.1613117114

Dovidio, J. F., & Gaertner, S. L. (2000). Aversive racism and selection decisions: 1989 and 1999. *Psychological Science, 11*(4), 315–319. https://doi.org/10.1111/1467-9280.00262

Dreher, G. F., & Cox Jr., T. H. (1996). Race, gender, and opportunity: A study of compensation attainment and the establishment of mentoring relationships. *Journal of Applied Psychology, 81*(3), 297–308. https://doi.org/10.1037/0021-9010.81.3.297

Durante, F., & Fiske, S. T. (2017). How social-class stereotypes maintain inequality. *Current Opinion in Psychology, 18,* 43–48. https://doi.org/10.1016/j.copsyc.2017.07.033

Durante, F., Tablante, C. B., & Fiske, S. T. (2017). Poor but warm, rich but cold (and competent): Social classes in the stereotype content model. *Journal of Social Issues, 73*(1), 138–157. https://doi.org/10.1111/josi.12208

Fang, R. T., & Saks, A. M. (2020). Class advantage in the white-collar labor market: An investigation of social class background, job search strategies, and job search success. *Journal of Applied Psychology.* Advance online publication. https://doi.org/10.1037/apl0000842

Fiske, S. T., Cuddy, A. J. C., Glick, P., & Xu, J. (2002). A model of (often mixed) stereotype content: Competence and warmth respectively follow from perceived status and competition. *Journal of Personality and Social Psychology, 82*(6), 878–902. https://doi.org/10.1037/0022-3514.82.6.878

Gaertner, S. L., & Dovidio, J. F. (Eds.). (1986). The aversive form of racism. In *Prejudice, discrimination, and racism* (pp. 61–89). Academic Press.

Giazitzoglu, A., & Muzio, D. (2020). Learning the rules of the game: How is corporate masculinity learned and enacted by male professionals from nonprivileged backgrounds? *Gender, Work & Organization*, 1–18. https://doi.org/10.1111/gwao.12561

Gilbert, J. A., & Lownes-Jackson, M. (2005). Blacks, whites, and the new prejudice: Does aversive racism impact employee assessment? *Journal of Applied Social Psychology, 35*(7), 1540–1553. https://doi.org/10.1111/j.1559-1816.2005.tb02183.x

Goudarzi, S., Pliskin, R., Jost, J. T., & Knowles, E. D. (2020). Economic system justification predicts muted emotional responses to inequality. *Nature Communications, 11*(1), 383. https://doi.org/10.1038/s41467-019-14193-z

Granovetter, M. S. (1973). The strength of weak ties. *American Journal of Sociology, 78*(6), 1360–1380. https://doi.org/10.1086/225469

Gray, B., & Kish-Gephart, J. J. (2013). Encountering social class differences at work: How "class work" perpetuates inequality. *The Academy of Management Review, 38*(4), 670–699. https://doi.org/10.5465/amr.2012.0143

Handley, K. (2018). Anticipatory socialization and the construction of the employable graduate: A critical analysis of employers' graduate careers websites. *Work, Employment and Society, 32*(2), 239–256. https://doi.org/10.1177/0950017016686031

Hebl, M. R., & Dovidio, J. F. (2005). Promoting the "social" in the examination of social stigmas. *Personality and Social Psychology Review, 9*(2), 156–182. https://doi.org/10.1207/s15327957pspr0902_4

Hout, M. (1984). Status, autonomy, and training in occupational mobility. *American Journal of Sociology, 89*(6), 1379–1409. https://doi.org/10.1086/228020

Ingram, P. (2021, January 1). *The forgotten dimension of diversity*. Harvard Business Review. https://hbr.org/2021/01/the-forgotten-dimension-of-diversity

James, E. H. (2000). Race-related differences in promotions and support: Underlying effects of human and social capital. *Organization Science, 11*(5), 493–508. https://doi.org/10.1287/orsc.11.5.493.15202

Johnson, S. E., Richeson, J. A., & Finkel, E. J. (2011). Middle class and marginal? Socioeconomic status, stigma, and self-regulation at an elite university. *Journal of Personality and Social Psychology, 100*(5), 838–852. https://doi.org/10.1037/a0021956

Jost, J. T., & Banaji, M. R. (1994). The role of stereotyping in system-justification and the production of false consciousness. *British Journal of Social Psychology, 33*(1), 1–27. https://doi.org/10.1111/j.2044-8309.1994.tb01008.x

Kosik, A. (2021, June). *America's worker shortage is real and getting worse by the day, US Chamber CEO says*. CNN. https://www.cnn.com/2021/06/01/economy/worker-shortage-us-chamber-of-commerce/index.html

Kossek, E. E., & Lautsch, B. A. (2018). Work-life flexibility for whom? Occupational status and work–life inequality in upper, middle, and lower level jobs. *The Academy of Management Annals, 12*(1), 5–36. https://doi.org/10.5465/annals.2016.0059

Kraus, M. W., & Keltner, D. (2009). Signs of socioeconomic status: A thin-slicing approach. *Psychological Science, 20*(1), 99–106. https://doi.org/10.1111/j.1467-9280.2008.02251.x

Kraus, M. W., & Stephens, N. M. (2012). A road map for an emerging psychology of social class. *Social and Personality Psychology Compass*, *6*(9), 642–656. https://doi.org/10.1111/j.1751-9004.2012.00453.x

Kraus, M. W., Torrez, B., Park, J. W., & Ghayebi, F. (2019). Evidence for the reproduction of social class in brief speech. *Proceedings of the National Academy of Sciences*, *116*(46), 22998–23003. https://doi.org/ 10.1073/pnas.1900500116

Krieger, N., Waterman, P. D., Hartman, C., Bates, L. M., Stoddard, A. M., Quinn, M. M., Sorensen, G., & Barbeau, E. M. (2006). Social hazards on the job: Workplace abuse, sexual harassment, and racial discrimination—A study of Black, Latino, and White low-income women and men workers in the United States. *International Journal of Health Services*, *36*(1), 51–85. https://doi.org/10.2190/3EMB-YKRH-EDJ2-0H19

Laurison, D., & Friedman, S. (2016). The class pay gap in higher professional and managerial occupations. *American Sociological Review*, *81*(4), 668–695. https://doi.org/10.1177/0003122416653602

Lei, R. F., & Bodenhausen, G. V. (2017). Racial assumptions color the mental representation of social class. *Frontiers in Psychology*, 8. https://doi.org/10.3389/fpsyg.2017.00519

Loignon, A. C., & Woehr, D. J. (2018). Social class in the organizational sciences: a conceptual integration and meta-analytic review. *Journal of Management*, *44*(1), 61–88. https://doi.org/10.1177/0149206317728106

Long, H. (2021). *It's not a 'labor shortage.' It's a great reassessment of work in America.* Washington Post. https://www.washingtonpost.com/business/2021/05/07/jobs-report-labor-shortage-analysis/

Madera, J. M., King, E. B., & Hebl, M. R. (2012). Bringing social identity to work: The influence of manifestation and suppression on perceived discrimination, job satisfaction, and turnover intentions. *Cultural Diversity and Ethnic Minority Psychology*, *18*(2), 165–170. https://doi.org/10.1037/a0027724

Major, B., & O'Brien, L. T. (2005). The social psychology of stigma. *Annual Review of Psychology*, *56*(1), 393–421. https://doi.org/10.1146/annurev.psych.56.091103.070137

Martin, S. R., Innis, B. D., & Ward, R. G. (2017). Social class, leaders and leadership: A critical review and suggestions for development. *Current Opinion in Psychology*, *18*, 49–54. https://doi.org/10.1016/j.copsyc.2017.08.001

Mazzella, R., & Feingold, A. (1994). The effects of physical attractiveness, race, socioeconomic status, and gender of defendants and victims on judgments of mock jurors: A meta-analysis. *Journal of Applied Social Psychology*, *24*(15), 1315–1338. https://doi.org/10.1111/j.1559-1816.1994.tb01552.x

McDaniel, M. A., Whetzel, D. L., Schmidt, F. L., & Maurer, S. D. (1994). The validity of employment interviews: A comprehensive review and meta-analysis. *Journal of Applied Psychology*, *79*(4), 599–616. https://doi.org/10.1037/0021-9010.79.4.599

McLaughlin, H., Uggen, C., & Blackstone, A. (2012). Sexual harassment, workplace authority, and the paradox of power. *American Sociological Review*, *77*(4), 625–647. https://doi.org/10.1177/0003122412451728

McLaughlin, H., Uggen, C., & Blackstone, A. (2017). The economic and career effects of sexual harassment on working women. *Gender & Society, 31*(3), 333–358. https://doi.org/10.1177/0891243217704631

Miller, C., & Roksa, J. (2020). Balancing research and service in academia: Gender, race, and laboratory tasks. *Gender & Society, 34*(1), 131–152. https://doi.org/10.1177/0891243219867917

Mullainathan, S., & Shafir, E. (2013). *Scarcity: Why having too little means so much.* Macmillan.

Mohr, T. S. (August 25, 2014). *Why women don't apply for jobs unless they're 100% qualified.* Harvard Business Review. https://hbr.org/2014/08/why-women-dont-apply-for-jobs-unless-theyre-100-qualified

Offermann, L. R., Kennedy, J. K., & Wirtz, P. W. (1994). Implicit leadership theories: Content, structure, and generalizability. *The Leadership Quarterly, 5*(1), 43–58. https://doi.org/10.1016/1048-9843(94)90005-1

Oh, J., & Ingram, P. (2019). Who's the boss? The effect of gender, race, and class on workplace authority. *Academy of Management Proceedings, 2019*(1), 14361. https://doi.org/10.5465/AMBPP.2019.14361abstract

Ostrove, J. M., Adler, N. E., Kuppermann, M., & Washington, A. E. (2000). Objective and subjective assessments of socioeconomic status and their relationship to self-rated health in an ethnically diverse sample of pregnant women. *Health Psychology, 19*(6), 613–618. https://doi.org/10.1037/0278-6133.19.6.613

Pedulla, D. S., & Pager, D. (2019). Race and networks in the job search process. *American Sociological Review, 84*(6), 983–1012. https://doi.org/10.1177/0003122419883255

Peterman, D. E. (2018). Socioeconomic status discrimination. *Virginia Law Review, 104*(7), 1283–1357.

Phillips, L. T., Martin, S. R., & Belmi, P. (2020). Social class transitions: Three guiding questions for moving the study of class to a dynamic perspective. *Social and Personality Psychology Compass, 14*(9), 1–18. https://doi.org/10.1111/spc3.12560

Pinsker, J. (2020, March 2). Why so many Americans don't talk about money. *The Atlantic.* https://www.theatlantic.com/family/archive/2020/03/americans-dont-talk-about-money-taboo/607273.

Pitesa, M., & Pillutla, M. M. (2019). Socioeconomic mobility and talent utilization of workers from poorer backgrounds: The overlooked importance of within-organization dynamics. *Academy of Management Annals, 13*(2), 737–769.

Raposa, E. B., Erickson, L. D., Hagler, M., & Rhodes, J. E. (2018). How economic disadvantage affects the availability and nature of mentoring relationships during the transition to adulthood. *American Journal of Community Psychology, 61*(1–2), 191–203. https://doi.org/10.1002/ajcp.12228

Reeves, R. V. (2018). *Dream hoarders: How the American upper middle class is leaving everyone else in the dust, why that is a problem, and what to do about it.* Brookings Institution Press.

Rivera, L. A. (2015). Go with your gut: Emotion and evaluation in job interviews. *American Journal of Sociology, 120*(5), 1339–1389. https://doi.org/10.1086/681214

Roberts, B. W., Kuncel, N. R., Shiner, R., Caspi, A., & Goldberg, L. R. (2007). The power of personality: The comparative validity of personality traits, socioeconomic status, and cognitive ability for predicting important life outcomes. *Perspectives on Psychological Science, 2*(4), 313–345. https://doi.org/10.1111/j.1745-6916.2007.00047.x

Robone, S., Jones, A. M., & Rice, N. (2011). Contractual conditions, working conditions and their impact on health and well-being. *The European Journal of Health Economics, 12*(5), 429–444. https://doi.org/10.1007/s10198-010-0256-0

Rockmann, K. W., & Ballinger, G. A. (2017). Intrinsic motivation and organizational identification among on-demand workers. *Journal of Applied Psychology, 102*(9), 1305–1316. https://doi.org/10.1037/apl0000224

Rosette, A. S., & Livingston, R. W. (2012). Failure is not an option for Black women: Effects of organizational performance on leaders with single versus dual-subordinate identities. *Journal of Experimental Social Psychology, 48*(5), 1162–1167. https://doi.org/10.1016/j.jesp.2012.05.002

Ross, M., & Bateman, N. (2019, November 5). *Meet the low-wage workforce.* Brookings. https://www.brookings.edu/research/meet-the-low-wage-workforce/

Rubenstein, A. L., Eberly, M. B., Lee, T., & Mitchell, T. R. (2015). Looking beyond the trees: A meta-analysis and integration of voluntary turnover research. *Academy of Management Proceedings, 2015*(1), 12779. https://doi.org/10.5465/ambpp.2015.20

Schaeffer, K. (2020, February 7). *6 facts about economic inequality in the U.S.* Pew Research Center. https://www.pewresearch.org/fact-tank/2020/02/07/6-facts-about-economic-inequality-in-the-u-s/

Schmitt, N., Rogers, W., Chan, D., Sheppard, L., & Jennings, D. (1997). Adverse impact and predictive efficiency of various predictor combinations. *Journal of Applied Psychology, 82*(5), 719–730. https://doi.org/10.1037/0021-9010.82.5.719

Schneider, B. (1987). The people make the place. *Personnel Psychology, 40*(3), 437–453. https://doi.org/10.1111/j.1744-6570.1987.tb00609.x

Shoss, M. K. (2017). Job insecurity: An integrative review and agenda for future research. *Journal of Management, 43*(6), 1911–1939. https://doi.org/10.1177/0149206317691574

Signorello, L. B., Cohen, S. S., Williams, D. R., Munro, H. M., Hargreaves, M. K., Blot, W. J. (2014). Socioeconomic status, race, and mortality: A prospective cohort study. *American Journal of Public Health, 104,* e98–e107. https://doi.org/10.2105/ajph.2014.302156

Smith, E. B., Menon, T., & Thompson, L. (2011). Status differences in the cognitive activation of social networks. *Organization Science, 23*(1), 67–82. https://doi.org/10.1287/orsc.1100.0643

Steele, C. M. (1997). A threat in the air. How stereotypes shape intellectual identity and performance. *The American Psychologist, 52*(6), 613–629. https://doi.org/10.1037//0003-066x.52.6.613

Stephens, N. M., Fryberg, S. A., Markus, H. R., Johnson, C. S., & Covarrubias, R. (2012). Unseen disadvantage: How American universities' focus on independence undermines the academic performance of first-generation college students. *Journal of Personality and Social Psychology, 102*(6), 1178. https://doi.org/10.1037/a0027143

Stone-Romero, E. F., Stone, D. L., & Salas, E. (2003). The influence of culture on role conceptions and role behavior in organisations. *Applied Psychology, 52*(3), 328–362. https://doi.org/10.1111/1464-0597.00139

University of Michigan. (2021). *Clothes Closet | University Career Center.* https://careercenter.umich.edu/content/clothes-closet

U.S. Census Bureau. (2019, December 4). *Income, poverty and health insurance coverage in the U.S.: 2018.* https://www.census.gov/newsroom/press-releases/2019/income-poverty.html

Vázquez, A., & Lois, D. (2020). Prejudice against members of a ridiculed working-class group. *British Journal of Social Psychology, 59*(4), 992–1017. https://doi.org/10.1111/bjso.12373

Warren, T. (2015). Work-life balance/imbalance: The dominance of the middle class and the neglect of the working class. *The British Journal of Sociology, 66*(4), 691–717. https://doi.org/10.1111/1468-4446.12160

Waterfield, B., Beagan, B. L., & Mohamed, T. (2019). "You always remain slightly an outsider": Workplace experiences of academics from working-class or impoverished backgrounds. *Canadian Review of Sociology, 56*(3), 368–388. https://doi.org/10.1111/cars.12257

Weininger, E. B., & Lareau, A. (2009). Paradoxical pathways: An ethnographic extension of Kohn's findings on class and childrearing. *Journal of Marriage and Family, 71*(3), 680–695. https://doi.org/10.1111/j.1741-3737.2009.00626.x

Whitely, W., Dougherty, T. W., & Dreher, G. F. (1991). Relationship of career mentoring and socioeconomic origin to managers' and professionals' early career progress. *The Academy of Management Journal, 34*(2), 331–351. https://doi.org/10.2307/256445

Williams, D. R., Mohammed, S. A., Leavell, J., & Collins, C. (2010). Race, socioeconomic status, and health: complexities, ongoing challenges, and research opportunities. *Annals of the New York Academy of Sciences, 1186*, 69–101. https://doi.org/10.1111/j.1749-6632.2009.05339.x

Williams, D. R., Priest, N., & Anderson, N. (2019). Understanding associations between race, socioeconomic status, and health: patterns and prospects. In *The Social Medicine Reader*, (Vol. II, 3rd ed., pp. 258–267). Duke University Press. https://doi.org/10.1037/hea0000242

Word, C. O., Zanna, M. P., & Cooper, J. (1974). The nonverbal mediation of self-fulfilling prophecies in interracial interaction. *Journal of Experimental Social Psychology, 10*(2), 109–120. https://doi.org/ 10.1016/0022-1031(74)90059-6

CHAPTER 11

EFFECTS OF STEREOTYPES, INTERGROUP BIAS, AND CULTURAL RACISM ON UNFAIR DISCRIMINATION AGAINST NATIVE AMERICANS

Dianna L. Stone
Universities of New Mexico, Albany, and Virginia Tech

Kimberly M. Lukaszewski
Wright State University

Julio C. Canedo
University of Houston Downtown

Dianna Contreras Krueger
Tarleton State University

ABSTRACT

Native people in the U.S. and the Americas experience numerous problems gaining and maintaining employment, and their employment problems exacerbate difficulties associated with poverty, food and housing insecurity, alcohol or drug addiction, health, and unfair discrimination (Reclaiming

Forgotten Minorities in Organizations, pp. 329–372
Copyright © 2023 by Information Age Publishing
www.infoagepub.com
All rights of reproduction in any form reserved.

Native American Truth, 2018). As a result, the primary purposes of this chapter were to: (a) present a model of the factors thought to affect unfair discrimination against Native Americans in organizations, (b) review the existing theory and research on these issues, (c) offer hypotheses to facilitate research on the topic, and (d) present practical strategies that might be used to decrease unfair discrimination and enhance the inclusion of Native Americans in organizations. Our model was based in theories of social cognition, social categorization, and cultural racism. As a result, it predicts that unfounded negative stereotypes about Natives are important determinants of employment decisions about them. Similarly, social categorization theory predicts that dominant group members (e.g., European Americans) denigrate outgroup members to boost their own self esteem (Turner et al., 1987). Further, the theory of cultural racism argues that dominant groups in a society (e.g., European Americans in the United States) determine the values, standards, norms, and when a nondominant group's (e.g., Natives) cultural values do not live up to these cultural standards, they are viewed as substandard and experience unfair discrimination in organizations. Hypotheses to guide research, and implications for future research and practice are considered.

"May the Stars Carry Your Sadness Away" —Chief Dan George

The quote just noted reflects the profound sadness expressed by many Native Americans in the United States (Chief Dan George, n.d.). One reason for this sadness is that in the 1500–1600s European colonists overpowered their tribes, confiscated their lands, and upended their societies (Reclaiming Native American Truth, 2018). Another reason is that the U.S. has engaged in ethnocide and attempted to annihilate Native Americans and eradicate all aspects of their culture and traditional ways of life (Reclaiming Native American Truth, 2018). Further, in recent years, their numbers have dwindled so much that many people view them as "forgotten or invisible minorities," and a large number of non-Natives have never met a Native American person (Reclaiming Native American Truth, 2018). For example, results of surveys revealed that even though there are 6.9 million Native Americans (hereinafter referred to as Natives) in the U.S. (U.S. Bureau of Census, 2020), people have limited personal experience with them, and the lack of contact perpetuates unfounded stereotypes about them (Reclaiming Native American Truth, 2018). Negative stereotypes about Natives are also reinforced by the media (e.g., TV, film), and shaped by non-Native's distance from Native reservations. Tribal reservations are typically located in very remote or rural areas so many non-Natives never venture to these distant regions (e.g., South Dakota, Alaska, New Mexico, Arizona) (Reclaiming Native American Truth, 2018). It merits noting that we use the term Native in this chapter rather than the terms American Indian or Native American because philosophers (Vizenor, 1991) and Native researchers (Boje & Boje,

2001) argue that the term "Native" best represents the shared experiences of the modern indigenous people of North America.

Natives also experience numerous problems in our society including high levels of poverty, unemployment, lack of education, alcohol addiction, food and housing insecurity, and social discrimination in society and organizations (e.g., Equal Employment Opportunity Commission [EEOC], 2020; Postsecondary National Policy Institute [PNPI], 2021). For instance, Natives have the highest poverty rate in the U.S. at 25.4%, and their median earnings is $36,252 compared to the median earnings of $52,176 for all ethnic group members (EEOC, 2020). One reason for this is that many of their assets and resources (e.g., land, food sources) were appropriated by European colonists who subjugated and relegated them to tribal reservations (Muhammad, 2019).

The educational levels of Natives also lag far behind members of other ethnic groups (e.g., African Americans, Asian Americans) (PNPI, 2021). For example, on average, less than 65% of Native students graduate from high school each year, and very few go on to college (Education World, 2020). However, in recent years more young Natives are receiving Associates Degrees because there are a growing number of tribal and community colleges located near reservations (e.g., Dine College, Bay Mills Community College) (PNPI, 2021). This trend should be very helpful to tribes over time because some of these individuals are likely to return to reservations to bolster the economy and employment opportunities (Moreno, 2019). Natives are also more likely to have serious health problems and die at younger ages than others in our society (Indian Health Services, 2019; youth.gov, 2020). For example, many Natives suffer from chronic illnesses including diabetes, stress, liver disease, obesity, chronic respiratory disease, and mental illness (Indian Health Services, 2019). Despite these difficulties, only 64% of non-Native respondents believe that the U.S. should do *more* to help Natives overcome their plight (Reclaiming Native American Truth, 2018).

There has been considerable research in organizational behavior (OB) and human resource management (HR) on unfair discrimination against ethnic minorities (e.g., African Americans, Dipboye & Colella, 2005; Hispanic Americans, Guerrero & Posthuma, 2014) in organizations. However, most of this research has focused on African Americans because they were brought to this country by the transatlantic slave trade, and experienced the unspeakable bonds of slavery (Bell, 2013). Other research has examined the degree to which women, older workers, and other ethnic minorities (e.g., Asian Americans, Cheng & Thatchenkery, 1997) experience unfair discrimination or are unfairly treated in organizations. However, relatively little research in OB or HR has considered the biases or unfair treatment of Natives in organizations (Findling et al., 2019; Muller, 1998). Despite the lack of research, approximately 54% of Natives report that they have experienced unfair discrimination in the employment process (e.g., hiring, pay rates) during the last year (National Public Radio, 2017).

In recent years, there has been some research on Native views about business, their leadership style, and entrepreneurial behaviors, but these articles did not directly address issues of unfair discrimination in organizations (Black & Kennedy, 2019; Gladstone, 2012, 2021; Gladstone & Pepion, 2017, Kennedy et al., 2017; Stewart et al., 2017). However, there has been a paucity of research on Natives in the social sciences as a whole (e.g., sociology, political science, psychology), and some researchers have noted that they have been one of the most neglected groups in social research (Peterson & Duncan, 2001). One reason for this is that they make up a small subset of the population (6.9 million out of 300 million) (U.S. Bureau of Census, 2020), and another is that few researchers have access to Native people because they live in very remote locations. It is unfortunate that there is limited research on the biases experienced by Natives because studies have shown that unfair discrimination has serious negative consequences for their emotional, psychological, and physical health-related outcomes (e.g., depression, alcohol and drug use, suicide) (Findling et al., 2019).

Although Natives have not received much attention in organizational research, results of surveys have shown that they experience recurring problems in work-related settings (Bureau of Labor Statistics, 2019). For example, they are more likely to be unemployed (e.g., the unemployment rate for Natives is 6.6% compared to 3.9% for the whole U.S. population), and less likely to be hired than members of other ethnic groups (Bureau of Labor Statistics, 2019). Further, when they are hired, they are more likely to be relegated to low skill dead end jobs than others. For instance, Natives are overrepresented in low skilled service jobs (25% of Natives versus 18% of others) that have low pay rates, few benefits, and limited opportunities for advancement (Bureau of Labor Statistics, 2019). They are also underrepresented in high skilled positions (e.g., managerial or professional positions) (25% Natives versus 40% others) and are more likely to work in physically dangerous jobs in natural resources (e.g., gas and oil), construction, and maintenance occupations (13% Natives versus 9% others) (Bureau of Labor Statistics, 2019). Thus, we believe that research is needed to determine the reasons for the employment problems experienced by Natives.

Even though Natives often experience unfair discrimination and exclusion from organizations, research has revealed that they have many unique skills and abilities that are likely to add value to organizations. For instance, they have been extremely creative over time, and invented thousands of products that have made important contributions to our society (e.g., aspirin, corn, rubber, kayaks, cable suspension bridges, contour farming, quinine, raised-bed agriculture, baby bottles, syringes, oral contraceptives, and so forth) (Kiger, 2019). Natives are also close to nature and the environment and may have the skills needed to help alleviate some of the problems associated with severe climate change in our world. They may also have long term survival skills that can be used to help organizations survive economic downturns, and volatility in business and natural environments.

One notable example of how Natives have added value to organizations is the example of the Navajo Code talkers in World War II (Intel.gov, 2021) These individuals were bilingual members of the military, and they used the little-known Navajo language to transmit secret tactical coded messages between military units. The Japanese were unable to decode these messages because very few people understood the complex Navajo language, and it was not recorded in writing at that time. As a result, the code talkers were able to improve the speed of encryption, decryption, and they facilitated secret communications across units. Historians have argued that they helped the U.S. win the war in the Pacific and helped expedite the end of World War II which saved thousands of lives (Intel.gov, 2021). Thus, we believe that the inclusion of Natives in organizations may add unique skills and insights that can be used to enhance innovation in organizations and overcome some of the challenges that they face.

Purpose of Present Chapter

In view of the many employment problems experienced by Natives and their potential to add value to organizations, the primary purposes of the present chapter are to (a) propose a model of factors thought to affect unfair discrimination against Natives in organizations, (b) review the existing theory and research on these issues, (c) offer hypotheses to guide future research, and (d) present practical strategies that might be used to decrease unfair discrimination and enhance the inclusion of Natives in organizations.

Sources of Unfair Discrimination Against Natives

Previous research has suggested that there are several basic reasons for the unfair discrimination experienced by Natives (Al-Asfour et al., 2021). One potential reason for unfair discrimination against Natives is that they are more likely to face prejudice, stereotypes, and stigmas in the employment process than European Americans (Al-Asfour et al., 2021). Another is that members of the dominant group in U.S. society (European

Americans) are likely to denigrate Natives in order to enhance their own social identity and self-esteem (Tajfel, 1982). A third reason is that members of the dominant group in the U.S. (e.g., European Americans) sets the values, norms, and standards in society, and they evaluate Natives (or other out-group members) negatively if their cultural values do not live up to these standards (Barker, 1981; Stephan & Stephan, 2013). Given that Native's cultural values are quite different than European American values, their culture is often viewed as inferior, and they are frequently viewed as having a primitive culture in our society. Each of these reasons for unfair discrimination will be considered in our model which will be described below.

MODEL OF UNFAIR DISCRIMINATION AGAINST NATIVES IN ORGANIZATIONS

Our model is based on an integration of the models of social cognition (Miller & Brewer 1984), social categorization (Tajfel & Turner, 1979), and cultural racism theory (Balibar, 2008; Barker, 1981; Taguieff, 2001). A depiction of the model is noted in Figure 11.1. Quite simply, our model predicts that when we encounter people, we categorize them into social groups in order to understand them and (understand them and our place) (Tajfel & Turner, 1979). For instance, we spontaneously divide people into groups based on culture (e.g., European Americans, Natives), physical characteristics (e.g., gender or ethnicity), social achievements (e.g., occupation or political affiliation), or other distinctions. The categorization process is often very quick and automatic, and research has shown that people recognize another person's race within one or two seconds (Macrae & Bodenhausen, 2000). Categorization and the assignment of people into groups is important because we are dependent on social groups for our survival, self-identity, and the satisfaction of our needs for belonging (Brewer, 2008). As a result, we are also motivated to categorize ourselves into some groups and not others which is known as self-categorization (Tajfel, 1982).

Once individuals are assigned to social groups then stereotypes about the group are elicited. Stereotypes are defined as "largely false, overgeneralized beliefs about members of a category that are typically negative" (Ashmore & Del Boca, 1981). For example, if one is assigned to the group based on their Native ethnicity then they are likely to be stereotyped as lazy, unintelligent, dishonest, criminals, addicted to alcohol, and environmentally conscious (e.g., Laxson, 1991; Merskin, 2001; Tan et al., 1997). On the other hand, if one is assigned to a group based on their European American ethnic background, they are likely to be stereotyped as friendly, intelligent, hardworking, generous, talkative, materialistic, arrogant, and

Figure 11.1

Model of Stereotypes and Intergroup Bias Against Native Americans

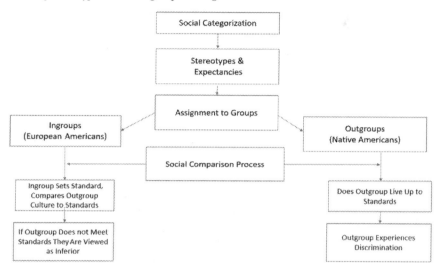

obsessed with guns (Wojnar, 2008). Next, stereotypes about these individuals are believed to evoke expectancies about the person which are anticipatory beliefs about an individual's behavior (Miller & Brewer, 1984). Further, the social categorization model predicts that stereotypes and expectancies are used to assign groups into two distinct social categories (i.e., ingroups and outgroups). For example, based on their high levels of social status and power in the United States, European Americans are likely to be assigned to ingroups (dominant group), and it is expected that Natives will be assigned to outgroups (nondominant group) because they are often viewed as having relatively low power and social status.

The social categorization model also argues that once individuals are assigned to ingroups and outgroups, then there is a comparison of the two social groups. Further, membership in these groups is thought to affect a person's self-concept and social identity (Turner et al., 1987). For example, a person is likely to have a positive self-concept and high levels of self-esteem if they are a member of Mensa, a group of high IQ individuals. Social identity is "that part of an individual's self-concept which derives from his/her knowledge of membership in a social group (or groups) together with the value and emotional significance attached to that group membership" (Tajfel, 1982, p. 255).

Social identities determine how we categorize people into ingroups and outgroups, and influence how we treat group members. Not surprisingly, this categorization process often results in intergroup bias. Intergroup bias refers to "the systematic tendency to evaluate one's [ingroup] or its members more favorably than [an outgroup] or its members" (Hewstone et al., 2002, p. 576). Further, intergroup bias typically results in unfair discrimination against outgroup members. However, there are several potential reasons for this process. One explanation is that people think about ingroups and outgroups in "us" versus "them" terms, and favor ingroups members or denigrate outgroup members to boost their own self esteem (Turner et al., 1987).

Another explanation is based on the sociological or anthropological theory of "cultural racism" (e.g., Barker, 1979, 1981). This theory predicts that some cultures are perceived to be superior to others, and cultures that have values that are different from the superior group are viewed as inferior or second-rate. Stated somewhat differently, the cultural racism model suggests that when the nondominant groups' cultural values do not live up to the dominant groups' cultural standards, they are viewed as sub-standard and experience unfair discrimination in organizational settings. For instance, in the U.S. society, the European American culture (e.g., white middle-class Protestants of European descent) has become the dominant culture because they a long history of achievements and accomplishments, and the accumulation of wealth which are some of the primary symbols of success in a culture. In contrast, Natives are often characterized as a nondominant culture because they were overwhelmed and subjugated by Europeans, and do not have a history of achievement or the accumulation of material wealth. As a result, cultural racism theory suggests that the dominant group is likely to view Natives as culturally backward or inferior and perceive that their misguided values are the primary cause of their poverty.

As might be expected, the dominant group sets the cultural values and standards in a society, and these cultural standards are used to evaluate other groups (e.g., Natives, African Americans) (Barker, 1981). For example, the dominant European American culture in the U.S. stresses individualism, competitive achievement, autonomy, egalitarianism, materialism, an emphasis on work over family, and a future time orientation (Trice & Beyer, 1993). However, Native culture is very different from European American culture, and emphasizes cooperation, generosity, welfare of the group over the individual, a circular time orientation (i.e., all energy recurs over time), and a lack of emphasis on materialism (Attneave, 1982; Stone et al., 2020). Given the differences in these cultures, our model predicts that the dominant group will view Natives as second-rate because they do not meet the cultural standards of European Americans. For example, based on European-American values and standards, members of this culture are likely to judge others on the extent to which they exhibit competitive behaviors or accumulate wealth. However, Natives are unlikely to meet these standards because their culture emphasizes cooperation rather than competition, and they are less likely to value materialism than European Americans (Laxson, 1991). Thus, based on the theory of cultural racism, our model posits that European Americans are likely to view Natives negatively and unfairly discriminate against them in organizations (Barker, 1981).

In summary, we based our model on an integration of social cognition (Miller & Brewer, 1984), social-categorization theory (Tajfel & Turner, 1979), and the model of cultural racism (Barker, 1981). These three theories make very similar predictions about the bases for unfair discrimination against Natives in organizations, but the underlying motives in the theories are somewhat different.

Considerable research on unfair discrimination in the U.S. has been based in the social cognition and social-categorization models (Miller & Brewer, 1984; Tajfel & Turner, 1979). However, very little research in the U.S. has based predictions about unfair discrimination on the model of cultural racism. Thus, we believe that using the model of cultural racism provides a unique explanation for why Natives are often denigrated in U.S. society. It merits noting that the cultural racism model has received a great deal of attention in Europe, but has not received the same amount of attention in the United States. Thus, we believe that our model makes a key contribution to the literature because it is based on an integration of social cognition, social categorization, and cultural racism theories.

Although we believe that our model provides a unique explanation for why Natives are discriminated against in organizations, we maintain that the predictions in the model need to be tested before generalizations are made. As a result, in the following sections we present the limited research that tests the relations in our model, consider gaps in that research, and offer specific hypotheses that can be used to guide future research.

Stereotypes as Predictors of Unfair Discrimination

One major source of discrimination against Natives and other outgroup members is that they are often stereotyped and stigmatized in work-related settings (Stone et al., 1992). We defined stereotypes in the section above, but define stigmas as the discrepancy between one's actual and virtual identity or deeply discrediting marks associated with a particular quality (Goffman, 1963; Jones et al., 1984).

Our model posits that when one encounters a new person, they assign them to a social category (e.g., man, woman, European American, Native). Categorization can be defined as the way that "mental representations (cognitive schemata) influence the way in which information about target persons is stored, organized, and processed" (Stone et al., 1992, p. 391).

Further, our model maintains that once a person is assigned to a social category then stereotypes about the person are elicited. The model also suggests that stereotypes are used in combination with category membership to generate job-related expectancies about the target person. These expectancies are anticipatory beliefs about the individual's potential to perform a job (Higgins & Bargh, 1987). As a result, if the person is categorized as a Native and the stereotypes about him/her are negative (e.g., person is unintelligent or lazy) then decision makers are likely to expect that the person will not be motivated or able to perform a job. Job expectancies are extremely important elements in the model because they are thought to bias employment decisions about the person. Thus, if the job expectancies about Native applicants are negative then they will be less likely to be selected for a job, receive challenging job assignments, or receive high pay rates.

Attributes of Natives That Influence Stereotypes and Stigmas

Social psychological models (Jones et al., 1984) maintain that there are a number of attributes associated with a person that affects stereotypes and stigmas about them. For instance, Jones et al., (1984) argue that some of these attributes include: aesthetic qualities (e.g., skin color, weight), concealability, and danger or peril. However, we believe that several other attributes may influence stereotypes of Natives including their spirituality, and the degree to which they are perceived to have a blemished character (Goffman, 1963).

Aesthetic Qualities

Aesthetic qualities refer to the extent to which Natives are perceived as attractive or unattractive, and it can be argued that the aesthetic appeal of Natives is likely to influence how they are perceived and treated in organizations (e.g., Jones et al., 1984). In support of this argument, theory and research on physical attractiveness (e.g., Hosoda et al., 2003; Stone et al., 1992) suggest that the more a person is perceived as attractive the more that others will react positively to them in the employment process. We believe that a number of factors may influence the perceived attractiveness of Natives, and two of those factors are skin color and physical weight. The relation between these two factors and unfair discrimination against Natives will be considered below.

Skin Color. In U.S. society, skin color is a major factor that affects perceived attractiveness, and also influences perceptions of social status and worthiness in organizations (Chen et al., 2020). For instance, research has found that people with light skin color are perceived as more attractive than those with dark skin color in the U.S. and many other societies (Stone et al., 1992). It is also a sign of social status, intelligence, and moral worth (Reece, 2017). Likewise, people with brown or dark skin color are viewed as less attractive, and are often perceived to have lower social status, diminished intelligence, and are more likely to be criminals than their light skinned counterparts (Hochschild, 2006). This phenomenon is known as "colorism" in the U.S., and many ethnic group members (e.g., African Americans) believe that their skin color is a major cause of unfair discrimination in organizations (Lee & Fiske, 2006; Stone et al., 2020).

In view of these findings, we believe that Natives who have brown or dark skin color skin will be perceived as less attractive, stereotyped more negatively, and will be less likely to receive positive outcomes in the employment process than those with light skin color. Interestingly, Natives' skin color varies between white and black, and is usually categorized as various shades of brown. One reason for this is that Natives have married Europeans for over 500 years, and many of them can be categorized as mestizo (e.g., person who has a combination of European and indigenous ancestry) (Mexico Daily Post, 2020). It merits noting that the term red skin is a misnomer because it does not actually reflect the color of Natives' skin, and it is considered a pejorative term for Natives in the U.S. and Canada (Shapira, 2016). Even though Natives may not have a red skin color, our model predicts that those who have brown or dark skin color are more likely to be stereotyped negatively and relegated to low levels jobs in organizations than those with light skin color (Ray & Preston, 2009).

Considerable research has provided support for the fact that individuals with brown or dark skin color are more likely to be stereotyped as lazy, unintelligent, unreliable, aggressive, dirty, and are more likely to be perceived as dishonest than those with white or light skin color (e.g., Dovidio & Gaertner, 1986; Maddox & Gray, 2002; Peffley & Hurtwitz, 1998). In addition, research by Ortiz and Telles (2012) found that individuals who had dark skin color were more likely to experience unfair discrimination than those with light skin color. Similarly, research by Timberlake and Williams (2012) revealed that Latin American and African applicants who had brown or dark skin color were more likely to be viewed as violent criminals than those from Europe or Asia who had light skin color. Results of other studies revealed that individuals with dark skin color were viewed as less competent, received lower wages, and were more likely to be assigned to low level jobs than those with light skin color (Hersch, 2011; Lee & Fiske, 2006). Interestingly, research in Canada (Shields, 2011) and Europe (Zschirnt & Ruedin, 2016) has also revealed that the biases against those with dark skin color exist across nations.

Taken together, these studies suggest that Natives who have brown or dark skin color are likely to be viewed as less attractive, stereotyped more negatively, and experience higher levels of unfair discrimination than those with light skin color. However, we know of no empirical research that has examined this prediction with respect to Natives in organizational settings. Thus, we believe that research is needed to determine if Natives' skin color affects their perceived attractiveness or biases employment decisions about them. Thus, we offer the following hypothesis to foster future research.

H1: Natives who have dark skin color will be (a) viewed as less attractive, (b) stereotyped more negatively, and will be less likely to be (c) hired, (d) assigned to high level jobs, (e) mentored, or (f) included in work groups than those who have light skin color.

Weight. Another factor that is likely to affect the attractiveness of Natives is that many of them are overweight or obese (American Psychological Association [APA], 2021; U.S. Department of Health and Human Services Office of Minority Health [OMH], 2018). Some recent research revealed that, at least, 33% of Native people are obese (U.S. Department of Health and Human Services, 2018). In U.S. society, those individuals who are overweight or obese are stereotyped negatively (i.e., lazy, unintelligent, and lacking self-discipline), and are not perceived to live up the cultural standards that stress people should be thin or a normal weight (Krueger et al., 2014). Thus, Natives who are overweight or obese are more likely to be viewed as unattractive and stereotyped negatively in the employment process than those who are thin or normal weight (Roehling et al., 2007).

In recent years, many Natives have become overweight because they have adopted the European American lifestyle which involves a sedentary routine, and consumption of fast foods which are high in processed fat (Center for Disease Control and Prevention [CDC], 2020). Given that reservations are located in remote locations, they often have little access to fresh fruits and vegetables, and many have abandoned their traditional Native foods (e.g., corn, squash, and beans) in favor of less healthy alternatives (Goetz, 2012).

In support of these arguments, a number of studies have found that weight-based bias affects the perceived attractiveness of individuals and employment related decisions about them (Krueger et al., 2014; Roehling et al., 2007). For instance, research has indicated that weight-based bias affects hiring decisions (e.g., Flint et al., 2016); compensation (e.g., Judge & Cable, 2011); performance ratings (e.g., Rudolph et al., 2012); promotion decisions (e.g., Katsaiti & Shamsuddin, 2016); and discipline or discharge (e.g., Lindeman et al., 2017). Further there is evidence that weight-based bias is not just a problem in the United States, but occurs around the world (Roehling et al., 2007). For example, research revealed that weight-based bias affects employment decisions in Canada (e.g., Chu & Ohinmaa, 2016), China (e.g., Lee, & Zhao, 2017), Europe (e.g., Hiilamo et al., 2017; Katsaiti & Shamsuddin, 2016), and South Africa (e.g., Henry & Kollamparambil, 2017).

Although there has been considerable research on weight-based bias (Krueger et al., 2014), we know of no empirical research that has examined the impact of weight on the perceived attractiveness and/or employment decisions about Natives. Being overweight may also create a double disadvantage for Natives who have dark skin color. Thus, we offer the following hypothesis to guide future research:

H2: Natives who are overweight will be perceived as (a) less attractive, (b) stereotyped more negatively and less likely to be (c) hired, (d) assigned to challenging jobs, (e) mentored, or (f) included in work groups than those who are normal weight.

Concealability

Another factor that is likely to influence the way that Natives are perceived and treated in organizations is the degree to which they can conceal their Native heritage (Jones et al., 1984). Concealability refers to the extent to which an individual's native ethnicity is hidden or not apparent to others (cf. Jones et al., 1984). In some cases, Natives' ethnic background is highly visible to others because their physical characteristics reflect those of the prototypical Native (e.g., brown skin color, straight black hair, high cheekbones, dark brown wideset eyes) (Access Genealogy, n.d.). However, researchers have argued that many Natives are indistinguishable from European or Hispanic Americans because their physical characteristics are more consistent with the prototype of these groups than Natives (e.g., they have light skin color, blue eyes, light hair color) (Hanson & Rouse, 1987). As a result, their Native ethnicity may not always be apparent to others, and we believe that when Natives can conceal their ethnicity, they are less likely to experience negative stereotypes and reactions from others than when they cannot conceal their identity. There has been relatively little empirical research on the concealability of one's ethnicity, but studies in the U.S. have found that raters expressed more negative attitudes toward strongly identified racial minorities than those who were weakly identified (Kaiser & Pratt-Hyatt, 2009).

Similarly, research in Canada found that visible minorities were more likely to experience discrimination and prejudicial attitudes than non-visible minorities (Kunz et al., 2000; Lalonde et al., 1992; Pruegger & Kiely, 2002). Research also revealed that ethnic group members who were highly identified reported more vulnerability to discrimination than those who were less highly identified (Operario & Fiske, 2001). Thus, we can infer from these findings that when Natives can conceal their ethnicity, they will be less likely to be stereotyped negatively or receive unfavorable employment decisions than when they cannot conceal their ethnicity. In spite of these arguments, we believe that a concealment strategy may evoke negative reactions from others when their ethnicity is eventually revealed to others. One reason for this is that raters may perceive that initially concealing one's ethnicity is a form of deception or dishonesty, and their cultural norms and behaviors may violate others' expectations (Stone & Colella, 1996).

There has been very little research on the effects of concealing one's ethnicity on employment decisions, and we know of no empirical research on Natives' use of a concealment strategy. Therefore, we offer the following hypotheses to guide research.

H3: When Natives' ethnicity is not apparent to others, they will be (a) stereotyped more positively, more likely to be (b) hired, (c) assigned to high level jobs, (d) mentored, or (e) included in work groups than when their ethnicity is apparent to others.

H4: When Natives are able to initially conceal their ethnicity, but their ethnicity is revealed at a later point in time, raters will react more (a) negatively to them and (b) perceive that they are more dishonest than when they initially revealed their ethnicity.

Danger or Peril

Another factor that is likely to affect how Natives are perceived and treated in organizations is the extent to which they are believed to be dangerous (Jones et al., 1984). Research has shown that Natives are often viewed as threatening because the media and historical representations portray them as "blood thirsty savages" (Hanson & Rouse, 1987). Thus, they may be more likely to be perceived as menacing than some other ethnic group members (e.g., Asian Americans, European Americans). In addition, they may be stereotyped more negatively when they are perceived as threatening than when they are not (Stephan & Stephan, 1985).

Research has noted consistently that Natives are often stereotyped as savages who are fierce, predatory, cultureless, and animalistic (Josephy, 1968; Laxson, 1991; Merskin, 2001; Strickland, 1998; Vrasidas, 1997). Other research found that raters often view Natives as warlike people or warrior fighters who are immoral or the "zero point in human society" (Hanson & Rouse, 1987, p. 36). Still other research revealed that Puritans equated Natives with Satan who opposed God's work (Hanson & Rouse, 1987), and they were viewed by other colonists as red devils who were hostile, vengeful, depraved, and sinful (Vrasidas, 1997).

Sociologists (Bar-Tal, 1990; Volpato et al., 1990) have argued that one consequence of assigning outgroups (e.g., Natives) to an extremely negative category is delegitimization. Delegitimization is the process of constructing a "categorization of groups into extreme social categories which results in their exclusion in society" (Volpato et al., 1990). It also provides a moral basis for harming or annihilating the delegitimized groups (Volpato et al., 1990). For instance, Bar-Tal (1990) suggested that delegitimization occurs when people are (a) dehumanized (e.g., called uncivilized savages), (b) characterized by extremely negative traits (e.g., idiots, parasites), and (c) viewed as less human than other groups (e.g., Natives are red devils). He also argued that when an ingroup (e.g., European Americans) views an outgroup (e.g., Natives) as evil then their feelings of threat become intensified, and they may aggress against the outgroup to prevent any potential danger posed by them. This process provides one possible explanation for why over 20 million Natives were annihilated by the Spanish and the English during the colonization of the Americas and may explain why Natives are viewed as invisible minorities today.

Further, sociologists argue that aggression imposed by the ingroup escalates or becomes violent over time (Bar-Tal, 1990). One potential cause of this process is ethnocentrism which is typically defined as an attitude that one's own group, ethnicity, or nationality is superior to others (Webster, 1997). For instance, when European Americans perceive that their group is superior to Natives, then they are likely to denigrate Natives which arouses fear and hatred of them (National Humanities Center, n.d.). In addition, European Americans may not view Native culture as fully legitimate in U.S. society, and some people refer to their culture as dead or dying (National Humanities Center, n.d.).

Although we know of no specific empirical research on the consequences of viewing Native culture as an illegitimate culture, portrayals of Natives in films, TV, and advertising often represents them as dangerous savages or ruthless criminals (Green, 1993). As a result, these unfounded perceptions are likely to bolster negative stereotypes and unfavorable job expectancies about them. These perceptions may also lead to low self-esteem among Native people, along with dysfunctional social interactions, and high rates of incarceration. For instance, research has shown that Natives are incarcerated at a rate that is 38% higher than the national average, and they constitute the majority of the prison population in 19 states (Vaisvilas, 2021). They are also more likely to experience hate crimes and violence from others than any other ethnic group (Kumar, 2021). For instance, they are 2.5 times more likely to experience violent crimes and at least 2 times more likely to experience rape or sexual assault crimes compared to all other groups (American Indian Affairs, 2021). In addition, homicide is the third leading cause of death among Native women between 10 and 24 years (Stumblingbear-Riddle, 2018).

Given that viewing a culture as illegitimate often results in violence toward members of the culture, we believe that these perceptions may also influence hostility toward Natives in organizational settings. For example, we maintain that the more others view Native culture as illegitimate, the more that Natives will experience bullying, harassment, recurring personal criticism, and victimization.

In the previous section, we argued that when Natives are viewed as dangerous, they are more likely to be stereotyped negatively and experience unfair discrimination in the employment process. We also believe that when their culture is viewed as illegitimate, they will experience more hostile behaviors (e.g., bullying, harassment, recurring criticism) than when their culture is not viewed as illegitimate. We know of no empirical research on the extent to which these perceptions about Natives lead to unfavorable job-related decisions about them, so we offer the following hypotheses to foster research on the topic.

H5: When Natives are perceived as dangerous, they will (a) be stereotyped more negatively and will be less likely to be (b) hired, (c) assigned to high level jobs, (d) mentored, or (e) included in work groups more than those who are not perceived as threatening.

H6: When Native culture is viewed as illegitimate, they will be more likely to experience (a) bullying, (b) recurring personal criticism, (c) harassment, (d) victimization, and (e) unfair discrimination in work organizations than when their culture is viewed as legitimate.

Blemishes of Character

Another attribute that is likely to affect how Natives are perceived and treated in organizations is the extent to which they are thought to have a blemished character (Goffman, 1963). In his seminal work on stigmas, Goffman (1963) argued that individual character is synonymous with one's integrity, reputation, or personality, and reflects the degree to which the person is honest, reliable, or has a strong will (Goffman, 1963). Thus, a blemished character is a deeply discrediting characteristic stemming from low levels of integrity and/or a weak will (e.g., drug and alcohol addiction, mental illness). Interestingly, one reason that these traits are viewed as a blemish of character is that people typically assume that individuals have personal control over them (Goffman, 1963).

Research on stereotypes of Natives suggests that others often perceive that they have a number of blemishes of character including alcohol and drug addiction, dependence on government support, and high rates of illegal behavior or spousal abuse (Dixon, 2020; James et al., 1994; Tan et al., 1997). For instance, some research has referred to Natives as "Whiskey" Indians who are drunks and doomed to become alcoholics (Josephy, 1968, Laxson, 1991; Tan et al., 1997). Research also revealed that they are viewed as coddled wards of the state (Josephy, 1968) who get free money from the government throughout their lives and cannot make it on their own in mainstream society (Tan et al., 1997). They are also represented as dishonest people who are unreliable and criminals with psychological problems (Angermeyer & Matschinger, 2004; Dijker & Koomen, 2003; Hanson & Rouse, 1987; Hinton et al., 2000; Whaley, 1997). Thus, stereotypes of Natives indicate that when they are perceived to have a number of character deficiencies others may believe that they will not be able to perform jobs in organizations.

Although there has been some research on Natives' blemishes of character (e.g., alcoholism, mental illness), results of that research have shown that these stereotypes are unfounded (Fleming, 2006). Further, most of the same research has been conducted in social not organizational contexts. Thus, we believe that more research is needed to determine if these perceived character flaws affect employment-related decisions, and we offer the following hypotheses to guide future research.

H7: When Natives are viewed as having a blemished character, they will (a) be stereotyped more negatively and will be less likely to be (b) hired, (c) assigned to high level jobs, (d) promoted, (e) mentored, or (f) included in work groups more than those who are not perceived as having a blemished character.

Spiritual Beliefs

Although most of the stereotypes that are attributed to Natives are viewed as extremely negative (e.g., they are unintelligent, lazy, criminals) there is one important attribute that may result in positive perceptions about them (Smith, 2006). Research has shown that people often view Natives as deeply devoted to their spiritual beliefs which includes a reverence for nature, mother earth, and all living creatures (Smith, 2006). Thus, we believe that the view that Natives are spiritual people should have a positive impact on perceptions of them, and employment decisions about them.

Most Natives have spiritual belief systems rather than formalized religions like European Americans (e.g., Catholicism, Judaism, Protestantism) (Smith, 2006). Members of different tribes have unique spiritual beliefs, and some tribes combine their spiritual beliefs with Catholicism or other formal religions. However, their spiritual values differ from Christian values, and they often believe that (a) there is no distinction between the spiritual world and the natural world, (b) there is some form of deity who may not be in same form as the God in Christianity (e.g., creator or great spirit), and (c) moral guidelines should be fluid and flexible. Given these spiritual beliefs, research has revealed that they have been stereotyped as the "noble savage" who is innocent, respectful of the environment, and at one with nature (Fleming, 2006; Hanson & Rouse, 1987; Laxson, 1991; Merskin, 2001; Mihesuah, 1996; Strickland, 1998). Results of research also indicated that, in some cases, they are viewed as wise (Fleming, 2006) noble heroes, brave, and good people who live close to nature (Hanson & Rouse, 1987).

Interestingly, recent research has compared the stereotypes of several different ethnic groups (e.g., European Americans, African Americans, Mexican Americans, and Natives) (Stone-Romero et al., 2020). Results of this research found that Natives were stereotyped more positively on several dimensions than African Americans, and Mexican Americans including (a) reliability, (b) cognitive ability, and (c) social skills, but less positively than Chinese Americans (Stone-Romero et al., 2020). Similarly, the findings of the study revealed that Natives were viewed as higher in terms of status than Mexican Americans, but not Chinese Americans. Results of the study also found that Natives were viewed as more collective and having higher levels of integrity than European Americans (Stone-Romero et al., 2020).

Taken together, these results suggest that not all stereotypes of Natives are negative, and they may be perceived more favorably in terms of reliability, cognitive abilities, and social skills than members of some other ethnic groups (e.g., African Americans, Mexican Americans) (Stone-Romero et al., 2020). Further, they may be rated as higher in terms of collectivity and integrity than European Americans.

Although the findings of this study are very interesting, the researchers did not identify the reasons for these different stereotypes. As a result, we believe that additional research is needed to determine if Natives' perceived spirituality influences others' reactions to them. In order to foster that research, we present the following hypotheses:

H8: When Natives are viewed as deeply devoted to their spiritual beliefs they will be viewed as having higher levels of (a) integrity, (b) reliability, and (c) collectivity, and (d) more likely to receive positive employment decisions than when they are not perceived to be committed to their spiritual beliefs.

H9: When Natives are perceived to revere nature, they will be viewed as having higher levels of (a) integrity, (b) reliability, (c) collectivity, and more likely to experience (d) positive employment decisions when they are not thought to revere nature.

In summary, in the sections above we argued that Natives are stereotyped primarily in negative ways, but perceptions that they are spiritual may result in positive stereotypes about them. As might be expected these stereotypes affect ratings of Natives and the degree to which they experience unfair discrimination in organizations. Further, there is a lack of research on Natives in the social sciences, especially organizational behavior, and human resource management, and we hope that our model will foster additional research on the employment experiences of Natives in organizations. In order to facilitate that research, we offered hypotheses to guide future research on the topic.

Consistent with our model, we also believe that stereotypes are only one reason that Natives experience unfair discrimination in organizations. Other reasons are based on social-categorization theory (Tajfel & Turner, 1979), and the model of cultural racism (Bailibar, 2008). These theoretical explanations will be reviewed in the sections that follow.

Social Categorization View

Next, our model predicts that stereotypes are used to assign groups into two distinct social categories (i.e., ingroups and outgroup) (Turner et al., 1987). For example, European Americans are typically assigned to the ingroup (i.e., dominant group) in the U.S. because they are viewed positively, and have high levels of social status, power, and material wealth. In contrast, Natives are often assigned to the outgroup because they are often viewed negatively, and have relatively low levels of power, social status, and material wealth. Consistent with social categorization theory, our model also argues that once individuals are assigned to ingroups and outgroups, then there is a comparison of these two social groups. Further, it predicts that members of the ingroup are motivated to maintain a favorable social identity for their group and ensure that outgroup members are viewed negatively (Tajfel & Turner, 1979). As a result, individuals enhance their social identity and self-esteem by increasing the positive image of their own group (e.g., European Americans) and/or denigrating the image of outgroup members (Natives) (Tajfel, 1982; Tajfel & Turner, 1979). This process allows ingroup members to maintain control over power, privileges, and material resources in society.

However, research has shown that the motivation to enhance an ingroup's positive image by putting outgroup members down affects intergroup interactions and may result in negative consequences for outgroup members (e.g., hatred, dehumanization, unfair discrimination, exploitation, or annihilation of members) (Hutchison & Abrams, 2003). As a result, if outgroup members are vilified by the ingroup they should be more likely to experience intergroup bias and unfair discrimination in organizations.

Differences in Cultural Values as a Cause of Unfair Discrimination

Our model also predicts that there are dramatic differences in the cultural values and norms between the dominant group (e.g., European Americans) and nondominant groups (e.g., Natives) in our society, and these differences are likely to elicit negative perceptions and unfair discrimination in organizations (e.g., Tajfel, 1982; Thomas & Chrobot-Mason, 2005). The primary reason for this is that the dominant group (e.g., European Americans) control the norms, standards, and rewards in a society, and evaluate nondominant groups (e.g., Natives) on the degree to which they live up to these standards. If an outgroup does not meet the standards set by the dominant group, then they are viewed as inferior or unworthy of rewards and outcomes. Thus, our model suggests that outgroup members are viewed negatively and stigmatized because their cultural values do not meet the dominant group's standards in a society. One consequence of this comparison is that the dominant group maligns or degrades members of the outgroup which leads to unfair discrimination in organizations.

Given these differences, we compare the cultural values of European Americans and Natives in the sections below. However, prior to discussing the dominant cultural values of European American and Native cultures, we want to emphasize that our discussion is based, on average, not absolute cultural values. Cultural values reflect widely held norms, roles, and beliefs that affirm what is desirable in a culture (Betancourt & López, 1993), and the majority of those in the culture endorse these values. However, there are within group differences in the culture so one cannot assume that all members of a culture share a specific cultural value (Betancourt & López, 1993). Thus, our discussion of cultural values is based, on average, and may not apply to all individuals within a culture.

Dominant Cultural Values in the United States

The U.S. is dominated by Western and Northern European ideologies and cultural values (Cox, 1993; Stone-Romero et al., 2003; Trice & Beyer, 1993) including: competitive achievement, rugged individualism, self-reliance, practicality, materialism, and rationality in decision making. Thus, the European American worldview dominates prevailing ideology in the United States, and members of the dominant culture set the standards, and evaluate the degree to which Natives live up to those standards. For example, if European Americans value material wealth and Natives do not, then Natives will be viewed as inferior because their culture does not emphasize the values of the dominant group. In order to understand this process, we review the cultural values of European Americans in the sections that follow, then compare Natives' cultural values to European American beliefs. We also highlight the dissimilarities in these two sets of cultural values, identify the consequences of these differences, and offer hypotheses to guide future research on these issues

European American Values: Competition, Cooperation, and Practicality. On average, two of the primary values of European American (or U.S.) culture are competitive achievement and practicality. Members of the U.S. culture believe that competition plays an important role in achievement because it motivates individuals to pursue excellence (Stone-Romero et al., 2005). They are also intolerant of idleness, laziness, and slothfulness (Trice & Beyer, 1993; Weber, 1958). However, this ideology does not emphasize all types of achievement, but stresses practical accomplishments at work, and material rewards. Individuals are expected to strive for success at work because it offers a source of self-respect, material rewards, challenge, growth, and personal fulfillment (Trice & Beyer, 1993). Similarly, the U.S. culture values practicality and getting things done (Trice & Beyer, 1993). Activities that are impractical (e.g., artistic or musical expression) are rarely valued, and individuals who stress academic pursuits or theory are often disparaged in society (Trice & Beyer, 1993). Further, individuals who are not competitive or do not strive for achievement are viewed as useless or "good-for-nothing" in the U.S. culture (Kossek & Lobel, 1996; Stone-Romero et al., 2003).

Natives' Values: Competition, Cooperation, and Practicality. Although the dominant culture (e.g., European American) in the U.S. stresses competitive achievement, Native culture is very different and typically emphasizes cooperation and ingroup harmony among families and tribal members (Verbos et al., 2011). Whenever possible, they avoid competitive acts and aggression, and some tribes view competition as rude or improper behavior (Burk, 2007). Others believe that it is acceptable to win at games once in a while, but not all of the time (Burk, 2007). However, their emphasis on cooperation and group harmony may create internal conflict for those Natives who try to fit in to work organizations that are dominated by European American value systems (Pewewardy, 2008).

Given that Natives' cultural values do not emphasize competitive achievement, European Americans are likely to view Native culture as inferior to their own. One reason for this is that European Americans view competition as a key motivating factor, and they use competitive reward systems in organizations to inspire high levels of performance. As a result, European Americans are likely to believe that Natives will not be motivated by competitive reward systems and will not strive for high levels of performance in organizations. As a result, Natives may not be viewed as suitable for jobs, and are likely to experience unfair discrimination in organizations.

Native culture is also less likely to stress practicality, and more likely to accentuate artistic expression than European American culture (Laxson, 1991). For example, Natives' revere artistic expression, and indigenous art is used as a means for Natives to express their societal values and customs (Laxson, 1991). For example, they use a wide variety of mediums (e.g., sculpture, paintings, basketry, textiles, pottery), and many examples of their visual art forms focus on their reverence for the animals (e.g., bears, coyotes, turtles, horn toads), and the interrelationship of all living creatures. Most of the original forms of Native art were designed for practical purposes (e.g., pottery used for water or cooking), but these practical tools and vessels still included artwork as embellishments. In view of Natives' emphasis on artistic expression, European Americans are likely to view Native culture as frivolous because artistic activities are not always valued in the dominant society, and those who pursue these endeavors are often disparaged by the culture (Laxson, 1991).

Although we believe that the arguments noted above are reasonable, we are not aware of any empirical research that has examined the effects of differences in Natives' and European American values regarding competitive achievement and practicality on reactions to Natives and unfair discrimination in organizations. Thus, we offer the following hypotheses to guide future research.

H10: When Natives stress artistic expression which is inconsistent with the dominant groups' standards regarding practicality they will (a) be stereotyped more negatively, (b) experience more unfair discrimination, and will be less likely to be (c) hired (d) assigned to high level jobs, (e) mentored, or (f) included in work groups more than those whose values are consistent with the dominant groups' values.

European American Values: Individualism, and Self-Reliance. Two other dominant cultural values in the U.S. are individualism and self-reliance (Trice & Beyer, 1993). On average, European American culture emphasizes individualism which accentuates the importance of the individual, personal rights, equity in allocating outcomes, and the right to be free from social and organizational controls (Trice & Beyer, 1993). Individualism also stresses independence, autonomous behavior, and priority given to personal rather than group goals (Triandis, 2001). Further, individualism in the U.S. culture is often coupled with values regarding self-reliance, and separateness so that one's social identity comes from the self rather than the family or group (Triandis, 1994). In addition, work is an extremely important part of the U.S. culture because it provides a context for achieving individual goals including success and self-fulfillment (Trice & Beyer, 1993). However, if Natives do not emphasize individualism and self-reliance, they are likely to be viewed as "freeloaders" in the society because they depend on others (e.g., governmental assistance) (Stone-Romero et al., 2003) more than European Americans.

Natives Cultural Values: Collectivism and Interconnectedness. Natives are more likely to emphasize collectivism than European Americans (Yamauchi, 1998). Those who value collectivism place the needs and goals of the group over the needs and desires of individuals (Triandis, 1994), and emphasize loyalty, working toward the common good, and helping one another. In contrast, individualistic cultures stress the needs and desires of individuals over the group, and highlight the importance of independence, freedom, and self-reliance (Triandis, 1994).

Given that Natives often endorse collective values, they also place a great deal of importance on the interconnectedness and interdependence of all things (Hain-Jamall, 2013), and there is a concerted emphasis on collective achievement (Pewewardy, 2002). For instance, they honor people who have made significant contributions to the group or community rather honoring their individual achievements (Dvorakova, 2019; Pewewardy, 2002). They also try to avoid calling attention to themselves (Burk, 2007), and prefer working in groups to working alone (Pewewardy, 2002). Cross-cultural researchers argue that the differences in collectivism and individualism have a profound influence on individuals' attitudes and behaviors (Triandis, 1994). As a result, those who value individualism stress that people should be able to solve problems or accomplish tasks on their own without having to rely on others for assistance (Triandis, 1994). They are also expected to be self-reliant and to "pull themselves up by their bootstraps" when they encounter obstacles. In contrast, individuals who value collectivism stress that people should work together in harmony, and become part of an interdependent group (Triandis, 1994). Collectivists also exhibit more loyalty and helping behaviors than individualists and are more likely to work toward the common good rather than individual goals (Triandis,

1994). Further, collectivists do not believe individuals are just separate units that should be interdependent from one another (Triandis, 1994).

In view of the European American emphasis on individualism, they are likely to expect that people will be more motivated by self-interest rather than group goals (Trice & Beyer, 1993). As a consequence, the dominant group in the U.S is likely to set standards based on their own individualistic or self-interested values and perceive that Natives who emphasize collectivism will be less motivated and have lower levels of performance in groups than those who stress individualism (Al-Asfour et al., 2021). As a result, they may rate Natives negatively and unfairly discriminate against them in the employment process. We know of no empirical research that has directly examined the degree to which differences in cultural values regarding collectivism and individualism affect motivation and performance expectations, and unfair discrimination against them in organizations. Thus, we offer the following hypothesis:

> **H11:** When Natives emphasize collectivism and which are not consistent with the dominant groups' individualistic values then they (a) are stereotyped more negatively, (b) experience more unfair discrimination, and will be less likely to be (c) hired (d) assigned to high level jobs, (e) promoted, (f) mentored, or (g) included in work groups more than those whose values are consistent with the dominant groups' values.

European Americans' Values: Rationality in Decision-Making and the Use of Science as a Way of Knowing. European Americans are, on average, more likely to highlight rationality in decision-making and science as a way of knowing than some other ethnic groups members (e.g., Natives) (Cascio & Aguinis, 2005; Trice & Beyer, 1993; Weber, 1958). Given this value system, dominant group members often create formal rules and procedures designed to (a) avoid favoritism or partiality, (b) enhance fairness in decision-making (Weber, 1958), and (c) separate the job from the job holder (e.g., organizations should not consider employees' personal needs when making decisions) (Weber, 1958). Although the use of standardized rules and procedures may increase fairness, they may also create problems because they set a negative tone in organizations, and employees may work to rules rather than organizational goals (Katz & Kahn, 1978). Further, when jobs are separated from job holders, employment decisions are based on impersonal criteria, and people are expected to give their primary attention to work rather than their family or personal needs (Weber, 1958). However, research has indicated that when organizations do not consider employees' family lives when making decisions, they will be more dissatisfied and have greater turnover intentions than when the organization considers their families when making employment decisions (Allen, 2001).

Apart from these values, the U.S. culture highlights that individuals should not express their emotions or personal feelings at work (Stone-Romero, 2005). However, research has shown that the suppression of emotions may be related to adverse attitudes and health-related outcomes such as job dissatisfaction, job stress, hypertension, heart disease, emotional exhaustion, and burn out (Jeung et al. 2018). Consistent with their values regarding rationality, European American culture also accentuates that decisions should be based on science rather than nonscientific ways of knowing (e.g., instinct, authority, folklore, spirituality, or traditionalism) (Trice & Beyer, 1993). The U.S. culture places a great deal of importance on science because it is a means of producing technologies that solve practical problems, and it gives people a sense of control over unpredictable events (e.g., the environment) (Trice & Beyer, 1993). Given their fervent views about science, European Americans often view cultures that use nonscientific ways of knowing (e.g., folklore, tradition, instinct, religion, personal experience) more negatively than those who use science (Trice & Beyer, 1993). For example, the dominant culture in the U.S. is likely to view Native culture as primitive or backward if they use nonscientific (e.g., folklore, instinct, spirituality) ways of knowing.

Natives Values: Coupling Nonscientific and Scientific Ways of Knowing. Although most members of the dominant culture in the U.S. stress science as a way of knowing, Natives' cultural values emphasize that science is important, but it should be coupled with other nonscientific ways of knowing in order to understand a phenomenon (Garroutte, 2015; James, 2006). Further, they believe that nonscientific ways of knowing, and science complement one another, and individuals should take extended periods of time to analyze the spiritual and scientific sides of an issue in order to completely understand the world around them (James, 2006).

Given that most members of the dominant culture in the U.S. are steadfast about their beliefs in science, they are likely to perceive that Natives have asinine or superstitious belief systems because they do not emphasize that science is the primary way of knowing. As a result, they may be skeptical of Natives' intelligence and wisdom, and perceive that their culture is archaic. Further, these views may lead European Americans to view Natives negatively and unfairly discriminate against them in the employment process. Even though these arguments are reasonable, we know of no empirical research that has assessed the consequences of viewing Native culture as superstitious or primitive on unfair discrimination in organizations. Thus, we propose the following hypothesis to guide research.

H12: When Natives' beliefs about science are consistent with the dominant groups' views that science is the only way of knowing, then Natives will (a) be stereotyped more negatively, (b) experience more unfair discrimination, and will be less likely to be (c) hired (d) assigned to high level jobs, (e) promoted, (f) mentored, or (g) included in work groups more than those whose beliefs are consistent with the dominant group's opinions.

European Americans' Communication Style. On average, members of the dominant culture in the U.S. emphasize that people should use a direct communication style and be assertive when talking with others so that they can gain attention and power (Kochman, 1981). Members of the culture are not typically comfortable with silence, and often fill those moments with idle comments about the weather or sports (Kochman, 1981). Overall, the dominant communication style is informal, linear, relies on logic, and views those who use emotion or communicate with excitement as weak willed (Kaplan, 1966; Stewart & Bennett, 1991). Further, when members of non-dominant groups use an indirect or quiet communication style they may be perceived as disinterested or uninvolved in the discussion even though they may be very passionate about a topic (Kaplan, 1966).

Natives' Communication Style. In contrast to European Americans, research has shown that Natives have a very restrained and indirect communication style (Kochman, 1970; Locust, 1988). Their indirect style gives them a chance to evade a question that is too personal or refuse a request without offending another person (Darnell, 1998). Natives also use long periods of silence in their communication patterns, and European Americans are extremely uncomfortable and suspicious of silence (Kochman, 1970). As a consequence, European Americans often misinterpret the meaning of Native's silence as lack of intelligence or disinterest in a topic (Basso, 1970). However, Native culture dictates that people should be quiet or silent, and unemotional when speaking with others even when they are very passionate about a topic (Elliott, 1992). Further, research has shown that Native culture specifies that people should not look others directly in the eyes because such behavior is rude or disrespectful (Kochman, 1970).

Given that European Americans and Natives have very different communication styles, and norms (e.g., silence, avoiding eye contact), members of the dominant culture may develop very negative views about Natives when communicating with them. For example, they may misconstrue Native's silence and unemotional language as disinterest in a topic and perceive that the lack of direct eye contact is a sign that they are sneaky or dishonest. As a result, they are likely to view Natives negatively and discriminate against them in the employment process. We are not aware of any empirical research on this issue, so we make the following prediction to guide future research.

H13: When Natives use an indirect communication style that involves long periods of silence and unemotional language, they will (a) be stereotyped more negatively, (b) experience more unfair discrimination, and will be less likely to be (c) hired (d) assigned to high level jobs, (e) mentored, or (f) included in work groups than when they use a more European American communication style (e.g., direct, assertive communication style).

European American Values: High Emphasis on Materialism. Research has shown that European Americans place a great deal of importance on materialism and acquiring wealth and possessions (Trice & Beyer, 1993). Materialism is often defined as a set of values and goals that focus on wealth, products, brands, image, and status (Kasser, 2016). Weber (1958) argued that Europeans and European Americans value materialism because their Protestant heritage stresses that those with a great deal of wealth are prized in the eyes of God.

Psychological research has also revealed that highly materialistic people believe that owning and buying things are a necessary means of achieving important life goals such as such as happiness, success, and self-fulfillment (Meyers, 2000). Other studies have shown that people use materialism as a way of conveying impressions that they are successful (Kasser, 2016), and, in some cases, they use purchases to manage the impression that they emphasize socially valued outcomes (e.g., they purchase Teslas or Toms shoes to show that they are socially conscious) (Kasser, 2016; Meyers, 2000). Other studies revealed that people are materialistic in order to adapt or cope with anxiety-provoking life situations (e.g., insecurity, death, difficult family relationships) (Kasser, 2016). Still other research found that highly materialistic people care more about building relationships with things than people (Meyers, 2000).

Social researchers also argue that materialism is the primary cause of many of our problems in the U.S., and often results in lower levels of well-being and higher levels of physical and mental health challenges (Jaworski, 2016). Jaworski (2016) also argues that the problem is that people in the U.S. have equated happiness with purchasing new products, and the satisfaction from purchasing things only lasts a very short period of time. Then, they become unhappy again, and this generates a desire for new things (Jaworski, 2016).

Natives' Values: Low Emphasis on Materialism. Natives, on average, are less likely to value materialism than European Americans, and many are suspicious of individuals who collect large numbers of material possessions

(Aldern, 2010). Some tribes even have ceremonies where members give most of their possessions away, and other tribes burn all of a deceased person's money at a funeral to show that money has no significance in life or death (Aldern, 2010). Natives also value generosity, balance, and prefer giving than receiving gifts. For example, Natives who dance at pow-wows often give members of the audience small tokens of their appreciation for attending the event. Further, Natives do not believe in saving money if others need it right now (Aldern, 2010). Apart from these values, they place a great deal of importance on reciprocity which means that when they receive a gift, they believe it is rude not to give one in return (Yan, 2005).

One result of the differences in values regarding materialism between Natives and European Americans is that the dominant group may view Native culture as underdeveloped because they do not believe in acquiring material possessions or wealth. The primary reason for this is that European Americans believe that individuals should maximize their personal wealth in order to survive, be happy, and lead a good life. One of the authors' colleagues relates a story of Native workers who were supposed to work for a week, but only came to work Monday through Wednesday because they thought they made enough money in three days, and did not need to work anymore (Stone-Romero, personal communication, 2021). In view of European American's emphasis on materialism, they use monetary reward systems to motivate people in organizations, but these types of rewards may not be as motivating for Natives as much as their counterparts. As a result, the dominant group may view Natives negatively because they expect them to have lower levels of performance in organizations than others. As a result, they may discriminate against or exclude them in the employment process.

Although we believe that these arguments are reasonable, we know of no empirical research that has examined the degree to which differences in cultural values regarding materialism affect ratings of Natives or unfair discrimination against them in the employment process. Therefore, we propose the following hypothesis:

H14: When Natives' cultural values regarding materialistic wealth are not consistent with the dominant groups' standards, they will (a) be stereotyped more negatively, (b) experience more unfair discrimination, and will be less likely to be (c) hired (d) assigned to high level jobs, (e) mentored, or (f) included in work groups more than those whose values are consistent with the dominant groups' values.

European American Values: Control Over the Environment and Animals. In the U.S. society, members of the dominant group believe that people should control the environment and use environmental resources and animals to reduce their workload or enhance their personal wealth (e.g., profit from the use of fossil fuels, cattle). There is also a belief that humans are superior to animals, and they should have power over them (Austin & Flynn, 2015). As a result, animals in U.S. society are expected to serve the utilitarian needs of people, and have been used as a source of food, transportation, leather, clothing, and hard labor. Until recently, there has also been little concern for the environment which has led to life-threatening problems associated with climate change. Despite these problems, the dominant U.S. culture is still clinging to their views about using and exploiting the environment for personal gain, and they often view Native culture as substandard because they do not share the European American value system (Wilson, 1998).

Natives' Values: Show Respect and Care for the Environment and Animals. Even though European Americans believe that people should use the environment and animals for their benefit, Natives stress that people should respect and care for the environment and animals (Booth, 2003). They also believe in the interrelatedness of the environment and all living beings (humans and nonhumans) (James, 2006), and feel that there should be strong bonds between the well-being of nonhumans, humans, and the environment (James, 2006). Natives also value a reciprocal relationship with nature which permeates every aspect of their lives, and they believe that the land is not really a separate place, nor a means of survival, but it is part of their being (Allen, 1979, as cited in Booth, 2003).

In view of the extreme differences between the dominant culture's views about the environment and those of Natives, European Americans may view Natives as foolhardy or unintelligent because they do not use the environment and animals to enhance their wealth. As a result, they are likely to view Native culture as primitive which may lead to unfavorable views about Natives and unfair discrimination against them in the employment process. Although these arguments are reasonable, we know of no empirical research that has examined the degree to which differences in cultural values about the environment and animals affect reactions to Natives and unfair discrimination against them in organizations. There, we offer the following predictions to guide future research.

H15: When Natives' beliefs about the environment and animals are inconsistent with European Americans' beliefs that the environment and animals should be used to enhance personal wealth, they will (a) be stereotyped more negatively, (b) experience more unfair discrimination, and will be less likely to be (c) hired (d) assigned to high level jobs, (e) promoted, (f) mentored, or (g) included in work groups than when their beliefs are consistent with the dominant group's views.

In summary, we based our model on the theories of social cognition, social categorization, and cultural racism. Taken together these theories predicted that Natives are often discriminated against in organizations because most of the stereotypes and views about their culture are negative. Further, our model argued that Natives may experience unfair discrimination in organizations because ingroups denigrate them in order to enhance their own self-esteem or boost the image of their own group. Finally, based on the model of cultural racism, our model argued that Natives may experience unfair discrimination in organizations because their cultural values do not live up to the dominant cultural values in the society. Although we believe that these predictions are plausible, research is needed to examine the relations in the model before generalizations are made. Thus, we offered hypotheses to guide future research on the issues.

Although research on these issues is clearly important, we also believe that our model has important implications for practice in organizations. Thus, we consider these implications in the section below.

IMPLICATIONS FOR PRACTICE

We believe that a greater understanding of the bases for unfair discrimination against Natives has important implication for setting policies and designing HR practices in organizations. Thus, we consider some of the organizational mechanisms that might be used to overcome unfair discrimination against them in organizations.

Mechanism 1: Decreasing Negative and Unfounded Stereotypes About Natives

Our model predicts that one of the primary reasons that Natives are discriminated against in organizations is that they are categorized and stereotyped negatively in the employment process. Thus, we believe that organizations should develop mechanisms for overcoming and eliminating unfounded stereotypes about them. We believe that this would enable decision-makers to develop accurate perceptions about the knowledge, skills, and abilities of Natives which should have a positive impact on employment decisions about them.

Consistent with previous models (e.g., Porter et al., 1975; Stone & Colella, 1996; Stone et al., 2020; Stone et al., 1992), we believe that organizations might use a number of mechanisms to modify inaccurate stereotypes about Natives. For example, they might use training programs to make decision makers aware of their stereotypes and show them that their beliefs about Natives are erroneous. Further, they might increase personal contact between Natives and others so that employees can gather individuating information about Natives and see that they are actually highly motivated skilled individuals. Contact can be increased through assignments to formal work groups, affinity groups, or participation in social events that allow all employees to get to know Natives. Another method for overcoming negative stereotypes about Natives is to publicize their special contributions to organizations and show how they have been successful in their jobs. Although we fully expect that these mechanisms will modify negative beliefs about Natives, additional research is needed to examine their effectiveness.

Mechanism 2: Decreasing the Degree to Which Dominant Group Members Denigrate Natives

Our model also predicts that dominant group members denigrate Natives and other nondominant groups in order to enhance their self-esteem and social identity. As diversity has increased in organizations, there has also been a rise in rude, abusive, racist, and bullying behaviors among employees (Kabat-Farr &Labelle-Deraspe, 2021). Many of these behaviors are targeted toward outgroup members, and have created numerous problems including decreased productivity, loss of top talent, and a decrease in satisfaction and motivation among some employees (Dipboye & Colella, 2005). As a result, when dominant group members attempt to bolster their self-esteem by putting others down, they are creating a climate of hostility and intimidation for Natives and others in organizations.

Thus, we believe that organizations need to take steps to prevent dominant group members from disparaging Natives and others. One mechanism for doing this is to hold them accountable for inappropriate behavior and comments about outgroup members (Cox, 1993). Along with increased accountability, organizations should also require that all employees undergo civility training to ensure that they do not harm or defame others. Such training should explain the standards that organizations use to evaluate incivility in organizations and highlight the rewards and penalties that organizations use to encourage appropriate behavior (Walsh & Magley, 2020). In addition, organizations might create "ally" systems that allow others to be an ally or report abusive or disparaging behaviors and comments about individuals (Collins et al., 2021). One reason for such a system is that people may be reluctant to report supervisors who have maligned them or other individuals who have defamed them, but allies may be more comfortable reporting harmful behaviors.

We also believe that individuals or groups should be encouraged to base their social identity and self-esteem on their contributions and accomplishments in organizations rather than the vilification of out-group members. As a result, we maintain that organizations should use more recognition and reward systems to praise employees and decrease the extent to which their self-esteem is based on disparaging comments by others. Although we believe that training, holding people accountable, and increasing the use of recognition systems may be effective mechanisms for decreasing the vilification of outgroup members, we also believe that research is needed to test the effectiveness of these strategies.

Mechanism 3: Decreasing Degree to Which Dominant Groups Set the Standards in Organizations

Our model predicts that a third mechanism that might be used to decrease unfair discrimination in organizations is to ensure that organizational standards are set by a diverse group of members not just the dominant group. As noted above, we believe that Natives are discriminated against in organizations because they do not live up to the norms, values, and standards set by the European American dominant group. For instance, in the typical U.S. organization, European Americans set the standards based on their own cultural values and expect others to live up to their norms about dress, hairstyle, language, custom, religion, and behavior. These requirements incorporate an inherent hostility toward those who are different or do not meet European American standards (Giroux, 2006). Giroux (2006) argued that the societal culture in the U.S. reflects a culturally racist stance that treats European American culture as normative, and encourages cultural assimilation to the dominant (i.e., superior) culture.

One way to decrease the extent to which the dominant group sets the standards in organizations is to make sure that there are diverse group members at all levels in organizations. For example, all managerial teams should include members of diverse groups so that they help set the goals and behavioral standards for the organization (Herdman & McMillan-Capehart, 2010). Further, all HR policymaking teams should include a diverse set of viewpoints and values. The primary reason for this is that the current policies may seem to be neutral, but they often have a disproportionately negative effect on members of diverse groups. For example, those who develop HR policies typically set performance standards, and require that employees have "an appropriate work appearance." As a result, they set requirements for employee grooming, dress, language, and accommodations for disabilities or religious observances. If these policies are developed by a diverse set of people in organizations, they are more likely to consider differences in hairstyles, dress, language, and religious observances than if they are developed only by European Americans.

For instance, many U. S. organizations provide time off for Christian religious observances (e.g., Christmas) because that is the primary religion of the dominant European American group. However, if HR policymaking teams include diverse members, they are more likely to provide time off for all types of religious observances not just Christian observances (e.g., Native religious celebrations, feast days, and dances, Jewish high holy days, and Muslim holy days and observances). Similarly, current policies regarding hairstyles are based on European American standards about hairstyles and hair lengths (e.g., hair should be short and straight), and ethnic minorities are required to conform to these standards. However, many ethnic group members, including Natives, wear their hair longer or have different hair types or hairstyles than European Americans. Thus, the current hairstyle standards are likely to have a negative impact on members of these groups. Given that this is a pervasive problem in organizations, a number of states and cities have passed laws prohibiting race-based hair discrimination (e.g., California, New York, New Jersey, Michigan, Wisconsin, Illinois and Kentucky as well as Cincinnati, Ohio, and Montgomery County, Maryland).

In the section above, we provided two examples of how European American standards put Natives and other ethnic group members at a disadvantage in organizations. As a result, we believe that including Natives and other diverse members on policymaking committees may decrease these problems. Even though these suggestions seem plausible, research is needed to determine their effectiveness, and we offer the following hypothesis to guide research.

H16: When organizations with diverse members, including Natives, establish policies and practices they will (a) decrease unfair discrimination against Natives, and (b) enhance the inclusion of Natives and all diverse group members.

In summary, although there may be a variety of mechanisms that can be used to decrease unfair discrimination and enhance the inclusion of Natives in organizations, we highlighted three specific mechanisms that are likely to meet these goals. First, we argued that overcoming negative stereotypes about Natives and ensuring that decision-makers have an accurate perception of their skills and abilities may decrease unfair discrimination. In particular, we maintained that the (a) use of training programs, (b) increasing personal contact with Natives in work and social groups, and (c) publicizing their many successes in organizations should help overcome unfounded negative perceptions about these individuals. Second, we argued that organizations might decrease unfair discrimination against Natives by holding people accountable for their disparaging statements and behaviors that expose these individuals to ridicule or unfairly harms their reputations (Cox, 1993). Third, our model predicted that another mechanism that might be used to decrease unfair discrimination is to ensure that organizational standards are set by a diverse group of members not just the dominant group. In order to achieve this goal, we believe that organizations should include diverse members on all policymaking committees and ensure that they have a voice in establishing performance and other standards (e.g., grooming, hairstyle, dress, language, religious accommodations).

CONCLUSION

Natives are a truly a forgotten minority and are almost invisible in U.S. society. They also have numerous problems gaining and maintaining employment which leads to high poverty and unemployment rates, housing and food insecurity, and numerous health-related problems (e.g., diabetes, stress, liver disease, alcoholism, and mental illness). Despite these serious problems, little research in the social sciences (e.g., organizational behavior, human resource management, psychology, sociology) has examined the reasons for the unfair discrimination and exclusion of Natives in work organizations. Thus, we proposed a model of the factors that are likely to affect unfair discrimination against these individuals.

Our model was based on an integration of theories of social cognition, social categorization, and cultural racism, and suggested that unfair discrimination against Natives stems from multiple sources. One source is that Natives are often stereotyped as lazy, unintelligent, dishonest, addicted to alcohol, or criminals, and these negative stereotypes influence job related expectancies about them. Further, our model suggests that individuals are typically assigned to ingroups and outgroups based on their culture, social achievements (e.g., occupations, wealth attainment), power, and social status, and so forth. Given that Natives have relatively low social status and social power in our society they are likely to be assigned to nondominant outgroups, and European Americans are typically assigned to the dominant ingroup because they have high levels of social status and power.

Further, our model argues that once individuals are assigned to ingroups and outgroups, there is a comparison of these two social groups. The comparison of the social groups determines how group members are treated, and often results in intergroup bias. Intergroup bias refers to "the systematic tendency to evaluate one's [ingroup] or its members more favorably than [an outgroup] or its members" (Hewstone et al., 2002, p. 576). Further, intergroup bias typically results in unfair discrimination against outgroup members.

The model also predicts that the social comparison of ingroup and outgroup cultures results in unfair discrimination because the dominant ingroup is viewed as superior to the outgroup, and outgroup members that do not live up to the values and standards set up by the dominant group are viewed as inferior. As a result, members of the outgroup are viewed as substandard, and discriminated against in organizations. Given that Native people do not typically share the cultural values of the dominant European American group, then their culture is likely to be regarded as culturally backward or primitive by members of the dominant culture, and these perceptions affect unfair discrimination in organizations.

Despite the predictions in the model, little research has examined the effects of the factors just noted on unfair discrimination against Natives in organizations. Thus, we offered a number of specific hypotheses to examine the relations noted in our model. We also suggested a number of practical strategies that might be used to overcome unfair discrimination against Natives and increase their inclusion in organizations. It is our hope that this chapter provides a greater understanding of the reasons Natives are excluded in organizations, and helps organizations decrease the biases against them. We also hope that it will help organizations utilize the many skills and talents that they bring to the workforce, and enable Natives to decrease their unemployment, poverty, and health-related challenges.

REFERENCES

Access Genealogy. (n.d.). *Native American history and genealogy.* Retrieved April 1, 2021, from https://accessgenealogy.com/native-american

Al-Asfour, A., Tlaiss, H. A., & Shield, S. W. (2021). Work experiences of Native Americans: A qualitative study. *Journal of Career Development, 48*(2), 105–119.

Aldern, J. D. (2010). *Native sustainment: The north fork mono tribe's stories, history, and teaching of its land and water tenure in 1918 and 2009.* Prescott College.

Allen, T. D. (2001). Family-supportive work environments: The role of organizational perceptions. *Journal of Vocational Behavior, 58*(3), 414–435.

American Indian Affairs. (2021). *Indigenous people and violence.* Retrieved April 3, 2021, from https://www.indian-affairs.org/indigenous-peoples-and-violence.html

American Psychological Association. (2021). *Ethnicity and health in America series: Obesity in the Native American community.* Retrieved April 5, 2021, from https://www.apa.org/pi/oema/resources/ethnicity-health/native-american/obesity

Angermeyer, M. C., & Matschinger, H. (2004). The stereotype of schizophrenia and its impact on discrimination against people with schizophrenia: results from a representative survey in Germany. *Schizophrenia Bulletin, 30*(4), 1049–1061.

Ashmore, R. D., & Del Boca, F. K. (1981). Conceptual approaches to stereotypes and stereotyping. In D. L. Hamilton (Ed.), *Cognitive processes in stereotyping and intergroup behavior* (pp. 1–35). Hillsdale, NJ: Erlbaum.

Attneave, C. (1982). American Indians and Alaska Native families: Emigrants in their own homeland. In M. McGoldrick, J. Pearce, & J. Giordano (Eds.), *Ethnicity and family therapy* (pp. 55–83). Guilford Press.

Austin, R. L., & Flynn, C. P. (2015). Traversing the gap between religion and animal rights: Framing and networks as a conceptual bridge. *Journal of Animal Ethics*, *5*(2), 144–158.

Balibar, É. (2008). Racism revisited: Sources, relevance, and aporias of a modern concept. *PMLA/Publications of the Modern Language Association of America*, *123*(5), 1630–1639.

Barker, M. (1979). Racism—The new inheritors. *Radical Philosophy*, *21*, 2–17.

Barker, M. (1981). *The new racism.* Junction Books.

Bar-Tal, D. (1990). Causes and consequences of delegitimization: Models of conflict and ethnocentrism. *Journal of Social Issues*, *46*(1), 65–81.

Basso, K. H. (1970). "To give up on words": Silence in western Apache culture. *Southwestern Journal of Anthropology, 26 (3)*, 213–230.

Bell, R. (2013). The great jugular vein of slavery: New histories of the domestic slave trade. *History Compass*, *11*(12), 1150–1164.

Betancourt, H., & López, S. R. (1993). The study of culture, ethnicity, and race in American psychology. *American Psychologist*, *48*(6), 629–637.

Black, S. L., & Kennedy, D. M. (2019). Supply Chain Management and Native American Entrepreneurs. In R. J. Miller, M. Jorgensen, & D. Stewart (Eds.), *Creating Private Sector Economies in Native America: Sustainable Development through Entrepreneurship* (pp. 170–184). Cambridge University Press.

Boje, D. M., & Boje, D. M. (2001). *Narrative methods for organizational & communication research.* SAGE.

Booth, A. L. (2003). We are the land: Native American views of nature. In H. Selin (Ed.), *Nature across cultures: views of nature and the environment in non-western cultures* (pp. 329–349). Kluwer.

Brewer, M. B. (2008). Social identity complexity and outgroup acceptance. In U. Wagner, L. R. Tropp, G. Finchilescu, & C. Tredoux (Eds.), *Improving intergroup relations: Building on the legacy of Thomas F. Pettigrew* (pp. 160–176). Blackwell.

Bureau of Labor Statistics. (2019). *American Indians and Alaska Natives in the U.S. labor force.* Retrieved April 5, 2021, from https://www.bls.gov/opub/mlr/2019/article/american-indians-and-alaska-natives-in-the-u-s-labor-force.htm

Burk, N. M. (2007). Conceptualizing American Indian/Alaska Native college students' classroom experiences: Negotiating cultural identity between faculty and students. *Journal of American Indian Education*, *46*, 1–18.

Cascio, W. F., & Aguinis, H. (2005). *Applied psychology in human resource management.* Prentice Hall.

Center for Disease Control and Prevention [CDC]. (2020). *Adult obesity facts.* Retrieved April 15, 2021, from https://www.cdc.gov/obesity/data/adult.html

Chen, H. Y., Robinson, J. K., & Jablonski, N. G. (2020). A Cross-cultural exploration on the psychological aspects of skin color aesthetics: implications for sun-related behavior. *Translational Behavioral Medicine*, *10*(1), 234–243.

Cheng, C., & Thatchenkery, T. J. (1997). Why is there a lack of workplace diversity research on Asian Americans? *Journal of Applied Behavioral Science, 33,* 270–276.

Chief Dan George. (n.d.). *Chief Dan George quotes and sayings.* Retrieved from February 15, 2021, from https://www.inspiringquotes.us/author/3730-chief-dan-george

Chu, F., & Ohinmaa, A. (2016). The obesity penalty in the labor market using longitudinal Canadian data. *Economics & Human Biology, 23,* 10–17.

Collins, J. C., Zhang, P., & Sisco, S. (2021). Everyone is invited: Leveraging bystander intervention and ally development to cultivate social justice in the workplace. *Human Resource Development Review, 20*(4), 486–511.

Cox, T. H. (1993). *Cultural diversity in organizations: Theory, research, and practice.* Berrett-Koehler.

Darnell, R. (1988). *Implications of Cree interactional etiquette* [Unpublished Master's thesis]. University of Alberta.

Dijker, A. J., & Koomen, W. (2003). Extending Weiner's attribution-emotion model of stigmatization of ill persons. *Basic and Applied Social Psychology, 25*(1), 51–68.

Dipboye, R. L., & Colella, A. (2005). The dilemmas of workplace discrimination. In B. Dipboye & A. Colella (Eds.), *Discrimination at work: The psychological and organizational bases* (pp. 425–462). Erlbaum.

Dixon, T. (2020). Media stereotypes: Content, effects, and theory. In M.B. Oliver, A. A. Raney, J. Bryant (Eds.) *Media effects: Advances in theory and research* (4th ed., pp. 243–257) Routledge.

Dovidio, J. F., & Gaertner, S. L. (1986). *Prejudice, discrimination, and racism.* Academic Press.

Dvorakova, A. (2019). Identity in heterogeneous socio-cultural contexts: Implications of the Native American master narrative. *Culture & Psychology,* 1–22.

Education World. (2020). *Reporters' notebook: Native Americans struggle, build pride.* Retrieved March 1, 2021, from https://educationworld.com/a_issues/school/schools012.shtml

Elliott, J. H. (1992). *The old world and the new: 1492–1650.* Cambridge University Press.

Equal Employment Opportunity Commission. (2020). *American Indians and Alaskan Natives in the American workforce.* Retrieved February 10, 2021, from https://www.eeoc.gov/special-report/american-indians-and-alaskan-natives-american-workforce

Findling, M. G., Casey, L. S., Fryberg, S. A., Hafner, S., Blendon, R. J., Benson, J. M., Sayde, J. M., & Miller, C. (2019). Discrimination in the United States: Experiences of Native Americans. *Health Services Research, 54,* 1431–1441.

Fleming, W. C. (2006). Myths and stereotypes about Native Americans. *Phi Delta Kappan, 88*(3), 213–217.

Flint, S. W., Čadek, M., Codreanu, S. C., Ivić, V., Zomer, C., & Gomoiu, A. (2016). Obesity discrimination in the recruitment process: "You're not hired!" *Frontiers in Psychology, 7,* 647–657.

Garroutte, E. M. (2005). Defining "radical indigenism" and creating an American Indian scholarship. In S. Pfohl, A. Van Wagenen, P. Arend, A. Brooks, & D. Leckenby (Eds.), *Culture, power, and history: Studies in critical sociology* (pp. 169–198). Brill Academic Publishers.

Giroux, H. (2006). *America on the edge: Henry Giroux on politics, culture, and education.* Springer.

Gladstone, J. S. (2012). *Old Man and Coyote barter: An inquiry into the spirit of a Native American philosophy of business* [Unpublished doctoral dissertation]. New Mexico State University.

Gladstone, J. S. (2021). Native American transplanar wisdom: A pragmatic view and application. In A. Intezari, C. Spiller, & S. Yang (Eds.) *Practical wisdom, leadership and culture: Indigenous, Asian and Middle-Eastern perspectives* (pp. 61–77). Routledge.

Gladstone, J. S., & Pepion, D. D. (2017). Exploring traditional Indigenous leadership concepts: A spiritual foundation for Blackfeet leadership. *Leadership, 13*(5), 571–589.

Goetz, G. (2012). *Nutrition a pressing concern for American Indians.* Retrieved April 2, 2021, from https://www.foodsafetynews.com/2012/03/nutrition-a-pressing-concern-for-american-indians/

Goffman, E. (1963). *Stigma: Notes on the Management of Spoiled Identity.* Prentice-Hall

Green, M. K. (1993). Images of American Indians in advertising: Some moral issues. *Journal of Business Ethics, 12,* 323–330.

Guerrero, L., & Posthuma, R. A. (2014). Perceptions and behaviors of Hispanic workers: A review. *Journal of Managerial Psychology, 29*(6), 3–30.

Hain-Jamall, D. A. (2013). Native-American & Euro-American cultures: A comparative look at the intersection between language & worldview. *Multicultural Education, 21*(1), 13–19.

Hanson, J. R., & Rouse, L. P. (1987). Dimensions of Native American stereotyping. *American Indian Culture and Research Journal, 11*(4), 33–58.

Henry, J., & Kollamparambil, U. (2017). Obesity-based labour market discrimination in South Africa: a dynamic panel analysis. *Journal of Public Health, 25*(6), 671–684.

Herdman, A. O., & McMillan-Capehart, A. (2010). Establishing a diversity program is not enough: Exploring the determinants of diversity climate. *Journal of Business and Psychology, 25*(1), 39–53.

Hersch, J. (2011). The persistence of skin color discrimination for immigrants. *Social Science Research, 40*(5), 1337–1349.

Hewstone, M., Rubin, M., & Willis, H. (2002). Intergroup bias. *Annual Review of Psychology, 53*(1), 575–604.

Higgins, E. T., & Bargh, J. A. (1987). Social cognition and social perception. *Annual Review of Psychology, 38*(1), 369–425.

Hiilamo, A., Lallukka, T., Mänty, M., & Kouvonen, A. (2017). Obesity and socioeconomic disadvantage in midlife female public sector employees: A cohort study. *BMC Public Health, 17*(1), 1–10.

Hinton, L., Guo, Z., Hillygus, J., & Levkofl,.S. (2000). Working with culture: A qualitative analysis of barriers to the recruitment of Chinese-American family caregivers for dementia research. *Journal of Cross-Cultural Gerontology, 15,* 119–137.

Hochschild, J. (2006). When do people not protest unfairness? The case of skin color discrimination. *Social Research, 73,* 473–498.

Hosoda, M., Stone-Romero, E. F., & Coats, G. (2003). The effects of physical attractiveness on job-related outcomes: A meta-analysis of experimental studies. *Personnel Psychology, 56*(2), 431–462.

Hutchison, P., & Abrams, D. (2003). Ingroup identification moderates stereotype change in reaction to ingroup deviance. *European Journal of Social Psychology, 33*(4), 497–506.

Indian Health Services (2019). *Disparities.* Retrieved February 22, 2021, from https://www.ihs.gov/newsroom/factsheets/disparities/

Intel.gov. (2021). *1942: Navajo code talkers: Inventors of unbreakable code.* Retrieved March 2, 2021, from https://www.intelligence.gov/index.php/people/barrier-breakers-in-history/453-navajo-code-talkers

James, K. (2006). Identity, cultural values, and American Indians' perceptions of science and technology. *American Indian Culture and Research Journal, 30,* 45–58.

James, K., Wolf. W., Lovato, C., & Byers, S. (1994). *Barriers to workplace advancement experienced by Native Americans.* Retrieved April 10, 2021, from http://digitalcommons.ilr.cornell.edu/key_workplace/123

Jaworski, K. (2016). *The gender of suicide: knowledge production, theory and suicidology.* Routledge.

Jeung, D. Y., Kim, C., & Chang, S. J. (2018). Emotional labor and burnout: A review of the literature. *Yonsei Medical Journal, 59*(2), 187–193.

Jones, E. E., Farina, A, Hastorf, A. H., Markus, H., Miller, D. T., Scott, R. A., & French, R. (1984). *Social stigma: The psychology of marked relationships.* Freeman.

Josephy, A. M. (1968). *The Indian heritage of America.* Houghton Mifflin Harcourt.

Judge, T. A., & Cable, D. M. (2011). When it comes to pay, do the thin win? The effect of weight on pay for men and women. *Journal of Applied Psychology, 96*(1), 95–112.

Kabat-Farr, D., & Labelle-Deraspe, R. (2021). *5 Ways to reduce rudeness in the remote workplace.* Retrieved April 22, 2021, from https://hbr.org/2021/08/5-ways-to-reduce-rudeness-in-the-remote-workplace

Kaiser, C. R., & Pratt-Hyatt, J. S. (2009). Distributing prejudice unequally: Do Whites direct their prejudice toward strongly identified minorities. *Journal of Personality and Social Psychology, 96*(2), 432–445.

Kaplan, R. B. (1966). Cultural thought patterns in intercultural education. *Language Learning, 16*(1), 1–20.

Kasser, T. (2016). Materialistic values and goals. *Annual Review of Psychology, 67,* 489–514.

Katsaiti, M. S., & Shamsuddin, M. (2016). Weight discrimination in the German labour market. *Applied Economics, 48*(43), 4167–4182.

Katz, D., & Kahn, R.L. (1966). *The social psychology of organizations.* Wiley.

Kennedy, D. M., Harrington, C. F., Verbos, A. K., Stewart, D., Gladstone, J. S., & Clarkson, G. (Eds.). (2017). *American Indian business: Principles and practices*. University of Washington Press.

Kiger, P. K. (2019). 10 *Native American inventions commonly used today*. Retrieved March 10, 2021, from https://www.history.com/news/native-american-inventions

Kochman, T. (1970). *Cross-cultural communication: Contrasting perspectives, conflicting sensibilities*. Educational Resources Information Center.

Kochman, T. (1981). *Black and white styles in conflict*. University of Chicago Press.

Kossek, E. E., & Lobel, A. (1996). *Managing diversity*. Blackwell.

Krueger, D. C., Stone, D. L., & Stone-Romero, E. F. (2014). Applicant, rater, and job factors related to weight-based bias. *Journal of Managerial Psychology, 29*(2), 164–186.

Kumar, A. (2021, September 9). *Hate crime against Indian Americans continue to rise: FBI*. Retrieved September 15, 2021, from https://www.americanbazaaronline.com/2021/09/09/hate-crimes-against-indian-americans-continue-to-rise-fbi-446990/

Kunz, J. L., Milan, A., & Schetagne, S. (2000). *Unequal access: A Canadian profile of racial differences in education, employment, and income*. Canadian Race Relations Foundation.

Lalonde, R. N., Taylor, D. M., & Moghaddam, F. M. (1992). The process of social identification for visible immigrant women in a multicultural context. *Journal of Cross-Cultural Psychology, 23*(1), 25–39.

Laxson, J. D. (1991). How "we" see "them" tourism and Native Americans. *Annals of Tourism Research, 18*(3), 365–391.

Lee, T. L., & Fiske, S. T. (2006). Not an outgroup, not yet an ingroup: Immigrants in the stereotype content model. *International Journal of Intercultural Relations, 30*(6), 751–768.

Lee, W. S., & Zhao, Z. (2017). Height, weight and well-being for rural, urban and migrant workers in China. *Social Indicators Research, 132*(1), 117–136.

Lindeman, M. I., Crandall, A. K., & Finkelstein, L. M. (2017). The effects of messages about the causes of obesity on disciplinary action decisions for overweight employees. *The Journal of Psychology, 151*(4), 345–358.

Locust, C. (1988). Wounding the spirit: Discrimination and traditional American Indian belief systems. *Harvard Educational Review, 58 (3)*, 315–331.

Macrae, C. N., & Bodenhausen, G. V. (2000). Social cognition: Thinking categorically about others. *Annual Review of Psychology, 51*(1), 93–120.

Maddox, K. B., & Gray, S. A. (2002). Cognitive representations of Black Americans: Reexploring the role of skin tone. *Personality and Social Psychology Bulletin, 28*(2), 250–259.

Merskin, D. (2001). Winnebagos, Cherokees, Apaches, and Dakotas: The persistence of stereotyping of American Indians in American advertising brands. *Howard Journal of Communication, 12*(3), 159–169.

Mexico Daily Post. (2020). *Spain promoted mixed marriages with indigenous people 500 years before it was legal in the USA*. Retrieved February 24, 2021, from https://mexicodailypost.com/2020/07/10/spain-promoted-mixed-marriages-with-indigenous-people-500-years-before-it-was-legal-in-the-usa/

Meyers, A. R. (2000). From function to felicitude: Physical disability and the search for happiness in health services research. *American Journal on Mental Retardation*, *105*(5), 342–351.

Mihesuah, D. A. (1996). Commonalty of difference: American Indian women and history. *American Indian Quarterly*, *20*(1), 15–27.

Miller N., & Brewer, M. B. (1984). *Groups in contact: The psychology of desegregation.* Academic Press.

Moreno, M. A. (2019). America's forgotten minority: Indigenous youth perspectives on the challenges related to healthcare access, widespread poverty and public misinformation regarding native Americans. In E. Stamatopoulou, D. Angel, V. Lopez-Carmen (Eds.), *Global indigenous youth: Through their eyes* (pp 185–214). Columbia University.

Muhammad, D. A. (2019). *Racial wealth snapshot: American Indians/Native Americans.* Retrieved February 1, 2021, from https://ncrc.org/racial-wealth-snapshot-american-indians-native-americans/

Muller, H. J. (1998). American Indian women managers: Living in two worlds. *Journal of Management Inquiry*, *7*(1), 4–28.

National Humanities Center. (n.d). *Becoming American: The British Atlantic colonies, 1690–1763.* Retrieved April 1, 2021, from http://nationalhumanitiescenter.org/pds/becomingamer/peoples/text3/indianscolonists.pdf

National Public Radio. (2017, November 14). *Poll: Native Americans see far more discrimination in areas where they are a majority.* Retrieved January 22, 2021, from https://www.npr.org/2017/11/14/563306555/poll-native-americans-see-far-more-discrimination-in-areas-where-they-are-a-majo

Operario, D., & Fiske, S. T. (2001). Ethnic identity moderates' perceptions of prejudice: Judgments of personal versus group discrimination and subtle versus blatant bias. *Personality and Social Psychology Bulletin*, *27*(5), 550–561.

Ortiz, V., & Telles, E. (2012). Racial identity and racial treatment of Mexican Americans. *Race and Social Problems*, *4*(1), 41–56.

Peffley, M., & Hurwitz, J. (1998). Whites' stereotypes of Blacks: Sources and political consequences. In J. Hurwitz & M. Peffley (Eds.), *Perception and prejudice: Race and politics in the United States.* Yale University Press.

Peterson, G., & Duncan, R. (2001). American Indian representation in the 20th and 21st Centuries. In C. Menifield (Ed.), *Representation of minority groups in the U.S.* (pp. 111–126). Austin & Winfield.

Pewewardy, C. (2002). Learning styles of American Indian/Alaska Native students: A review of the literature and implications for practice. *Journal of American Indian Education*, *41*(3), 22–56.

Pewewardy, C. (2008). *Identity and names: We must define ourselves to escape linguistic imperialism.* Retrieved April 22, 2021, from https://tribalcollegejournal.org/19-3-beyond-names-uncovering-identity-resource-guide/

Porter, L. W., Lawler, E. E., & Hackman, J. R. (1975). *Behavior in organizations.* McGraw-Hill

Postsecondary National Policy Institute [PNPI]. (2021). *Factsheet Native American students.* Retrieved January 10, 2021, from https://pnpi.org/native-american-students/

Pruegger, V., & Kiely, J. (2002). *Perception of racism and hate activities among youth in Calgary: Effects on the lived experience.* City of Calgary Community Strategies.

Ray, B., & Preston, V. (2009). Geographies of discrimination: Variations in perceived discomfort and discrimination in Canada's gateway cities. *Journal of Immigrant & Refugee Studies, 7*(3), 228–249.

Reclaiming Native American Truth. (2018). *A project to dispel America's myths and misconceptions.* Retrieved March 1, 2021, from https://rnt.firstnations.org/

Reece, R. (2017). *By the numbers: Skin tone and racial advantage.* Retrieved March 21, 2021, from https://scalawagmagazine.org/2017/08/by-the-numbers-skin-tone-and-racial-advantage/

Roehling, M. V., Roehling, P. V., & Pichler, S. (2007). The relationship between body weight and perceived weight-related employment discrimination: The role of sex and race. *Journal of Vocational Behavior, 71*(2), 300–318.

Rudolph C. W., Baltes B. B., Zhdanova L. S., Clark M. A., & Bal A. C. (2012). Testing the structured free recall intervention for reducing the impact of bodyweight-based stereotypes on performance ratings in immediate and delayed contexts. *Journal of Business Psychology, 27,* 205–222.

Shapira, I. (2016, May 19). *A brief history of the word 'redskin' and how it became a source of controversy.* Retrieved January 11, 2021, from https://www.washingtonpost.com/local/a-brief-history-of-the-word-redskin-and-how-it-became-a-source-of-controversy/2016/05/19/062cd618-187f-11e6-9e16-2e5a123aac62_story.html

Shields, J. (2011, February). *Entering the labour market: The association of immigrant class, gender, and country of birth with employment outcomes* [Paper presentation]. Annual meeting at Local Immigrant Partnership (LIP) Conference, Toronto, Canada.

Smith, H. (2006). Introduction: The primal religions. In P. Cousineau (Ed.), *A seat at the table: Huston Smith in conversation with Native Americans on religious freedom* (pp. 1–5). University of California Press.

Stephan, W. G., & Stephan, C. W. (1985). Intergroup anxiety. *Journal of Social Issues, 41*(3), 157–175.

Stephan, W. S., & Stephan, C. W. (2013). An integrated threat theory of prejudice. In S. Oskamp (Ed.), *Reducing prejudice and discrimination* (pp. 23-46). Psychology Press.

Stewart, E. C., & Bennett, M. J. (1991). *American cultural patterns: A cross-cultural perspective.* Nicholas Brealey.

Stewart, D., Verbos, A. K., Birmingham, C., Black, S. L., & Gladstone, J. S. (2017). Being Native American in business: Culture, identity, and authentic leadership in modern American Indian enterprises. *Leadership, 13*(5), 549–570.

Stone, D. L., & Colella, A. (1996). A model of factors affecting the treatment of disabled individuals in organizations. *Academy of Management Review, 21*(2), 352–401.

Stone, D. L., Lukaszewski, K. M., Krueger, D. C., & Canedo, J. C. (2020). A model of factors thought to affect unfair discrimination against immigrants in organizations. In D. L. Stone, J. H. Dulebohn, & K. M. Lukaszewski (Eds.), *Research in human resource management: Diversity and inclusion in organizations* (pp. 331–360). Information Age Publishing.

Stone, E. F. (2005). Personality-based stigmas and unfair discrimination in work organizations. In R. Dipboye & A. Collela (Eds.), *Discrimination at work: The psychological and organizational bases* (pp. 255–280). Psychological Press.

Stone, E. F., Stone, D. L., & Dipboye, R. L. (1992). Stigmas in organizations: Race, handicaps, and physical unattractiveness. In K. Kelley (Eds.), *Advances in psychology* (Vol. 82, pp. 385–457). North-Holland.

Stone-Romero, E. F., Stone, D. L., Hartman, M., & Hosoda, M. (2020). Stereotypes of ethnic groups in terms of attributes relevant to work organizations. In D. L. Stone, J. H. Dulebohn, & K. M. Lukaszewski (Eds.), *Research in human resource management: Diversity and inclusion in organizations* (pp. 59–84). Information Age Publishing.

Stone-Romero, E. F., Stone, D. L., & Salas, E. (2003). The influence of culture on role conceptions and role behavior in organizations. *Applied Psychology, 52*(3), 328–362.

Strickland, C. (1998). Aspects of diversity, access, and community networks. In C. Ess & F. Sudweeks (Eds.), *Proceedings cultural attitudes towards communication and technology* (pp. 135–146). University of Sydney, Australia.

Stumblingbear-Riddle, G. (2018). *Standing with our sisters: MMIWG2S.* Retrieved March 15, 2021, from https://www.apa.org/pi/oema/resources/communique/2018/11/standing-sisters#:~:text=Mark%20Daines%20voiced%20in%202017,women%20aged%2025%20to%2034.

Taguieff, P. A. (2001). *The force of prejudice: on racism and its doubles* (Vol. 13). University of Minnesota Press.

Tajfel, H. (1982). Social psychology of intergroup relations. *Annual Review of Psychology, 33*(1), 1–39.

Tajfel, H., & Turner, J. C. (1979). An integrative theory of intergroup conflict. In W. Austin & S. Worchel (Eds.), *The social psychology of intergroup relations* (pp. 33–47). Brooks/Cole.

Tan, A., Fujioka, Y., & Lucht, N. (1997). Native American stereotypes, TV portrayals, and personal contact. *Journalism & Mass Communication Quarterly, 74*(2), 265–284.

Thomas, K. M., & Chrobot-Mason, D. (2005). Group-level explanations of workplace discrimination. In R. Dipboye & A. Collela (Eds.), *Discrimination at work: The psychological and organizational bases* (pp. 63–88). Psychological Press.

Timberlake, J. M., & Williams, R. H. (2012). Stereotypes of US immigrants from four global regions. *Social Science Quarterly, 93*(4), 867–890.

Triandis, H. C. (1994). *Culture and social behavior.* McGraw-Hill.

Triandis, H. C. (2001). Individualism-collectivism and personality. *Journal of Personality, 69*(6), 907–924.

Trice, H. M., & Beyer, J. M. (1993). *The cultures of work organizations.* Prentice-Hall.

Turner, J. C., Hogg, M. A., Oakes, P. J., Reicher, S. D., & Wetherell, M. S. (1987). *Rediscovering the social group: A self-categorization theory.* Basil Blackwell.

U.S. Bureau of Census. (2020). *Facts for features: American Indian and Alaska Native heritage month: November 2020.* Retrieved April 1, 2021, from https://www.census.gov/newsroom/facts-for-features/2020/aian-month.html

U.S. Department of Health and Human Services Office of Minority Health [OMH]. (2018). *Obesity and American Indians and Alaska Natives.* Retrieved April 2, 2021, from https://minorityhealth.hhs.gov/omh/browse.aspx?lvl=4&lvlid=40

Vaisvilas, F. (2021, March 17). *American Indians incarcerated at among highest rates in Wisconsin, as many as half the inmates in some jails.* Retrieved April 11, 2021, from https://www.greenbaypressgazette.com/story/news/native-american-issues/2021/03/17/native-americans-incarcerated-among-highest-rates-wisconsin/6841084002/

Verbos, A. K., Gladstone, J. S., & Kennedy, D. M. (2011). Native American values and management education: Envisioning an inclusive virtuous circle. *Journal of Management Education, 35*(1), 10–26.

Vizenor, G. (1991). *The heirs of Columbus.* Wesleyan University Press.

Volpato, C., Maass, A., Mucchi-Faina, A., & Vitti, E. (1990). Minority influence and social categorization. *European Journal of Social Psychology, 20*(2), 119–132.

Vrasidas, C. (1997). *The White man's Indian: Stereotypes in film and beyond.* Retrieved April 2, 2021, from http://files.eric.ed.gov/fulltext/ED408950.pdf

Walsh, B. M., & Magley, V. J. (2020). Workplace civility training: Understanding drivers of motivation to learn. *The International Journal of Human Resource Management, 31*(17), 2165–2187.

Weber, M. (1958). *The protestant ethic and the spirit of capitalism.* Scribner's.

Webster, Y. O. (1997). *Against the multicultural agenda: A critical thinking alternative.* Greenwood Publishing Group.

Whaley, A. L. (1991) Ethnic and racial differences in perceptions of dangerousness of persons with mental illness. *Psychiatry Services, 4,* 1328–1330.

Wilson, J. (1998). *The earth shall weep: A history of Native America.* Grove Press.

Wojnar, L. (2008). *Students face U. S. stereotypes abroad.* Retrieved March 11, 2021, from http://wesleyanargus.com/2008/10/21/ students-face-us-stereotypes-abroad/

Yamauchi, L. A. (1998). Individualism, collectivism, and cultural compatibility: Implications for counselors and teachers. *The Journal of Humanistic Education and Development, 36*(4), 189–198.

Yan, Y. (2005). The gift and gift economy. In J. Carrier (Ed.), *The handbook of economic anthropology* (pp. 246–261). Edward Elgar.

youth.gov. (2020). *Physical and mental health.* Retrieved January 30, 2021, from youth.gov/youth-topics/american-indian-alaska-native-youth/physical-mental-health

Zschirnt, E., & Ruedin, D. (2016). Ethnic discrimination in hiring decisions: A meta-analysis of correspondence tests 1990–2015. *Journal of Ethnic and Migration Studies, 42*(7), 1115–1134.

ABOUT THE AUTHORS

Julio C. Canedo, PhD, is an Associate Professor of Management at the Marilyn Davies College of Business of the University of Houston Downtown. He is certified in coaching, human resource management (HRM), and ethics. Member of academic and professional organizations like the Society for Industrial and Organizational Psychology, the Academy of Management, the Southwest Academy of Management, and the Houston Hispanic Chamber of Commerce. He published the book *The Intelligent Startup—A New Model of Coordination for Tomorrow's Leaders*. His research has been published in such outlets as *Organizational Dynamics*, the *Journal of Managerial Psychology, Research in Human Resource Management, AIS Transactions on Human-Computer Interaction*, the *Journal of Business and Entrepreneurship*, Oxford University Press, and TIP The Industrial-Organizational Psychologist. He has presented his work in conferences of the Academy of Management, the Southern Academy of Management, the Midwest Academy of Management, and the Southwest Academy of Management. Also, he has presented his work in sponsored corporate events in Latin America and provides training (pro bono) to the Houston-Galveston area members of Workforce Solutions. In addition, he serves as reviewer for *Human Resource Management Review, Human Resource Management, Research in Human Resource Management, Journal of Managerial Psychology, Psychological Reports, and Management Research*. He is member of the editorial board of *Human Resource Management Review, Research in Human Resource Management*, and the *Journal of Managerial Psychology*. Finally, he serves as Associate Editor of the *Organization Management Journal* and coeditor of *Research in Human Resource Management*.

Shannon Cheng, MA, is a PhD candidate in Industrial-Organizational Psychology at Rice University. Her research interests focus on diversity, inclusion, and well-being from a multilevel perspective—working to understand the individual-level and what challenges marginalized individuals are experiencing at work, the interpersonal-level and how people from different backgrounds can better serve as allies for each other, and the organization-level and how organizations can create more inclusive cultures and policies that support employee performance and well-being.

Henrique Correa (PhD, University of Warwick, Warwick Business School) is the Steinmetz Professor of Operations and Supply Chain Management at the Rollins College's Crummer Graduate School of Business. Professor Correa previously taught at the FGV Business School and at the University of São Paulo (both in Brazil). He has also served visiting appointments at MIP Business School, Politecnico di Milano (Italy), FIA Business School (Brazil), IPADE Business School (Mexico), Porto Business School (Portugal), the University of Warwick Business School (UK), IESA (Venezuela), IE Business School (Spain), among other institutions. His research interests include global supply chain management and flexible operations. He has published in academic journals including the *International Journal of Operations and Production Management*, *Expert Systems and Applications*, *Applied Soft Computing*, *Journal of Modeling in Management*, *International Journal of Operational Research*, *International Journal of Logistics Systems Management*, *International Journal of Logistics Economics, and Globalization,* among others. Correa has authored and coauthored 11 books and textbooks in the fields of operations strategy, service operations, operations management, and global supply chain management. He has also consulted with many multinational companies such as Unilever, Diageo, Ferrero Rocher, General Motors, 3M, Hewlett-Packard, Embraer, Brazil Foods, Natura & Co., Monsanto/ Bayer, Beiersdorf, and Pepsico.

Abby Corrington is an Assistant Professor of Management in the School of Business at Providence College. She studies diversity and inclusion in the workplace, in contexts ranging from social interactions to the hiring process. She helps provide employees, allies, organizations, and society as a whole with information and strategies that are effective at improving workplace experiences for all. She is the author of over 20 publications and her work has been featured in the *Harvard Business Review*.

Cristina Rosario DiPietropolo (DBA—Crummer Graduate School of Business, Rollins College) is the Founder and CEO of Leader Essentials Group, an executive consulting firm specializing in collaborating and executing strategies with their clients. She has extensive experience across multiple industries and is highly skilled in the areas of strategic planning and human resource management. She also has over ten years of teaching experience as a university professor specializing in Human Resource Management, Organizational Behavior, Practices of Management & Leadership in Entrepreneurship, Business Management, International Management, Strategic Planning, Productions Operations Management, and Labor-Management Relations. Cristina also has significant experience in supply chain management and logistics specializing in ocean transportation of cargo from Europe, Asia, Central, and South America into the Bahamas and Caribbean basin. Her combined U.S. and international expatriate experience conducting business in the Caribbean has given her the ability to view business from a global perspective. She earned her Doctorate in Business Administration at the Crummer Graduate School of Business, Rollins College in Winter Park, FL. Her research focused on investigating interviewer bias towards military veterans by assessing the degree to which military service experience influences hiring managers' selection decisions (either positively or negatively) in U.S. organizations.

James H. Dulebohn is a Professor of Human Resource Management at the School of Human Resource Management and Labor Relations at Michigan State University. He received his PhD in Human Resource Management and Organizational Behavior from the University of Illinois. His research focuses on leadership in organizations, virtual teams, HR metrics, electronic-human resource management, and other related issues. Results of his research have been published in the *Journal of Management, Human Resource Management Review, Journal of Applied Psychology, Personnel Psychology*, and the *Academy of Management*. He is currently the coeditor of the *Research in Human Resource Management* series and serves on the editorial boards of the *Journal of Management, Human Resource Management Review, Group and Organizational Management*, and the *Journal of Managerial Psychology*. He and his coauthors won the best paper award for their research on authentic and servant leadership in the *Journal of Management*.

Naomi Fa-Kaji is a postdoctoral researcher in the Department of Psychological Sciences at Rice University and a Rice University Academy of Fellows Junior Fellow. She received her PhD in Organizational Behavior from Stanford University. Her research examines intergroup hierarchies—particularly race and gender hierarchies—and explores the mechanisms through which social inequality is maintained, as well as the ways in which it might be reduced.

Robert C. Ford (PhD—Arizona State University) is Professor of Management Emeritus at the University of Central Florida and Visiting Professor of Management at Rollins College. Across his career, Bob has been an active contributor to the knowledge base of management, to his profession, and his community. Besides publishing several books, he has authored or coauthored over 100 refereed publications in both top research and practitioner journals. In recognition of his work in services management, he was twice awarded the W. James Whyte Visiting Research Fellowship at the University of Queensland, Australia. In service to his profession, Bob has served the Academy of Management (AOM) as editor of *The Academy of Management Executive*, Chair of both the Management History and the Management Education and Development Divisions, Chair of Placement, Chair of the Ethics Adjudication Committee, and cofounder of the Community of Academy Senior Scholars (CASS). He has also been active in the Southern Management Association (SMA), where he held every elected office, including president. In recognition of his contributions to the SMA, Bob was awarded SMA's Distinguished Service Award and elected a SMA Fellow. Most recently, he was awarded the Richard M. Hodgetts Distinguished Career Award by the Management History Division.

Cristina M. Giannantonio is a Professor of Human Resource Management in the Argyros School of Business and Economics at Chapman University. She is an Associate of the Thompson Policy Institute on Disability and Autism at Chapman University. She is the coauthor of *Autism in the Workplace Creating Positive Outcomes for Generation A* published in 2020 as part of the Palgrave Explorations in Workplace Stigma series. Dr. Giannantonio's research interests include autism in the workplace, extreme leadership, and image norms. Her research has been published in academic journals, including the *Journal of Management*, *Personnel Psychology*, and *Personnel Review*. She was the coeditor of the *Journal of Business and Management* from 2004–2016. Dr. Giannantonio and Dr. Hurley-Hanson's book *Extreme Leadership: Leaders, Teams, and Situations Outside the Norm* was published by Edward Elgar Publishing in 2014.

Amy Jane Griffiths is a licensed psychologist (PSY 24536) and a Nationally Certified School Psychologist. She obtained her doctorate in Counseling, Clinical, and School Psychology from the University of California, Santa Barbara. Dr. Griffiths is an Assistant Professor in the Attallah College of Educational Studies and a research affiliate at the Thompson Policy Institute on Disability. Prior to her work at Chapman University, Dr. Griffiths served as a director for an intervention and residential program designed to support teens and young adults with disabilities as they transition into adulthood. Her scholarly and research interests are focused on the question: *How can we prepare children from underserved populations for resilient futures?* This is explored by understanding school system intervention (e.g., psychological well-being and mental health, targeted intervention, program evaluation), as well as career and transition planning and intervention.

Michele L. Heath is an assistant professor of management at Cleveland State University. Her research interests include the role of leadership, governance, culture, conflict, team composition, change management, and other core management concepts. Michele's research has been published in several scholarly journals including *Health Policy & Technology, Information Systems Management, Behaviour and Information Technology,* and *American Journal of Business.* Her work has appeared in the following proceedings: Qualitative Research in Organizations and Management, Americas Conference on Information Systems, Southern Management Association Midwest Association for Information Systems, and Academy of Management. Prior to entering the academic field, Michele worked at Ernst & Young and KPMG.

Mikki Hebl is the Martha and Henry Malcolm Lovett Professor of Psychological Sciences and Management. Her research focuses on workplace discrimination and the ways both individuals and organizations can remediate such discrimination and optimize diversity and inclusion. She has approximately 200 publications, 21 teaching awards (including one of the most prestigious national awards called the Cherry Award), research grants from NSF and NIH, and several gender-related research awards.

Amy E. Hurley-Hanson is an Associate Professor of Management in the George L. Argyros School of Business and Economics at Chapman University. She is an Associate in the Thompson Policy Institute on Disability and Autism at Chapman University. She is the coauthor of *Autism in the Workplace Creating Positive Outcomes for Generation A* published in 2020 as part of the Palgrave Explorations in Workplace Stigma series. She is the coeditor of the book *Extreme Leadership: Leaders, Teams, and Situations Outside the Norm.* She was the coeditor of the *Journal of Business and Management* from 2004–2016. Dr. Hurley-Hanson was chosen as an Ascendant Scholar in 2000 by the Western Academy of Management.

Catrina Palmer Johnson received her PhD in Organizational Management from Rutgers Business School —Newark and New Brunswick. Her research focuses on how gender and racial disparity affect mentorship relationships in the academy, as well as the effects of criminal history on individuals' ability to acquire meaningful work. Johnson has taught introductory management and guest lectured two diversity courses: women leading in business and managing diversity. Prior to entering academia, she served as an academic advisor at a midwestern university and a research associate at a consulting firm.

Eden King, PhD is the Lynette S. Autrey Professor of Industrial-Organizational Psychology at Rice University. She is pursuing a program of research that aims to make work better for everyone. This research—which has yielded over 100 scholarly products and has been featured in outlets such as the *New York Times*, *Good Morning America*, and *Harvard Business Review*—addresses three primary themes: (1) current manifestations of discrimination and barriers to work-life balance in organizations, (2) consequences of such challenges for its targets and their workplaces, and (3) individual and organizational strategies for reducing discrimination and increasing support for families. In addition to her scholarship, Dr. King has partnered with organizations to improve diversity climate, increase fairness in selection systems, and to design and implement diversity training programs. She is currently coeditor of the *Journal of Business and Psychology* and the immediate past-President of the Society for I-O Psychology.

Dianna Contreras Krueger received a PhD in Business Administration, Organizational and Management studies attending The University of Texas at San Antonio and an MA in Psychology attending Stephen F. Austin State University. Her research focuses on selection and diversity in organizations. She is currently an assistant professor of management at Tarleton State University. Results of her research have been published in the *Journal of Applied Psychology*, the *Journal of Business and Entrepreneurship*, the *Business Journal of Hispanic Research*, and *The Wiley Blackwell Handbook of the Psychology of the Internet at Work*.

Kimberly M. Lukaszewski received her PhD from the University at Albany, State University of New York. She is a Professor of Management at Wright State University. Her research is focused on electronic human resources and diversity issues. Her work has been published in journals such as the *Human Resource Management Review, the Journal of Managerial Psychology, Journal of Business and Psychology, the Journal of Business Issues, the Journal of the Academy of Business Education, AIS Transaction in Human-Computer Interactions and Communications of the Association for Information Systems.* She currently serves on the editorial boards of *Journal of Managerial Psychology, Research in Human Resource Management, Journal of Human Resource Education*, and served as a guest editor of a special issue of *Journal Managerial Psychology* on social issues, for three special issues of *AIS Transactions Human Computer Interactions* on HRIS and e-HRM.

Lindsay Mathys is an undergraduate student at Rice University, majoring in Biological Sciences. Her research interests focus on allyship and inclusion surrounding mental health and well-being. Lindsay has also conducted research in a clinical psychology setting at the Texas Children's Hospital Brief Behavioral Intervention program and hopes to continue advocating for mental health inclusion within the medical field, especially in underserved communities.

Sara Mendiola is an undergraduate student at Rice University. She is expected to graduate with a BA in Psychology and Social Policy Analysis in May 2021. Her research interests are mental health, diversity and inclusion, immigration, and social issues in the United States. Past research experience includes work on diversity and inclusion with the Hebl/King lab, early language education with Rice University, the Texas Policy Lab, and Alief ISD, and quality of voter experience with Rice University and the Harris County Clerk's Office.

Eli Mendoza is an undergraduate student majoring in Psychology at Rice University. His research interests include examining barriers to accessibility for disabled persons as well as how those barriers affect their health and productivity in order to promote inclusivity and show how accessibility affects all people. He also is interested in looking at the intersections of martial arts, spirituality, and government throughout history.

Christoph A. Metzler. Since March 2012 Christoph works at the German Economic Institute in Cologne and is currently employed as a senior consultant. Prior he studied business and economic education and worked as a research assistant focusing on empirical data analysis and evaluation at the University of Mannheim. He pursued and completed his PhD in business administration at the University of Siegen. Christoph Metzler has worked with various national and international clients in research projects to further the participation of people with disabilities at the working place. These clients include charitable and self-help organizations for the disabled, representatives of employers and trade unions as well a joint project as part of the German Israeli national cooperation. He has served in several advisory boards in related research projects and has close connections to the community of German disabled. His research interests are in research to promote the participation of disabled individuals on the labor market, the role of SME in Germany and the chances and challenges in the current era of digital transformation. In his research he endorses quantitative and qualitative methods.

Petra M. Moog. Since October 2007 Petra Moog is Professor at Siegen University, Chair for Family Business and Entrepreneurship. She studied economics at the University of Cologne. On top she completed the International Master CEMS/MIM at Universitá Commerciale Luigi Bocconi, Milano (Italy) before finishing her PhD in Cologne. She has been a research fellow at MIT, Cambridge. She worked as PostDoc at Zurich University (Switzerland) and at the SME Research Institute in Bonn. Petra Moog teaches Entrepreneurship and Family Business, as well as Empirical Research Methods. She worked at various universities, i.e. ITAM Mexico, UNEC Azerbaijan, and so forth. She is the director of the PhD Graduate School in SME research at Siegen University and the director for the Master Program on SME and Entrepreneurship Management. Petra Moog is editorial board member of JFBS and SSHO, and a reviewer for different academic journals, conferences, and institutions like SNF or DFG, the author of several books, edited volumes, and journal articles. She is a Member of the STEP Program and Senior Research Fellow at the Institute for Development Strategies/Indiana University. Her research interests are in Family Business and Entrepreneurship, SMEs, and Academic Spin-offs, mostly theory-based and empirically driven.

Brian Murray, PhD, is associate professor of management in the Satish & Yasmin Gupta College of Business at the University of Dallas. He was formerly the university's vice president and CFO and was board president for CARES, a multiple employer self-funded healthcare benefits association. His research includes studies of employee attitudes, retirement savings behavior, skill-based pay, leadership and performance management, and work implications for employees who are family caregivers for individuals with special needs. His work has been published in journals including the *Academy of Management Journal*, *Personnel Psychology*, *The Leadership Quarterly*, *Decision Sciences*, and *Human Resource Management Review* among others. He was coeditor for the *Research in Human Resource Management* volumes *Leadership: Leaders, Followers, and Context* and *Managing Team Centricity in Modern Organizations*. He earned his PhD from Cornell University.

Linnea Ng is an assistant professor at Lawrence University and a former Graduate Research Fellow of the National Science Foundation. Her research examines diversity and discrimination in the workplace, centered on understanding how both individuals and organizations can promote equitable experiences for all.

Daniela Petrovski is a Doctoral Candidate in the School of Human Resource Management at York University in Toronto, Canada. Her research interests include creativity and aesthetics, training and development, gender inequality, employment of people on the autism spectrum disorder, critical pedagogy in higher education, workplace deviance, psychologically healthy workplaces, and other emerging issues in human resources management. Her papers on some of these topics have been accepted at conferences such as Academy of Management (AoM), and Administrative Sciences Association of Canada (ASAC).

Cassandra N. Phetmisy is a PhD student in Industrial-Organizational Psychology at Rice University. She broadly researches how employees experience and respond to stressors in the workplace. She particularly focuses on topics related to financial stress, resilience, discrimination, and voice.

Her research and contributions have appeared in *Industrial and Organizational Psychology*, *The Cambridge Handbook of Workplace Affect*, and *Journal of Management Studies*.

Deborah E. Rupp, PhD, joined the George Mason University faculty as Professor of Psychology in the Fall of 2019. She was formerly Professor and William C. Byham Chair in Industrial-Organizational Psychology and Research Integrity Officer at Purdue University; and before that, Associate Professor of Psychology, Labor/Employment Relations, and Law at the University of Illinois at Urbana-Champaign. Her research has focused on legal issues surrounding human resource management and equal employment opportunity; organizational justice, behavioral ethics, and corporate social responsibility; as well as issues surrounding testing and assessment by organizations. Her research has been cited in U.S. Supreme Court proceedings, and she has consulted to myriad organizations around the world. She has published six books and over 100 papers and chapters, sits on the editorial boards of five journals, and is the former Editor-in-Chief of *Journal of Management*. She also served on the Executive Board of the Society for Industrial and Organizational Psychology, and currently sits on the advisory boards of Amazon Conservation Team, Pinsight, the Thornton Institute for Assessment Centers, and the Georgia Tech Work Science Center.

Elisabeth R. Silver is a PhD student studying Industrial/Organizational Psychology at Rice University. Her research focuses on diversity and discrimination in educational, medical, and organizational contexts, with an emphasis on gender, race, and class. She has published in a variety of journals, including *Journal of the American Medical Association Network Open, Public Health and Nutrition,* and *Sex Roles*.

Dianna L. Stone received her PhD from Purdue University, and is now a Research Professor at the University of New Mexico, a Visiting Professor at the University of Albany, and an Affiliate Professor at Virginia Tech. Her research focuses on diversity in organizations, electronic human resource management, privacy in organizations, and cross-cultural issues. Results of her research have been published in the *Journal of Applied Psychology, Personnel Psychology, the Academy of Management Review, Organizational Behavior and Human Decision Processes,* and *Human Resource Management Review*. She is currently the coeditor of *Research in Human Resource Management,* a research series in human resource management and related fields. She is also the Associate Editor of *Human Resource Management Review,* and the former Editor of the *Journal of Managerial Psychology*. She is a Fellow of the Society for industrial and Organizational Psychology, the American Psychological Association, and the Association of Psychological Sciences. She has been awarded the Scholarly Achievement Award and the Sage Service Award in the Gender and Diversity Division of the Academy of Management. She also won the Trailblazer Award in the PhD Project.

Nicole Strah is an Assistant Professor of Management at UNC Charlotte. She received her PhD in Psychology from Purdue University, specializing in Industrial-Organizational Psychology and completed a Postdoctoral Research Fellowship at George Mason University›s Industrial and Organizational Psychology program. Her research interests revolve around diversity and inclusion, perceptions of justice and fairness, and the intersection between psychology and employment discrimination law. She has published in several respected journals, including the *Journal of Applied Psychology*, the *Journal of Vocational Behavior*, and *Industrial and Organizational Psychology: Perspectives on Science and Practice*.

Erika N. Williams is an assistant professor of management at the University of Southern Indiana. Her research interests include entrepreneurship, women entrepreneurs, entrepreneurial decision-making, and the workplace experiences of historically marginalized populations.

Nicole C. Jones Young received her PhD in Management, Organizational Behavior from the University of Connecticut. Her scholarship is concentrated in the area of diversity and selection, specifically related to marginalized populations and organizational inclusion. Her current research focuses on understanding the implications of a criminal history in the selection process from multiple perspectives such as those of the employer and the formerly incarcerated. Another research interest focuses on diversity and inclusivity in organizations such as in the academic business school pipeline. Young has taught courses in organizational behavior and diversity and inclusion in the workplace. Prior to entering academia, she worked in human resources in the financial services, consumer product goods, and professional sports industries.

Printed in the United States
by Baker & Taylor Publisher Services